Charles Adolphus Row

The Nature and Extent of Divine Inspiration

As Stated by the Writers, and Deduced from the Facts, of the New Testament

Charles Adolphus Row

The Nature and Extent of Divine Inspiration
As Stated by the Writers, and Deduced from the Facts, of the New Testament

ISBN/EAN: 9783337181048

Printed in Europe, USA, Canada, Australia, Japan

Cover: Foto ©Lupo / pixelio.de

More available books at **www.hansebooks.com**

THE
NATURE AND EXTENT

OF

DIVINE INSPIRATION,

AS STATED BY THE WRITERS,

AND

DEDUCED FROM THE FACTS,

OF THE NEW TESTAMENT.

BY

THE REV. C. A. ROW, M.A.,

OF PEMBROKE COLLEGE, OXFORD, AND LATE HEAD MASTER OF THE
ROYAL GRAMMAR SCHOOL, MANSFIELD.

LONDON:
LONGMAN, GREEN, LONGMAN, ROBERTS, AND GREEN.
1864.

PREFACE.

Why should revelation and science be such sworn enemies? Why should the battle-field be gradually widening, and the strife growing more deadly? Why? Because men of science have pursued a different course, with respect to their investigations in nature, from that followed by the divine in his searching the Scriptures for the purpose of examining into the nature of Divine inspiration.

The geologist has taken spade and hammer in hand, and investigated for himself; he has raked the bowels of the earth, uncovered the hid treasure, and left it to tell its own story. The astronomer has directed his telescope, with untiring perseverance, to the heavenly bodies, and allowed them, in their own inimitable way, to declare the glory of God. But the divine studies his Bible differently: he has preconceived ideas of what a revelation ought to contain, and, in his zeal for the preservation of his view of Divine truth, he has at one time condemned, and at another persecuted, those who have propounded truths deduced from science, because they stood out in contradiction to his views of Divine revelation; and when at last the voice of science has become irresistible, he has endeavoured to twist the Scriptures to make them accord with her latest discoveries. Hence the tendencies of many thoughtful and learned men of the present day. Hence the destructive theories which are ever and anon propounded, tending to unsettle the minds of thousands, and shaking their faith in the reality of a Divine revelation, while they offer nothing in return but a cold and barren rationalism.

The writer of the following pages has attempted to study the Christian Scriptures as the naturalist studies God's natural laws. He has taken the New Testament, and examined its contents, to see what evidence it would afford respecting the nature of its own inspiration. He has dug for the hid treasure, with no preconceived opinions. He has discussed the à priori question for the purpose of ascertaining the solidity of the foundation of existing theories, and of inquiring into the extent of our knowledge of the mode in which a revelation of the Infinite would be communicated to the finite; and the facts of the case, as presented by the Christian Scriptures, have fully borne out the conclusions at which he has arrived.

He has found in the person of the Redeemer the highest conceivable form of inspiration—the highest and most glorious manifestation of Deity to the finite mind. Revelation has been made in Him, and not merely by Him. Redemption has been purchased through Him.

He has summoned the Apostles as witnesses, carefully weighed their testimony; and has inevitably arrived at the conclusion that, while they testified as men to the facts which they had seen and heard, they possessed an unction from above, not according to the development-theory, which attributes inspiration to every one who surpasses his fellow-men in genius, acquirements, or profundity of thought, but supernatural enlightenment of such a kind, and to such an extent, as to leave no doubt that their inspiration was objectively imparted, and was a thing wholly distinct from any subjective endowment of the mental capacity;

that their inspiration was imparted through the agency of supernatural gifts, which, though neither destroying their individual personality nor controlling their language, nor bestowing infallibility on their conduct, afforded them an assistance proportionate to their need, and led them into "all the truth," and so fulfilled our Saviour's promise (which was never intended to extend to every truth, but to "the truth" —the particular truths of the Christian revelation); that these gifts, varying in their operations, and in their degrees, from human to superhuman and miraculous agency, were possessed in their fulness by Apostles, and that they were imparted in inferior measures to the early infant Church, one person possessing one gift, and another another; and that the possession of an inferior gift often led these early Christians to suppose that they were equally inspired with the Apostles, and hence the sectarian spirit which prevailed, and the daring defiance of even apostolical authority.

But inspiration was not confined to the act of recording the things written: the silences of the Scriptures are inspired. No uninspired writer could have refrained from detailing certain things respecting which the silence of the New Testament is absolutely unbroken.

He has found that our Lord appointed the Apostles to be witnesses of the great facts of His ministry, His death, and His resurrection. He has examined the Gospels, and found that they are the embodiments of the results of this apostolic testimony.

He has examined the Epistles, and found that they contain the results of that inspiration which communicated to the Apostles all the deep truths of their Master's kingdom. But while he has found in them the fulfilment of the promise to lead them by supernatural guidance into all the truth of the gospel, he has discovered evidence no less direct that the individuality of the writers was neither superseded nor overwhelmed by the presence of inspiration.

The author has viewed with pain the steady march of the spirit of unbelief, veiled under the specious pretext of honouring Christianity as the highest among the developments of man. He has felt that this honouring of the Redeemer as the highest of human teachers, while He claims to be a teacher come from God, is to mock Him by arraying Him in the robes of spurious royalty. He has therefore asked the Evangelists, "How did you originate your conception of that glorious Christ? How did you conceive that picture of the perfect man, dying in agony and degradation, and succeed in enthroning Him in royal dignity on the throne of God? Is it true that you, fishermen of Galilee, created the first conception, and that others, with plastic hand, by the aid of myths and human developments, have elaborated the great ideal?" He has asked all the systems of thought or feeling possessed by the ancient world to labour with united effort, and assert their claims to be the progenitors of a Christ. All have, with unanimous voice, declined the proffered honour. All are ready to produce what is of earth, earthly: all confess their inability to give birth to the Lord from heaven.

Such is the work which the writer now introduces to the public. If it should become the means of freeing the mind of the thoughtful student of the Scriptures from those difficulties with which the theories of men have encircled them, his highest wishes will have been gratified; for he is fully convinced that, if the Christian Scriptures be stripped of all those strange things with which zealous but mistaken men have shrouded them, if they be allowed to have free course, they will most certainly be glorified.

CONTENTS.

CHAPTER I.
Introduction.

The importance of the question respecting the nature of inspiration, 1.
The inductive method the correct mode of prosecuting the inquiry, 2.
The nature and limits of the investigation, 3.

Causes of the diversity of opinion as to the nature of inspiration, 5.
Abstract reasonings incorrect guides to facts, 6.

CHAPTER II.

The inadequacy of all human conceptions of the Infinite a limitation to the extent of truth which can be communicated in a Revelation.

The distinction between the Infinite and the finite, 7.
The conceptions in which a revelation is made cannot represent the Divine realities themselves, but are only approximations to them, 8.
The distinction between the natural and the moral attributes of the Creator, 9.

The conceptions used in a revelation must be imperfect human conceptions, 10; must convey relative, not absolute, truth, 11; must be analogical representations of truth, 12.
The nature of our conceptions of the Divine attributes, 13.

CHAPTER III.
Different theories as to the Extent of Divine Inspiration.

The term "plenary inspiration" ambiguous, 15.
Definition of "inspiration," 16.
Great mental endowments not inspirations, 18.
Definition of "verbal inspiration," 20.
The consequences which flow from the theory, 22; its modifications, 23.

The views of those who, while they believe in the inspiration of the Scripture, yet reject verbal inspiration, stated, 25.
Inspiration is not a mere intensification of the ordinary faculties, 29.
Distinction between inspiration and sanctification, 31.

CHAPTER IV.

The Possibility of a Divine Revelation, and the Mode adopted in its communication.

The question of the Divine origin of a revelation distinct from the mode of its communication, 33.
Statement of objections to the possibility of a miraculous revelation, 34.
The limits within which human experience and analogical reasonings are bounded, 37.
Reasonings founded on the Divine attributes will not conduct us to the facts of nature, 40.
Uniform action in conformity with law and order stated to be the only worthy conception of the mode of the Creator's acting, 42.
God not a mere mechanist or chemist, 43.
A perception of the Divine personality is the foundation of religion, 44.
The creation of the finite must have been one great deviation from previously existing invariable law, 45.
The possibility of creative acts proves the possibility of a miraculous revelation, 46.
God never works in nature by a double instrumentality, 49.
The expenditure of labour imposed by God as the condition of the discovery of truth, 51.
Similar analogies will be found in revelation, 50, 52.
A moral revelation possible, 53; it does not involve the use of a double instrumentality, 54.
The gospel discovers the motives which render obedience to the moral law possible, 56.
A revelation will receive the necessary Divine attestation, 58.

CHAPTER V.

The Impossibility of arguing from the Divine Attributes to the Facts of Nature invalidates all such arguments when applied to the Facts of Revelation.

Abstract reasonings would lead us to construct a universe wholly different from the actual universe of the Creator, 59.
Such reasonings equally inconclusive as to what He must do in communicating a revelation, 60.
We cannot reason to the facts of nature from our conceptions of Almighty power, 62; infinite wisdom, 62; perfect goodness, 66.
Imperfections exist in the universe of the Creator, all-powerful, wise, and good, 63.
All attempts to explain the existence of evil only remove the difficulty one step backwards, 68.
God will manifest Himself as Revealer, analogously to the mode in which He has manifested Himself as Creator, 70.
It is impossible to reason from the Divine perfection as to the particular mode in which a revelation must be communicated, 71.
The Divine Worker employs the most unexpected agencies in effectuating His purposes in creation and providence, 73.
The waste in creation, 74.
In communicating a revelation, the Creator cannot deny His moral perfections, 75.
The limits of our powers of reasoning on such subjects, 78.
No single Divine attribute an adequate representation of the whole of the Divine character, 79.
The above illustrated in the case of the doctrine of the Atonement, 80.
Human conceptions of benevolence and justice not an adequate representation of those attributes as they exist in God, 81.
The assertion that the conceptions in every revelation must be human conceptions no limitation to the omnipotence of God, 83.
All such conceptions must partake of the nature of anthropomorphism, 86.

The Christian Scriptures written on the assumption of this principle, 88.
The Christian revelation consists of an objective fact, 89.

Spiritual truth taught in the Scriptures through material imagery, 91.
General conclusions which follow from the previous reasonings, 93.

CHAPTER VI.

The theory of Verbal Inspiration contrary to the mode of the Creator's acting in Creation and Providence.

The written and oral teaching of the Apostles equally inspired, 96.
The theory of verbal inspiration cannot be proved from its being desirable that it should have been so communicated, 98; nor because such a mode of communication would have precluded liability to mistake its meaning, 99; (man has been created to be a fellow-worker with God, 101;) nor from considerations of the Divine goodness, 104; nor because the Scriptures must be infallible guides to truth, 105.
Their claim to speak with authority rests on their having received a Divine attestation, 107.

Such an attestation must be miraculous. The nature of a miracle, 108.
The claims of a revelation attested by miracles, 111.
Verbal inspiration cannot be proved from reasonings founded on the Divine perfections, 112; nor because the Scriptures are called "God's word," 113.
The varied nature of the contents of the Christian Scriptures, 116.
The degree of inspiration proportioned to the subject-matter, 117.
The highest form of inspiration exhibited in our Lord's person, 118.
The true nature of inspiration must be learned from the facts and declarations of the New Testament, 119.

CHAPTER VII.

The Incarnation is the great objective Manifestation of Deity to the finite mind. The Person of Christ exhibits the highest form of Inspiration.

The mode in which the Christian revelation differs from all previous Divine communications, 123.
The perfections of God, as far as they can be comprehended by the finite mind, are manifested in the Incarnation, 125.
Deity in His essential nature invisible to man, but manifested in Christ, 126.
The representations of the synoptic Gospels on this subject, 129.
The word of life the subject of apostolic testimony, 130.
Christ the image of the invisible God, 131.

Unsearchable riches of Divine knowledge manifested in His person, 132.
The fulness of the Godhead manifested in His human nature, 133.
God manifest in the flesh, 134.
The Christian revelation not a theory, but a fact, 135.
The inspiration which was the result of the indwelling of Deity in our Lord's person, 137.
Our Lord's assertions respecting the nature and extent of His own knowledge, 138.
The views presented by the synoptic Gospels, 139.

CHAPTER VIII.

The Nature of our Lord's Knowledge derived from the Inspiration of the Spirit. Its two recorded limitations.

Our Lord's human nature created, and therefore finite, 142.
The purpose for which it received the fulness of inspiration from the Spirit, 143.
The first limitation of His human knowledge, as asserted by St. Luke, 144.

The second limitation, asserted by St. Mark, 145.
The real nature of that limitation, 146.
St. Mark's words contradict no truth of the Incarnation, 148.
Contrast between our Lord's inspiration and that of the prophets and apostles, 148.

CHAPTER IX.

The Nature of the Inspiration of the Apostles. The Apostles witnesses. Our Lord's promises. The Sources of St. Paul's apostolic Knowledge.

Belief in the gospel founded on a human and a Divine testimony, 150.
The Spirit testified by the exertion of miraculous power, 151.
The Apostles testified to facts of which they had been actual witnesses, 152.
No human testimony can exist without an act of recollection, 153.
Facts, as facts, do not admit of greater or less degrees of truth, 155.
The difficulty of correctly reporting discourses, when not copied down at the time when they were delivered, 156.
Our Lord's promises to the Apostles of supernatural assistance, 158:—
1st, of supernatural aid to their memories, to enable them to recollect the discourses of our Lord, 161.

2nd, of the witness of the Spirit to corroborate their human testimony, 162.
3rd, of supernatural guidance into the knowledge of the truths of the Christian revelation, 163.
4th, to discover events yet future, 165.
5th, promise of supernatural assistance when called on to defend themselves in courts of justice, 167.
Promises of inspiration not vague, but definitely limited to the things which are Christ's, 166.
The contrast between St. Paul and the original Apostles, 168.
St. Paul's knowledge both of the truths and of the facts of the gospel not derived from human sources, but from inspiration, 169.

CHAPTER X.

The Spiritual Gifts—their character.

The statements of St. Paul respecting the nature of the spiritual gifts, 172.
Their communication was the fulfilment of our Lord's promise of supernatural inspiration, 173.

The inspiration conferred by them not confined to the Apostles, 177.
Nor were they imparted to all in equal degrees, 179.
They were distinct spiritual endowments, 180.

CHAPTER XI.

The Spiritual Gifts the chief source of Apostolic Inspiration. The Nature of the Inspiration imparted by each gift.

The nature of the gift of tongues, and the phenomena by which it was accompanied, 181.
The purposes for which it was designed, 184.
The gift of interpretation, 186.
The gift of wisdom the gift preeminently apostolic, 186.
The gift of prophecy the second great spiritual endowment, 189; its precise nature, 190.

The spiritual gift of knowledge, 191.
The two miraculous gifts—their distinction, 193.
The gift of discerning of spirits, 195.
The gift of faith, 196.
The spiritual gifts, in their exercise, were subject to the control of the rational will, 198; were permanent mental endowments, 201.
The calmness with which their exercise was attended, 202.

CHAPTER XII.

The Limits of the Inspiration conferred by the Supernatural Gifts.

They were limited to a definite subject-matter, 203.
The knowledge conveyed by them was limited within the functions of the respective gifts, 204.
The possession of a gift did not secure its right use, 206.
The cause of resistance to apostolic authority, 207.
Their possession did not convey a general infallibility, 208.
The supernatural direction which they afforded the Apostles in their ministry, 209.
Errors in conduct compatible with inspiration, 212.
St. Peter at Antioch, 113; his inspiration did not hinder him from compromising Christian truth by his conduct, 215.

The quarrel between Paul and Barnabas, 217.
St. Paul's last visit to Jerusalem—the plan formed to obviate his danger, 220.
The conduct of all parties concerned inconsistent with the consciousness of possessing supernatural guidance on this subject, 225.
The spiritual gifts afforded no supernatural guidance on questions of chronology, 226.
The nature and extent of general promises, 228.
The difficulties of St. Stephen's speech, 230; their proposed solutions, 231.
General promises not to be construed to the letter, 234.

CHAPTER XIII.

General Character of the Gospels, and the Nature of their Inspiration: their Inspiration not Verbal.

The Gospels contain the results of the highest form of inspiration in our Lord's words and actions, 235.
If the facts of the Gospels are true, they preserve the results of that inspiration, 236.
The peculiar phenomena presented by the Gospels, 237.
Difficulties with which the theory of

verbal inspiration is attended when applied to the Gospels, 238, whether we assume that the Evangelists wrote independently, 241, or with the intention of supplementing each other, 243.
The peculiar character of St. John's Gospel, 244; its bearing on the present question, 245.

CHAPTER XIV.

Examination of Parallel Passages in the Gospels, with a view to determine the Nature of the Inspiration by the aid of which they were composed.

Comparison of the Evangelists' accounts of the institution of the Eucharist, 247.
The parable of the vineyard, 252.
The agony in the garden, 254.
The inscription on the cross, 257.
The miracle at Gadara, 259.
The miracle at Jericho, 263.
The events of the Passion, 265; and of the Resurrection, 270.
The night of our Lord's last Passover, 270.

The death of Judas, 272.
The history of the centurion's servant, 273.
The cure of a woman with an issue of blood, 274; of the demoniac child, 277; of the daughter of the Syrophenician woman, 280.
The cleansing of the Temple, and the cursing of the barren fig-tree, 282.
St. Matthew's genealogy, 283.

CHAPTER XV.

The Silences of the Gospels proofs of their Inspiration.

The Gospels are selections from an extensive mass of materials, 285.
The necessity that the Apostles should have been guided in making this selection, 286.
The character of the silences of the Gospels, 287.
Their silence as to our Lord's personal appearance, 288.
The silence respecting the history of our Lord's youth and early manhood, 290.

The silence respecting our Lord's brethren, 291.
The silence respecting Lazarus's knowledge of the unseen world, 292.
The silence respecting the nature of our Lord's sufferings, 293.
Other silences of the Gospels, 294.
These silences can only be accounted for on the supposition that the Evangelists were supernaturally hindered from breaking them, 295.

CHAPTER XVI.

The View which the Facts of the Gospel would suggest to a careful reader, who had not previously perused them, respecting their Origin and the Mode of their Inspiration.

The theory of their mythic origin, 298.
The Gospel miracles not mythic, 299.
Their mythic origin contradicted by their general contents, 299.
Difficulties in the way of believing any one of the Gospels contains the mythic story of which the other Gospels are later modifications, 301.
Difficulties in the way of considering the common narrative, freed from its miracles, as the original story, 302.
The Jesus of the Gospels no mythic creation, 304.

The phenomena presented by the discourses consistent with our Lord's promise to assist the memories of the Apostles in recollecting them, 306.
The phenomena presented by the facts present all the variations of human testimony, 309.
The results of the evidence as bearing on the theory of verbal inspiration, 311.
The character of St. Luke's Gospel, and the sources from which it was derived, 314.

CHAPTER XVII.

The gradual Enlightenment of the Apostles in the great Truths of the Christian Revelation.

Our Lord's promise implies that the enlightenment of the Apostles would not be sudden, but gradual, 318.
The Apostles at first ignorant that the gospel was to be preached to the Gentiles, 320.
The importance of the truth of the calling of the Gentiles, 323.

The gradual development of this truth in the Apostles' minds, 326.
St. James's Epistle an exemplification of the mode of teaching Christian truth in the Jewish Church, 331.
Their first enlightenment qualified the Apostles to preach the gospel to the Jews only, 332.

CHAPTER XVIII.

Nature and Extent of full Apostolic Inspiration.

St. Paul's assertions respecting his own inspiration considered in—2 Cor., xii. 2-4, 333; 1 Cor., ii. 6-16, 335; Eph., iii. 1-11, 339; Col., i. 25-28, 343; Titus, i. 1-3, 344; Phil., iii. 8-10, 345; 1 Thess., ii. 13, 347; 1 Cor., xiv. 37; 2 Cor., xi. 17, & xiii. 2-3, 350; Gal., iv. 14, & 2 Tim., iii. 14-17, 351.

The objective nature of the truth communicated by inspiration, 336–342.
Truths discovered by revelation do not extend to the knowledge of God revealed by the created universe, 341, 344.
The Apostle an ambassador, 350.

CHAPTER XIX.

The Human Element in Apostolic Inspiration.

The individuality of the writers a human element in the Epistles, 354.
The undeniable presence of that individuality in the Epistles of St. Paul, 355; St. John, 358; St. Peter, 359; St. James, 361.
The distinction between the Divine and human elements in the Epistles, 362.
Examination of the Divine and human elements in 2 Cor., i. 5-24, 365; Phil., i. 3-18, 368; Phil., ii. 17-30, 369; Col., iv. 7-9, 370; 1 Thess., iii. 1-8, 371.

The precise weight attached by St. Paul to his own experience and example, 372.
Comparison between St. Paul and Jeremiah, 373.
The difference of the styles of the Apostles, 376; their different modes of stating and reasoning on the same truth, 378.
The mode of quoting the Old Testament adopted by the writers of the New, 379.
The Book of Revelation, 382.

CHAPTER XX.

The Results of the preceding Inquiries on existing Theories of Inspiration.

The effects of the present spirit of inquiry, 383.
The danger of evading difficulties, 385.

The Church of Rome an impressive warning to the discouragers of investigation, 386.

The danger to which the assumption of the theory of verbal inspiration exposes Christianity, 387; it occasions scepticism among scientific men, 389.

The assertions of Scripture respecting the nature of its own inspiration are in accordance with the facts of the New Testament and the analogies of nature, 390.

CHAPTER XXI.

The Christ of the Gospels no creation of the unassisted powers of the human mind.

General statement of the views of those who maintain the human origin of Christianity, 393.
Christianity, as an existing fact, requires that an account of its origin should be given, 395.
The nature of the developments of purely human ideas, conceptions, and feelings, 396.
Human developments require long periods of time for their completion, 399.
Christianity originated in an historic age, 402.
The greatness of the interval which separates Christianity from any previously existing system of thought or feeling, 403.
The problem to be solved by those who assert a human origin of Christianity—the creation of the conception of the Christ of the Gospels, 406.
The conception of the suffering Christ, 408.
The conception of the perfect human Christ, 411.
The conception of the Divine Christ, as portrayed in the Gospels, 415.

The greatness of the work accomplished by the Evangelists, 417.
The nature of the elements out of which Christianity must have originated, if it be a human development, 419.
Neither the Egyptian tone of thought, 420, nor the Indian, 421, nor the Chinese nor Persian, 422, nor the Grecian, 423, nor the Roman, 426, nor the Jewish, 427, could generate the conception of a Christ.
The historical conditions of the problem, 429; illustrated by the slow growth of English nationality, 432.
The conception of the Christ of the Gospels incapable of being produced by the fusion together of every element then existing in the world, 433.
The Jewish Church of the prophets would have been inadequate for its production, 435.
The historic Christian Church presents no appearance of having been able to generate the conception of a Christ, 436.
Conclusion, 437.

THE
NATURE OF INSPIRATION

INDUCTIVELY CONSIDERED.

CHAPTER I.

INTRODUCTION.

THE question respecting the nature and extent of Divine inspiration is one of enlarging and deepening interest. Among the theological questions of the day, it occupies a place of the highest importance. With an extensive class there is a tendency to push the inspiration of the Scriptures to the extremest limits of verbalism. Others, on the contrary, are using their strongest efforts to represent the supposed inspiration of the New Testament as nothing but a product of the unassisted reason of man. Whatever view we take on this question, our opinions as to the character of the Christian religion must be materially affected by the opinions which we entertain respecting the nature of the inspiration of the New Testament. Our views as to the degree and the mode of the inspiration of the Christian Scriptures must also exert a powerful influence on the principles of interpretation which ought to be applied for the elucidation of their meaning. When the unbeliever is directing the strongest attacks against the Sacred Volume, it is necessary that the defender of the fortress should be acquainted with the nature of the works which he is called upon to protect, and should carefully avoid occupying unnecessary, extended, or dangerous positions. The chief objections which are urged against Christianity, and which cause great difficulties to the minds of many, are not objections against the essence of Christianity as a Divine revelation, but owe their entire weight to certain interpretations of detached portions of its contents, which interpretations have originated in particular theories respecting the mode of the inspiration of the Scriptures. The question as to the nature of the inspiration of the New Testament may be considered as the great theological question of the day.

The utmost variety of opinion has been maintained respecting the nature and degree of the inspiration under the influence of which the New Testament has been composed. Have such opinions the foundation of certainty, or are they mere assumptions based on uncertain evidence? On what principles have these theories been assumed? Many of them are founded on considerations supposed to arise out of the probabilities or the necessities of the case. It is not even pretended that the greater portion of such opinions are the result of careful inquiry into the facts presented by the pages of the New Testament: they are based on mere grounds of supposed antecedent probability.

Now universal experience has proved that, except within the region of strict demonstration, the principles of induction are the only safe guides to truth in every department of human knowledge. Why should not those principles be applied to the New Testament Scriptures, with a view to ascertain from those Scriptures themselves the nature of the inspiration under the influence of which they have been written? Mere assertions and theories applied to the study of the natural universe have led those employing them, not to the discovery of truth, but into endless mazes of error. Why should assumptions and theories, which have been utterly discarded as guides to truth in every matter of inferior moment, be still retained as the only safe modes of determining the nature of the inspiration under the influence of which the New Testament Scriptures have been composed?

Ancient philosophers indulged in useless speculations as to what the universe must be. They thought that the mere deductive powers of the human intellect were adequate to the investigation of its laws. Nature obstinately refused to give a response to such a mode of investigation: endless metaphysical jargon was the result, but no great truth was discovered. Our present knowledge of the universe has been attained, not by theorizing as to what that universe ought to be, but by investigating what it actually is.

According to the statements of our common histories, when Queen Elizabeth entered London on her accession to the throne, she was presented with a copy of the New Testament. This gift she thankfully received. In addition to this gift, there was presented to her a petition purporting to come from four supposed prisoners, Matthew, Mark, Luke, and John, praying that their imprisonment, which they had been suffering, might be brought to a termination. The Queen replied that before she complied with the prayer of the petition she would consult the prisoners themselves, and hear from their own mouths whether they desired the liberty which was sought for them. This determination was certainly not unreasonable. In the same manner, before we assume that the writers of the New Testament have written under the influence of this or that particular mode of inspiration, it seems no less reasonable to ask the writers themselves, under what degree and particular mode of inspiration they assert that they have actually written. It would be absurd to assume for them an inspiration which they themselves may possibly disclaim.

Such an inquiry we propose addressing to the writers of the New Testament.

We do not purpose to extend this inquiry to the Scriptures of the Old Testament. It will be strictly limited to the writers of the New Testament alone. We propose to inquire—

I. Whether there are any grounds of antecedent certainty which can aid us in determining the nature of the inspiration which must have been afforded to the authors of the Christian Scriptures, if they are a revelation from God.

II. We shall inquire of the writers themselves, what assertions they make respecting the nature and degree of the inspiration under the influence of which they wrote.

III. We shall investigate what is the nature and degree of the inspiration which the facts of the New Testament presuppose to have been required for its composition; and we shall compare the evidence which the facts present with the assertions of the writers themselves, and with the antecedent probabilities of the case.

IV. We shall inquire into the possibility of the New Testament having originated out of the action of influences purely and entirely human.

There are two extreme limits within which all views as to the nature of the inspiration of the New Testament must be contained. One view asserts that every idea, word, thought, and expression, as they came from the penmen themselves, are the direct inspiration of the Holy Spirit. If this view be carried out consistently, there can be no human element whatever in the Christian Scriptures. They must be absolutely, in every part of them, the word and dictation of God. The only thing which man can have had to do with their composition is to copy down with pen, ink, and paper what the Spirit of God has dictated. Consequently everything contained in the New Testament must be alike infallibly certain, whether it be religious doctrine or precept, or statements of historic fact, or anything which we may read there in the remotest degree connected with the proper subject-matter of the New Testament revelation, and even in statements connected with scientific truth. Throughout the whole, therefore, whether it be thought, fact, or style, not the smallest error can exist, as being the infallible dictation of the Spirit of God, to whom the penmen acted in no other character than that of amanuenses.

But, according to the opposite line of thought, when divested of all ambiguities of expression, the authors of the New Testament were no otherwise inspired than as men of lofty genius, such as Shakespere and Milton, were inspired. Persons holding these opinions maintain that there is a sense in which every man of exalted genius is an inspired man. According to these views, no other inspiration was possessed by the writers of the New Testament beyond an inspiration of this description, or beyond what the possession of superior powers, or being endowed with larger degrees of spiritual insight, may afford to one man above another. These sentiments, expressed in words devoid of ambiguity, mean that the writers of the New Testament were wholly devoid of the aid of any species of supernatural inspiration.

Few persons at the present day take the ground that the writers of the New Testament were simple barefaced impostors. The age in which it can be asserted that the whole of Christianity is a cunningly devised fable, invented by crafty men, is passed away. The most extreme men of the present time admit that its authors were animated by benevolent intentions, and perhaps inspired by an inspiration analogous to the inspiration of genius. Most modern unbelievers allow that Christianity forms the highest development to which the human race has yet succeeded in attaining. The next higher growth to which man can attain will be one which will be reached under their own guidance.

Now it is impossible that views thus widely differing respecting the character of such a book as the New Testament can have originated in an examination of the contents of the book itself. The book is one of no inconsiderable dimensions. The facts presented by it are large and extensive. It seems to be impossible that conclusions of so opposite a character should have been arrived at respecting the authorship of the same book, with so extensive a mass of materials to assist in the formation of a judgment. Nothing can be wider than the diversity of the opinions in question. One party asserts that the whole contents of the book is without one human element —everywhere and entirely divine. The other party is equally confident in their assertion that the entire book is without one divine element—everywhere and entirely human.

Such a disagreement respecting the nature of the same facts can only have originated in theories assumed on *à priori* grounds, quite independently of a calm and impartial examination of the contents of the book itself. It is impossible that any study of the book could have suggested two theories respecting the nature of its contents so fundamentally and radically opposed. The facts and phenomena presented by the New Testament, by the investigation of which a judgment might be arrived at, are so extensive, that the usual theories which are propounded as to the nature of the inspiration of its writers cannot have been deduced either from the assertions of the writers themselves or from the facts and phenomena presented by them. They must have been the result of *à priori* considerations as to the degree of inspiration with which such a book ought to have been composed. The theories have not been deduced from the facts, but the facts have been tortured into agreement with the theories.

From what cause has this resulted? Evidently from this: —Speculation is easy; investigation is laborious: man is naturally disposed to adopt the easier course. But while men have contented themselves with speculating on what the universe ought to be, instead of patiently inquiring what it actually is, nothing but the most grotesque theories or barren speculations have resulted from their attempts to unfold its secrets. Systems called by the name of sacred systems of the universe have frequently been propounded, but they have conducted the speculators further and further from the true view of the universe of the Creator! Similar speculations have been employed for the purpose of ascertaining the nature of the inspiration with the aid of which the New Testament has been composed. Can we be justified in applying to the elucidation of the inspiration of the New Testament a system of investigation which has been exploded as a guide to truth in every other department of knowledge? It becomes therefore a subject of the highest interest, on the supposition that the Creator were pleased to make a supernatural revelation, to ascertain whether any grounds of antecedent certainty exist which will enable us to determine what must be the nature and extent of that revelation, or the mode which must be adopted in its communication. It will be found that our grounds of antecedent knowledge on this subject are of a very narrow and limited description. On such a subject we require not mere probabilities, but demonstrations, or well-ascertained analogies.

CHAPTER II.

THE INADEQUACY OF ALL HUMAN CONCEPTION OF THE INFINITE A LIMITATION TO THE EXTENT OF TRUTH WHICH CAN BE COMMUNICATED IN A REVELATION.

THERE is one fundamental limitation under which every revelation must be communicated. This limitation has all the self-evidence of axiomatic truth. It is founded on the essential difference between the finite and the infinite. A revelation to man must be expressed in conceptions not of the infinite, but of the finite. The distinction between the infinite and the finite is not a difference of degree, but of kind. The finite cannot comprehend the infinite*.

Between the ideas of the finite and the infinite not only an impassable gulf is fixed, but there is an essential difference of nature. If a revelation of the infinite is made to the finite, the truths which are revealed must be expressed in conceptions relative to the finite mind. The necessity of this is founded on the truth that the infinite ideas of God cannot be represented adequately by the imperfect conceptions of man. The ideas of the human mind can form no adequate measures of the eternal reality.

In all human modes of conceiving the infinite, we attempt to arrive at an approximate idea of the infinite by successive additions of the finite. But no successive additions of finite added to finite will make up the total of the infinite. The very notion of infinite is inconsistent with the idea of totality: of the true nature of that total it is impossible to form even a conception. After any amount of successive additions,

* This subject has been most ably handled by Mr. Mansel, in his Bampton Lectures "On the Limits of Human Thought," as an argument against rationalistic speculation. The principles laid down by Mr. Mansel are equally important as proving the futility of attempts to determine on abstract grounds what must be the contents of a revelation, and the mode which must be adopted in its communication. Man's inability to conceive the nature of the infinite must form a necessary limit to the possibility of a revelation.

we are still indefinitely remote from the idea of infinity. Successive additions of portions of time piled one on the other will make no adequate representation of the actuality of eternity. No continuous enlargement of successive space will make up the total of immensity. No accumulations of finite power will image to the mind the reality of the Almighty. The infinite must differ from the finite, not only in conception, but in nature. An actual conception of the nature of the infinite by the finite must therefore be an impossibility.

If therefore a revelation be made of the infinite so as to be comprehensible by man, it is necessary that the unlimited and perfect ideas of the Divine mind should be translated into the limited and imperfect conceptions of the human. The conceptions of the human mind neither are nor can be the divine realities themselves. The utmost which the human mind can attain to must be an analogical expression of those realities, or they may be represented by approximation.

It follows as a necessary consequence, from the distinction which exists between the ideas of the finite and the infinite, that, if God makes a revelation of himself, the ideas employed in making that revelation cannot be the absolute and infinite ideas of God himself, but such ideas of the human mind as are the best representations and the nearest approximations to the conceptions as they exist in the mind of the Creator. If they were ideas actually measuring and representing the infinite, they could not be introduced into the finite understanding. Any other class of ideas except that which is finite and limited would be simply incomprehensible to the human mind; they would fail to convey any conception to the understanding. The ideas, therefore, in which a revelation is conveyed must be imperfect and inadequate conceptions of the reality of the Divine nature. They cannot be the ideas as they exist in God, but such conceptions only as man is capable of comprehending.

The nature of the actual relationship between the finite conceptions of man and the conceptions of the Creator, and in what degree the thoughts of the human mind can approximate to the divine realities, are questions on which we need not enter. The point which is essential to be observed in relation to our present inquiry is, that between human conceptions and their realities as they exist in God there is a difference, not merely of degree, but of kind.

But it may be contended that there is a distinction between the attributes of the Creator. To some of those attributes the idea of infinite may be properly applied. Those to which the term "infinite" properly belongs are not capable of being taken cognizance of by the finite understanding. But it may be urged that the proper term to denote His moral attributes is not "infinite," but "perfect." Now, although it is true that the mind of man can form no conception of the infinite, yet it may be able to form an adequate conception of the perfect. The eternity of God, His power, His wisdom, may be infinite, and as such utterly incomprehensible as to their actual existence by man. But His goodness, His holiness, His truth, His benevolence are not correctly designated as infinite, but as perfect. It is contended that while the one of these cannot be adequately represented by any formula of human thought, the representations of the other are capable of being embraced by the human mind, or at least are nearer approximations to the divine realities.

Now the truth of a portion of this position we are not prepared to dispute. But although a distinction between the ideas of the infinite and the perfect really exists, yet the perfect attributes of God are the attributes of the unlimited and infinite Being. Our conceptions of the perfect are conceptions derived from the attributes of beings who are limited. The Being of the Creator is absolute, infinite, unconditioned; the being of the creature is relative, finite, conditioned. The moral attributes of the Creator and the creature must partake in this essential distinction of character. Although perfect may be the best term to denote the moral attributes of the Creator, yet the conception of perfection, when applied to God, must be different in kind from that conception when applied to the creature. The attributes of God must be the perfect attributes of the infinite Being. The attributes of man are imperfect attributes of the finite. In proportion to the difference between the finite and the infinite, the creature's conceptions of even the moral attributes of God must be imperfect representations of the realities as they exist in the Divine mind. How a perfect moral attribute exists in an infinite Being cannot be distinctly conceived by a finite comprehension.

Although then we are ready to admit that the moral attributes of God are not infinite, but perfect, and consequently that it would be more correct to say that God is perfectly (not infinitely) holy, or that He is perfectly (not infinitely) good, yet we must not overlook the fact that these attributes are the perfect attributes of the infinite Being; consequently the actual conception of the divine reality of those attributes can only be conceived of in the human mind in terms of the limited and the imperfect.

It follows as a necessary consequence, that, in representing such truth to the human understanding in a divine revelation, such imperfect and finite conceptions of the mind of man must be employed to represent the perfect attributes of God as are not exact measures of the attributes themselves, but the best which the mind of man can furnish for their representation. Man has no other conceptions by which they are capable of being imaged to his mind.

It will be unnecessary for our present purpose to determine whether the various attributes of the Creator exist in the Divine mind independently, or whether they flow from a single principle in the Divine mind, of which they are only modifications. If, instead of existing in the Divine mind independently, those attributes are only modifications of a common principle, it will greatly increase the difficulty in representing in human conceptions the perfections of the Infinite. How the Infinite exists in Himself, what is the nature of the absolute and the unconditioned, and of the moral perfections existing in an infinite Being, are points entirely beyond the limits of human apprehension. How the Infinite was first moved to the creation of the finite, when previously nothing but the Infinite existed, is among the secrets which, although man strain his utmost powers to determine, are beyond the limits of finite powers to grasp or even to conceive.

From these considerations we arrive at the conclusion that the Creator must have formed the creature subject to one condition. That condition is that the creature must exist, conceive, and think, not as infinite, but as finite; and that between the perfection of the Creator and the creature a gulf must exist, the profundity of which it is impossible for man to fathom. Consequently every conception which the creature forms of the Creator must be subject to this condition. No conception, therefore, which man can form can be an adequate representation either of the mode of the actual existence or of the attributes of God.

It is a necessary deduction from this truth, that, if the Creator condescended to reveal Himself to the creature, the ideas in which that revelation would require to be communicated cannot be the infinite or the perfect conceptions of the absolute Being, but the imperfect and relative conceptions of the finite mind. All revelations from God to man must be subject to the previous condition which renders the existence of the created possible, that, the conceptions of man being finite, all the thoughts, ideas, and conceptions contained in the revelation must be finite likewise, and, as being finite, cannot fully represent the conceptions of the infinite and eternal God.

If, then, we were to assume that the Christian Scriptures have been communicated with the highest degree of Divine inspiration, and even that every word composing them was the express dictation of the Divine Spirit, and that every conception contained in them was His express suggestion to the human mind, yet on this assumption there is one necessary limitation as to the knowledge which that revelation would convey, one human element in that knowledge—that the ideas composing the revelation can only be adequate representations of the divine realities as far as the ideas and conceptions in the mind of man approximate to being adequate representations of the realities in the mind of God.

It follows from the necessity of the case, that the revelation must be a relative and not an absolute revelation. The truths which it contains must be expressed in inadequate human conceptions, and not in divine realities. To enable man to receive an absolute revelation from God, he must cease from the very condition of his being. Instead of being the finite, he must become the infinite. None but the infinite can comprehend the Almighty as He is. The being who can comprehend Him must himself be infinite.

The whole of man's knowledge is limited, finite, and human. The whole of his conceptions and ideas, however complicated, have originated in three sources alone. They have sprung either out of the perceptions of external things by the mind itself, or from the reflex action of the mind upon these perceptions, or from the feelings and affections of the mind and its own self-consciousness acting upon them.

Out of these three sources every thought, idea, and conception of man has originated. All existing ideas in their utmost complexity are combinations of thought arising out of one or more of these three sources. The external has combined with the internal, and the internal with the external. The ideas of necessity and freedom, of moral and physical, of cause and effect, of time and space, of happiness and misery, of holiness and sin, of finite and infinite, have all issued from one of these sources or several in combination. In such terms the truths of every revelation must be expressed. The only question is, In what degree has the Creator created these original conceptions of man so as to be representations and analogies of the realities in His own glorious being?

The truths, therefore, which are communicated in any revelation must be analogies more or less remote from the actualities themselves. They cannot be perfect representations of the infinite God, even if we assume the revelation to have been communicated with the highest possible degree of inspiration. They must be such ideas and conceptions as the mind of man is capable of conceiving, and which the perfection of the Divine knowledge sees to be best suited for conveying to the mind of man the amount of truth respecting the Divine nature and perfections which the Creator intended to disclose. The vehicle employed in the communication of truth must be conceptions as they exist in the mind of man, not as they exist in the mind of God. If the ideas were not finite human ideas, they would be without the power of conveying meaning to the mind of man. Even the idea of infinite used in the revelation must be the human conception of infinity, and not the divine reality. The nearest approximation to the idea of infinity which man possesses is a series indefinitely prolonged, without ever actually ending, which in neither direction has bounds or limits. This is man's only positive notion of infinity. But it is not its reality, but its approximation.

Such an idea is the highest which we can conceive of the Creator. We can only form a conception of His existence as without limits in past or future time. Our notion of Him as the Almighty is the human conception of power, but without limits to that power. All power which is conceivable or limited does not represent a positive idea of the Almighty power. Although the manifestations of His power which we behold are presented to us under the condition of limitation, it must be free from this limit in its actual existence in Him. The only conception which we can form of His wisdom is wisdom without limits. All actually conceivable wisdom, therefore, is not the adequate representation of the wisdom of God. Every positive conception of existence, wisdom, or power which man is capable of forming, being conceived under the condition of limitation, cannot possibly represent the attributes of the infinite.

When we want to form an idea of God's moral character, we add on to the conception of His infinite Being the notion of perfection. This idea of perfection applied to the infinitude of God is the human idea of perfection indefinitely extended. The positive view which we take of it is the denial of all the imperfection to which all finite perfection is necessarily subject. Such is the highest conception which the human mind can form of the moral perfections of the Creator. It is equally impossible to form an adequate positive conception of the perfect in the Infinite mind as to form a positive conception of the infinite itself.

By such conditions, therefore, the contents of a revelation, whatever may be the degree of its inspiration, must be limited, and in conceptions of this description it must be expressed. No revelation is possible to man which does not contain one human element—the representation of the infinite in the inadequate ideas of the finite. To suppose the contrary is to assume the possibility of God's making a contradiction.

But before we inquire whether there are any self-evident grounds of certainty, by means of which we are entitled to infer the nature or the extent of the inspiration through which the revelation must be communicated, previously to all examination of the facts presented by the revelation itself, it will be necessary to inquire into the nature of the various views of the mode in which we can conceive that inspiration is capable of being communicated to man. We shall then be better able to estimate the value of any theories as to the extent in which inspiration has been vouchsafed for the communication of a revelation.

CHAPTER III.

DIFFERENT THEORIES AS TO THE EXTENT OF DIVINE INSPIRATION.

It has been very extensively held that the Christian Scriptures have been written under the influence of an inspiration designated as plenary inspiration. The term plenary inspiration, used as a description of the Divine method of communicating a revelation, is one of no inconsiderable ambiguity. According to the context in which the expression occurs, it may be not incorrectly used to denote any conceivable degree of inspiration whatever.

It is hardly possible for any one to believe that any particular book, such as the Christian Scriptures, has been written under the influence of inspiration at all, and not to hold that the inspiration under the influence of which it must have been composed is plenary. The term "plenary inspiration" means full inspiration; if, therefore, we use the expression in its unqualified sense, it cannot mean anything short of what is designated by the term "verbal inspiration."

When we use the expression verbal inspiration, we mean that every word, thought, conception, and expression in the Scriptures is the absolute dictation of the Spirit of God, and that the writers of the different books in the Bible have merely copied down what the Divine Spirit dictated to them. Inspiration in this sense is the highest form in which we can conceive of inspiration as communicated. It represents it as so complete, that all the faculties of the human soul are entirely superseded by the action of the inspiring Spirit. In this sense therefore the inspiration may be said to be full, absolute, and complete. If therefore, by the expression plenary inspiration, we intend to denote the fullest form of inspiration, it will be more correctly designated by the expression verbal inspiration.

But this is not the sense which is usually intended when it is asserted that the Christian Scriptures have been composed under the influence of plenary inspiration. Something short of verbal inspiration is usually intended.

But as soon as we qualify the expression, the term loses all definite meaning. In a qualified sense it is difficult to conceive that any one who believes in the inspiration of the Christian Scriptures can believe that they have been delivered to man by any other than a plenary inspiration. If they are inspired at all, they must have been fully inspired as far as it was the Divine purpose to communicate supernatural knowledge. If God intended to make any revelation, it is not conceivable that He has not communicated fully what He intended to reveal, or that He has not given the necessary amount of inspiration to communicate that knowledge. If the inspiration therefore were not plenary, it would be the same thing as to suppose that God has purposed to reveal truth, but that He has withheld the degree of inspiration necessary for its communication.

Still, when plenary inspiration is spoken of as a distinct form of inspiration from verbal inspiration, we use an ambiguous term. If we concede that the Scriptures are not verbally inspired, we concede that their inspiration cannot be plenary, because, in whatever degree the inspiration is less than verbal, a degree of inspiration must have been employed less than the fullest form of inspiration. The fullest form of inspiration would have required that every word, thought, and expression, even that the style in which the Scriptures are composed, should be the work of the Spirit of God. In whatever degree we admit in them the existence of any element of which He is not the complete and absolute Author, we detract from the fulness of the inspiration. Its amount then becomes a question of degree. In the strict sense of the term, therefore, plenary inspiration cannot be anything short of verbal inspiration.

Now what do we mean when we assert that the Scriptures have been composed by the aid of supernatural inspiration? We intend by that expression that there is an element in them which the unassisted powers of the human mind never would have produced by the simple exercise of its natural powers. We conceive of the influence as one by which an intelligent mind introduces new truths, new forms of thought, and new feelings into the mind of another by agencies different from the action of the ordinary mental powers. We imply also that the inspired person has a consciousness that the feelings, truths, and conceptions in question have been introduced into his mind by an external influence distinct from the powers of the mind itself.

If we say that a book has been composed by the aid of inspiration, and intend by that expression only to assert that it has been composed by some secret influence belonging to the mind itself, and arising out of its natural powers, we employ a term essentially fallacious. Latent powers exist in the mind, the action of which we cannot refer to any known law; but we understand a wholly different thing from the exertion of any power of this description when we assert that the Scriptures have been composed by the aid of inspiration. Our present inability to assign such phenomena to the action of any known law affords no ground for believing that they act independently of law. To call such phenomena by the term inspiration is to confound together ideas essentially differing in meaning.

It is not uncommon, however, to use the term in a metaphorical sense. But when it is so used, we are never in danger of mistaking its meaning. In this sense we speak of the inspirations of the poet and of the man of genius. By such an expression we intend to express the suddenness of the conceptions, or the unknown powers of mind in which they originate. Such expressions are never intended to convey that the thought has originated in any source different from the natural powers inherent in the mind. In the same manner the powers which have originated great discoveries and inventions have been designated by the term inspirations; and so have perceptions of truths which have the nature of intuitions, which are perceived at a glance by men of lofty powers, but which men of inferior intellect are compelled to arrive at by long and painful deductions. Different theories may be invented to account for the origin of all such thoughts; but whatever explanation we may accept, they must be the result of some great law of the human mind differing entirely from what we mean when we speak of thoughts, conceptions, or ideas being communicated by means of *divine inspiration.* When, then, it is asserted that the Christian Scriptures have been composed under the influence of divine inspiration, if we use that term and only intend to convey the meaning that it is the same influence, only higher in degree, as that by the aid of which any ordinary book of man is composed—if we intend by that expression nothing more than that they have been composed by the aid of genius, or of deep spiritual insight or superior power of intuition, but by no influence acting on the mind from without and differing in character from its other powers,—it is to delude ourselves and others by a fallacious use of words. We can only consistently mean, when we use the term inspiration to denote the mode of the composition of the Scriptures, that they have been composed by the aid of another personality acting on the mind, whose action has produced results which the mind would have failed to produce except as the result of His operation, and that it is a direct communication from God, differing from the ordinary mode of His operation on the soul.

It is necessary to keep this distinction in view, because there is a sense in which every ordinary power of the human mind is an inspiration from God: " an inspiration from the Almighty giveth man understanding." All our mental powers being God's gifts, in this sense of the expression, they may be said to be derived from His inspiration. But, although all the human powers may be said to be derived from an inspiration from the Almighty, nothing would be more absurd than to speak of ordinary books, or even works which are the creations of the highest genius, as composed by the aid of divine inspiration.

We must also be careful to distinguish between certain natural states of human progress and enlightenment under the direction and guidance of Divine Providence, and supernatural communications of truth made to man by inspiration. No two conceptions can be more fundamentally distinct.

Perhaps no more dangerous attack has been opened on the authority of divine revelation than the attempts made by numerous writers of the present day to represent these as flowing from the same influence as inspiration, and of substantially the same authority. It is well known that a large class of writers who claim to believe in revelation represent all the great developments of man as essentially divine, and among these developments assign Christianity a high rank. Still the views which are advocated imply that there is no essential difference in kind between them.

Such writers assert and maintain that all the great races of men have been endowed by the Creator with certain great mental qualifications, which have gradually elaborated certain great points of the national character. According to these views, all past forms of civilization have not only been under the general superintendence of the providence of God, but have had God for their author, and have been looked upon by the Divine Being with actual and positive approbation. Thus he has endowed the Oriental with his genius for metaphysical speculation; the Greek with his exquisite taste for beauty, and his genius for philosophy; the Roman with his special talent of political constructiveness; the Hebrew with his moral sense, and his monotheistic perceptions, and his personal religion. Out of these elements, all partaking of a divine character, have been developed Christianity and modern civilization. In some sense or other, all these special endowments may be received as inspirations from God. By this mode of representing the matter, the human is not deified, but the divine is reduced to the standard of humanity.

The same class of thinkers take a similar view of the developments of the Christian Church; they are all alike designed by its Founder, and divine. The Christianity of the earlier centuries, the Christianity of the middle ages, the Christianity of the Romish Church, the Christianity of the Greek Church, the Christianity of the Reformation, are all necessary developments of the great idea, are all the results and workings of the universal inspiring Spirit. The great principle maintained is, Whatever has habitually prevailed among large masses of men must have been divine, and therefore derived from an inspiration from God.

It is a great truth, that every event which happens has a special place in the dispensations of Divine Providence. All things which occur, every endowment which man possesses, have been and are regulated by the powerful hand of the Creator. He makes all things subservient to the great purposes of His providence. "The Most High ruleth in the kingdoms of men, and giveth them to whomsoever He will, and setteth up over them the basest of men." Every event of Providence, the whole combined agency of man, has been rendered subservient to the introduction of His great revelation. The gospel was revealed in the fulness of the times. This involves an overruling influence exerted over all human things, the nature of which must remain for ever unknown to man. How God in His ordinary providence acts on the human mind, without interfering with its freedom, is a depth the profundities of which we cannot penetrate. But to represent these influences as of a similar nature to those which we mean when we speak of a revelation communicated by inspiration is to confound together conceptions essentially distinct.

We must also be careful to observe the distinction between the conceptions of inspiration and superintendence. Each may exist without involving the other. A man may be inspired, and yet have no general superintendence exerted over him in communicating to others the things which were supernaturally discovered to his mind. A general superintendence may be exerted over a man's mental operations, and no new truth or feeling may be imparted to him. Inspiration and superintendence may coexist in the same mind, and yet their influences may be entirely distinct. By inspiration fresh truths are introduced into the mind. Superintendence regulates those already there.

But supposing God to have made a revelation by supernatural inspiration, we must examine the nature of the views held as to the degree in which such inspiration has been communicated. The believers in the supernatural inspiration of the Christian Scriptures divide themselves into two classes: one of these holds that they must have been communicated by what is called verbal inspiration; the other maintains that a human element of some kind exists in them, together with a divine one. We will proceed to lay down what ought to be the complete theory of verbal inspiration.

Of all the theories of the manner in which inspiration has been communicated, this theory is the most complete; it leaves nothing unaccounted for; it eliminates out of the conception of inspiration everything human. As a theory it is beautifully consistent. According to the opinions of those who believe that this theory is the true account of the mode of the inspiration of the Christian Scriptures as they issued from the hands of those who transcribed them, they must have been completely and in every part the work of the Holy Spirit. The only human agency employed in their production must have been the simple act of copying what the Spirit of God dictated. Every word, assertion, and declaration in them are His positive word, assertion, and declaration. Facts, doctrines, precepts, references to history or chronology, quotations from writers sacred or profane, allusions to scientific truth, visions or prophetic declarations, mere references to the most ordinary actions of life, according to this view, are not the work of man, but of Omniscience. The only use which has been made of human agency in the composition of the book has been to copy down with pen, ink, and paper what has been dictated by the Divine Spirit.

By some of those who entertain this view the theory has been pushed to the full length of asserting that the autographs, as they came from the hands of the inspired penmen, must have been devoid of a single inaccuracy or mistake. Such persons carry out the theory to its legitimate consequences; and it is difficult to see how a person holding it can be satisfied with less. If it is absolutely necessary that a divine revelation should be communicated with all the accuracy of verbal inspiration, there is no reason why it should not both have dictated the entire contents of the Christian Scriptures and superintended their transcription. Nor can any reason be given why such a superintendence should not have been exerted over their transcription and translation to the present day, as to have prevented every human element of error from impairing the accuracy of this perfect transcript of the Divine mind. The only reason which can be given is, that it would have involved a perpetual miracle. But why, if it were necessary, should not a perpetual miracle be wrought? We have something very like one in the continual separate existence of the Jewish people during a space of 1800 years, scattered as they are in every climate and through every nation.

But while the theory of verbal inspiration has been constructed for the purpose of eradicating every conceivable human element in the structure of the Scriptures, many of its supporters shrink from carrying it out to its full and legitimate consequences; they feel that the facts as they exist in the Scriptures are hard to reconcile with the theory. While, therefore, they are ready to maintain that they have been generally dictated by the Spirit, they hesitate to assert that the style of these writings is His work. But if the theory be correct, on what conceivable principle can its supporters hesitate to ascribe the style of the Scriptures to the Divine Spirit? Every sentence in them has been dictated by Him. Every declaration has nothing in it human, but is wholly divine. But if every word be a divine dictation, and the influence of the minds of the writers has been completely superseded under the agency of inspiration, the style in which they have been composed requires to be accounted for. The existence in them of a peculiar style is an undeniable fact. It must be either human or divine. It must be that of the individual writers or that of the Spirit of God.

It follows that if the whole contents of the Christian Scriptures be the dictation of the Spirit, without the intermixture of any human element, the style in which the thoughts are conveyed cannot be that of the persons whose names are prefixed to the books, but the composition of the Divine Spirit. But if He is the author of the style, the perfection of the divine ought so far to transcend that of any human style as the ordinary works of God transcend those of man. To make the theory perfect, it must be assumed that the style in which the Scriptures have been composed must be an exhibition of this perfection. Mahommed makes the pretension in his Koran, that the style in which it is composed is actually divine, and that its excellence is a proof of the divine origin of the book. In making this assertion, he is consistent with his own principles; for he affirms that the contents of his revelation have formed from eternity a portion of the Divine mind. But the theory does not require the assertion of the absolute perfection of the style. The separate works of God are not necessarily absolutely perfect. We are only compelled to claim for it the same degree of perfection which is displayed in the other Divine operations. According to the theory of verbal inspiration, in whatever degree the divine mode of working transcends the human, the divine style ought to be similarly distinguished from the styles of imperfect and fallible men.

To admit less than this, is to admit the presence of a human element of some kind in the composition of the Scriptures. Many of the advocates of the doctrine of verbal inspiration hesitate to carry it out in this manner to its legitimate consequences. But it may be asked, On what principle of consistency do they stop short of pushing the theory to these consequences? Those who hold the theory are ready to argue in its support, If the Scriptures contain any, even the smallest amount of imperfection, how shall we know where that imperfection ends? From the supposed cogency of this argument, it is inferred that the Scriptures can only have been composed under the influence of verbal inspiration.

But the argument admits of being applied in another direction with equal cogency. It may be urged, the style is either human or divine. If the style is human, there is a human element in the structure of the Scriptures; and if one human element exists, who shall assign its limits? If there are faults in the poetry, if any particular passage might have been expressed with greater perspicuity, if inaccuracies of grammar exist, who shall say that such inaccuracies may not extend to a genealogy, a date, or a fact? Imperfections must be the result of human, and not of divine agency; and if one single mark of human agency be admitted, the theory of verbal inspiration is subverted. If such a theory must be assumed as an explanation of the mode of the inspiration of the Scriptures, it must not be used only as far as it is convenient, and then abandoned; it must be fully carried out to its legitimate consequences. Its correct statement requires that the style, no less than the substance, of the Scriptures should be the work of God.

But the phenomena presented by the Scriptures have produced various modifications in the theory. After the theory has been modified, its precise nature is difficult of definition. Perhaps those who make the modifications seldom realize to themselves the full extent in which those modifications destroy the theory itself. It is then the common resource to conceal the indistinctness of the theory behind the ambiguous phrase of "plenary inspiration." The object kept in view is to make the smallest concession possible to the presence of a human element. If any portion of the theory be at hopeless issue with a palpable fact, that portion has been abandoned: by this surrender its consistency has been marred. It then becomes extremely difficult to give to the view maintained a clear and distinct expression.

It has been conceded by persons professing to hold this

theory, that some human element may have entered in a low degree into the structure of the Scriptures; but such an influence has been exerted over this human element by the Spirit of God as to eradicate out of it all the defects to which, as human, it is liable: but no clear explanation is offered, what is the precise nature of that influence. A human something is supposed to exist in the structure of the Scriptures, but the defects to which it is liable are counteracted by a divine influence; but we are not told what is the nature of the influence. Language of this kind supplies us with no distinct conception on which we can reason; it furnishes us with nothing but vague generalities. Divested of ambiguities, it is difficult to see how this view differs from that of verbal inspiration.

The most distinct view which can be formed of what is intended by such a statement is, that some thoughts and modes of expression in the Scriptures must be admitted to be human. Those thoughts and conceptions, however, in a manner of which no distinct idea can be formed, have undergone such a constant revision by the Spirit of God as to have become divested of their human character.

We will explain what we apprehend that the propounders of such a theory intend, by an illustration:—An incorrect time-piece has been constructed, and set working. The force of the springs, if left to the natural result of their own operation, would cause the time-piece to go either too fast or too slow, or, from defects in the works, it might cause inequalities of motion. But the maker of the time-piece, by applying forces external to the machinery, counterbalances its imperfections, and produces the result of correct time. He effects this by applying to the time-piece a power from without, producing an influence in an opposite direction to that exerted by the springs exactly sufficient to counterbalance their irregularities. In like manner the human elements employed in communicating a revelation, if left to their natural operation, would produce various degrees of imperfection; but as in the time-piece the action of external forces counterbalances the defects of the machinery and the inequalities of its motion, so the agency of the Spirit of God constantly exerts a counterbalancing influence on the imperfection of the human agencies employed in communicating a revelation. In the one case we can clearly comprehend the nature of the agencies employed; in the other case, the imperfection of our conceptions of them hinders us from forming any rational conclusion as to their nature, and destroys the force of the analogy.

But there is a numerous class of persons who believe in the divine character of the Christian revelation, but who deny that the nature of the inspiration under the influence of which it has been communicated is verbal inspiration. We will state their leading opinions.

Such persons maintain that the great end and purpose for which a divine revelation would be communicated is limited to the clear discovering and the correct statement of those truths which form the peculiar and exclusive subject-matter of a divine revelation. Inspiration, therefore, would not be a general influence exerted over the whole powers of the mind, nor would it confer a general infallibility on persons under its influence, but it would be strictly limited to the communication of the special truths forming the subject-matter of the divine revelation.

There are two modes through which the Creator may discover Himself to man. One of these is the manifestation of the Divine character and perfections made by means of the works of creation. The other is the discovery of His character and will by communicating truth to the mind directly by inspiration.

Now persons holding such opinions maintain that the truths which are discovered through the manifestation which God has made of His character and perfections in creation and providence form a revelation which has a distinctive character. The truths discovered are all confined within a particular range of subject-matter. On many subjects on which man feels the profoundest interest, such as his future condition beyond the grave, they communicate to him little or no information. The mode in which man learns the truths communicated by this natural revelation of God is a careful study of the laws of the universe by the exercise of the ordinary faculties of the mind.

Now it is asserted that everything which we know of the character of God, as discovered by creation and providence, leads us to the conclusion that those things which He has given man ample opportunities to discover by the careful use of his natural faculties He would not discover to him by a supernatural revelation. It is inconsistent with the perfections of God to employ a double set of means for producing a single result. The use of double means for the production of a single result is the effect of finite imperfection. The proper subject-matter for a supernatural revelation, therefore, is that class of truths respecting which the works of creation and providence afford us no information, or which the human faculties are unable to deduce from those works. To suppose that God will reveal by inspiration what He has already revealed by creation, and which He has furnished man with faculties to discover for himself, is to assume it possible that the Creator will employ a double agency for the purpose of effecting a single result, which is the refuge of imperfect power or of imperfect wisdom.

Now in making a discovery of the character or the will of God to the mind of man, two things, according to the views in question, are essentially necessary—an objective manifestation of Himself made by God, and a subjective communication of that manifestation imparted to the mind of man.

The objective manifestation of God in the created universe consists in the works of creation and providence. The knowledge of the Divine character and perfections is communicated to the human mind through the exercise of its rational powers in the study of those works. But the manifestation of His perfections to the human mind by a supernatural revelation will involve an objective manifestation of God, the meaning of which will be communicated to the mind, not by the exercise of the ordinary faculties, but by inspiration. To such a manifestation, therefore, inspiration will be strictly limited.

Now, if the Creator be pleased to make a supernatural revelation of Himself, that revelation must be made relatively to the faculties of those for whom it is intended; it could not be an absolute, but a relative revelation. It must have a special object and a particular purpose. Consequently, if God determined in Himself the extent of truth which He had resolved to communicate, those who believe in the divine inspiration of the Scriptures, while they deny their verbal inspiration, maintain that the inspiration would be strictly limited to the special subject-matter which God intended to disclose, and to the faculties through the agency of which He purposed to make the disclosure. If, therefore, the revelation was made in a form which either admitted or required the intermixture of other subject-matter with its contents besides the special truths which it was the Divine purpose to disclose, they consider that divine inspiration would only be afforded to the truths forming the proper subject of the divine communication. Consequently, if it is assumed that the Christian Scriptures contain a revelation from God, and that for special reasons those Scriptures have been composed in an historical form, many subjects may be introduced into them external to the proper subject-matter of a revelation, for the recording of which the assistance of supernatural inspiration may not have been afforded. The necessity for inspiration would only extend to that portion of them in which the truths which it was the special purpose of God to reveal were contained.

Different views are taken by persons who believe in the reality of a divine revelation, as to the manner in which the inspiration itself has been afforded. According to one view, the revelation has been communicated in all its fulness, once and for all, to the mind of the inspired person; and after he has been once perfectly taught the contents of the revelation, he has been left to the exercise of his ordinary faculties in making known to others those contents. Others think it more probable that, after the contents of the revelation have been communicated to the mind, a constant supernatural guidance has been afforded whenever the revelation was communicated to others, so far as to avoid the danger arising from the imperfection of the human faculties, and to communicate that revelation with absolute truth and correctness. The inspiration by which the Christian Scriptures have been revealed may have been communicated in this manner. The whole of the divine truths contained in them may have been clearly discovered by one original act of inspiration, and then left to the action of the ordinary faculties of the mind; or those faculties may have been assisted, whenever those truths were communicated to others, by the presence of supernatural inspiration, allowing other elements in different measures and degrees to coexist with that inspiration.

Different opinions are held as to the degree in which such assistance has been afforded. As we are imperfect judges of the extent in which God would be pleased to make a revelation, so we must be equally imperfect judges of the extent in which He would be pleased to exercise such guidance over the persons employed in communicating it. All that can be asserted with certainty is, that to whatever extent it is the purpose of God to reveal Himself, His purpose, whatever it may be, will certainly be accomplished. Any modification, therefore, of view respecting the Divine purposes as to the extent of the revelation will render necessary a corresponding modification as to the instrumentality through which those purposes have been accomplished.

The revelation contained in the Christian Scriptures is in an historical form. As they contain a great variety of matter, different portions of the matter contained in them may have required different degrees of inspiration for the assistance of the writers in their composition. Some portions of the Christian Scriptures consist of accounts of facts which have actually occurred; other portions are descriptions of feelings which have been experienced by the writers. Some portions consist of precepts for the regulation of conduct; other portions profess to be revelations of great truths. They likewise contain allusions to various customs, manners, and historical events. The Epistles contain details of the conduct of the writers when placed in particular situations. Now the contents of the Christian Scriptures being of this varied description, different opinions are held by those who believe that they have been communicated under the influence of supernatural inspiration, as to what degree elements thus widely different in character have required that supernatural assistance should be afforded to the authors. With persons who believe that God never employs unnecessary means to effectuate His ends, it would be a probability almost approaching to certainty that God would proportion the aid of inspiration to the requirements of the different subject-matters contained in the Scriptures. The allusion to an ordinary matter of fact or to some historical detail lying within the powers of the ordinary faculties of the writers would require the aid of a far less degree of supernatural assistance than the statement of some great truth respecting the Divine character and perfections. Among those, therefore, who are firm believers that the Christian Scriptures have been communicated by the aid of divine inspiration, it may still be an open question as to the extent in which particular portions of the Scripture have participated in that inspiration.

It has been asserted that the correct view of inspiration is, that the spirit of man is penetrated in all its functions and powers by the Spirit of God, and thereby all its thoughts, conceptions, and powers are elevated to a height to which they would otherwise be incapable of attaining. According to this theory, inspiration consists in a preternatural elevation of the existing powers of the human mind.

We are quite unable to determine to what extent truths which lie beyond the reach of our present faculties would be discoverable by the mind if the powers of those faculties were indefinitely multiplied. A large amount of truth, of a similar description as that with which we are at present acquainted, would undoubtedly be thrown open to our view; but whether the intensification of our faculties would enable us to penetrate into new and distinct regions of truth, we have no data to determine.

We therefore cannot concede that it is an adequate account of what we mean when we assert that a revelation has been communicated by inspiration from God, to define the influence by which the revealed truths have been communicated as a simple intensification of the existing faculties of man. Such an increase of power, while it might have greatly enlarged our knowledge of present truths, might have admitted us to the acquaintance of no new species of truth. The Holy Spirit might penetrate and intensify all the existing powers of the mind, and yet they might leave us in the dark on various subjects respecting the Divine character and perfections of the highest importance for us to be informed on.

But if inspiration consisted simply in a communication of an increase of power to the ordinary faculties of the mind, one element essential to a divine revelation would be wanting. The person thus inspired would not be sensible that the source of his additional knowledge would be the testimony of a personality external to his own mind. He could have no direct evidence that the truths communicated to him were imparted by God. Such truths, therefore, would have no higher authority to bind the conscience than those discovered by the ordinary course of our mental operations. In the case of a revelation of the Divine will, we want to have distinct evidence that it is God who is speaking, and not man. Although He may employ certain portions of man's ordinary mental powers in communicating a revelation, its very notion implies a direct sense of the presence of God in the mind of him to whom the revelation is imparted.

We do not deny that the effect of inspiration on the human mind may be to intensify the existing powers, and call them into a far more vigorous action. Such an effect seems to have been produced on the writers both of the Old and New Testaments. But if we restrict inspiration to the production of this result, we make no sufficiently clear distinction between it and the ordinary operations of the mind of man.

The supporters of this theory hold a very extensive communication of an inspiration of this description. Many are of opinion that in this sense most of the great writers in the world's history, who have produced beneficial results, have been inspired. The view is closely connected with that to which we have already alluded, which confuses between God's providential government of the world and the results of supernatural inspiration.

To one more theory we must make a brief allusion—that which identifies the ordinary operation of God's Spirit in sanctifying the heart with the results of divine inspiration.

Into the profound depths of this question we shall not enter. It would require to be discussed in a separate treatise. We shall only make two observations respecting it.

The action of the Holy Spirit in new-creating the heart must unquestionably open to the intellect discoveries of spiritual truth substantially new. The new feelings and affections implanted in the soul must introduce a fresh body of truth into the understanding. If the renovation of the human mind imparts to it a fresh spiritual sense, a fresh body of truth by this influence must be discovered by the mind precisely proportionate to the change wrought in the feelings and affections in the soul. So far the influence exerted may be similar.

But if we restrict inspiration to an influence of this description, we shall unduly narrow the limits of what we mean when we speak of God's making a supernatural revelation. Such an expression implies the direct imparting by God of objective truth to the mind, not a mere creation of subjective feelings and affections which throw their light into the human understanding. That such influence may be closely allied to that which we designate by the expression divine inspiration, we are far from denying; but it were to confound ideas essentially distinct to confine it to such influence, and to assert that it gives a full account of those phenomena which we designate by the term divine inspiration. One essential element it would leave entirely wanting—the distinct perception by the mind possessed of inspiration that it was God who was imparting truth to the mind by a direct personal agency.

Such then are some of the theories which are held by those who believe in the supernatural inspiration of the Christian Scriptures respecting the nature of that inspiration. No opinion is at present expressed as to the truth or the fallacy of those views. They have been stated because, in examining the nature of the inspiration of the writers of the New Testament, it is necessary that we should have a distinct view of these various theories.

In determining the question as to the nature and extent of the inspiration vouchsafed to the writers of the Christian Scriptures, if we assume that they are a revelation from God, there are only two modes of inquiry open to us. First, what is the degree of light which is thrown on the subject by any antecedent certainty or antecedent probability which the mind possesses independently of all inquiry into the nature of the facts presented by the Christian Scriptures? Secondly, supposing that the Scriptures are authenticated as a revelation from God, what assertions do they make respecting the nature of the inspiration under the influence of which they have been composed, and what degree of inspiration do the phenomena contained in the Scriptures necessarily presuppose to have been afforded to the writers?

We will now proceed to examine what degree of antecedent certainty we possess as to the nature and degree of the inspiration of a revelation, supposing that it is the purpose of God to communicate a revelation of Himself to man.

Now the amount of the inspiration through which a revelation has been communicated to man is a question quite distinct from the divine origin of the revelation itself. Our belief as to whether a revelation has been made by God to man must be entirely dependent on the evidence afforded as to its reality. A revelation professing to come from God must be sufficiently attested as having Him for its author, before any one can be called on to believe in its divine character. We cannot be satisfied with a mere declaration of any person claiming to publish a revelation that he is under the influence of inspiration as a sufficient ground for believing that he is so. Something more than mere assertion is positively required. But the determination of the nature and degree of the inspiration with which a revelation has been given is a matter entirely distinct from the sufficiency of the evidence on which a belief in its divine origin rests. If the attestation to any revelation that it is of divine origin is sufficient, our belief that it is such a revelation in no way depends on our views as to the nature and extent of the inspiration under the influence of which it has been communicated.

This distinction has been frequently overlooked. It has often been asserted that the denial of a particular mode of inspiration is equivalent to the denial of the divine origin of the revelation itself. But the question whether any particular person is authorized to publish a revelation from God, or whether any particular book contains an account of such revelation, is a point which must be determined wholly by evidence. It resolves itself into the inquiry, Have we, or have we not, sufficient evidence that such a particular person has been authorized by God to publish a revelation of His will? Can he produce the broad seal of Almighty God, guaranteeing to us the truth of his divine commission?

CHAPTER IV.

THE POSSIBILITY OF A MIRACULOUS INSPIRATION, AND THE MODE ADOPTED IN ITS COMMUNICATION.

THE certainty that a revelation has been made by Almighty God must ultimately resolve itself into the question, whether it has received a miraculous attestation. Such an attestation is the only means whereby the reality of a divine commission can be directly proved. Other evidence, such as the moral character of the revelation, may afford corroboration to the proof; but the moral character of a revelation alone would be powerless to assure us of its divine authority, or to render it binding on the conscience, without the support of a miraculous testimony. A miracle denotes the finger of God. A revelation guaranteed by a miraculous testimony must be believed to be such, whatever questions may be raised as to the extent of the inspiration through which it has been communicated. The degree of the inspiration can have nothing to do with the evidence on which the reality of the miracles rests.

But it is extensively held that the human mind possesses antecedent grounds of certainty, which render all inquiry into the evidence of a supposed revelation unnecessary, and a miraculous attestation to such a revelation impossible. The ground on which such an assertion is made is, that the universe is regulated by one unvarying principle of law or order, from which all deviation is impossible. A divine revelation supernaturally communicated, or a miracle as the evidence of such a revelation, would be a violation of the established law and order by which the universe is regulated. From this principle no deviation has taken place within the experience of man. It is not asserted that human experience is cognizant of all the actings of God, or even with a considerable portion of them; but it is assumed that the experience of man with respect to the subjection of the created universe to unalterable law is a fair representation of all the actings of God which do not come within the range of that experience.

From these premises it is assumed that action in conformity with law and order is an essential attribute of the Divine mind, and that everything contained within the universe must be an exhibition of this portion of the Divine character. It is deduced as a consequence from these premises, that if the Creator were to violate the existing order of the universe, He would deny an essential attribute of His own nature. But as a supernatural revelation, from its very conception, must be a deviation from the universal law and order by which the universe is governed, every miracle performed in attestation of such a revelation must be an additional violation of this principle. If, then, from its very conception, a miraculous revelation must be a violation of previously existing law, it follows on indubitable grounds of antecedent certainty, that both such a revelation itself and the only evidence which can support it are impossibilities, being repugnant to the known character of God.

This reasoning is frequently supported by other minor

considerations. It is urged that it is more worthy of the Creator that He should only act in conformity with law, than that He should deviate from it, in effectuating His purposes. It would be a reflection on His wisdom, if, after having once established a particular order, He had any necessity for its violation. It is urged that it presents a far more glorious view of the Divine perfections if we assume that there never has been any occasion for the interference of the Creator, in altering the existing laws of the universe, since the period when He first created it. It gives the highest ideas of the Divine power and wisdom if we suppose that the Creator, in His primitive act of creation, so regulated the universe by law that it has ever since continued to evolve itself in steady subjection to those laws, which have been laid down with such perfect wisdom as never to have required one special interference from the hour of creation.

Now, on what are these views based? Have they any grounds of positive certainty on which to rest? Are the reasons alleged self-evident truths or uncertain probabilities?

We have no intention to deny that on some subjects grounds of antecedent certainty exist, which are valid evidence on which the mind must rest prior to all inquiry as to fact. If such principles possess the evidence of demonstration, the mind is unable to refuse its assent to them; but such grounds of belief must be self-evident truths, or capable of demonstration from self-evident principles. They must not be mere probabilities, which, when they are applied as exponents of the modes of the action of the Creator, lead to results which experience testifies to be universally untrue.

The objection resolves itself into two parts. First, it is contrary to the Creator's character as a lover of law and order to manifest Himself at all in any other manner than that in which He has manifested Himself in the creation and government of the universe. Secondly, that any miraculous attestation to such a supposed revelation is, for the same reason, impossible.

Now it must be conceded that, as far as man's knowledge of the created universe extends, one universal principle of law and order is the rule by which the Creator manifests Himself in its creation and providence. Every phenomenon with which we are acquainted in the universe is the effect of law. The inanimate universe is regulated by universal laws of unvarying constancy, no deviation from which has ever come under the cognizance of man. Those laws contain within them the principle of their own preservation. There is one unvarying sequence of cause and effect. With respect to the sensient creation, the same general principle prevails. But here our knowledge is less complete. The free will of man interferes with the operation of mere physical laws. It presents phenomena of a character entirely distinct from the results of those operations. Free will, as a cause, differs in its entire conception from mere physical sequence. Our conception of a personal God involves the highest exercise of free will. The free spontaneity of His will has produced creation; but how and when the various orders of beings have been brought into existence we have no positive data to determine. Theories in abundance have been propounded; but whatever knowledge may be hereafter obtained on the subject, the evidence as to their origin which is possessed from an induction of facts is wholly insufficient to entitle the theories which have been propounded on the subject to be reckoned among established truths. They are only deductions from probabilities or remote analogies.

Those who propound the views of which we have been speaking assert that species have been evolved successively, without any fresh creative act, from species previously existing, and that the higher forms of being have been gradually developed from the lower, in ever-increasing perfection, until at last the production of man has been the crowning result of these successive developments. This assertion, however, is a theory, of which the proof, if not wholly wanting, must be pronounced to rest on evidence indefinitely small. The paucity of the data on which the theory is erected, compared with the vast extent of the theory itself, is of a very surprising character. Those who hold the contrary opinion maintain that each separate species has come into existence by a separate creative act. The opponents of this view reply, that the number of these species requires such a number of creative acts as to render such a supposition improbable.

But on what observed facts does the former of these theories rest? on what is the opinion founded? On the observed laws of order which the inanimate creation obeys. But have we a knowledge of the laws by which the entire universe is governed? If not, by what right do we extend our inferences from such laws into regions essentially distinct? Our observations are confined to existing phenomena, and lie entirely beyond the region of creative acts. To extend inferences drawn from existing phenomena into the region of creative acts is to assume as true what ought to be proved. Positive proof that species have been evolved from species by the action of general laws, there is none. No fact of such transformation can be adduced. Geology supplies no direct evidence of such transformations. No one instance has yet been found of an organized being in a state of transition from one species to another.

But because the natural universe, as far as it has come under observation, obeys the law of order, and is regulated by a necessary sequence of causes and effects, it has been affirmed that every other portion of the universe must have been evolved in conformity with the same law. Such an inference has been said to be not in conformity with probability merely, but with analogy.

It must be admitted that analogy is a much higher ground for belief than bare probability; but we are entitled to ask whether we have any evidence or experience sufficiently extended to assure us that in such a case the analogy will hold. Considering the infinite variety of modes in which it may please the Creator to manifest Himself, an analogy derived from one single mode of His manifestation can be no certain guide to one of an entirely different description. Before, therefore, we can assume that the whole of the manifestations of the Creator in the universe are simple manifestations of law and order, and that He never manifests Himself by occasional deviations from them, we require evidence of a positive, and not of an analogical character. Before we can apply analogical evidence in such a case, we must be certain that the facts from which the analogies are derived are fair representations of the conduct of the Creator. We must be sure that our field of vision is not a narrow corner of the universe, but that it commands an extensive view of its general principles. In this case the extent of our knowledge is too limited to admit of such an application. The theory does not profess to be founded on an induction of facts, and is wholly inapplicable to creative acts.

Our finite experience is of a nature far too limited to enable us to judge what is or what is not antecedently probable with respect to the Creator in matters of this description, or to assume on such data that God cannot deviate from such laws as our limited experience of His actings has induced us to consider as the laws which regulate His conduct. This experience is a safe guide to truth within its legitimate bounds; extended beyond the limits of those boundaries, it leads to inferences not resting on certainty, but bare probability.

Unless a divine revelation or a miracle were a deviation from the ordinary law of the Creator's acting, it would lose its essential character as a revelation or a miracle. It is the very essence of the nature of miracles that they should be such a deviation: it forms the groundwork of our conception of them. As man's experience is finite, it is evident that an infinite amount of the actings of God must lie beyond its range. He cannot, therefore, be in a position to lay down the laws of what is, or what is not, possible with God. The experience of man can only bring under our observation what is a mere sample of the actings of the Creator.

We have therefore no grounds for assuming that the actings of the infinite Being, which in past eternity must have been as infinite as Himself, are all of one and the same character, or that their nature can be adequately represented by the small number of them which have come under our limited observation. We are ready to grant that a deviation from law and order in the mode of the Divine actings has never come under scientific experience. Yet it is too much to assume, from this experience, that the eternal Creator, in all the modes of His self-manifestation in the course of a bygone eternity, can never have acted otherwise than in conformity with that experience.

From the nature of the case our inductions respecting the past actings of the Eternal and the Infinite must be of a far less general nature than those of the Indian king who, on the strength of the evidence of his contracted experience, pronounced that the existence of ice was an impossibility. It was beyond the limits of his experience; but his experience was no measure of the universal experience of man. He argued from analogy. That analogy held good within the range of the circumstances to which it was applicable; it led to untrue inferences when it was assumed as a universal measure of things. In a far greater degree any conclusions founded on the limited experience of man, as to what must have been the mode of the acting of the Infinite and the Eternal throughout the infinitude of the present and the past, must be founded on an induction far too limited to enable us to assert what is or is not possible with God. Who will venture to assert that, in the eternity of the past or in the infinitude of the present, the Divine mode of acting may not have presented a character entirely different from any manifestation which has taken place within the limited sphere of our finite view? To assert that our experience is an adequate measure of the mode of the Divine acting is a conclusion far too wide to be founded on mere probability or analogy. Such a conclusion requires the support of an evidence which is unattainable by man.

It is impossible, therefore, on the foundation of any experience which is attainable by man, to arrive at the conclusion that law or order is so essential a conception of the Divine nature that any deviation from them is repugnant to our conception of the Divine attributes, and therefore antecedently impossible. But the theory under discussion presupposes that they are such essential qualities of the Divine mind, that any deviation from them involves a contradiction. On both points the evidence is imperfect. We do not know on any evidence which must command the assent of the understanding, even if the Creator's actings had been founded on these principles, that it is self-contradictory that he should act in a different manner. The assertion that such is the invariable mode of the acting of the Creator is founded on an induction which extends only as far as the experience of man. Beyond that experience lie the infinite actings of God in the eternity of His existence. This assertion is of the same class as numerous other *à priori* assertions, which are found to be utterly groundless when they are tested by experience. To justify us in assuming that the Creator cannot deviate from those laws which have come under human observation in the government of the universe, we ought to have evidence nothing short of demonstration that such deviation must be repugnant to the Divine perfections.

It cannot be proved that the evidence which we possess, that the love of law and order is so essential an attribute of the Divine mind as to render all deviation from it on the part of the Creator impossible, exceeds the evidence which we possess of the other attributes of God; or that conclusions founded on this portion of the Divine character will be more certain guides as to what has been the actual conduct of the Creator than conclusions professedly deduced from the other perfections of His nature. But those conclusions founded on the other attributes of God, when pushed to their strict logical consequences, are found to be incorrect guides to the actual facts presented by the universe. Why, then, should such principles be assumed as correct guides in determining questions respecting the possibility or the impossibility of a divine revelation?

It is impossible to deduce the facts of the actual structure of the universe by *à priori* arguments derived from our human views of the Divine perfections. To adduce a few examples. The power of the Creator is infinite. We might infer, therefore, that every exertion of His power ought to contain distinct traces of His infinity. No one exertion of that power ought to admit of increase, or contain traces of defect. But, according to our modes of conception, every exertion of that power is not a display of infinite power; it is only such a display of power as the necessities of the case demand.

In like manner, it is an undoubted truth that the Almighty is infinitely wise. Shall we infer from this attribute that every created thing as it exists in the universe must have had the whole treasures of this infinite wisdom expended on it? If this conclusion be true, the Creator could not make ever-increasing displays of the profundity of His wisdom. Because God is infinitely wise, no person will maintain that in each special manifestation of His wisdom the whole resources of that wisdom must be displayed. In the manifestation of his wisdom displayed in His works, we observe degrees of wisdom actually employed. If we were able to comprehend the works of the Creator taken as a whole, we might discover in them the resources of infinite wisdom. But the works of the Creator, taken as a whole, do not exist to finite minds. There is not only the past eternity in which He has operated, but there is the eternity yet to come, in which he will never cease from His glorious manifestation. But man can only conceive of them under the limitation of time. The resources of infinite wisdom cannot be displayed in special acts. Even in any existing state of the universe, the profundities of His wisdom are not exerted in any single manifestation, but they will require an eternity in which they will be unfolded.

Another attribute of the Creator, which the supporters of the theory we are impugning are the foremost to maintain, is His goodness. That God is perfectly good is a great truth at the foundation of religion.

But will it be maintained by the supporters of this theory, that in every creative act of God we find a perfect manifestation of the attribute of goodness? On the contrary, all their views of the universe are based on the supposition that in His actual working God commences with lower beginnings, and advances to more perfect displays of goodness. The universe, as it comes under human observation, is no perfect display of that attribute. Arguments deduced from that attribute by strict logical consequence would lead us to infer a different structure of the universe from that which actually exists. We might argue from the existence in the Creator of the attribute of perfect goodness, united with infinite wisdom and power, that the existence of evil, whether moral or physical, would be utterly impossible. For this conclusion we have far higher grounds of antecedent probability than that a miraculous revelation is impossible, because the love of law and order are attributes of the Almighty.

The argument which infers from the perfect goodness of the Creator, united with His infinite wisdom and power, that evil could not exist in the universe of which He is the Creator and Governor, would lead us to a conclusion which contradicts the actual phenomena of that universe as they come under our observation. Evil exists in the universe of the all-powerful, the all-wise, and the all-perfect God, however contrary it may be to our ideas of antecedent certainty that it would exist. If we cannot infer from the attributes of infinite power, wisdom, and perfect goodness in the Creator that evil cannot exist in the universe of which He is the author, we are in no position to argue that a supernatural revelation or miracles wrought in its attestation are impossible, because the love of order and law are conceived of by us as among the attributes of God.

But the asserters of this opinion maintain that the unalterable and universal dominion of law and order in the universe affords the most perfect conception which we can form of that universe as framed by the creative power of God, and as governed by the wisdom of His providence. They assume that the highest conception which can be framed of the wisdom and power of the Creator is, that He so formed the universe at the beginning, and impressed its laws on it with that perfection of wisdom, that they have by their own self-acting evolved every existing thing, without the necessity of a single subsequent interposition of the Creator's hand. It is asserted to be the highest possible view which we can take of the character of God, that by one act of creation He has accomplished His work, and that the creation has since evolved itself according to His eternal laws, without the necessity of His special intervention. It would undoubtedly denote a higher degree of wisdom in a human artist, if he could not only form an instrument or piece of machinery fully capable of executing its purpose, but which also possessed the power of generating a new piece of machinery out of itself in endless succession, equally capable of executing the intentions of the original contriver. Because it is assumed that such a view is the highest which can be taken of the intelligence and power of the Creator, it is taken for granted that it is the only one in conformity with which He can act in the government of the universe.

If this theory be correct, it follows that any variation from this law would imply a lower display of the perfection of God. But a revelation or a miracle is a deviation from established order previously existing; it involves a special intervention of the Creator. His original contrivances must therefore have been imperfect, to render such a special intervention necessary. His work was not perfect from the first; but as the Creator is perfect, no work involving imperfection can be His. A revelation, therefore, and miracles wrought in attestation of it are impossible.

Such reasonings might have considerable cogency if we had sufficient evidence that the Creator had no other perfection beyond that of the most perfect of mechanists. A mechanist who can make a machine so perfect as never to require rectification, which contains within itself the powers necessary for its own reparation, and which, in addition to these extraordinary properties, could evolve out of itself in endless succession other similar machines, would undoubtedly display greater resources of wisdom and power than one who could only make a machine without the other properties in question. Such a mechanist would be the most perfect of mechanists; he would make a single machine, and retire from action for ever; his perfection would be so great, that even if he were to cease to exist, he would not be found wanting!

But in reply we ask, Is the only view which we can take of the character of the Creator that of a perfect mechanist or chemist? Has He no moral attributes through which to display the glories of His being? May He not make a manifestation of them, as well as of His wisdom and His power? Has He not also a personality? Is not the absolute freedom of His will a most glorious attribute of His nature? May not a manifestation of the self-determination of His free will be as glorious a display of His character as an invariable acting in conformity with order and law by physical sequence? May He not stand in other relations to His creatures than those of a simple mechanist or a chemist? May He not also manifest Himself to them in the capacity of a Father? His character as Father of rational beings is a most glorious attribute of the Eternal. Is it not possible that He may appear more glorious in some one or in all of these aspects than by a mere exhibition of Himself as the most perfect mechanist, whose perfection was so great that He needed to act only once, and then for ever sink into inactivity, and be to us as though He existed not? Such possibilities are worthy of being seriously reflected on before the theory in question is propounded as the only possible account of the Divine conduct.

It by no means follows that, because such a view may give us the most exalted idea of the Creator as a mechanical contriver, it is the best means of displaying the other perfections of His nature, or that the simple idea of God as the most perfect of mechanical contrivers is the most glorious manifestation of the Creator. Nothing is more necessary, in order that the mind of man may have perfect trust in God, than that it should have a most distinct and constant perception of His personality. A sense of the Divine personality forms the foundation of all feeling towards Him in the capacity of a Father. It is surely equally important that His creatures should be capable of contemplating their Creator as a Father, as that they should view Him as the most perfect of mechanical contrivers. But unalterable continuity of action destroys man's sense of personality. The pure spontaneity of will is not most clearly manifested by the action of immutable and eternal law. Action in conformity with never-deviating law, unless corrected by other influences, has a tendency to produce the belief that the action is mechanical or dynamical, not spontaneous or free. Occasional interruptions in the continuity of the action of God may be necessary as evidence of the personality of the Creator. If, therefore, He be anything else than a mere mechanist, it may be no diminution of His perfection to interrupt the law and order of the universe by occasional manifestations of Himself, and to instruct His creatures by means of a supernatural revelation.

But even on the theorizer's own representation of his theory, it contains in it one weak point, which brings it to inevitable ruin and destruction. On his own principles, there has been at least one interruption of the law and order of all things. The universe is not the result of blind necessity or chance, but the work of an intelligent Creator. Creation, therefore, had a beginning. There once was a time, however remotely distant, when finite existence began to be. The only way in which this consequence can be evaded is to break down the distinction between the finite and the infinite, and to take refuge in pantheism. Before the commencement of the finite, the infinite existed alone. The infinite must once have evolved the finite. The laws which the Creator has impressed on created things may have been so perfect as never to have required any interference on His part from the first act of creation by any fresh exertion of creative power or special interference of His providence. But one interruption of law and order has taken place, when the Creator produced the finite. Prior to the creation of the finite, law and order subsisted only in the bosom of the Infinite.

The creation of the finite must have been the greatest of all conceivable interruptions of that state of order which previously existed. Hitherto creative power had never energized in the upholding of the finite. But if one interruption, and that the greatest of all interruptions, of order previously existing has taken place, and in it the Creator has been essentially glorious, why may He not, in the unknown depths of His wisdom, make other interruptions, and in them appear equally glorious? As He has once become the author of the natural revelation, why may not He become the author of a new moral and spiritual creation? A new moral and spiritual creation is surely as worthy an occasion for the exertion of creative energy as the production of the material universe.

In making these observations we have no intention of disputing the truth of the assertion that manifestations in conformity with law and order are the only manifestations made by the Divine mind in the material universe, as far as scientific experience has yet penetrated. But how can we know that it is not the necessary condition of enabling the human mind to grasp a distinct conception of the personality of God, that a general principle of acting in conformity with law, united with occasional deviations from such a mode of action, should be the mode in which the Creator manifests Himself to His creatures? What actual experience have we of creative acts? Distinction between species exists as a fact in creation. The generation of new orders can be as readily accounted for by an exertion of the creative power of God as by a gradual evolution of one species from another by the agency of natural laws. Why, then, are creative acts deemed incredible? Unless pantheism is the true solution of the existence of the universe, one creative act there must have been; and if one, why not more? And if creative acts be not incredible, how can miracles be impossible? Variations from existing laws may even be necessary to enable us to appreciate the fulness of the beauty of the usual laws of order under which the Infinite has manifested Himself. Variation itself seems to be one of the necessary conditions of perception. What is it which gives us a sense of the beauty of the law and order by which the universe is regulated and governed? Our power of comparing it with irregularity and disorder.

We conclude, therefore, that we have no grounds of antecedent certainty which can justify us in drawing the conclusion that the uninterrupted observance of law in the universe is so glorious a representation of the character of God as to amount to a demonstration that all deviations from it are impossible in Him, nor from its existence in the material universe can there be any adequate grounds for inferring that a discovery of Himself by means of a revelation attested by miracles is impossible with God, or involving any violation of the Divine attributes.

But we are entitled to draw a contrary inference. If God has once in the course of His actings deviated from the order previously existing, we infer with inevitable certainty that what He has done once He may do again. He has once made this deviation, when He created the finite; He may, therefore, make another deviation for the purpose of effecting a new moral and spiritual creation.

A revelation, therefore, accompanied with miracles wrought in attestation of it, contradicts no known truth respecting the Divine nature. Miracles could prove no adequate attestation of a divine commission, if the usual mode of the Divine acting was not in conformity with law. If their performance was frequent, our notion of law, and consequently our idea of a miracle, would be subverted. The assumption, therefore, that a revelation with a miraculous attestation is impossible, is a mere theory unsupported by evidence : it rests for support on no intuitive truth, nor can it be demonstrated to be a consequence of such truth.

There is one antecedent probability, respecting the mode of communicating a revelation, which has the self-evidence of an axiom. To whatever extent it was the purpose of God to reveal Himself in a revelation, that purpose, in whatever revelation He was pleased to make, He would fully and effectually accomplish.

Such a proposition simply asserts that, in the case of a Being who is infinitely powerful and wise, His purposes and the effects resulting from those purposes are necessarily coincident. With the Almighty, to will is to accomplish. He has the most perfect knowledge of the means by which His volitions can be effectuated. His infinite power gives Him an absolute command of those means. He can therefore have neither impediment nor hindrance in the execution of His designs. To whatever extent the Creator has determined to reveal Himself, that purpose He must have thoroughly and completely effected. If this were not the case, there must exist a limitation either to His power or His knowledge.

But before we can apply this truth for the purpose of determining the nature of the revelation, or the instrumentality through which it has been communicated, we must know the extent of truth which it was the Divine purpose to reveal. But we are no adequate judges af the amount of truth which God must communicate to man. We cannot, therefore, determine the precise extent in which it would please God to make a revelation of Himself. We can only know what He ought to reveal, by ascertaining from His own declarations what He has been pleased to reveal. We shall then be fully justified in concluding that the Divine purposes have been fully carried into effect in every communication which possesses evidences of being a divine revelation.

It is also a truth of the highest antecedent certainty, that neither in the subject-matter of a revelation nor in the means employed for its communication can the Creator act contrary to the moral attributes of His nature. There are many points connected with those attributes, which, as we have seen, lie beyond the range of the human understanding; but, within the limits of that understanding, it is a universal truth that the Creator can only act according to the moral perfections of His nature. If we were to assume that God could act otherwise, it would be equivalent to the admission that God can act without motives. The moral attributes of the Deity must be the motives of the Divine conduct. The imperfection of our understandings impairs the force of our conclusions when we attempt to argue to things as they must exist from the separate attributes of God, because we are unable to determine the bearing of one of those attributes on another. But within those limits where the mind has adequate powers of judgment, we may safely conclude that whatever professes to be a revelation from God, and contradicts the Divine attributes in their great and essential bearings, brings with it direct evidence of untruthfulness and imposture. The principle is only dangerous when it is pushed into regions of thought where the limited intelligence of man renders him an incompetent judge either of the Divine attributes themselves or of the general system of the Divine government.

We may also assume on principles of analogy, united with considerations derived from the Divine character, that if it pleased God to communicate a knowledge of Himself by a supernatural revelation, the knowledge which He was pleased to communicate by such a revelation would not be extended to those subjects the knowledge of which the human mind was able to attain by means previously imparted.

The evidence of this truth rests on direct analogy, derived from God's mode of action as Creator and Preserver of the universe, supported by considerations deduced from His infinite wisdom and power. The force of such an analogy, derived from actual manifestations of the Creator, as to what His conduct would be in other similar manifestations, differs entirely in point of evidence from a mere antecedent probability. It reaches little short of certainty when the analogies themselves fully coincide with conclusions respecting the Divine conduct which we should deduce from the Divine perfections. If God has acted in a particular manner in one case, it affords a probability, amounting to a certainty, that He will act in the same way in a similar case when the same perfections of His nature are involved.

Now we observe that, in His works of creation and providence, the Creator never uses a double set of means for the purpose of effectuating the same end; He can have no occasion to do so. Infinite power furnishes Him with every possible resource for effectuating His purposes. No possibility is beyond the reach of Omnipotence. Whatever can be, He can effectuate and call into being. His infinite wisdom gives Him the most perfect knowledge of the means suited for carrying His purposes into effect. There is no possible contrivance which He does not know, and which, knowing, He cannot create. There is no possible result which He does not foresee, and against which He cannot provide. Consequently whenever God acts He has the most perfect knowledge of the means which He uses, and of the mode in which His purposes

E

can be effectuated, and the most perfect power to create the means and adapt them to their respective uses. The means which the Creator uses, therefore, cannot fail to effectuate His ends; consequently He cannot have occasion to use a double instrumentality.

In conformity with this great principle are the facts of nature. Whether the operation be great or small, we always see the Almighty working by a single set of instruments. He never makes provision for the possible failure of one instrumentality, by providing another to aid or supplement it. No two sets of means are provided for producing the same result. The simplicity of the Divine operations always stands in marked contrast to the multiform contrivances of man. This is the uniform mode of the Divine agency, whether we trace the operations of the Almighty in the force with which He propels a planet, in the wondrous contrivances with which He has constructed the bodies of animals and vegetables, or in the minute structure of a microscopic animalcule.

The use of a double set of means for effectuating the same end is the result of a consciousness of imperfection of power or wisdom in the operator. Such consciousness of imperfection cannot exist in the Almighty. When man provides a double instrumentality or multiform contrivances for the execution of the same work, he does so under the fear that one of his instruments may fail in producing that which he is seeking to effectuate, or owing to his imperfect command of means. If we were certain that one instrumentality would effect our purpose, or if all means lay freely at our disposal, it would be a deficiency of wisdom to provide a variety of contrivances; but neither fear as to the result of His operations, nor deficiency of wisdom, is possible with the Creator.

The same mode of operation which God employs as Creator and Preserver of the universe we should expect that He would employ in communicating a revelation of His will. As it is inconsistent with His perfections to employ two distinct and separate means for effectuating the same end in creation, so it is in the highest degree improbable that He would communicate the same truth to man by two methods wholly and entirely distinct. What the perfections of the Divine nature have prompted Him to do in the one series of acts, the same perfections will prompt Him to do in a similar course of action. If the same God is the author of creation, providence, and revelation, we should find Him displaying in each alike the same power and wisdom. He would not provide man with adequate means of attaining truth by natural revelation, and then provide a wholly different means of attaining to the same truths by means of a supernatural revelation. What, therefore, God has provided man with adequate means of learning by the use of his natural faculties, by the study of the created universe, that knowledge He would not communicate by a wholly different instrumentality—that of inspiration.

Still less is it conceivable that the infinitely wise Creator would use two different methods of discovering the same truth to man, the one of which would render necessary a great degree of exertion on his part in the discovery of truth, and the other would discover the same truth without any effort on the part of man being needful. If there are two methods of doing the same thing, a laborious one and an easy one, the easy one will be adopted, the laborious one avoided. Who would trouble himself with the laborious investigations of geology, if its truths could be read in the pages of a supernatural revelation? Who would undertake the laborious exertion of research in all the great branches of science, if God had provided a shorter, an easier, a more royal road to the attainment of truth? All the most valuable of the truths which man discovers by the exercise of his natural powers require exertion for their discovery. If these truths were also discovered by divine revelation, the necessity of laborious exertion would be entirely superseded.

All the great truths to which man has attained by the use of his natural faculties have required a great expenditure of labour for their discovery. The exercise of the higher powers of the mind in the discovery of those truths is the divinely appointed means by which, in the natural course of things, the knowledge of them is attainable. Few persons unacquainted with these subjects can form an adequate idea of the amount of labour by which the great discoveries in mathematical and physical science have been effected.

The expenditure of labour as the necessary condition is the universal law which the Creator has imposed in the attainment of every ordinary branch of human knowledge. The higher the truth the greater is the labour necessary for its acquisition. God has placed His book of nature open for man to read it, but He has not intended that he should read it without the exertion of all his mental powers. Man's discoveries in the kingdoms of nature and providence have been vast; but they have been effected by means of the highest energy and exertion. Is it to be supposed, then, that God would ordain a laborious method for the discovery of truth, and supersede His own appointed method by discovering those truths by a supernatural revelation?

We may lay it down, therefore, as a condition by which the extent of a divine revelation will be limited, that God will not communicate to man by inspiration the knowledge which He has already given him ample means of acquiring by the exercise of his natural powers. The inspiration, therefore, with which a revelation would be communicated would not be extended to matters adventitious to the proper subject-matter of that revelation.

It follows as a necessary consequence that the truths of physical science would form no proper subject-matter of a divine revelation, nor would be communicated to man by supernatural inspiration. God has already provided man with a distinct and separate instrumentality, affording him ample means of attaining the knowledge of those truths—the laborious exertion of the powers of his mind on the phenomena presented to him by God in the book of nature. To suppose that the Creator has ordained this laborious method of arriving at these truths, and then discovered them by a preternatural revelation, would be little short of ascribing to Him an act of folly of which man would not be guilty.

If this view of the case be correct, numerous objections against divine revelation, arising out of difficulties suggested by physical science, at once fall to the ground. The discovery of the truths of physical science is no proper function of inspiration; it belongs to the natural faculties of man, for which they are completely adequate. An inspired writer, therefore, if he has occasion to mention matters connected with scientific truth, may use popular language and popular conceptions on such subjects, even when they involve an incorrect scientific theory. A remarkable instance of such usage occurs in the Gospels, in the history of the cure of the woman with an issue of blood. To this we will recur in its proper place. It is no function of revelation to correct scientific errors, or rather errors which exist through the want of scientific knowledge. We have already proved that revealed truth must be communicated to man in ordinary human language. The expression "in hell," εἰς ᾄδου, involves an incorrect scientific theory. It is an expression derived from heathen mythology, and denotes "the house of Hades or Pluto." The sacred writers use the words in their popular sense, without being committed to their incorrect theory. The occurrence of such modes of statement can form no possible objection against Christianity as a divine revelation.

For similar reasons we infer that, in a revelation itself, truth will not be so revealed as to supersede all necessity for the exertion of man's mental powers on the subject-matter of that revelation. Labour is ordained by God as the road to knowledge. We cannot, therefore, assume, because God has made a supernatural revelation of truths not discernible by the natural faculties, that He meant to supersede the necessity of the active exercise of man's mental powers on those truths.

It will perhaps be objected that, on these principles, the communication of moral truths to man by means of a supernatural revelation, if not impossible in itself, is a mode of acting which the Creator would not adopt, as involving the use of two sets of instruments for the production of the same result.

It has been asserted as an objection against Christianity, that a revelation of moral truth is impossible, because the conceptions of moral truths must previously exist in the human mind before they can be introduced into the mind from an external source. Unless such moral conceptions existed in the mind, the mind would have no ideas wherewith to comprehend the external communication. It has been further urged, that conscience is the one and exclusive source of all moral obligation; and if conscience is the source of all moral obligation, moral truth can have neither force nor power as communicated by a supernatural revelation.

The objection in this form is a most patent fallacy. It is equally powerful against the possibility of communicating any kind of truth, as against the possibility of discovering moral truth by revelation. The argument would be equally efficacious to prove that it is impossible to teach or communicate the truths of Euclid, because the primary conceptions connected with mathematical science must previously exist in the mind before the teacher can operate with success. God, in ordaining the laws of the human mind, has mutually adapted the objective and the subjective to each other. The eye cannot see without an object; the object is modified from what it actually is by the eye. Moral truth, doubtless, could not be revealed to man, if he had not a moral nature. Man's possession of a conscience gives to morality a binding force. But conscience pronounces judgment on the various moral truths presented to it for its decision. Whatever truth the understanding presents to the conscience, the conscience pronounces on its validity.

But our immediate inquiry is not whether it is possible that God can make a moral revelation, but whether His doing so involves the use of a double instrumentality in the sense in which we have already proved that it is not the mode of the Divine acting.

The full discussion of this would render necessary the discussion of one of the deepest of revealed doctrines, the depravity of man, and the mode in which that depravity has been occasioned. The Scriptures assert its existence as a fact. Revelation declares that free will, the glorious image of the Divine freedom, has been imparted to man by his Maker, and, through the abuse of that freedom, the moral constitution of man has been impaired. The balance of his powers, as they were established by his Creator, has been subverted. It is one of the conditions of the creation of freedom, that man should have a derived power of working on his own being. If the assertions of the Scriptures respecting man are correct, this difficulty is dissipated.

In speaking of moral truth, two points must be kept distinct, which there is great danger of confounding. There is the moral truth or the moral duty itself. There is the motive by which the moral truth is enforced on the practice. What Christianity asserts is, that the moral truths which man knows, he is powerless to effectuate without the aid of the motives which she alone is powerful to supply. Human testimony fully confirms the first of these assertions.

To what extent are the natural faculties of man, devoid of supernatural illumination, capable of discovering the great truths of morals?

There is no moral truth which Christianity teaches which does not commend itself to the human conscience. When such a truth is propounded to the conscience, it cannot help pronouncing that it is a reasonable duty. When the conscience hears the great truth announced, "Thou shalt love thy neighbour as thyself," it is compelled to pronounce that the command is reasonable.

But while man must admit this obligation, there are in man's present state other principles within him which render him unwilling to practise it. This admission of obligation, united with disobedience to its injunctions, constitutes the essence of guilt.

If the records of existing literature were examined, they would be found to contain a large portion of moral truth. Numbers of precepts contained in revelation, not indeed propounded as a great code of human duty, but in a detached form, have been discovered by persons who have not had the benefit of a direct revelation.

But while the mere knowledge of moral truth has existed, man's unassisted powers have been unable to discover any motive sufficiently powerful to enable him habitually to practise what conscience has pronounced to be a matter of obligation.

The highest motive which heathen philosophers have been able to discover, to enforce the practice of virtue, has been the conception of its moral beauty. They were unable to sanction it by the realities of a future state. They could only appeal to its tendencies to produce happiness in this world. Of the nature of the love of God, as a motive to holiness, they were ignorant. Mere appeals to the excellency of virtue were the imperfect substitute. They were the highest motive with which they were acquainted. They freely confessed its feebleness. Man's impetuous passions easily broke through the weak restraint. The moral law of conscience, to use the expression of St. Paul, "was weak through the flesh." Man was corrupt, and reason and philosophy failed to discover any motive powerful for his reformation. On this point the language of philosophers is the language of despair. They feel themselves powerless to act on the vulgar herd. They might discuss curious points of morals with their select disciples, but they were utterly destitute of motives through which to preach to man a resurrection to holiness, or even to render their own principles powerful to influence their own conduct. Seneca preached high morality, dwelt in a marble palace, and justified Nero's murder of his mother.

But although, in man's present condition, the motives furnished by natural light are wholly powerless to effectuate the moral law as a binding influence on the conduct, it by no means follows that they were equally powerless in the original constitution of man. God created him a free agent, and through that free agency he has become an independent worker. Even the present constitution of man—that state which man by his free agency has induced—points to what was once the rightful supremacy of conscience. Permitted free agency has subverted its dominion. Free agency and the possession of a rational will have made man a cause. They have enabled him to operate on his own being.

A motive powerful to impart strength to the present weakness of man, but absent from every system of morals, it is the purpose and the glory of revelation to supply. Revelation withdraws the curtain which veils the unseen world, and with powerful reality discloses the great truth of man's responsibility. Revelation denies not the beauty of virtue, but it creates a motive powerful to strengthen, to quicken, and to animate the inmost recesses of the human heart—the love of God in Christ. Revelation discloses in morals a new creation—infinite love dying for the unholy, a glorious Christ freely offering himself as a sacrifice for man. What man's natural powers have been unable to invent, revelation has created — a motive powerful to animate the lifeless body of morality—the law of love—Christ, through his death and resurrection, become the Lord both of the dead and living. Christian morality now centres in Christ's glorious person. The creation of a motive powerful to enforce moral obligation has been attended with a corresponding enlargement of the bounds of morality itself—"Love one another, as I have loved you."

Shall we, then, assume that the Creator has failed in the execution of His work, and not created a motivity adequate to enable man to yield obedience to the moral law? Is His purpose therefore void of its effect? We answer, He has created free agency in man, subject to the necessary conditions which free agency involves, and His purpose is the creation of that free agency. Shall we assume that He has supplemented an imperfect operation by a double instrumentality? Having first created man with a motive which was inadequate, has He provided an adequate one by revelation? We reply, By His creative act He has created free agency in man, subject to the conditions which it involves. By revelation He has created motivity adequate to obedience, without impairing the free agency which He has created. In producing obedience in the holy, in generating holiness in man, and in overthrowing the dominion of moral evil, the Creator works by a single instrumentality, by motives which are the sole product of revelation, which, when firmly embraced by the human mind, are powerful to render the moral law the living guide of the life of man—the great truths which

He has disclosed in bygone ages by inspiration, and has consummated in the revelation of the Gospel.

It is also a matter of antecedent certainty that, if it pleased the Creator to make a supernatural revelation of His will, He would adopt the necessary means for authenticating that revelation with the stamp of His own authority. He would provide that those for whom it was intended might be under no uncertainty that its truths proceeded from Him. Without such an authentication, the end and purpose of making the revelation would entirely fail of attaining their object. The proper authentication of the revelation must therefore form a substantial portion of the Divine plan. Unless sufficient evidence were afforded that the revelation was from God, it would be the same as if it had never been communicated.

But respecting the amount of truth which God would communicate in a revelation we have no other grounds of antecedent certainty to guide us. Before we can determine such a question, we must know the nature of the Divine purposes, and be able to penetrate to the remote depths of the Divine mind. But who can presume to penetrate into the council-chamber of the Most High? All theories propounded on such a subject can be no better than mere guesses, founded on more or less of supposed probability, respecting which certainty is not attainable by man.

CHAPTER V.

THE IMPOSSIBILITY OF ARGUING FROM THE DIVINE ATTRIBUTES TO THE FACTS OF NATURE INVALIDATES ALL SUCH ARGUMENTS WHEN APPLIED TO THE FACTS OF A REVELATION.

THIS involves a truth of the utmost importance for the determination of the mode in which inspiration must be communicated. If antecedent assumptions, founded on our views of the Divine attributes, fail to conduct us to the facts of nature as they actually exist, they must be wholly impotent to determine what must be the facts of a revelation. If we were to reason as to what the universe must be from those attributes, we should construct a universe widely different from the one which the Creator has actually formed. As this has a most important bearing on our estimate of what, on mere grounds of antecedent probability, we might expect in a divine revelation, we will adduce a few instances of the utter fallacy of all such reasonings.

It would seem to be antecedently probable, that the attribute of perfect goodness in the Creator would render it necessary that He should communicate to man the greatest possible degree of happiness which he was capable of receiving. This would appear more probable when we consider that His goodness cannot possibly be impeded by defects either in His power or His wisdom. What impediment can obstruct Omnipotence? If the Creator is absolutely good, wise, and powerful, we should not only naturally conclude that no evil existed under His government, but that every creature was actually enjoying the greatest amount of happiness of which its nature was capable.

The same argument would lead us to conclude that there could be no degrees of happiness in the universe, but that every creature must have been alike endowed with happiness by its Creator. If God be almighty, all-wise, perfectly good, and perfectly just, how can He bestow on one being a greater degree of happiness than He has bestowed on another? No grounds of merit can be the reason of His preference. If He has done so, it must be at the expense of the attribute of equity.

On similar grounds we might assume that we should find no progressive happiness in the universe, but that the greatest possible degree of happiness had been communicated at once. If God is perfectly good, nothing but limitations in His power or His wisdom can hinder Him from the most perfect display of goodness in each particular instance.

On similar grounds we might argue that the Creator must

have communicated to man the greatest amount of knowledge which he was capable of receiving. For the same reasons we might infer that all were endowed with equal faculties for its attainment, and that the highest possible degree of knowledge had been communicated at once. On similar antecedent views of the Divine attributes we might infer that God had not made the acquisition of knowledge difficult, because it is so desirable. On the same grounds we might infer that such knowledge did not require to be communicated by revelation at all, but that the Divine goodness rendered it necessary that all desirable knowledge should have been communicated from the very first. From such reasonings we might build a universe wholly different from the one which has been actually erected by the Almighty. Such conclusions would seem to follow with inevitable certainty from reasonings on separate attributes of the Creator; but, when tested by His acts, they totally fail us in unfolding the actualities of His creative works.

If then we make similar assumptions as to what God must do in communicating a revelation, on the ground of our human views as to the perfection of the Divine attributes, and argue from those views of perfection what the particular acts of the Divine Being must be in communicating a revelation of His will, we shall wander as far from the truth, with respect to the actual facts of that revelation, as similar modes of argumentation on the same attributes would cause us to wander from the actual facts exhibited in God's creative and providential kingdoms. From such reasonings we might draw the most varied inferences as to what God must reveal, and the mode which must be employed by Him in making that revelation. But our only means of knowing what perfect goodness requires God to do in any particular case is by inquiring what He has actually done. In the same manner, our only means of knowing what amount of knowledge God must communicate, if He be pleased to make a revelation, is by ascertaining what amount of knowledge He has actually communicated, either by the study of the works of nature or by examining the pages of an authenticated revelation.

We are equally devoid of all grounds of antecedent probability to guide us, if it were the Creator's pleasure to make a revelation, what would be the means employed in communicating this revelation, or whether the revelation would consist of a simple divine element, or to what extent a human element might be united or mixed up with the divine one.

The argument from our human view of the Divine attributes to facts as they exist, or deductions from single Divine attributes as to what must or ought to be, universally fail when brought to the test of things as they actually exist. It is hardly possible to conceive of any assertion which could have a higher degree of antecedent probability than that evil could not exist in the universe of a perfect Creator. No probability as to the mode which God must adopt in communicating a revelation can have an amount of evidence at all comparable with this. But evil does exist. Its existence has proved a sore trial to the faith of the good in every age. The intellect of man has vainly endeavoured to fathom this profound mystery from the earliest dawn of human thought. With our present faculties, it is impossible to deduce the actualities of existence from considerations derived from the attributes of God. Our reasonings are based on our finite views of single and separate attributes in the Creator. We are unable to take a combined view of the complicated whole, or to deduce what must be the necessary result of their complicated action. We are equally unable to grasp the Divine works taken as a whole; and until we can do so it is impossible to form an opinion as to the relations which detached portions of them bear to the Divine perfections. Until we can comprehend both of these subjects, our reasonings as to what God must or must not do in particular cases are necessarily futile.

The clear perception of this truth is of the utmost importance in forming a judgment as to what God must or must not do in communicating a revelation of His will. Most assertions made on this subject rest on precisely the same foundation as similar assertions made as to what must be His conduct as Creator and Preserver of the universe. A large portion of the views usually maintained as to what must be the nature of a divine revelation are bare probabilities of this description. Nothing was more common in former times than for ingenious writers to construct systems of the universe founded on their views of what the Divine attributes require that it should be. Nothing has been more fallacious than these systems as exponents of its actual facts. In a similar manner, it has been a general practice to construct systems based on antecedent data of what must be the mode of communicating a divine revelation, and what must be the contents of that revelation. Why should this latter mode of procedure lead to results more satisfactory than the former? Research as to the actual facts presented by the universe has proved the resultlessness of such reasonings. Similar investigation into the actual facts of revelation will prove no less destructive to the latter.

It is so important to perceive the utter resultlessness of this species of argument as a guide to truth as to the actualities of creation and providence, that we must adduce the chief instances in which such reasonings would conduct us to conclusions utterly opposed to facts as they actually exist in nature.

First, as to our conception of almighty power. There is nothing which almighty power cannot effectuate which does not involve a contradiction. We may argue from this attribute that the universe cannot contain a defect which it was in the power of the Omnipotent to have prevented. But defects do exist, which it is impossible to say that almighty power could not have hindered. Could not almighty power have framed otherwise the imperfect organisms which we see in nature? Could not Omnipotence have prevented the monstrosities which not unfrequently are produced in the animal and vegetable kingdoms? Arguing from *à priori* principles, we should draw the conclusion that every exhibition of God's power must be absolutely free from every conceivable defect. Such conclusions, however, will inadequately represent the facts of nature.

Similar conclusions will follow from abstract arguments derived from the perfect wisdom of the Creator. The Creator is not only perfectly wise, but He unites infinite wisdom with infinite power. Infinite wisdom gives the Creator boundless skill. Nothing is beyond His power of contrivance. Infinite power enables Him both to create and use the means which His wisdom suggests. Every resource is at His command.

From the existence of these attributes in the Creator, if we argue on antecedent principles and frame a system of the universe in conformity with their conclusions, we should infer that there could not exist in the universe one single imperfection which it was within the power of either of those attributes to have prevented. We might infer that an imperfect work of any description could not have proceeded from the hands of infinite wisdom and power. This would lead us to the conclusion either that such imperfect works did not exist in the universe of God, or that, where they did exist, they must be the result of the operation of another worker than God.

But how stand the facts of the case? As we contemplate the universe, is it free from every imperfection which infinite power and wisdom united could not have obviated? When we see with our eyes defects in the animal or the vegetable kingdoms, shall we, on the strength of our reasoning, deny their existence, or say that God is not the author of them? Shall we assert that everything in the universe which, to human apprehension, denotes imperfection cannot be the workmanship of God? Shall we say of every imperfect organism which exists in animals or vegetables, that God did not make it thus? When we see a man lame, blind, or a cripple, or with some other defect in his bodily structure, shall we say that God did not make that man? If God has not made these organisms thus, who has? Have they made themselves? Are their defects owing to their being evolved through the operation of imperfect laws? Did not God make those laws? Shall we say that the devil has made them thus?

The facts are undeniable, and are to be found widely scattered through every department of nature. The Divine workmanship presents the most wonderful exhibitions of the operation of the Creator; but perfection is not the universal rule of actual existence. Some endeavour to account for the existence of these imperfections by the action of general laws, others by the existence of sin, others by the counteracting agency of an independent principle of evil. How do these considerations aid us to explain the difficulty? They remove it only one step further back. If they result from the action of general laws, if God is the Creator of the universe, He has ordained those laws in their imperfect operation. There, then, must have been a limit to His power or His wisdom. If those laws operate independently of Him, there is a plain limitation of His power. If they are dependent on Him, and they act imperfectly, how shall we say that He is not their author? If the imperfections are the result of sin, then sin itself has been permitted to enter and ravage the universe of which the Creator is the sovereign Lord. Could not Omnipotence and Omniscience have prevented such a result? The organisms in question, despite of their defects, are marvellous exhibitions of creative power and wisdom. Did God make the perfect portions of them, and sin the imperfect ones? In assuming such a power as sin, we assume the existence of a power of working in the universe, which owes its being to the Divine will, independent of the power of the Almighty, which He either cannot or will not control. If we ascribe these imperfections to the existence of an independent principle of evil, we at once assert that there is an agent operating in the universe independently of the Almighty, whose operations He is able neither to overcome nor restrain. By these solutions we do not explain the difficulty, but remove it one stage from our view.

But that God has built the universe and all things therein, is the great truth proclaimed alike both by natural reason and revealed religion. Whatever is done there, He must have been, and is, the doer of it. This truth stands on a higher ground than any truth merely deduced from our conceptions of His separate attributes. If an animal is born with two heads or with superfluous limbs, shall we venture to affirm that God did not make it? The organism itself contains mighty exhibitions of wisdom and of power. Who formed its vessels in all their complicated relationships? who assigned to each their respective functions? If they are not God's work, they must have either produced themselves or be the work of one who is not God.

The existence of these things in nature presents us with but three alternatives. Either the Creator has created the world subject to definite laws, and by means of these laws, without any further operation on His part, He has evolved all existing things: these laws have become deranged, maimed, and imperfect; and He has left the imperfection to itself, and He has ceased to exert over them either creative power or providence. Or He has permitted one who is not God to perform creative acts in His own universe. Or, for reasons unknown to us, in the regular exercise of His creative energy, He has formed the imperfect organisms Himself. To ascribe these things to the first of these causes is to admit a theory which banishes the Creator to a remote distance from His works, and, after all, obliges us to admit imperfection in His acting. To ascribe them to the second is to admit a theory which no devout theist will concede. It follows, therefore, that the organisms, with all their imperfections, must be the Creator's work, which, for reasons which we cannot penetrate, but which must be consistent with His infinite power and wisdom, He has made thus. We are inadequate judges, therefore, respecting the inferences which are to be deduced from the attributes of God as to the nature of the facts which must be presented by creation.

Reasonings, therefore, deduced from the attributes of God as to what must be the actualities of creation fail to conduct us to a knowledge of the created universe. The actual universe differs vastly from what we should have expected, on mere antecedent considerations derived from the Divine attributes, would have been the universe of the Almighty, the infinitely wise and benevolent God. Instrumentality is used to effectuate His purposes, such as we should never have expected; it contains what to human conceptions imply limitation of power, of wisdom, and of goodness, in the very midst of displays of the same attributes, which prove the reality of their existence in the Creator. These imperfections do not exist in the actual structure of the universe, but arise from the limitation of the human mind, and its inability to apprehend in their fulness both the perfections and the works of Him whose being and whose perfections are beyond the apprehension of the finite. These difficulties must ever exceed the powers of man to fathom. Our inability to reconcile all the facts of the universe with our conceptions of the perfection of the attributes of the Creator leads to one inevitable conclusion, that all reasonings from *à priori* views of what ought to be, to facts as they are, are inconclusive; they fail to conduct us to the truth of the universe as it has actually issued from the hand of its Creator.

But what follows? Shall we argue from our views of the attributes of the Creator that the perfection of these attributes, which have not rendered it necessary that He should produce a universe perfect according to human conceptions, must compel Him to make a revelation which fully realizes these human notions of perfection? Shall we insist that everything in that revelation must be squared according to our rule and plummet? Shall we assert, if it contains things which we should not have expected it to contain, or if it has been communicated in a manner less accurate than we may think desirable, or by a different mode of inspiration from that which we should have supposed antecedently probable, that a revelation, however strongly attested, cannot be a revelation from the Most High? We might as well assert that the universe cannot be His work. On the contrary, we will infer that reasonings which wholly fail in explaining the Divine conduct, as God actually exhibits it as Creator and Preserver of the universe, will be equally unsafe guides to truth when applied to what God must do as the author of a supernatural revelation.

Similar conclusions may be deduced from the human view of the Divine attribute of goodness. God is absolutely and perfectly benevolent and good; to this goodness He unites infinite power and wisdom. He has, therefore, at His command the most absolute means of most perfectly exhibiting this attribute in creation and providence. His benevolence prompts Him to produce the greatest possible amount of good; His wisdom enables Him to contrive the means suitable for its production; His power enables Him to create the means, and effectuate the full purposes of His will. Arguing, therefore, on our human views of these three separate Divine attributes, it follows as a legitimate conclusion, that every existing being in the universe is endowed with the highest degree of happiness of which it is capable.

Now no antecedent probability as to the mode which God must adopt in communicating a revelation has an equal degree of apparent certainty as that, if God is perfectly good, powerful, and wise, in the universe of which He is the Creator and Preserver, neither moral evil nor physical suffering would have been permitted to exist. Their existence at all, according to our conceptions, implies some limitation of the Divine goodness, power, or wisdom. Still greater is the degree of improbability that they would have been permitted to exist to the extent in which they actually do exist.

If we assume that perfect and absolute goodness exists in the Deity, united with power without bounds to effectuate, and wisdom to contrive, how is it possible that misery should have entered the kingdom of the Almighty? How is it that holiness is frequently in the deepest depression in that world in which the Creator has all things in His hands, and over which the Lord is king for ever and ever? The argument seems a near approach to demonstration. The perfect goodness of the Divine mind moves the Deity to the production of nothing but good. To the purity of the Divine character moral evil is utterly repugnant. His omnipotent power enables Him to effect whatever His goodness and holiness will, at least everything not involving a contradiction; His infinite wisdom gives Him the most perfect acquaintance with the means by which His ends can be accomplished, and of the tendencies of those ends. How, then, can moral or physical evil exist as the result of the creative power or providence of God, perfectly good and perfectly holy, with infinite power, and knowledge without limit? How antecedently improbable is it that moral evil should not only have entered, but actually have spread in the universe of that God to whom sin is utterly repugnant?

But sin, evil, and suffering do exist in the universe, and in a degree which is both painful and awful. Its existence is so palpable, it is so much the experience of daily life, that to attempt to prove it is a work of supererogation. Its existence is not a difficulty which lies hard on the Christian faith alone; it is no less perplexing to the philosopher. It bears equally hard on natural religion as on Christianity. Some, therefore, as a solution of the difficulty, have denied the existence of God. Others, forgetting that the difficulty lies equally at the seat of every system of theism, in consequence of the supposed difficulties which it presents, deny that the Christian religion is a revelation from God. Others endeavour to palliate by every conceivable device the amount of evil which actually exists. But can they deny that evil exists at all? Such a denial is the only thing which can really solve the difficulty. Little and great is all alike to the Creator. He could as easily have prevented a little evil as a great one. If they cannot deny its entire existence, to diminish merely the amount of evil will not help them. A Creator all-powerful, wise, and good could have prevented the smallest evil from entering the universe. Shall the denial of the existence of a Creator be the refuge to which we will have recourse? But the universe is full with the proofs of His being. To do so is to attempt to evade one difficulty by rushing into a greater. We might as well deny that the universe itself exists. Shall we assert that there is no real distinction between moral and physical evil, and that the existence of physical evil is a necessary consequence of the existence of finite being? Then, unless we can show that it involves a contradiction, we admit that a necessity exists independently of the will of the Creator, which even that will could not overcome; or we rush into the absurdities of pantheism.

But it has been asserted, as an explanation, that physical evil is the result of moral evil, and that moral evil owes its being to the independent freedom of the human will, and man's revolt from his Maker. That physical suffering is occasioned by moral evil requires proof; but supposing the latter portion of the assertion true, does this supposition get rid of the difficulty? does it do more than remove that difficulty backwards a single step. When God created the universe subject to the conditions to which He subjected it, had He not the most perfect knowledge whereto those conditions tended? Was not the subjection of the human mind to its existing conditions the result of the fiat of His creative power? Could He not have created it subject to other conditions? Unless the supposition involves a positive contradiction, the assertion that God could not have prevented the entrance of evil into the universe, or that He could not have acted otherwise than He has acted, is a direct limitation of the power of the Creator.

It has been urged that the free agency of moral beings could only have existed if they were created subject to the condition that considerable numbers of them would fall. Consequently, that the misery occasioned by the sinfulness of man is a necessary condition of his free agency. But have we any reliable evidence that it is so? Are such assertions better than conjecture? Even if it were so, we assign a limit to the power of the Creator. But on what evidence have we the assurance that the creation of free will could not be united with such a perception of the existence of goodness as to have placed an effectual barrier to the existence of evil? To assume that this was impossible, unless we can show that it involves a contradiction, involves either a limitation in the power of God or the assertion that something exists independently of His will.

But the difficulty has been explained by asserting that moral evil will be ultimately eradicated, and physical suffering compensated for in another state. But how does this assumption explain the present existence of either physical or moral evil in the universe of a perfectly powerful, wise, holy, and benevolent Creator? The point which requires solution is not how it can be compensated hereafter, but the fact of its present existence here, and how its existence is compatible with the attributes of perfect goodness and infinite power and wisdom in God. Could He not have prevented it altogether?

The only adequate answer which can be given respecting such difficulties is, that their solution transcends all the powers of the human understanding. Except to a very limited extent, we can arrive at no certainties, from arguments based on human views of the Divine attributes, as to what must be the Divine conduct in particular cases, or what is required by the action of those attributes as a complicated whole. We have abundant proof that infinite power, infinite wisdom, and perfect holiness are attributes of God, and that feelings towards God corresponding to those attributes are great duties of man. We know that a Being who is good must produce good by His creative acts; we know that such a Being cannot be tempted of evil. This should teach us humility in making positive assertions in matters beyond the reach of our faculties. But the only answer which can be given to the difficulties is, we are entirely unable to determine the mode in which the attributes of God must operate in every creative act of the Almighty.

If, then, reasonings founded on human views of the attributes of God lead us to incorrect views as to the facts of creation and providence, and if we should form from such reasonings most incorrect views as to the manner in which He ought to have created the universe, reasonings founded on similar views must lead to conclusions equally erroneous as to the mode which He must have adopted in discovering Himself by a supernatural revelation.

We will now consider what light is afforded by these principles on the subject-matter of a divine revelation, and the mode in which it must be communicated.

If the same God is the author of creation and providence, and the author of a revelation, we have the strongest antecedent certainty that as He displays Himself in the one He would display Himself in the other. This is founded on God's character as a moral agent. The action of the Divine attributes must be constant and invariable. With the all-perfect God capriciousness must be impossible. The Divine attributes must form the motives of the Divine conduct. Whatever difficulties we should find in the one, we should expect similar difficulties in the other. If reasonings founded on human views of the Divine conduct failed as guides to facts in the one, we should expect them similarly to fail in the other.

This analogy prevails through all the works of the Creator. We find it a rule pervading all the operations of intelligent beings, that their works must contain a general impress of their character. The difficulties which we find in them are all of a similar description. If, therefore, the antecedent probabilities of which we have been speaking are insufficient guides to enable us to arrive at the actual facts of God's creative acts and general government, we conclude that similar presumptions, when applied to the facts of a revelation, will be equally insufficient guides to unfold to us the actual facts of that revelation, or the mode of its communication.

Now, on what evidence do the usual theories that such and such things must necessarily form a portion of a Divine revelation, or that it must be communicated in this or that particular manner, rest?

Are the principles in question at all different in character from those which have been frequently applied to determine the manner in which God must have acted as Creator, and which have led to conclusions utterly at variance with the facts which the universe presents?

It has been often asserted that if God be the author of a revelation, it must be absolutely perfect according to human views of the perfection of the Divine character. But what evidence does this assertion rest upon beyond the very principles which, when they are applied to account for creation, totally fail in conducting us to the truth of what God has actually done. We cannot infer that each separate detail of a divine revelation must be perfect, more than we can infer that each separate detail of creation and providence must possess a distinct and separate perfection. Perfect it will undoubtedly be as far as God's purposes are concerned; for that is the same thing as asserting that whatever He purposes He accomplishes. But we are ignorant of the precise nature of those purposes, and therefore we are unable to measure it by a human standard of perfection.

It has been generally assumed that if God be the author of a revelation, every portion of it must contain an equally distinct statement of truth ; God cannot have employed mere relative truth in communicating with man ; the truth conveyed in the revelation must be absolute truth respecting His own moral character and perfections. But is this the rule by which the Creator acts in nature? Do apparent imperfections in nature, does the existence of moral evil and physical suffering, prove that the Creator is not infinitely powerful, wise, and good ? Are not many of the truths conveyed by God's actings in nature relative truths ? Particular stages of human civilization are only capable of low views respecting the Divine character. The views of moral obligation between man and man are of a similar description. It is thought unworthy of the Deity to use language, in a revelation of His will, accommodated to an imperfect civilization or imperfect spiritual and moral perception. Hence an objection is urged against considerable portions of the Old Testament as a divine revelation. On the other hand, those who maintain its divine origin endeavour to evade its supposed difficulties by assigning to such passages a degree of enlightenment and elevation of moral feeling which no person would naturally draw from the passages themselves.

The whole force of the objection arises from supposing that a revelation can contain truth expressed in terms as it absolutely exists in the Divine, and not expressed relatively to the human mind. When we clearly perceive that all the discoveries of a divine revelation must consist of relative truth, the only question which can exist is as to the degree of the accommodation. It is impossible to deny the principle that all revealed truth respecting God must be relative, and not absolute. This truth we have already proved.

In conformity with this mode of discovering truth by a supernatural revelation is the actual mode of the Divine working in creation and providence, as it is portrayed in the book of nature. The Creator has unquestionably commenced His operations with the lower forms of life, and with less complicated structures, and has advanced by slow and gradual stages to the creation of the higher. To the truth of this every discovery of science bears unequivocal testimony. Whatever conclusions we may arrive at from abstract reasonings on the Divine attributes, the actual operations of the Almighty as they come under man's observation in His works give one uniform testimony, that the Creator as a worker does not produce works abstractedly perfect, even according to human notions of perfection, but the law of His operations is to advance higher and higher, from stage to stage, in the kingdom of nature. God manifests Himself as a worker, not in time, but in eternity, ever manifesting fresh and unceasing displays of His glories. Human conceptions of perfection are applicable only to a being who exists in time.

If, then, as Creator and Preserver of the universe, God begins with that which is imperfect, and gradually advances by slow progress towards perfection, we may conclude that the same Divine worker will act in a similar manner in making a revelation of His will.

It has been argued from the supposed necessity that the Creator should display Himself in each of His particular operations as a perfect worker, that it is impossible that a human element should exist in a revelation which is wholly divine. The admission of a human element existing there is represented as a denial of its perfection, and therefore of its divine character.

Now on what foundation can such an assumption rest? We have already seen that all arguments from the human views of perfection to corresponding displays of perfection in the separate Divine operations are entirely futile. We have also already seen that, whatever apparent imperfection there exists according to man's estimate of it in the Divine operations, we should expect to find similar phenomena in a revelation of which the same moral Being was the author. To say that a human element cannot exist in union with a divine one in a revelation, is to assert that we are adequate judges of the means which infinite wisdom must employ in its operations.

But in creation and providence God employs agencies, for the purpose of effecting His designs, of a character such as we never should have expected. Who would have anticipated that the benevolent Author of all good would have employed earthquakes, volcanoes, storms and tempests, pestilence and war, for the effectuation of the most gracious purposes? Who would have imagined that the immense destruction of animal life would have been a means subservient to the most benevolent ends *? Nothing strikes the devout contemplator of the Creator's works as more contrary to what he should have antecedently expected than the existence on an enormous scale of what, contemplated in a human point of view, has been designated as a waste in creation. Vast numbers of things, formed with elaborate creative power and skill, seem formed for no other end than that they should perish, and, as far as man can see, effectuate no purpose in creation. No tongue can tell of the enormous expenditure of animal life in the ocean, in the air, and on the land. The number of eggs which the Creator has formed which never emerge into life is past all computation. Seeds, which are formed with admirable workmanship, and perish, are as numerous as the sand on the ocean shore. Infinite varieties of the most complicated organisms, or of the most elaborate structures, adorned with inconceivable beauty, have probably never been contemplated by an eye capable of appreciating their glories from the hour of their creation. Birds who have never emerged from primeval forest, shells buried in the profoundest depths of ocean, and insects in numbers numberless, too minute for human eye to behold, He has arrayed in robes of beauty, at which Solomon's, in all their glory, must stand abashed. The human mind eagerly asks, like Judas of old, To what purpose is this waste? Is it that the Creator, in the solitude of His infinitude, rejoices in the contemplation of the productions of His boundless power and of the results of His infinite wisdom? The Creator refuses to answer. He dwells in a depth impenetrable to man. To the height of His infinity who shall soar? To human apprehension, creation is full of waste; but who shall venture to assert that it is waste with God?

But, if such be the aspect of creation when contemplated by the limited faculties of man, who shall venture to assert

* See 'Plurality of Worlds,' *passim*.

that a similar aspect may not be presented by a divine revelation when viewed by the same faculties, if that revelation has the Creator of the universe for its author? If it contains things of which we cannot see the use, is that to be accepted as affording conclusive proof that it cannot come from God? If it contains means for effectuating His purposes such as we should not have antecedently expected, can that prove that it cannot have God for its author? If it does, the same argument proves that the universe is not the workmanship of the Most High. If in the created universe the Almighty has used earthquakes and volcanoes to effectuate the purposes of benevolence—if storms and desolations do His bidding—if He makes wars and revolutions subservient to the moral training of mankind—if creation abounds with what to human apprehension is a wasteful expenditure of power, who shall venture to assert that He, who is all-powerful and all-wise, cannot introduce a human element into a revelation, and use it as an instrument for the discovery of His will?

Whether, then, a revelation would be discovered in an historical form, whether it would contain dogmatic statements of truth, or would present us with a complete system of theology, whether its records would be confined strictly to the subject-matter of a supernatural revelation, or in what proportion the human and the divine would be interwoven in such a revelation, are questions which can be determined by no antecedent reasonings. Such reasonings would be equally fallacious, as we have found them, as guides to the structure of the universe. We are equally unable to determine through what agencies of the human mind the revelation would be communicated, of what kind would be the instruction afforded, whether a constant supervision would be exerted over every stage of its delivery, or whether it would be rapid or gradual in its communication. Antecedent certainty on such subjects we have none. If we wish to have definite views on them, our views must be deduced from the facts of an actually authenticated revelation. The absence of all *à priori* certainty on this subject is the necessary consequence of the limited human intellect being unable adequately to judge the conduct of the Infinite mind. This inability results from the human mind not possessing conceptions which are measures of the actualities as they exist in God, but only imperfect representations of them. Its antecedent judgments can only afford grounds of certainty when they are confined to the great outlines of the conduct and character of God. Limited thus, if a professed revelation contradicts such primary views of the Divine character, it cannot have God for its author. Supposing a revelation conceded to a pretended prophet indulgences which it denied to other men, if there was anything in it which plainly and palpably contradicted the Divine attributes taken as a whole—as that God looked with complacency on actions essentially immoral, or that the great Governor of the universe possessed a material body, or that He was not self-existent, or that anything existed independently of His will, or that He was in any way subject to finite limitation—this would be ample and sufficient proof that such a pretended revelation could have not had God for its author. But to be able in this manner to form a correct judgment on the general principles of the Divine character, and the contents of a revelation as in conformity with it, is a very different thing from being able to decide whether the minor contents of a revelation are consistent with particular attributes of God.

We know, on the highest evidence, that the Creator must be self-existent, almighty, and infinitely wise. We know that He must possess the moral perfections of perfect holiness, benevolence, justice, and truth. None of these perfections God can deny; for if He were to do so, it were to deny Himself. Certain assertions might distinctly deny these Divine attributes, and thereby afford palpable proof that they had not the sanction of Divine authority. The human mind is a fully competent judge that the distinct approbation of falsehood would be a contradiction of the Divine veracity, or that the holding one man responsible for the same thing for which he held another irresponsible, would be a contradiction of the Divine justice, or that the condemning a man for an action for which he was entirely irresponsible would be totally inconsistent with the character of Him who is the Judge of all the earth. If, again, a professed revelation were to assert that God had made particular men for the purpose of devoting them to everlasting suffering, such an assertion would be an unquestionable contradiction of the Divine goodness, and prove that the pretended revelation was not from God. But this is a very different thing from judging a particular act of the Divine conduct which forms part of a complicated whole, and affirming that our view of it contradicts the Divine character. Do we fully comprehend it in all its bearings? Do we know its ultimate issues? Can we sound the remote depths of the Divine perfections? It is one thing to assert that God cannot lie, and another that the doctrine of an atonement is demonstrably inconsistent with the Divine benevolence, or, because we cannot reconcile the existence of moral and physical evil with the Divine perfections, to deny the existence of a holy or an intelligent Creator.

If, therefore, we judge of what God reveals from what He actually does, a revelation of the Divine will may unite a divine element with a human one, involving various degrees of what may appear to human judgment imperfections. Before we can determine what effect certain supposed imperfections may have on disproving that a book containing such difficulties can be a divine revelation, we must have clear and indisputable evidence that they lie within the powers or the cognizance of the human faculties.

It is instructive to observe to what opposite results the same antecedent assumptions lead different minds. One class of mind assumes that an inspired revelation must correspond with certain *à priori* assumptions which have been formed respecting it, both as to the subject-matter of what the revelation must consist and as to the manner in which it must have been communicated. According to their view, the Christian Scriptures do not realize this ideal; therefore they are not a revelation from God. The other class make the same *à priori* assumptions. According to their view, the Christian Scriptures are from God; therefore they attempt to force the facts and phenomena of those Scriptures into conformity with the conditions under which they have assumed that a supernatural revelation must have been communicated.

Now the objections against the Divine character of Christianity for the most part resolve themselves into certain views of the Divine character and attributes, founded on antecedent reasonings, to which particular doctrines or statements in Scripture are said to be repugnant. Now antecedent assumptions, to be applicable to such a case, ought to be self-evident truth or demonstrations from such truths. It will not be sufficient that they should rest on a mere foundation of probability. When, then, we assume certain consequences as flowing from the attributes of the Creator, and apply those consequences as criteria for judging the contents of a supposed revelation, what is the nature of the evidence on which those judgments rest? Are they self-evident, demonstrative, or probable? If they are the latter merely, the objections can have no force to subvert the evidence by which a divine revelation is attested. But we must not only have evidence that our deductions are necessary consequences flowing from particular attributes in the Creator, but also have sufficient grounds for arriving at the conclusion that the action of the attribute from which our conclusions are deduced may not be modified by that of another attribute of the Divine mind. To enable us to form an adequate judgment on such subjects, we ought to have as our point of view a standing-point from whence we may be able to survey the complicated action of the attributes of the Divine mind, or else to be able to form a conception of the common principle in the Divine mind of which the various Divine attributes are manifestations or modifications. Until we can determine whether any single Divine attribute be a complete manifestation of the whole of the Divine character, our conclusions as to what God must or must not do in particular instances must be involved in uncertainty. It will be necessary to determine to what extent a particular Divine attribute may be modified in its action by another. What is the relationship which the Divine attribute of goodness bears to those of holiness or justice must be determined, before we can deduce any certain conclusions from either of them separately. The whole of the Divine character cannot be reduced by the human understanding to the action of any one of its single attributes.

The common objections brought against the Christian Scriptures are founded on the assumption that some one of the Divine attributes is a full and complete representation of the Divine character. The attribute most commonly assumed as being this full representation of it is the attribute of benevolence. It is asserted that all the other attributes of the Divine character are mere modifications of this single attribute.

But what right have we to make this assumption? Is it an assumption founded on any self-evident truth? Why may not holiness, or justice, or veracity be assumed as the single Divine attribute of which the others must be modifications or manifestations? Is the assumption that benevolence must be the single attribute of Deity founded on any self-evident principles, or any demonstration flowing from such principles? Is not the assumption rather made because it is a convenient assumption? To beings of greater purity than ourselves, perfect holiness may appear the most venerable attribute in the Divine mind.

But if the attribute of benevolence be the source from which all the other Divine perfections flow, it cannot be the mere human conception of such an attribute, but one of a wider and more comprehensive range, which includes justice, holiness, truth, and all the other Divine perfections in its wide embrace. According to our conceptions, justice and holiness differ from benevolence, not in degree, but in conception and idea. We can have no right, therefore, to assume a mere human conception of benevolence as the adequate conception of that attribute in the Divine mind which embraces in itself all the other perfections of the Divine nature, and then to measure every other doctrine or statement in the Christian Scriptures by such a standard. If we apply to other conceptions which have a human origin a standard of benevolence which is the strict human conception of that quality, and then apply it to principles entirely differing from it in conception, it is easy enough to make statements in the Scriptures contradict such supposed attributes of God. If we imagine an attribute of the Divine nature which is wholly different from any mere human conception of it, and apply it to other classes of conceptions not similarly modified, we can have no right to assign to such conclusions the evidence of demonstration. If it is the human idea of benevolence which we employ, the action of that attribute must be modified by considerations deduced from the other attributes of God.

On grounds such as we have been considering, it has been often asserted that the Scripture doctrine of the atonement contradicts the Divine attributes, and therefore it cannot have been revealed to man by God. We select this doctrine as a sample of many others. The two attributes in God, to which this doctrine has special relation, are His benevolence and His justice. It has been urged that it is inconsistent with the perfect benevolence of the Deity that He should require an atonement in order that He may pardon sin. If the Deity is perfectly benevolent, He can require nothing but repentance. It is also urged to be contrary to the Divine justice to inflict sufferings on one person as a satisfaction for sins committed by another.

Now into the profound depths of such questions we shall not enter. Our only concern with them is, what limits do they necessarily assign to the capacity of the human faculties to pronounce on such questions, and, consequently, of the powers of the human mind to form a judgment as to what must or must not be the contents of a Divine revelation, or the mode of its delivery? Now the conceptions of benevolence, justice, and the atonement are the human representations of those conceptions, and not the realities in the Divine mind. We are dealing entirely with those human representations. The Divine realities cannot be represented in our finite comprehensions.

If, then, we assume the human idea of benevolence as fully representing the actual attribute in the Divine mind, it is not difficult to make the assertion, that the Deity requires an atonement before He can pardon sin, contradict that attribute. With equal ease, the inflicting suffering on one entirely innocent, as a compensation for suffering which ought to be borne by the guilty, even when that suffering is borne voluntarily, may be made to contradict the human conception of the attribute of perfect justice. But the human conceptions of benevolence and justice are conceptions which are entirely distinct from each other; they have nothing in them in common. As they exist in man, they energize in a manner independent of each other; they can be represented by no common attribute of which we can form a distinct conception. Their requirements may frequently clash. If we suppose both of them to exist equally in the same mind, the strict feeling of justice demands that the reward of demerit should be rigidly dealt out to the offender. The feeling of benevolence requires that suffering should be annihilated, and happiness created. According to our human conceptions of these attributes, one of them cannot possibly be the common ground of the other; they may clash, but they cannot coincide. A common principle may exist in the Divine mind under the influence of which the claims of each may be modified. An atonement may be consistent with neither of the human conceptions of benevolence or justice; but it may be consistent with the complicated action of both, or with a common principle which forms their groundwork in God.

But when it is asserted that the doctrine of atonement contradicts either the Divine attribute of benevolence or of justice, this cannot be meant of a human conception of benevolence or justice, but of a higher conception, to which the name of benevolence has been given as an attribute which comprehends in its wide action all the other perfections of the Divine mind, and which is supposed to be an adequate measure and representation of the reality as it exists in God. If the doctrine of an atonement contradicted merely the human conceptions of benevolence or justice, it would prove nothing against the possibility of Christianity being a divine revelation. The objection only possesses cogency if it could be shown that it contradicted an attribute of benevolence which the human mind was capable of comprehending as an adequate exponent of all the other perfections of the Divine nature.

Such must be the character of the attribute of benevolence when we assert that it is the single attribute of the Divine nature. Such an attribute cannot be comprehended by man so as to enable him, from reasonings founded upon it, to draw definite conclusions respecting the Divine proceedings. It may be that such an attribute does exist in the Divine mind; but both its nature and mode of action must be quite incomprehensible to the human mind. If we survey the Divine conduct as regulated by the human conceptions of benevolence or justice, it may not be the precise result of the action of either of those attributes, but may be modified in conformity with the requirements of both. If the Divine conduct was the result of either single attribute, the doctrine of atonement might contradict that attribute; but if it is the result of the complicated action of different Divine perfections, we can have no evidence of such contradiction.

Our human conceptions of the Divine justice and holiness are not adequately represented by our human conception of benevolence. Fallacies of this kind arise from assuming that a human conception of a Divine attribute is an adequate measure of the depths of the Infinite mind, and then using that attribute as an adequate measure of the other perfections of the Almighty. Conceptions of this kind differ wholly from the class of conceptions to which we have already alluded, and which, from their distinctness and definiteness, are within the range of the human faculties to pronounce as to their agreement with the Divine character.

Various other doctrines in the Christian Scriptures have been objected to as inconsistent with the character of God. The greater proportion of these objections are based on a similar foundation of sand—that one or more of the Divine attributes adequately represents the perfections of the Most High, and that the human conception of those attributes is the perfect measure of the Divine reality.

We have only selected the doctrine in question as a sample

of such objections, founded on antecedent probabilities, on the strength of which it has been asserted that Christianity cannot be a revelation communicated by inspiration from God. With respect to all such objections there is one answer: the human understanding does not furnish us with any grounds of antecedent certainty as to the precise relationship which the conceptions in question bear to the attributes as they exist in God, and consequently we can have no evidence that, if such doctrines form a portion of a professed revelation, they are destructive of its claims to a divine origin. Objections of this kind are founded on precisely the same antecedent probabilities as those which, when they are applied as exponents of the Divine working in creation or providence, expressly contradict the realities of things as they exist in the universe, which forms the great revelation of the omnipotence and omniscience of the Creator.

Our being assured of the fallacy of such antecedent reasonings is of the highest importance, because those are of a precisely similar description, on the strength of which particular theories have been erected respecting the mode in which inspiration must have been communicated. If the one are unreliable, the others must be equally untrustworthy.

From these premises, therefore, we draw the general conclusion that it is impossible to reason on such conceptions as to what may or may not be possible in a revelation from God, or what will be the mode adopted for its communication, because the conceptions on which we reason are only metaphorical representations, made to the finite understanding, of the realities of the Divine mind.

We have already proved that if it pleased the Creator to communicate a revelation, there is one limitation under which that revelation must have been communicated—that the conceptions contained in it cannot consist of the Divine conceptions of His own attributes and perfections, but the best representations of the infinite and perfect ideas, as they exist in the Creator, which the limited and finite intellect of man is capable of affording. In asserting that every revelation must be subject to this precondition, and can only be made in conformity with it, we are not assigning a limitation to the powers of the Creator. The limitation has been imposed by the Creator on Himself; and it implies no defect of power in a worker to assert that His operations must be confined within limits which He Himself has imposed. These self-imposed limits which God has assigned to His own working are the preconditions under which He has created the finite. He might have created beings subject to different preconditions; but having once created them subject to certain limitations, they can only act in conformity with the laws imposed upon them by their Maker. To say that the Almighty could only make a revelation of Himself to man in conformity with existing laws of thought, is only the same thing as asserting that, the Creator having made man subject to certain laws of thought, as long as man continues to be man, the Creator can only communicate truth to him in conformity with those laws which He has Himself imposed on the human mind.

We will illustrate our meaning by an example from mathematical truth. The Creator of the human mind has preconditioned our conception of a triangle to be such that its three angles cannot but be equal to two right angles. It is therefore no limitation to the power of Omnipotence, to assert that it is impossible to make a triangle with its three angles equal to three right angles. Such a triangle would not simply be an impossibility, but a contradiction.

In the same way it is no limitation to the power of God to affirm that, when He has preconditioned the human mind to be only capable of conceiving in limited finite conceptions, it is impossible for Him to communicate to it an intelligible revelation in any other ideas than in the conceptions of the finite, or that it can be made by Him in the perfect conceptions of the Infinite mind. To assert its possibility is to assert a positive contradiction.

We know, therefore, with demonstrative certainty that every revelation made by God to man must employ as its vehicle for communicating truth the limited and imperfect conceptions of the human mind, and that to this extent a human element must exist in the Christian Scriptures. It follows, therefore, that if it pleased God to make a revelation of Himself to man, the truths communicated must undergo a process of translation from their divine realities into the corresponding human representations of them, which are the best counterparts of the Divine realities themselves. Such a revelation, therefore, must be limited to the discovery of such portions of the Divine character as the mind of man possesses ideas through which the representation of the Divine realities becomes possible. Consequently the truths contained in the revelation can only represent the Divine realities as far as the human thoughts have been preconditioned to be representations of those realities.

But we have already observed that all human conceptions have been derived from three sources—the mind's perception of external and material things, the feelings and affections of the mind itself, and the self-conscious acting of the mind on itself. These form the original source of all the conceptions that we possess, which are common between man and man, and through which thought, speech, and language become possible. Within the boundaries of such conceptions, therefore, the possibility of communicating truth to man, which was previously unknown, must be limited.

Now, in order that a revelation may be intelligible to man, it is necessary that it should be couched in those conceptions common to the human mind. If it were not so, it might be a revelation to an individual, but it could not be so to the human race. It would be impossible that its contents should be capable of communication by one man to another. It is, doubtless, possible, if such were the Creator's pleasure, to make a revelation to each separate individual. But the ideas in which such a revelation was communicated could not form subjects of common thought, and consequently could not form a written revelation. If such a revelation were made, it could not form a subject of teaching by man to man. All teaching must be made through the medium of intelligible thoughts, common between man and man. The teaching of a revelation by one man to another can only be effected through the medium of common subjects of thought capable of finding expression in intelligible language. If the thoughts in a revelation were not ordinary human thoughts, they could exist only for each separate person.

In every revelation which is designed for the use of the human race, it is necessary that the various conceptions which it contains should be derived from one or more of the three sources above mentioned. Its conceptions, therefore, will consist of ideas derived from the mind's conceptions of external things, or from its own feelings and affections, or from its own self-conscious actings, and be subject to all the necessary conditions of such classes of conceptions.

It follows as a necessary consequence, that, in every revelation of God communicated to the spirit of man, another human element must exist in it—that the conceptions, ideas, and thoughts in which that revelation is expressed are all derived either from man's conceptions of external things or from his moral perceptions, and that they only metaphorically represent truths as they exist in God. Whatever theory of inspiration is adopted, the necessity for this concession cannot be evaded.

It also follows, from the nature of the human mind, that the ideas and conceptions in which spiritual and divine truth is announced to man must partake of the character of anthropomorphism. This word is frequently used to denote grossly corporeal conceptions of the Deity; but its real meaning implies nothing more than that we conceive of God by means of conceptions which are originally derived from man. In this sense it is impossible that our conceptions of Him can have any other origin. To apply degrading or corporeal conceptions, derived from man, to the Creator, is to give a perverted view of His character and existence. But, in our zeal against the application of such conceptions to God, we are in danger of forgetting that it is a question of degree only, and that even our highest and most spiritual conceptions of God can claim no other origin. To represent God as possessed of body, parts, or passions, is degrading to His nature; but when we assert that He is of infinite power, wisdom, and goodness, let us not forget the real origin of the conceptions in question.

When, therefore, the Christian Scriptures speak of the perfections of God, the terms which they employ cannot be expressions directly denoting the Divine perfections themselves, but expressions originally derived from the material universe, or from the human mind, analogously expressing those perfections. When the Scriptures use the expression "Almighty," what is the conception which they are alone able to convey by it? Does it unfold the eternal reality of the Divine mind? The positive ideas of power which it conveys are all derived from the created universe. The power which could effect creation is the highest positive degree of power which the human mind can conceive of. The conception of that degree of power is the positive idea which is conveyed by the expression "Almighty." But that positive conception is a finite conception; it therefore does not adequately represent the idea of power as it exists in God. To supply this defect in our conception, we deny the existence of bounds to the power, and express this denial by the word "Almighty." This portion of the conception is entirely negative. The only positive conception, therefore, which the mind possesses is one derived from the created universe.

The human idea of existence, purged of its imperfections, must also be used analogously to represent the existence and being of the Creator. We add to the positive human conception the negative expressions of "absolute," "unconditioned," "infinite." The human idea of existence forms the only positive conception formed by the mind. By applying to it the expressions "absolute," "unconditional," "infinite," we endeavour to eliminate out of that conception the finite imperfections with which it is necessarily associated; but still our conception is the finite human conception.

The human ideas of goodness, holiness, purity, justice, mercy, and truth must be the positive portion of our conceptions when we speak of the moral perfections of the Most High. There is no other source whence the positive portion of those perfections can be derived than the conceptions of those affections as they exist in man. To free them from these imperfections as attributes of man, we apply to them the negative conception of infinite or perfect when they are applied to God. Still, by this process we do not destroy the human character of the positive conception. When we say that God is perfectly benevolent, good, and holy, we mean to assert that there are affections in Him corresponding to those attributes in man, which we endeavour to free from finite imperfection by qualifying them by the negative conception of perfect.

The only conception which man possesses of will is one derived from his own self-consciousness. This, when the negative conception of freedom from conditions and limitations is attached to it, is the only positive conception which can be used when mention is made of the will of the Creator.

The human notion of existence is one which is necessarily complicated with conceptions of time and space. Man cannot conceive of anything actual, except as existing in one or the other of those conditions. This notion is applied to the Creator, divested of the conditions which are necessarily involved in it as a positive human conception.

Throughout every revelation, therefore, the imagery in which God is spoken of must be imagery derived from the created universe or from the corresponding attributes in man. God cannot otherwise become the object of human thought. This is another human element which must necessarily form an ingredient in every revelation.

The Christian Scriptures are written on the assumption of the truth of these principles; they consequently even ascribe to God bodily organs, for the purpose of denoting those affections which in man are associated with the exercise of those bodily functions. This language is anthropomorphistic, but it is one which is clearly comprehensible. It only becomes dangerous when we mistake its nature and suppose that, instead of being only metaphorically applicable to God, it denotes realities existing in the Divine nature. Thus God is said to have eyes: the eye, to man, is the source of knowledge. By this image the perfection of the Divine knowledge is intended to be conveyed. God is said to have hands: this assertion is used to denote that God has those affections and energies of which hands in man are the most appropriate expression. God is said to be seated, to denote His sovereign power, because that is the mode in which sovereign dignity is displayed by man. In a similar manner all the bodily organs and material and mental portions of man's nature are used to denote perfections of the Most High.

This human element, therefore, must exist in every revelation, whatever be the degree of its inspiration.

The careful student of the Christian Scriptures cannot fail to be struck with the fact that there is something, which they designate as "the gospel," quite distinct from the contents of the Scriptures themselves. According to the New Testament, the Christian revelation consists of two portions, both accommodated to the finite understanding of man. The one of these portions is preeminently called the εὐαγγέλιον, or "good news," and consists of a succession of outward objective historical facts—the manifestation of incarnate Deity in human flesh, the historic life and death of Christ; the other consists of the record of those facts, and the comments on those facts—the actual written records of the New Testament itself. What the Christian Scriptures preeminently designate as the Gospel is not a body of doctrines or precepts, but the great historic fact of the manifestation of Christ as the revelation of Deity in His incarnate person. Of this we shall adduce proof hereafter: at present we assume its reality. Now if the Christian revelation be made in the Divine person of the incarnate Son of God, it is evident that such a revelation would be the nearest possible approximation to the realities of the Divine perfections which the finite intellect of man is capable of comprehending; but even high as such a revelation would be, still it must be limited to meet the conditions of man's finite nature. The perfections of incarnate Deity must be the highest reflections of the glories which flow from the invisible and incomprehensible fountains of Godhead. The perfections of God manifest in the flesh must be the highest possible displays which human thoughts can conceive, or human language can convey, of the incomprehensible glories of that Being whom none can behold and live; but while they are the representations nearest to the reality which the finite can receive of the infinite, they cannot be the infinite itself.

In making this manifestation of Himself to man, the agency employed by God consists in the fact of the Incarnation—the union of the infinite with the finite. Such a revelation would have no other limitation than the necessity that the Divine nature must be veiled in finite representations. As far as the infinite in God can be represented in human nature, the objective fact of the Incarnation must be its absolutely perfect representation. As an objective fact, it must be a revelation in itself, quite independently of all views taken of that fact by the percipient powers of the mind, in the same manner as the objective universe is a revelation of the Creator's glories quite distinct from any particular view which the mind forms of that universe.

But every objective existence involves a subjective view taken of that existence by the mind itself. There is the external universe as it exists in itself; there is the conception which the mind forms of that universe: there is the great fact of the Incarnation; there is the view which the mind of man conceives of the Incarnation.

Actual existence differs from our perceptions of that existence. Every object, as it exists in itself, receives a colouring through our percipient faculties. The actual perception which we form of things consists of the union of the objective and the subjective—of actual existence with the powers of perception. We are incapable of knowing actual existences otherwise than as they are coloured by the percipient powers of the mind. In conformity with this principle, the Christian Scriptures both contain the records of the revelation made by God in the person of Christ, and an exposition of the meaning of this great revelation of God, expressed in ideas and conceptions relative to the mind of man. The question here involved is one which must be kept quite distinct from all mere views of the degree of inspiration with which those Scriptures must have been communicated. Whatever be the degree of inspiration which has been afforded to their writers, an important human element must form portion of their contents; they must speak of heavenly things by their earthly representations. Even in the revealed commentary on the great fact of the Incarnation, this is the only medium of teaching which is possible.

This mode of teaching is most freely used in the New Testament Scriptures. They press every truth and metaphor which can be derived from earth into the service of delineating the unknown mysteries of the kingdom of heaven. At the same time they give us distinct warning that the imagery itself only metaphorically describes the Divine acts and character.

We will illustrate this mode of stating spiritual truth by a few examples. Various representations of the Deity are made in the Scriptures which in their literal sense assert His limitation under the conditions of time and space. Expressions are used which imply a limited presence in particular places and definite localities; but, while they are forced to use expressions of this description for the purpose of teaching us the relative truths which they are intended to convey, they guard against the error of our fancying that these truths are the ultimate realities of the Divine nature. While they assert that God dwells in heaven, they most emphatically declare that the heaven and the heaven of heavens cannot contain Him. They speak of the Spirit of God as poured out on the spirit of man. To pour is a conception which denotes a material action; it implies motion: it is properly applicable to the passage of a liquid from the thing containing it into another locality; it can, therefore, only by a remote metaphor denote an act of the Divine mind. But the laws of human thought necessitate the use of such metaphorical expressions in teaching spiritual truth. They may be, and are, imperfect instruments for teaching; but whether perfect or imperfect, they are the only ones which exist, and without them all knowledge of divine things would be impossible to man. A small or obscure light affords but imperfect vision; but if we have no other, we shall not see better by extinguishing it. A metaphor less remote than the idea of pouring might have been used; but, whatever degree of remoteness it might possess, it could only represent a divine idea by a similar analogy.

God is frequently said in Scripture to make the pure and holy soul His temple. The truth meant to be represented is the close union between it and God; but, although it is easy of apprehension, it is the plain case of an inadequate material conception used to denote a spiritual idea. In the same way the expressions of sitting on a throne, a divine fulness where He locally manifests His essential glory, acts of worship rendered in a material temple, the judgment-seat of a Roman governor ($\beta\hat{\eta}\mu\alpha$ $X\rho\iota\sigma\tau o\hat{v}$), and multitudes of other material conceptions of this description are the constant means used to represent spiritual truth. Expressions of this kind we are in little danger of mistaking for realities. Why should we convert into realities expressions which, although less obviously of a material origin, are of a precisely similar description?

But, while they use such teaching, the Scriptures emphatically warn us that God is a Spirit. They use a term which, while it was metaphorical and material in its first use, is now employed by us as the highest negation of all material form. In the same manner they use language respecting His moral perfections: they speak of His repentance, His anger, His wrath, His jealousy.

Now every one of these and kindred affections, applied to God, are attributes of the human mind, some of them implying considerable degrees of imperfection. As human affections, they necessarily imply the idea of change; but while the Scriptures use such expressions analogically to represent to us the Divine attributes or the Divine conduct, they emphatically assert that with God there is no variableness nor shadow of turning. In all His attributes and perfections, whatever God is, He is ever and unalterably the same.

In accordance with this principle, the first article of the Church of England defines the Deity as being without body, parts, or passions; and then defines His perfections by ascribing to Him the human conceptions of power, wisdom, and goodness, and eliminates as far as may be the human imperfection involved in the conceptions by adding to them the negative idea of the infinite. No effort of scientific definition can evade a necessity which is founded on conditions and limitations to which the human understanding has been created subject.

General Conclusions.

The following are the results of the foregoing reasonings as to the conditions under which a supernatural revelation must be communicated to man, and the limitations attending its communication :—

1. That as far as the Creator designed to make a revelation, He would fully realize His own purposes in making it.

2. That the conceptions through which the revelation must be communicated cannot be the Divine ideas themselves, but their analogous representations and approximations in human thought.

3. That to make the revelation an intelligible revelation to the mind of man, it must be made through the medium of human thoughts, conceptions, and ideas, more or less remotely representing the divine realities.

4. That, even on the highest theory of inspiration, the human origin of the conceptions in which a revelation must be expressed is a necessary human element in every conceivable revelation.

5. That a revelation must be authenticated by a miraculous attestation, if it is to have a binding obligation on the human conscience.

6. That we have no antecedent knowledge, amounting to certainty, as to the amount of truth which a divine revelation must contain.

7. That we have a very high degree of evidence that, in communicating a revelation, God would act in a manner analogous to the mode which He has already pursued in creation and providence.

8. That the evidence of a direct miraculous attestation given to a revelation is not affected by difficulties in its contents, which rest on no other foundation than uncertain probabilities.

9. That the only adequate ground which would justify the rejection of a supposed revelation, supported by an apparent adequate attestation, is that some portion of its contents palpably contradict self-evident truth respecting the Divine character and perfections, of which supposed contradiction the reason of man enables him to form an adequate judgment, and arrive at conclusions not based on probabilities, but on certainties.

10. That although the representation of divine truths by human conceptions of greater or less degree of imperfection must be a human element in every revelation, yet, if a revelation were communicated to the spirit of man by the Spirit of God, the analogies employed would be the best suited for conveying the nearest approximation to the divine truths.

11. That there is no evidence, nor any grounds of antecedent certainty possessed by man, either that a miraculous revelation is impossible, or that it cannot receive a miraculous attestation.

12. That we have no grounds of antecedent certainty to guide us as to the nature or degree of inspiration with which a revelation would be communicated.

13. But that the inspiration afforded would not be a greater degree of inspiration than that which was necessary for the effectuating the purposes of God in communicating a revelation.

14. That such truths as God has already communicated by natural means, and which He has already given man the power to discover for himself, would not form the proper subject-matter of a supernatural revelation.

15. That, according to analogies of God's conduct in creation and providence, inspiration would be confined to the proper subject-matter of the revelation itself, and would not be extended to mere collateral matter connected with the revelation.

16. That reasonings founded on certain human views of the Divine attributes as to what a revelation must contain, or what must be the mode of its delivery, are no less fal-

lacious than similar reasonings have proved as to the great facts of creation and providence.

17. That not only is there no antecedent presumption against the existence of a human element in a revelation, but the analogies of God's operations in creation and providence would lead us to infer the presence of such an element in every revelation of which the Creator and Preserver of the universe is the author.

18. That various assumptions which have been made respecting the extent of a divine revelation, and respecting the mode in which it must have been communicated, rest upon no solid basis of truth, but on mere probable grounds of belief; and when such probabilities are applied as exponents of God's works in creation and providence, they totally fail us as guides to truth.

These are the only truths, which are necessary deductions from the preceding reasonings, which bear directly on the question which we are now discussing. We are quite ready to admit that these reasonings involve considerations of the highest importance as to the mode of interpreting the Christian Scriptures. They are also worthy of the deepest attention as implying limits as to the extent in which the rational faculty in man can safely deduce consequences from the analogous representations of divine truth contained in the pages of a revelation. They raise an important question as to the reality of a large mass of metaphysical theology, and whether such theology consists of truths necessarily flowing from statements contained in revelation, or whether it is not mere barren speculations of the human intellect, extending its researches into regions far beyond the limits of its powers. However closely connected the discussion of the above deductions may be with these and similar questions, we must confine ourselves entirely to their bearing on the nature and extent of the inspiration under the influence of which the Christian revelation has been communicated.

CHAPTER VI.

THE THEORY OF VERBAL INSPIRATION CONTRARY TO THE MODE OF THE DIVINE ACTING IN CREATION AND PROVIDENCE.

WE must therefore proceed to examine the nature of the probabilities which are usually adduced as evidences of the truth of the theory of verbal inspiration. We observe, in the first place, that, assuming the truth of the facts as they appear in the New Testament, the written and the oral teaching of the Apostles must have been of precisely the same nature, and delivered with the same degree of inspiration. A considerable portion of the New Testament is derived from the oral teaching of the Apostles. The writers of the New Testament do not claim any higher degree of inspiration for their written than for their oral teaching, but, on the contrary, frequently put their oral teaching on a par, in point of authority, with their written teaching. If, therefore, the New Testament was composed under the influence of verbal inspiration, or the inspiration denoted by any of the cognate theories, the same inspiration likewise belonged to every branch of their oral teaching when the Apostles and other inspired persons were occupied in teaching Christian truth.

If, then, the Apostles were always under the influence of verbal inspiration whenever they taught Christian truth, the influence of inspiration must, during the greater portion of their lives, have nearly superseded the use of their ordinary faculties. According to the statements of the historians, they were generally employed in their Master's work; and if so, they must have ordinarily displayed the peculiar phenomenon of infallibility: whenever they conversed on any subject of religion, it was not the individual Apostle who was heard discussing and arguing, but the Holy Spirit.

It has been considered that the supposition that any inspired writing has perished involves a considerable difficulty. It is therefore inferred that the written teaching of the

Apostles must involve a much higher form of inspiration than their oral teaching; and it has been taken for granted that no portion of their written teaching has perished. The difficulty of supposing that the whole of the oral teaching of the Apostles was the result of so high a gift as verbal inspiration has led to these assumptions. Hints, however, are found in the New Testament that other writings were composed by the Apostles, besides those which we at present possess, and other men were recognized as inspired. If this be the case, such writings have perished.

But it is evident from the assertions of the Scriptures themselves, that many things communicated by a high form of inspiration are no longer in existence. Before the Gospels were committed to writing, the oral teaching of the Apostles and of the original witnesses formed the only standard of divine truth possessed by the Church. Our present Gospels do not contain a record of the whole of the actions of our Lord, or of the whole of the discourses uttered by Him. Those which have been recorded must have been a selection out of a much larger portion of inspired teaching. The writers have only recorded what appeared to them sufficient for the purpose of handing down to future ages the great truths of Christianity. It is plain, therefore, that the delivery of a truth by a high form of inspiration does not guarantee the perpetual preservation of that which must have been delivered under its influence.

Now on what principle can we assume, on the supposition of the truth of the facts as recorded in the New Testament, that the writings of inspired persons must possess an inspiration which does not extend to their oral teaching? The general teaching of the Apostles is frequently referred to in their writings as no less the result of assistance from on high than their written teaching. The early churches could have possessed no other knowledge of the facts of our Lord's life but the narratives of that life imparted to them by the original witnesses, before the present Gospels were committed to writing. The whole of the contents of the Gospels were most probably delivered orally before they were set forth in

H

their present form. A similar position must have been occupied by the oral preaching of the Apostles, before the composition of the Epistles, or before they had obtained general circulation. This oral teaching must have been the only authoritative standard of Christian truth which the Church was in possession of. Now it is impossible, on any sound principle, to assume that when the Apostles taught the very same truths, or declared the same facts, by word of mouth, they were not possessed of the same inspiration as when they wrote them. It must be admitted that whatever degree of inspiration was possessed by them in the one capacity was possessed by them in the other. If the theory of verbal inspiration be an accurate exponent of the degree of inspiration under the influence of which the Christian Scriptures must have been composed, it must be so because the Apostles were always verbally inspired.

The theory of verbal inspiration, therefore, is encumbered with the difficulty of supposing that the ordinary faculties of inspired persons were superseded during the greater portion of their lives.

One of the arguments adduced in proof of the necessity that the Christian Scriptures must have been communicated under the influence of verbal inspiration is, that it is exceedingly desirable that they should have been composed by the aid of the highest possible form of inspiration, so that they might contain nothing which is human, but only what is divine.

We have already seen that this is a position which cannot be realized even on the verbal theory. Every human element cannot be excluded, even if the inspiration afforded was actually verbal inspiration. The whole machinery of thought and conception must be human.

But it is a most unsafe guide to truth to argue because, according to ordinary human apprehension, it seems very desirable we should have certain things, that those things must be granted to us by God. The wisdom of God differs widely from the wisdom of man. Many things which seem to us most desirable to have been bestowed upon us, God has certainly not given. The number of additional blessings which we might think desirable is absolutely endless. To set up our views of what we think it desirable that God should do, and to infer from this that God must have done so, is to measure with our finite wisdom the wisdom of the Most High. Nothing, therefore, is more absurd than to infer that, because it may appear to human wisdom desirable that a revelation should be communicated under the influence of verbal inspiration, it follows as a necessary consequence that this is the mode which the Divine wisdom must have adopted in its communication.

It has been urged that a revelation which is designed to make men wise unto salvation, and which therefore must exert the most important influence on the happiness of man in the future world, should have been so communicated as not to leave the smallest doubt on the mind as to what was the meaning of any portion of its contents. It may seem that it is antecedently probable that it would be free from any difficulty; that every statement would have been made with the utmost possible plainness; that it would have propounded a system of theology for our belief, and rules of conduct for our practice, respecting which no doubt could have originated, and that it would have left nothing to be inferred by us. But we have as much right to infer that God has never placed man in a situation of difficulty by His creative and providential acts as to assert that a revelation must be free from difficulties.

But it has been asserted that the right reception of the truths of a divine revelation involves man's everlasting happiness in the world to come, and that truths invested with such unspeakable importance could not be communicated under a guidance inferior to that implied by verbal inspiration. In such a revelation every word must be verbally true, and the possibility of error must be rigidly excluded.

We readily grant the high importance of such a revelation, and of the truths which it contains; but this importance is no guide as to the means which God must necessarily employ in its communication. Will it be pretended that numbers of things in our present state do not exercise an influence of the highest importance on the future condition of man? Will not the character, the tastes, the habits and tendencies which we form in this life exercise the most important influence on our happiness in the world to come? Has man, in the formation of these things, any guidance like verbal inspiration to direct him? Why may we not as well infer from the same premises that God the Creator has never placed man in this position at all, as lay it down that it is inconsistent with His character that such things should enter into a revelation? The argument is equally good to prove that God could never have placed man in a position of difficulty or doubt, where he could run the risk of hazarding interests so infinitely momentous.

But it will be replied, the purpose of a revelation must be to remedy the original defects in the situation in which man has been placed by his Creator.

We answer, when we speak of defects in connexion with the works or the operations of the Almighty, we use such a term in reference to the imperfect views presented of those operations through the defects of the human understanding. We do not speak of defects in reference to the view taken of them by the Divine mind, or assert that there can really be any defect or imperfection in the Divine operations. To say that the purpose of God in making a supernatural revelation is to remedy the deficiencies of His working as Creator and Preserver of the universe is directly to ascribe imperfections to God, not in the human, but in the divine view of His own operations. We have therefore no right to assume that the difficulties which are presented to the human mind in the Divine mode of operation in creation and providence will be removed by a supernatural revelation, or that the same mode of communicating truth would not be adopted in one as in the other.

God intended to reveal Himself in creation; why is it not equally probable that He has provided us in creation with an infallible guide to conduct us to the knowledge of those truths which it was His purpose to reveal by His creative works? It will not be denied that the truths which God has thus revealed have a very deep and intimate bearing both on questions of religion and morality.

It would be far more just to conclude that God has always

had good reasons for placing man in a situation where he would have difficulties of this description to encounter, and that those difficulties which are presented in creation and providence would be found in a supernatural revelation of which God was the author.

But every analogy derived from creation and providence directly contradicts the supposition that God would provide everything ready made for man, without His own labour or exertion, in a revelation communicated by Him. On the contrary, we have the most abundant evidence that it is the Divine purpose that man should be a joint worker with Himself. God has imparted to man no gift of nature which does not require the aid of his own exertions to perfect. The highest and the best gifts of God require the greatest exertions on the part of man fully to realize their benefit. God has endowed man with glorious gifts of reason and of intellect. These are the noblest gifts which the Creator has bestowed on him. Does any gift which man possesses require greater exertion on his part in order that it may attain its perfect development? The gift will rust and almost perish unless kept in constant exercise. God has provided food for man in rich abundance; but all except the lowest kinds require man's co-operation in its production, and the higher the kind of food the greater degree of human co-operation is necessary. God has clothed the animals; He has not clothed man. Wherefore has He made this distinction? To man He has imparted the power of providing clothing for himself, and therefore He wills that he should exert that power. To the animals He has given no such power, and therefore He has provided them with clothing. Is it probable then that that Being, who, while He has provided man with the means of getting food and raiment, yet has denied him either without the exertion of the faculties with which He has endowed him, in the spiritual world has entirely altered the course of His conduct, and has provided him with truth all ready for his use, without the necessity of the exertion of those faculties with which He has invested him?

God, again, has endowed man with bodily powers and capacities. But even for the full perfection of those powers man's co-operation is necessary by exercise and exertion. In striking contrast is the mode in which God has imparted knowledge to the animal creation from that in which He has imparted it to man. To man He has communicated capacities for acquiring knowledge, rather than actual knowledge itself: man is not born with knowledge. To the animal creation the Creator has acted otherwise. Whatever knowledge they possess is the direct gift of their Creator, complete and entire like a verbal inspiration. It requires no co-operation on their part for its complete development. Thousands of generations of bees have existed. Their knowledge has not been progressive. Thousands of years ago their knowledge and skill were as great as it is now. They have made no progress during the interval. Their Creator has invested them at once with knowledge on some subjects which it has required man long ages to discover. The bee knew, ages before man, that the use of the hexagon in building involved the greatest economy of space. The youngest bee goes at once to its work perfectly taught by its Creator. But man arrives at this knowledge after deep study of geometry, and only after a succession of discoveries. The reason of this is, that man is created to be a fellow worker with God.

Nothing can be more striking to the thoughtful mind, in contemplating creation, than the extent to which it is evidently the pleasure of the Almighty that man should be a fellow worker with Himself. The whole kingdom of nature teems with evidences of this fact. It is one of the distinctive marks which separate the irrational races from the human. Everything in nature points to man as its archetype; but everything in nature no less distinctly requires man to become a fellow worker with God before it can be appropriated to its use. The earth is fitted for his abode, and stored with everything which his wants require; "but man must *subdue* it"*. The sea has been made by the Creator the highway of nations; but man must build his bark before he can traverse it and make it subservient to the purposes of intercourse. The Creator has fabricated the materials of steam; but man has invented the

* Gen. i. 28.

steam-engine. God created electricity, and endowed it with powers by which distance is annihilated; man has invented the telegraph. Metals in abundance God has stored in the earth for man's use; but man must invent before he can appropriate one of the Creator's gifts. Many of the harsher powers of nature stimulate this same activity in man, working, as God works, by unalterable law; man has to co-operate with Him to avoid the pressure of those laws on himself. The very difficulties of nature force man to be a fellow worker with God. Nature is full of difficulties, in order that man may be full of work to overcome them.

If such be the aspect of nature, why may not revelation also present similar features? If it is the pleasure of the Almighty that man should be His fellow worker in creation and providence, why may it not be likewise His pleasure that man should be a fellow worker with God in His character of Revealer? Man must be a co-worker with God before he can appropriate His gifts in nature; why may not the same necessity exist before he can appropriate the knowledge communicated by revelation? Difficulties exist in nature for the purpose of forcing man to become a fellow worker with his Maker; why may not similar difficulties exist in revelation for the purpose of effectuating the same end? If the very same difficulties exist in revelation as in nature, shall we without hesitation admit that nature is the workmanship of the Most High, and, because of the difficulties, deny that Christianity can have come down from the Father of light?

Shall we, with the verbal inspirationist, assume that that God who in creation and providence has hardly imparted to man a single gift which does not require his own co-operation for its perfection, has reversed the order of His operations in communicating a supernatural revelation, and provided man with every truth all ready to his hands, without the necessity of exerting any power with which he is invested? Analogy leads us to the conclusion that, if the God of creation and providence be the author of revelation, He would not invariably act by one rule in the one, and directly reverse it in the other. But the theory of verbal inspiration has been assumed to supersede the necessity of human agency in the study of divine revelation, and to present truth as much as possible ready made for man's use. If, therefore, the theory of verbal inspiration has been assumed as the mode in which a revelation must have been communicated because it presents truth as more ready for man's use than any other supposition, and requires less human exertion for its attainment, that theory is assumed in direct contradiction to the known actings of God in creation and providence. It therefore is so far from possessing antecedent certainty, that it has not even a low degree of antecedent probability that it would be the mode in which the Creator would communicate a supernatural revelation.

But it has been asserted that the goodness of God renders it antecedently probable that, if God made a revelation to man, and rendered man's everlasting happiness at all dependent on his reception of that revelation, not only would it be authenticated by the highest degree of external evidence, but it must be communicated with an inspiration not inferior in accuracy to verbal inspiration or some of its cognate theories. It has been asked, Can it be supposed that the Creator, if He has made such a revelation, has left in it anything dark and obscure for man to grapple with? Surely the goodness of God requires that the knowledge of its contents, or the reception of its truths, should not depend on any imperfections in the human intellect, but that truth should be communicated in the clearest and most distinct manner by God himself. These assumptions, if true, would have rendered all supernatural revelation unnecessary from the first. The argument from the Divine goodness is equally potent to prove that God must have endowed man with all requisite knowledge when He originally created him.

But we answer that, while it is an unquestionable truth that the Judge of all the earth will certainly do right, such important conclusions must not be assumed on what seems merely probable to us, but must rest on some certain grounds of evidence as to what has been the mode of the Divine procedure in analogous cases. Now whatever we know of God as Creator and Governor of the universe contradicts the supposition. Has not God the Creator left man ignorant of many subjects deeply affecting his spiritual well-being? Nor do the facts of the Christian Scriptures afford it any better support. Our Lord's mode of teaching in parables is expressly asserted to have been adopted from other reasons than because it was the plainest and the simplest method of communicating truth. If the argument possessed any real value, it would be effectual to prove that, if God made a revelation at all, that revelation must have been published in every part of the world, and proposed at once to the acceptance of every human creature. This we know He has not done: the mode of the Divine conduct, therefore, in making a revelation contradicts the supposition.

We are not now dealing, however, with the facts of the New Testament, but with our antecedent knowledge. The same principle which leads us to infer that the Scriptures must have been communicated by verbal inspiration equally requires that they must have been preserved in the same degree of accuracy in which they were originally communicated. If it be necessary, from considerations of the Divine goodness, that the Scriptures should have been verbally inspired, the same goodness would require that an infallible guide should have been provided for their interpretation. The Church of Rome carries this theory out consistently, and maintains that the difficult work of interpreting the Scriptures has not been left to the fallible judgments of ordinary men. According to her views, God has provided an infallible interpreter in herself. Her views on this subject have, in theory at least, the merit of consistency; and if these antecedent principles are correct, it is difficult to escape from the necessity of the conclusion. Against this conclusion the stern logic of fact raises its inexorable protest. The original assumption, therefore, rests on no grounds of antecedent certainty, and, as a probability, contradicts alike the facts of creation and providence and the pages of revelation.

It has often been asserted that if God be the author of the Scriptures, they must be infallible guides to truth, and that they must have been composed by the aid of verbal inspiration.

The whole force of the argument depends on an ambiguity in the expression. The expression "the Scriptures must be an infallible guide to truth" has a double meaning.

If the Scriptures be a divine revelation, they will be sufficient guides to truth. But in what sense of the word "truth" is this assertion intended? There is truth as it has been objectively communicated by God. There is truth in its abstract form, as it is the subject of revelation. There are also the several perceptions and apprehensions of that truth as it appears to the mind of different persons.

Now, supposing the Scriptures to be given by divine inspiration, the objective truths (not our views of them, or our deductions from them) would be the truths to which the term infallible or efficient guides is properly applied. If we say that these truths are infallible guides to man, we must be careful to define what we mean by that expression. They are infallible as far as God's purposes are concerned, but not necessarily infallible guides to every particular individual whatever may be his peculiar mental character. The very same thing may be an infallible guide to one man, which is far from being an infallible guide to another. How far anything can be an infallible guide to any particular person for the purpose of regulating his faith or his conduct, is a question purely relative. It will entirely depend on his character or his disposition. What may be an infallible guide to an inquiring, earnest, teachable man, to make him wise unto salvation, may be very far from being an equally infallible guide to a person of an opposite character. It frequently happens that orders which, to a faithful and intelligent servant, present no difficulty or ambiguity, are utterly insufficient for the guidance of a careless one. A revelation from God must always be a sufficient guide to man: its infallibility as a guide must depend on the disposition and the character of those to whom it is addressed. The more correct expression of this truth would be, "The Christian Scriptures, if they are a divine revelation, are a sufficient guide, and ought to be an infallible guide, to every man, to lead him into the road to life everlasting." It is impossible, therefore, from such data to infer the necessity of verbal inspiration. The only necessary inference is, that God has afforded sufficient inspiration.

It has been asserted as a proof that the Scriptures must have been written under the influence of verbal inspiration, that if they were not, the whole evidence of the truth of their contents becomes endangered. If any human element exists in them, the inquiry has been put, How can we be certain that they contain anything divine?

The truth of the Scripture as a divine revelation cannot be affected by any theory as to the mode in which inspiration was communicated in its composition. Its claims to be received as a revelation from God rest on the sufficiency of the attestation which it has received from Him. If God makes a revelation of His will, man is bound to receive and obey it, in whatever manner it may please the Divine wisdom to communicate it.

A sufficient attestation by God is the only ground on which a revelation possesses any claim to bind the consciences of man. The Christian Scriptures claim a miraculous attestation, quite independently of all questions as to the mode of their inspiration. If the attestation of a revelation were not miraculous, it would only bind the conscience of that person to whom it was communicated, and who possessed direct evidence in his own mind that the revelation was from God. God might give, if it pleased Him, an internal attestation to every particular individual that a revelation of His will had been made to him. The Christian Scriptures themselves lay claim to an internal evidence commending itself to the heart and conscience, in addition to their outward miraculous attestation. But this internal evidence is not the ground on which they claim a binding authority. That binding authority is expressly declared to be derived from their having received a miraculous attestation. This is directly asserted by our Lord himself. "If I had not done among them the works which none other man did, they had not had sin; but now they have no cloak for their sin." The miracles performed by our Lord, consummated by His own resurrection, and the miraculous powers with which

He subsequently invested the Apostles, constitute that attestation.

Now a real miracle is the full and sufficient attestation to a revelation, that it has God for its author. By it God places the stamp of His authority on the person who professes to have the revelation to communicate. A real miracle can only be performed by the great Governor of the universe, and by no inferior agent. The truth of this results from the following considerations.

A miracle is a suspension of the ordinary mode of the Creator's acting, and His acting by a different instrumentality. The established laws of nature are the mode through which the Creator acts. They are not merely the laws of His acting, but, to speak more correctly, they are the actings of God in conformity with law predetermined by His own will. God, in His universal energy, is ever present in those laws.

Now, if the laws of nature are only another word for the Divine energies themselves, any suspension of them can only be the result of a Divine act. A suspension of the laws of nature can therefore only be God ceasing to act by one method, and acting in another. A miracle, therefore, if it be a suspension of the ordinary laws of nature, or a deviation from them, must be a Divine operation denoting a special act of the Creator.

We do not here enter on the question of such miracles as may be of a doubtful character. A miracle may be a true miracle, but yet it may not be evidently miraculous to us. We speak only of such miracles as are unquestionable suspensions of the laws of nature. If the whole course of providence be the law of the Divine acting, and a miracle be a deviation from this ordinary mode of the Divine operation and the adopting of a different one, a miracle must give the Divine attestation to the person who is able to perform it. If a deviation from the ordinary laws of nature takes place at the word of a particular person, and those laws are the actings of the Creator, it proves the presence of God with that person at whose word the ordinary laws of nature are suspended. "This is the finger of God," is the natural language which will be uttered by every man when he witnesses an unquestionable miracle.

It will be admitted that a miracle is not more a divine act, nor more an exertion of a divine power, than the ordinary laws of providence are divine acts and exertions of divine power. No mistake is more common than to represent that a miracle is an *extraordinary* (*i. e.* extra great) exertion of a divine power. This error leads to an entire misapprehension of the true end and purpose of a miracle. The performance of a miracle is not intended to display power, but to afford proof of a special intervention of God. It is God really ceasing to act in one way, and acting in another. If a man announces that he will perform a miracle, for the purpose of attesting a commission from God, the performance of the miracle by the Creator under these circumstances, at the word of the person claiming to reveal His will, affixes His broad seal to the truth of the assertion of the person who professes to be empowered to communicate a revelation. If the laws of nature are God's laws—the ordinary modes of the Divine actings,—the power to perform a miracle must be a proof of a special commission from God. In a miracle, God manifests the reality of His personal will by suspending His ordinary mode of operating.

If miracles are actual Divine operations, and if none can interfere with the Divine actings but God himself, they can be performed by no inferior agent; they therefore afford a conclusive proof of a divine commission. The greatest unbeliever in existence, if he actually witnessed the cure of one born blind, and was certain that the cure had been effected by no other instrumentality than a word, would feel himself compelled to believe that the person at whose word the miracle had been performed was a messenger from God.

It follows that a true and genuine miracle, wrought at the word of a person claiming to have a divine commission, is an attestation by God to the reality of that commission. It enables us to know that what He asserts or commands is asserted or commanded on the authority of God. If a supposed revelation has a clear and certain miraculous attestation, its right to be received is established, quite distinct from any considerations as to the mode of its communication. The only question which can be raised is one of fact. Has the person claiming to be a prophet a miraculous attestation? Are the miracles which he professes to perform undeniable suspensions of the ordinary laws of nature? If he has a miraculous attestation, the mode in which the revelation has been discovered to the prophet's mind has nothing to do with our obligation to receive it.

The mode in which a particular revelation has been communicated to the prophet's mind is a simple question of the Divine will, and must be determined exclusively by the Divine wisdom. We are wholly inadequate judges of what the Divine wisdom requires God to do. When we see an act unquestionably divine, we may be sure that it is founded on the Divine wisdom. A miracle is such a divine act. An event of ordinary providence is another. Whatever elements a revelation attested by miracles contains, they have received the stamp of the Divine authority. If there be human elements in such a revelation, those human elements must have been placed there by God for a special purpose. It is not for man to attempt to improve on the works of God. Supposing such elements to exist, it is plainly God's intention that man should employ his faculties for the purpose of ascertaining their comparative value.

The assertion that if a human element exists in the Scriptures, it destroys all certainty as to the divine truths contained in them, is equivalent to limiting the Creator in the use of means. We ask, why cannot God combine a human and a divine element in a supernatural revelation? Can God only work by such means as we should use ourselves? The assertion that the presence of a human element in the Scriptures must nullify the divine one would only hold good if man had no faculties capable of discovering truth. We might as well assert that the evidences of revelation must be demonstrative, and not moral. But God has been pleased to give man few demonstrative truths to guide his conduct.

The evidence which He affords to man on most subjects is moral evidence. It admits of degrees. It is such as would be estimated differently by different minds. It is capable of being resisted. It requires a diligent search after truth, and a readiness to admit truth when found. This is the general mode in which God communicates truth to man in His ordinary dispensations. By what right do we assume that He reverses the whole mode of His procedure in communicating a revelation of His will?

Instead, therefore, of any presumption in the form of the theory of verbal inspiration arising from these considerations, all antecedent probabilities contradict the supposition that it would be the mode in which Divine revelation would be communicated. It is far more probable that truth in the pages of a supernatural revelation will present the same aspect as it does in God's revelation through the natural universe, and that it will require the same moral conditions in the recipient as other truths of equal importance, of which God has not afforded demonstrative evidence. The very introduction of a human element into the record of a revelation may be part and parcel of the same divine plan. It may be intended to make the discovery of truth in some degree relative to the moral character of the inquirer.

Our duties respecting a revelation depend on the degree of its attestation as coming from God, and not on the mode of its communication. If it is God's revelation, a reverent study of its contents is one of the highest of human duties. If it is sufficiently attested as divine, there can be no doubt that it has been communicated, and the human elements introduced into it, by the Divine wisdom; and although it may require careful study, yet the humble inquirer will be able to discover in it those truths which it was the intention of God to communicate for his illumination and guidance. If a human element has been admitted into the revelation, we may safely trust Omnipotence and Omniscience that it has been introduced in such a way as not to endanger the existence of what is divine.

It has been urged in support of the theory of verbal inspiration, that it is antecedently probable that this method would be employed, because it is a shorter and more compendious method of communicating truth. But we can have no ground of assuming, because, according to our conceptions, it may be the most direct method of communicating truth, that it must, therefore, be the mode which Infinite wisdom must necessarily employ. We may think it very convenient that every word in the Scriptures should have been a divine dictation; but to assume that it must be so, is to pretend that we are able to fathom the profound depths of the Divine mind.

But the supposition that there is an antecedent necessity that a supernatural revelation must be communicated by an inspiration no less exact than verbal inspiration is chiefly founded on the notion that we may form a human standard of perfection, and apply it to the dealings of God as the revealer of His will. Whatever does not come up to that standard of perfection is assumed as unworthy of the Creator.

According to human apprehension, a revelation communicated with all the accuracy of verbal inspiration may be considered perfect, compared with one which contains an admixture of different human elements. But how do we know that this is perfection in the way in which the Creator views it? We know that human standards of perfection very inadequately measure the realities of the Creator's works in the universe which He has formed; how do we know that they will be more trustworthy guides as to the facts of a supernatural revelation? The admission that God is perfect is a very different thing from asserting that the human standard of perfection must be realized in every one of the Divine acts. The Divine works are transcendent displays of the infinite power, wisdom, and goodness of the Creator; but as man is permitted to behold them, although the existing universe may be tending towards perfection, it is not perfect. Its law is progress. The facts of the universe prove that perfection does not now exist. On what ground, then, do we venture to assume that we must find in revelation the very opposite displays of the Divine actings to those which we actually find in creation and providence? If we were to find such phenomena in a revelation, would not their existence afford a strong antecedent probability that the revelation was a pretended one?

But it is a common argument in favour of the theory of verbal inspiration, that if the Christian Scriptures are a revelation from God, they must be God's word, and this renders it necessary that every word in them must be verbally inspired. If they are God's word, a human element cannot exist in them; they must be throughout absolutely and completely divine. If they are God's word, every expression in them must be absolutely true.

There is an ambiguity in the expression "God's word," which it will be necessary to remove. It may mean either God's own spoken word, or His will communicated through the agency of others.

The expression "God's word" cannot be properly applied to a divine revelation in the first of these senses. It cannot be God's spoken word in the same sense that an utterance of man is man's spoken word. It is the use of it in this sense alone that can afford any aid to the theory of verbal inspiration.

The expression is derived from the human use of the faculties of conception and of speech. To suppose that the great and infinite Spirit expresses Himself through a faculty of language is to represent Him as none other than ourselves. We might as well invest Him at once with bodily organs.

But if we use the expression as denoting God's conceptions, we have already proved that no revelation of God's infinite conceptions in their divine reality is possible to man. The divine realities must be translated into their nearest finite representations and approximations. To use the expression "God's word" in the same sense in which we use the expression "man's word," and apply it to a revelation of His will, involves an impossibility.

But the Scripture assertion, "God who cannot lie," involves a truth which lies alike at the foundation of theism and of revealed religion. The ambiguity which we have noticed is nothing less than an assumption of the whole question at issue.

When it is asserted that the Christian Scriptures are God's

word, the only correct sense which such an assertion can convey is, that they contain the general revelation of the Divine truth and will. They are God's word, because they contain His message to man. They embody the thoughts, ideas, and conceptions which it was His purpose to reveal. But if it is intended, by the expression that they are God's word, to imply that every idea, conception, and expression in them is as much the idea, conception, and expression of God as the expressions contained in a book composed by a human writer are the actual expressions of that writer, we use language the only effect of which must be to mislead.

When we employ the expression in a human sense, nothing can be the word of a writer in the strictest sense of that expression, except that which has been originally conceived, and then expressed in language, by that writer. If a writer expresses the thoughts of others in his own particular style, he is hardly entitled to designate them as his word, if we insist on the use of expressions verbally exact. We accuse of plagiarism a writer who borrows the conceptions of others without acknowledgment, and publishes them as his own. In the same manner, if one person supply the original conceptions, and another work them up into language, neither is entitled to claim the undivided authorship. If we use words in their strictest sense, both the conceptions and the language ought to be our own to entitle any particular expression to the designation of "our word."

But, in the ordinary use of language, expressions of this description are not used strictly, but in their popular sense. In this sense, when we use the expression "our word," we denote by it that the words employed express our meaning and intentions. If we send a message to a third person, and if the things which we intended to be communicated were honestly communicated, although the mode and conception and the language were those of the messenger, yet we should undoubtedly say that it was our message which was delivered, and we might honestly be held responsible for the consequences of it. In all such cases the truth is the essential point, not the language in which it is conveyed. A command may be given by a person in authority to his subordinates. They may communicate that command to others, each in different language from that originally given. Still the command is effectually the command of the superior, as long as it conveys the real purport of his orders, however great may be the variation in the expression. A person who was bound to obey the commands of such a superior, but who pleaded that he did not esteem the commands to be his, because the language in which they were conveyed was not precisely the same as those in which the original commands were given, would be justly punished for disobedience. To infer that, because it is asserted that a particular expression is the word or commandment of another, it must necessarily be expressed in that person's identical language and conceptions, is to assume that what is quite intelligible in a popular sense must be used with strict scientific propriety. To argue from the use of such a mode of expression to the particular mode in which the inspiration of the Christian Scriptures must have been communicated, is to assume the very point which it is necessary to prove.

The assertion that the Scriptures are the word of God cannot honestly be forced to mean more than that they contain the mind and intention of God. They are God's word communicated, not directly, but through the medium of a third person. This communication of the Scriptures, not immediately by God, but through the instrumentality of men, constitutes an essential difference between the sense in which they can be God's word and the sense in which a pure human utterance must be the word of man. The attempt to argue, because in a popular sense of the expression they are designated as the word of God, that therefore the modes of the expression and the style must be equally divine as the substance, is disingenuous and sophistical. In the case of a human author the expressions are not transferred through a second mind; in the case of the Christian Scriptures, whatever degree of inspiration we may claim for them, it is certain that the conceptions in them must have been transferred through the mind of the inspired person. The conceptions of the human author are entirely his own. In the case of a divine revelation, the conceptions have passed through a human medium; they cannot be God's conceptions, but their approximations in human thought.

It therefore by no means follows that, because the Scriptures are God's word, there cannot be a human element in them. The extent of such human element can only be ascertained by an appeal to the contents of the Scriptures themselves; it cannot be deduced from any grounds of antecedent probability.

We cannot assume, because the Christian Scriptures are a revelation from God, that inspiration has been afforded beyond the necessities of the case for the purpose of communicating those truths to man. All that we can infer is, that the record of the revelation contains those truths which it was the Divine purpose to reveal, and that they are so revealed as to be a guide to the humble inquirer as to the true way to life everlasting. But whether the inspiration with which they have been communicated has been verbal inspiration, or inspiration in another form, is a point which we have no grounds of antecedent certainty to enable us to determine from such premises.

Now the variety of subject-matter contained in the pages of the New Testament is very great. There is the account of our Lord's life and ministry, and of the discourses uttered by Him, given us in the four Gospels, interspersed with occasional reflections of the writers. It contains likewise another historical book, the Acts of the Apostles, which gives us an account of the planting of the most important Christian churches, and details the proceedings of some of the most eminent missionaries. These books contain a very considerable number of historical allusions. Then follow the Epistles, in which we find, in a very unsystematic form, doctrinal statements, precepts, allusions to events well known to the writers of the Epistles and those to whom they are addressed, statements of feelings and experiences, observations on events passing in the Church, directions about matters of business, and salutations. Lastly, one book professes to be entirely prophetical. The mode of instruction adopted in these books is of a most varied character. The truths treated of extend over the widest possible field, from the deepest truths of God to the most ordinary events of daily life.

Now, such being the contents of the book, it would seem antecedently probable that a book which consists of such a vast variety of matter would not be written under the influence of a uniform degree of inspiration, but that the degree of inspiration would be in accordance with the requirements of the subject-matter. Nothing is more contrary to our notions of wisdom than an undue expenditure of power. In human things, when we see a power applied out of all proportion to the effect intended to be produced, we consider it a deep reflection upon the skill of the designer. No engineer would employ an engine of 200 horse-power to lift a weight which required only the exertion of fifty. No one would think of employing a man with the powers of Sir Isaac Newton to discharge the duties of a copying-clerk. The Divine operations in nature are all founded on similar principles—the proportion of means to ends. The same principle may even be traced clearly enough in the book of revelation itself. The Christian Scriptures never represent God as doing for man what man can do for himself. It is therefore highly antecedently probable that we should find God acting by the same principle as to the degree of inspiration with which He communicates a revelation of His will, and proportioning the Divine assistance to the requirements of the subject-matter.

To illustrate this argument by an example taken from the New Testament itself:—In the eighth chapter to the Romans St. Paul confessedly treats of some of the most profound truths of religion. In part of the sixteenth chapter he is occupied in simply sending salutations to Christian friends. It is hardly possible to conceive of subject-matter more widely differing in character. Are we to assume that that God who carefully proportions means to ends in nature and providence, has afforded the same amount of supernatural guidance to discover to an apostle the deepest truths of revelation and to enable him to write, " Salute them which are of Aristobulus' household," or " The salutation of me, Paul, with my own hand"? To assume that both passages have received an equal degree of supernatural assistance in their composition is to make a deep reflection on the Divine wisdom. We may infer, therefore, that it is antecedently probable that the degree of inspiration afforded would vary according to the subject-matter.

Now, if the great revelation of Christianity is made in the person of our Lord, it is antecedently probable that in His person and teaching would be exhibited the highest possible form of divine inspiration. That revelation, as we have already intimated, the Christian Scriptures assert to consist of two parts: the one consists in the revelation of the Divine character and perfections made in the person of Christ; the other in the various discourses uttered by Him, and in the doctrines taught by Him. To the truths as they flowed from the lips of our Lord the highest form of inspiration would necessarily belong, if in his person He is God incarnate. As far as human ideas can express those truths, they must be expressed in our Lord's teaching with the greatest possible precision. Whatever degree of knowledge of the Divine character and perfections the human mind is capable of understanding, it is antecedently probable that the highest degree of that knowledge would be communicated in the teaching of Christ. No difficulties would impede Him in his teaching of truth, except those which the Creator has imposed as the necessary conditions and limits of human thought. He would be fully able to present to man the best view of the Divine realities which the human mind could possibly attain to. If the mind of man is only capable of attaining an analogous knowledge of truth, the analogies used by Him in its communication would be the best which the whole range of human conception could supply for their representation. Whatever may be the precise relation of our human conceptions to the divine realities, such a teacher would afford us the nearest approximation to the realities themselves.

But, as the thoughts of man must be human, and not divine, even such a teacher must be limited in his teaching by the essential conditions of human thought. However divine the teacher, he must be limited by those conditions which God has imposed on His own acting.

But, subject to this limitation, the teaching of one who unites the Divine nature with the human must involve the highest form of possible inspiration. Consequently it would be a probability, amounting to a certainty, that the inspiration which dwelt in Christ must have been higher than that with which any other messenger from God would be endowed.

As our Lord's person, life, and teaching must involve the highest form of inspiration, the only thing which is necessary is, that the history of His life and the records of His teaching should be transmitted to us with entire accuracy. In that case we should possess a revelation authorized by the highest form of inspiration, whatever might be the degree of inspiration afforded to those who recorded the history of our Lord's life or reported His discourses.

The preceding observations prove that we have very limited grounds of antecedent certainty as to what must be the subject-matter of a divine revelation, or the extent of the inspiration with which it must be communicated, or to what extent a human element might exist in an historical revelation like the Christian. Our only true means of determining what God must do in any given case is by carefully inquiring what He has actually done in creation and in providence. What the same Being has done in the one case, it is in the highest degree probable that, within certain limits, He will also do in the other. But the only means which we possess which can certainly lead to a satisfactory result is the examination of the sacred writers themselves as to what they assert respecting the nature of their own inspiration, and by carefully investigating the facts actually presented by that revelation.

If the same God be the author of creation, providence, and the Christian revelation, we may conclude that the same method which will conduct us to the knowledge of the Creator and Preserver of the universe would be the most likely to conduct us to the knowledge of the same Being as the revealer of His will. In creation and providence, the mode by which we ascertain the laws of the Divine acting is by a careful induction of facts. Why should the most careful study of God's actings in creation and providence be the only mode of attaining a knowledge of the Divine conduct in the one, and why should not the study of the facts and phenomena of revelation be the road to truth as to the mode of the Divine acting in the other? Why should we assume on mere grounds of probability the mode and degree of inspiration which has been afforded for the composition of the Scriptures, and not inquire of those Scriptures themselves what is the mode and degree of inspiration with which they assert that they have been written? Why should such modes of investigating truth be false in creation and providence, and certain guides when applied to revelation? Is there any rational ground for refusing to accept the testimony of the Scriptures in such a case? Why are we to assume that they have been composed under a greater or less degree of inspiration than they themselves actually claim? If we assume that they are devoid of the inspiration under the influence of which they positively assert that they have been written, it is equivalent to a denial that they are a divine revelation at all. But what right have we, on the other hand, on mere probable grounds distinct from their own testimony to assume that they have been composed with the aid of a higher inspiration than they actually claim, or with an inspiration which they may possibly disclaim? Many motives may influence a human author to induce him to disclaim the powers which he possesses. This cannot be the case with an author who is divine.

But it may be urged, their testimony on this subject is neither sufficient nor distinct. Is, therefore, the degree of their inspiration to be determined on grounds which, when applied to the works of creation and providence, conduct us to nothing but error and delusion? If it is correct that the Scripture testimony as to the nature of their own inspiration is indistinct, it is useless to have recourse to guides which will conduct us to erroneous conclusions as to other departments of the Divine conduct. Our appeal must be, on the contrary, to a careful analysis of the facts presented by the Scriptures, to enable us to arrive at a judgment of the nature and degree of inspiration by the assistance of which they have been composed. Now, we ask, why should not the facts of the Christian Scriptures be made the subject of a careful induction to enable us to determine the nature of their inspiration, in the same manner in which the phenomena of creation and providence must be subject to induction to enable us to determine the mode of the Creator's acting? Why should the facts of a divine revelation be twisted into conformity with an antecedent theory? Why should not our theory, as in all other cases where man has attained to correct knowledge, be formed as the explanation of the facts? Has the application of theories to the solution of the systems of creation and providence been so fruitful in the discovery of truth as to encourage us to apply similar principles to the solution of important truths connected with the Christian revelation? All our correct knowledge of the kingdom of nature has been the result of careful study and analysis of facts; and through that analysis correct theoretic knowledge has been attained. All the truths of modern science have been discovered on this principle; why, then, should not a similar principle be applied to ascertain the nature of the inspiration under the influence of which the Christian Scriptures have been composed, on all points which have been left doubtful by the assertions of the writers of those Scriptures? The right mode of determining this question is by an application of the inductive method to the facts of revelation, and by ascertaining from the testimony of the writers themselves the degree of inspiration by which they were guided, and under the influence of which they wrote.

If, therefore, the Scriptures are silent as to the mode of their own inspiration, the only method of arriving at the truth as to what degree of inspiration was necessary for their composition is a careful induction and analysis of the facts which they contain. A principle which is the source of all the knowledge which man possesses cannot be a dangerous one to apply to the elucidation of the question of inspiration.

We will therefore proceed to inquire what the Christian Scriptures themselves inform us respecting the nature of the revelation itself, the mode of its communication, and the extent of the inspiration afforded for its communication. We will then examine the facts and the phenomena presented by the revelation itself, and endeavour to deduce a theory of inspiration from the testimony of these facts. The only assumption which we shall make will be, that the Christian Scriptures have received a miraculous attestation, sufficient to prove them to be a revelation from God.

We will first of all unfold a subject to which we have already alluded, as it forms the groundwork of all correct views on the subject of inspiration.

CHAPTER VII.

THE INCARNATION IS THE GREAT OBJECTIVE MANIFESTATION OF DEITY TO THE FINITE MIND. THE PERSON OF CHRIST EXHIBITS THE HIGHEST FORM OF INSPIRATION.

IT has been already observed that the Christian Scriptures assert that the positive objective revelation of God has been made in the person of Jesus Christ. The fact that this revelation of God is objective in Christ's person forms the groundwork of the assertions of the Christian Scriptures. They declare that Christ is God manifest in the flesh. As far as the incomprehensible truths of the Infinite are capable of being imaged or grasped by the finite understanding, those truths, as an objective revelation, are manifested in the person of the God-man, in His life on earth, His death and resurrection, and they ever will continue to manifest themselves in His divine person. The Christian Scriptures represent that this great manifestation of the Infinite in the person of the finite not only contains the highest revelation of the glories of the Godhead possible to men, but that it is designed for the enlightenment of intelligences far superior to the human race—"that unto the principalities and powers in heavenly places might be known through the Church the manifold wisdom of God."

The truth that the person of Christ is God manifest in the flesh, forms the corner-stone of the Christian revelation. If the person of Christ be in this sense divine, it is evident that there will be exhibited in Him the highest possible form of divine inspiration. We must therefore examine the testimony of the New Testament on the subject.

One of the most remarkable passages in which that truth is directly asserted is the first chapter of the Epistle to the Hebrews :—

"God, who at sundry times and in divers manners spake in time past unto the fathers by the prophets, hath in these last days spoken unto us by His Son, whom He hath appointed heir of all things, by whom also He made the worlds; who being the brightness of His glory, and the express image of His person, and upholding all things by the word of His power, when He had by Himself purged our sins, sat down on the right hand of the Majesty on high; being made so much better than the angels, as He hath by inheritance obtained a more excellent name than they."

The translation of ἐν υἱῷ by the words "by His Son" is unquestionably incorrect. The evident intention of the sacred writer was to assert, not that God spoke by His Son, but in His Son, *i.e.* in the person of His Son, which is the evident meaning of the Greek no less than the evident intention of the writer.

In this passage the following statements are made by the apostolic writer respecting the nature of the Christian revelation.

The Christian revelation differs from all the other revelations of God to man, in the instrumentality through which it has been communicated. Former revelations were made through the instrumentality of inspired prophets: they gave utterance to the divine oracles. The Christian revelation has been communicated in the person of the Son of God. God has spoken unto us in His Son.

It differs also in the mode of its communication. Former

revelations were made at sundry times and in divers manners. πολυμερῶς, καὶ πολυτρόπως. By this expression is denoted the partial character of former revelations, both in the mode of their delivery and in the extent of their communications. No former revelation was made in the person of a prophet. God revealed Himself through him, but never in him. The Christian revelation is also contrasted with all former divine discoveries by the divine dignity of the person in whom and through whom it has been revealed. In it "God has spoken to us in His Son."

The Revealer of the Christian dispensation is the heir of all things. Through Him God has arranged the ages, and through Him, as the efficient cause, He has laid the foundation of the material globes. God, in speaking in His Son, has spoken in the person of one who is the brightness of the Divine glory, the express image of the Divine person, and who upholds all things by the word of His power.

The expression, " the brightness of the Divine glory" (ἀπαύγασμα τῆς δόξης), requires some explanation. It denotes that the glories of the invisible Creator, from the depths of His infinitude, shine forth visibly in the person of the Son. The Son is the outshining of that glory in such a manner as to be intelligible to finite comprehension. He is the ray of light flowing from the brightness of Him whom no created eye can behold, or created intellect apprehend.

The revealer of the Christian dispensation is also the express image of the Divine person—χαρακτὴρ ὑποστάσεως. The term ὑπόστασις denotes not only the person, but the subsistence of God. It is that which essentially constitutes the Divine nature. Of this Divine subsistence the Divine Revealer is declared to be the express image, or χαρακτήρ. By this expression is denoted that as the signet corresponds with the seal, so the great Revealer of the Gospel dispensation represents in His person the divine realities of the Almighty, as closely as the infinite can be represented in the finite.

The Apostle therefore distinctly asserts that the last great revelation is made to man in the person of Him who is God and man. In that person He is the manifestation to the finite understanding, as far as it is capable of comprehending the eternal God in the infinite depths of His existence. His perfections are visibly represented in the Divine person of the Revealer. The unveiled glories shine forth in Him, as far as they can be comprehended by the creature. He is the medium through whom the natural and moral perfections of the Godhead become comprehensible.

We next adduce, in proof of our position, the opening of the first chapter of St. John:—

"In the beginning was the Word, and the Word was with God, and the Word was God. The same was in the beginning with God. All things were made by Him, and without Him was not anything made that was made. In Him was life; and the life was the light of men. And the light shineth in darkness, and the darkness comprehended it not . . . . . And the Word was made flesh, and dwelt among us (and we beheld his glory, the glory as of the only begotten of the Father), full of grace and truth . . . . . No man hath seen God at any time; the only begotten Son, who is in the bosom of the Father, he hath declared Him."

St. John here expressly asserts that the person in whom the revelation of the Gospel has been manifested is incarnate Godhead. The apostle affirms the great truth which we have already proved, that the eternal and infinite Creator cannot possibly be adequately comprehended by the creature in the glories of His incomprehensible being:—"No man [none] hath seen God at any time." He can neither be made visible to the bodily eye nor comprehensible to the understanding as He exists in Himself. But the only begotten Son, who dwells in the bosom of the Father, has become the revealer in His incarnate person.

The Incarnation is here expressly asserted to be the great revelation of the Godhead. The Word (the Revealer) was in the beginning with God, and was God. He was made flesh, and dwelt among us. He was manifested in such a manner that we could behold His glory—the glory as of the only begotten of the Father. Such a mode of revelation differs from all mere discoveries made by inspiration to the spirit of man. Not only were the glories of the natural attributes of God manifested in the Incarnation, but St. John draws our attention to the fact that it formed chiefly a revelation of His spiritual attributes and moral perfections. The Revealer was " full of grace and truth." The Revealer " became flesh, and dwelt among us; and we beheld His glory, the glory as of the only begotten of the Father." The Father's perfections shone forth in Him in his incarnate nature, as the most adequate representation of the Infinite which can be made to the finite understanding.

But the very expression by which St. John designates the Revealer of the Christian dispensation is indicative of the same truth. He is the Word, or Logos—the manifester, declarer, and revealer. He is to the Infinite what man's word or reason is to the finite. The expression denotes His relationship to the Father. He is the visible manifestation of the invisible God, through whom all revelation of God is possible. To the Word, or Revealer, the apostle then ascribes divine perfections. He was in the beginning with God; and was God. Without Him no creative act has taken place; all things were made by Him, and conditioned through Him. He possessed in Himself inherent life. That life became the light of man. That power which endowed all things with life has become the light of men. He is the true light, which, by coming into the world, has enlightened every man. Although the Divine perfections are above the comprehension of the finite understanding, the divine Logos, issuing from the bosom of the Father, having His Father's perfections manifested in His divine person, has become, by the Incarnation, the revelation of the Father.

We will next adduce the testimony, not of an inspired writer, but of our Lord himself.

In John xiv. our Lord declares, " I am the way, the truth, and the life: no man cometh unto the Father, but by me. If ye had known me, ye should have known my Father also: and from henceforth ye know Him, and have seen

Him. Philip saith unto Him, Lord, show us the Father, and it sufficeth us. Jesus saith unto him, Have I been so long time with you, and yet has thou not known me, Philip? He that hath seen me hath seen the Father; and how sayest thou, then, show us the Father? Believest thou not that I am in the Father, and the Father in me? The words that I speak unto you I speak not of myself; but the Father that dwelleth in me, He doeth the works. Believe me that I am in the Father, and the Father in me; or else believe me for the very works' sake."

The apostles, grounding their opinion on the literal language of the Old Testament, had formed the idea that the infinite God, in His eternal being and uncreated perfections, was capable of being visibly beheld by man. So late as the close of our Lord's ministry, they had been unable to grasp the full truth of the Divine infinity. They were still strangers to the great truth, that no man hath seen God at any time. After they heard our Lord assert that He was the way, the truth, and the life, and the only means of access to the Father, that if any man had known Him he would have known the Father also, and that henceforth they both knew Him and had seen Him, Philip, thinking not only that the finite mind could grasp the Infinite, but that He could be seen by mortal eye, said unto Him, "Lord, show us the Father, and it sufficeth us."

Our Lord's reply is an express declaration that whatever can be seen or known of the Father is embodied in Him. "He that hath seen me hath seen the Father." "If ye had known me, ye should have known my Father also; and from henceforth ye know Him, and have seen Him."

Our Lord therefore declares Himself to be the only visible and intelligible representation of the invisible God. The apostles had seen the Father; but what they had actually beheld was the manifestation of incarnate Deity in the person of Jesus Christ. It was Christ they had known, conversed with, and whose divine perfections they had witnessed in every relation of life. Our Lord asserts that those who had witnessed the perfections exhibited by Himself had actually seen and witnessed all that man can behold of the perfections and of the person of the invisible God.

The wish expressed by Philip was doubtless to have a manifestation made by God to the apostles similar to those which had been made "at sundry times and in divers manners unto the fathers." He had misread the ancient Scriptures, and thought that the appearances which were recorded there were manifestations of the real existence of the great Unseen. He wished to have a new exhibition of the visible glories of Sinai.

Our Lord's answer is a mild rebuke :.—"Have I been so long time with you, and yet hast thou not known me, Philip? Have you derived no more correct knowledge of what God is, that you are still craving for a visible manifestation? Believe me, every one who has seen me, and beheld the spiritual glories of my person, has seen all that created mind can comprehend, of the 'King eternal, immortal, invisible, who dwelleth in light which no man can approach unto, whom no man hath seen or can see.' God does not consist in a glorious form: He is an infinite Spirit. There is no visible representation of Deity, but my divine person and my divine perfections. The Divine glories consist in the deep spiritual perfections of His infinite nature. I am 'the brightness of the Father's glory, and the express image of His person.' Believest thou not that I am in the Father, and the Father in me?' If you have not beheld the Father's glories in me, believe me for the sake of the works which I do."

When the New Testament Scriptures speak of seeing God, they do not mean beholding Him by the outward eye of sense. Their unequivocal assertion is, No man hath seen God at any time. Even man's mental eye cannot embrace within its spiritual vision the realities of the Infinite, the Unconditioned, and the Absolute. But whoever has beheld the glories of the Saviour's person has witnessed the outshining of the glories of the Father. Those glories are exhibited in the moral perfections of Jesus Christ. In His divine person, therefore, is made the clearest representation which man can behold of the glories of the depths of Deity.

But although assertions of this kind are chiefly made in the Gospel of St. John, yet all the accounts of our Lord's ministry as recorded in the synoptic Gospels are based on the same assumption, that both in His teaching and in His works He speaks and acts with the authority of incarnate Deity. But while these Gospels do not contain such distinct assertions that He is God, they represent Him throughout as acting as God. They do not expressly assert, but, what is equally satisfactory, they presuppose this truth as the foundation on which their view of the character of Jesus Christ is erected. They exhibit the human aspect of His person; but while they bring this prominently forward, they portray both His teaching and acting to be of such a character as would be quite inappropriate to be assumed by any human being, however highly he might have been gifted with inspiration. They uniformly represent His knowledge of divine things as immediate, and not derived to Him from any external authority.

But one passage, recorded by St. Matthew and St. Luke, in the character of its assertions bears out the more express declaration of the Gospel of St. John:—"All things are given unto me by my Father; and no man knoweth who the Son is but the Father; neither knoweth any man the Father, save the Son, and he to whomsoever the Son will reveal Him."

In this assertion of our Lord, He claims to be the sole channel through which all true knowledge of the Father is conveyed to man. The Father, He asserts, in His own nature is incomprehensible. "No man knoweth the Father but the Son." The Son, therefore, possesses a knowledge of the Father which is possessed by none but Himself. Every one who attains a knowledge of the Father, attains it through the Son. He is discovered only to him to whom "the Son is willing to reveal Him." This claim to be the sole and exclusive Revealer of the Father is made by our Lord, not simply in His divine or human nature, but in his incarnate person; for it is in that person that He is a rest to the weary and heavy laden. It is immediately after making this declaration that He invites such to come to Him for rest.

The next proof which we adduce is the first chapter of the First Epistle of St. John—" That which was from the beginning, which we have heard, which we have seen with our eyes, which we have looked upon, and our hands have handled of the Word of life (for the life was manifested, and we have seen it, and bear witness, and show unto you that eternal life which was with the Father, and was manifested unto us); that which we have seen and heard declare we unto you."

Words could hardly have been framed to declare more strongly that the Christian revelation consists of an objective fact, and that it is made in the divine person of our Lord, than the words here used by the apostle. The author of the Epistle declares that the subject respecting which he was about to write consists of Him who was from the beginning—the Word of life. But it is the Word of life in the Incarnation respecting whom he writes. It is the actual Word of life "which we have heard, seen with our eyes, looked upon, and which our hands have handled." Such a description only befits the Word of life in His incarnate person. "That which we have seen and heard," says he, "declare we unto you." The Word of life, which he had seen and handled, " was made manifest." " He was with the Father, and was made manifest unto us." He is therefore become the great objective revelation of God. This manifestation must have taken place in the Incarnation; because it is the Word of life as seen and handled by him, respecting whom he testifies. But He is the special revelation of God in His character as the life of the spiritual world : " The life was manifested." St. John bore witness of that " eternal life which was with the Father." Such assertions cannot possibly be restricted to the sense that our Lord is the revelation of the Father in His divine nature only. They are express that the revelation has been made in His incarnate person.

We next quote St. Paul as asserting the same truth (Col. i. 14-19) :—" In whom we have redemption through His blood, even the forgiveness of sins : who is the image of the invisible God, the firstborn of every creature : for by Him were all things created that are in heaven and that are in earth, visible and invisible, whether they be thrones, or dominions, or principalities, or powers : all things were created by Him, and for Him : and He is before all things, and by Him all things consist. And He is the head of the body, the church : who is the beginning, the firstborn from the dead; that in all things He might have the preeminence. For it pleased the Father that in Him should all fulness dwell."

It is evident that St. Paul is here speaking, not of our Lord's divine or human nature separately, but of His incarnate person. The apostle is speaking of Him through whose blood men have redemption and forgiveness of sins. He is also the head of the Church, the firstborn from the dead, in whom it pleased the Father that all fulness should dwell. These are characters of our Lord in his incarnation.

Now it is this incarnate person of our Lord which the apostle distinctly asserts to be the image of the invisible God. He is the image, representation, and likeness, and therefore the objective revelation, of the Father. The apostle distinctly asserts that God Himself in His eternal perfections is invisible. But he designates Christ as the image of the invisible God. The incarnate person of the Son, therefore, makes the invisible perfections of the Godhead visible to finite minds.

But the apostle further describes the Revealer of the Godhead as Him through whose blood man has redemption. He is (as the translation ought to have been rendered) the firstborn of the whole creation. He is the Creator of all things, visible and invisible; He is before all things, and in Him all things consist. He is the beginning; and all things were created both by Him and for Him.

The expression, "in Him all things consist," or hold together (συνέστηκε), means that the Revealer of the Godhead is Himself the precondition of all finite beings. Without Him all created things, or finite beings, would be unable to hold together or subsist. He is therefore the means through which the invisible and incomprehensible depths of Godhead are capable of being manifested to the finite universe.

The Son is therefore the image or representation of the invisible God in everything in which the Infinite mind is capable of being comprehended by the finite: as the same idea is elsewhere expressed by the apostle, "He was in the form of God."

The next passage which we shall adduce as testifying to the same view of the nature of the Christian revelation is Eph. iii. 8–11:—

"Unto me, who am less than the least of all saints, is this grace given, that I should preach among the Gentiles the unsearchable riches of Christ; and to make all men see what is the fellowship of the mystery, which from the beginning of the world hath been hid in God, who created all things by Jesus Christ: to the intent that now unto the principalities and powers in heavenly places might be known by the church the manifold wisdom of God, according to the eternal purpose which He purposed in Christ Jesus our Lord."

In this passage the apostle speaks of our Lord not only as a revelation of the deep things of God to the Church, but to higher intelligences than men. By means of the gospel revelation, through the instrumentality of the Church, is discovered the manifold wisdom of God. The gospel revelation, which it was his duty to preach among the heathen, is here described by the apostle as consisting in the unsearchable riches of Christ. In the person of Christ, therefore, there is a perfect depth of divine knowledge. These unsearchable riches, which are now made manifest in Christ, had been hidden in God. The revelation of these unsearchable riches which were hidden in the Godhead was made in consequence of an eternal purpose formed in the Divine mind, to make in Christ a display of His glories to the creature. The depths of that divine knowledge the apostle had before asserted were, "in other ages, not made known unto the sons of men, as" they are "now revealed unto the holy apostles and prophets by the Spirit." The revelation of the Gospel now makes manifest unto all men the unsearchable riches of Christ, which had been hid in God in eternal ages, so that they may all see the fellowship of the mystery which has been hid in God. These unsearchable riches are displays of divine perfection to men. But there was another purpose contemplated in this revelation. It was designed to make deep discoveries of truth to the angelic world. By this disclosure, unto the principalities and powers in heavenly places was made known by the church the manifold wisdom of God.

The same great truth is affirmed by the apostle in Col. ii. 9: " In him dwelleth all the fulness of the Godhead bodily."

The apostle is here dealing with a number of philosophizing Christians, who were endeavouring to incorporate various oriental systems with Christianity. The sects who, by their philosophizing notions, were subverting the simplicity of Christian truth, taught that the Godhead dwelt in a remote or unknown pleroma or fulness in peaceful silence, apart from matter and all creative works. How then had finite existence originated? It was an emanation from the Infinite. From the Divine pleroma various emanations had issued in different degrees, more or less remotely connected with the Divine essence. These were imperfect manifestations of the perfections of the invisible God. The more remotely these emanations were connected with the Godhead, the more nearly were they allied to material things. A remote emanation had at length generated the material universe. In matter the essence of evil dwelt. By the act of generating the material universe, all evil had been produced, and spirit had become imprisoned in the trammels of the flesh.

Speculations of this kind involved the principles of Pantheism or Dualism, or both united together. According to the views of these speculators, either all things had ultimately, though remotely, emanated from God, or matter must have existed independently of God, and was the source of evil. Such opinions were destructive of the Christian faith.

In opposition to these views, the apostle asserts that the fulness of the Godhead, the very pleroma itself, which these speculators viewed as so remote from the material creation, dwelt in the human nature of Christ. In his person, therefore, is the fulness of the manifestation of the Godhead as an objective revelation.

A similar argument may be deduced from the apostle's assertion (2 Cor. v. 19), "God was in Christ, reconciling the world unto Himself."

If God was in Christ, reconciling the world unto Himself, Christ in His atoning work must have been the visible manifestation of the attributes of God. Whatever perfections, therefore, Christ displayed in accomplishing the work of reconciliation, these perfections must be visible representations of the incomprehensible realities of the Divine mind.

Although the reading of 1 Tim. iii. 16 is doubtful, and consequently cannot be quoted as a conclusive authority, we will examine its testimony. If the reading were certain, that testimony would be conclusive:—

"Without controversy, great is the mystery of godliness: God was manifest in the flesh, justified in the Spirit, seen of angels, preached unto the Gentiles, believed on in the world, received up into glory."

The other reading (ὃς) seems hardly to convey sense. If therefore the common reading be the true reading, the apostle most distinctly asserts that the fact of the Incarnation is the objective revelation of God. But the evidence that this is the apostle's view becomes very strong when we take this and the other passages referred to in connexion with his declaration, 1 Tim. vi. 15, 16. Speaking there of the future manifestation of Jesus Christ, he says:—

"Which [manifestation] in his own times he shall show, who is the blessed and only Potentate, the King of kings, and Lord of lords; who only hath immortality, dwelling in the light which no man can approach unto; whom no man hath seen, nor can see."

The apostle makes, in this passage, the assertion that the blessed and only Potentate neither has been seen nor can be seen by man. His glorious perfections transcend all human powers of apprehension. "He dwells in the light which no man can approach unto; whom no man hath seen, nor can see."

That blessed and only Potentate will, in His own time (yet future), show another manifestation of Jesus Christ. The apostle, therefore, implies that this future manifestation of Christ will be a glorious display of the perfections of Him whom "no man hath seen, nor can see."

We next adduce, in support of our argument, 1 Cor. xv. 1–4: "Moreover, brethren, I declare unto you the gospel which I preached unto you, which also ye have received, and wherein ye stand; by which also ye are saved, if ye keep in memory what I preached unto you, unless ye have believed in vain. For I delivered unto you first of all that which I also received, how that Christ died for our sins, according to the Scriptures; and that He was buried, and that He rose again the third day, according to the Scriptures."

Some portion of the Corinthian church had embraced philosophizing principles, under the influence of which they denied the reality of a bodily resurrection from the dead. These principles must have asserted the inherent evil of matter, and, as such, that a material body was an unfit habitation for the human soul, and must therefore have been Pantheistic. Whatever they were, if they were carried out to their legitimate consequences, they were subversive of the Christianity which was taught by St. Paul. If the dead could not be raised, Christ could not be risen; and with the truth of Christ's resurrection the whole mass of Christian truth was closely interwoven, and fell to the ground if the belief in it was subverted.

The apostle, therefore, set himself to recall the Corinthians to the first principles of Christianity as taught by him. He reminds them that that gospel which they had received, in which they stood, and by which they were saved, did not consist in a mass of theories or of abstract doctrinal statements, but in an objective fact—the actual death and resurrection of Christ. He then recapitulates the evidence on which belief in that fact rested.

The apostle has here designated the fact of Christ's death and resurrection as the gospel: he recalls to their minds the gospel which he preached unto them; he delivered unto them what he also received, that Christ died and rose again. These were not theories, but objective facts. He therefore sets forth that, distinct even from all his teaching, there was an objective fact which constituted the gospel. This fact forms the groundwork of Christianity itself; it forms the very gospel of the grace of God.

There are many other passages in the New Testament which either assert or imply the view of the nature of the Incarnation for which we are arguing. To adduce these passages separately would be only to give a further consideration to evidence already adduced, by repeating over again the same assertions. If the passages already cited are not of sufficient force to prove that the Incarnation is, in the view of the writers of the New Testament, the great objective revelation of the perfections of the infinite God, it will be readily admitted that the other passages by themselves would not be sufficient to establish it.

We have proved, therefore, that it is laid down as a fundamental principle by the writers of the New Testament, that the great revelation of Deity has been made in the person of the incarnate Son of God. There are two objective revelations of the perfections of the Infinite. One revelation of God has been made by the created universe. That universe is a display of the power, wisdom, and goodness of its Author. It gives us evidences of Him as acting through the agency of law. But it is a manifestation of some portions of the Divine character and perfections to a far greater degree than of other portions of them. But the Scriptures inform us that, in addition to the manifestation made of Himself by the works of creation and providence, another partial revelation has been made by God's having spoken in sundry times and in divers manners unto the fathers through the prophets. The last and great revelation is not made in any of these partial manifestations. It consists in the incarnation of the Son of God, in His human life and death and resurrection—the objective manifestation of the glories of the infinite God. Whoever has seen Christ has seen the Father, as far as His perfections can be made comprehensible to the creature.

If this be a correct view of the teaching of the New Testament as to what constitutes the gospel revelation, the highest conceivable form of inspiration must be displayed in our Lord's own divine person. This is a necessary consequence of the permanent abiding of Deity in His human nature. If our Lord be not a prophet merely, but God manifest in the flesh, it is self-evident that our Lord, in His person and in His teaching, must present divine truth in the highest form in which it can be exhibited to the mind of man. The teaching is not the teaching of man merely, or of man supernaturally aided and assisted, but of one who, while He is man, is also God. The knowledge of truth could not have been derived to Him from without, but dwelt within Him. But this is not a conclusion resting on inference merely; it is the repeated assertion both of our Lord himself and the apostles. We will proceed to consider some of these assertions.

But, before we enter on that examination, we must make one remark. The teaching of our Lord in the Gospels is very extensive. It is recorded by four different biographers. Throughout the whole of that teaching, although we possess four separate records of it, not one single passage can be adduced which denotes the remotest consciousness on the part of our Lord that He derived one particle of truth from any source external to His own person. No such expression as "Thus saith the Lord" ever once passed from His lips. He speaks throughout with an inherent and direct perception of personal knowledge and authority. He does not speak or teach on any occasion as one who was conscious of inspiration merely, but as one who possessed divine authority inherent in His person.

The first assertion of our Lord which we shall adduce is John iii. 11–13: "Verily, verily, I say unto thee, We speak that we do know, and testify that we have seen; and ye receive not our witness. If I have told you earthly things, and ye believe not, how shall ye believe, if I tell you of heavenly things? And no man hath ascended up to heaven, but He that came down from heaven, even the Son of man which is in heaven."

In this passage our Lord asserts, not His own inspiration merely, but His own inherent knowledge of the deep things of God. The imagery in which the assertions are conveyed is taken from man's most intimate knowledge of the things of man: "We speak that we do know, and testify that we have seen." He makes no profession, therefore, of deriving His knowledge from such a kind of inspiration as was claimed either by prophets or apostles. The declaration is equivalent to the assertion that He was acquainted with divine truth by direct intuition. He declares that He has ascended up to heaven; that He has come down from heaven; and that He is in heaven. He uses expressions, therefore, which denote the clearest knowledge of the realities of heavenly things. He speaks as if the spiritual world was open to His view. His knowledge of it is intimate and perfect: it corresponds to human knowledge derived from direct vision.

In John viii. the following assertions of our Lord are recorded:—"I speak to the world those things which I have heard of Him." "As the Father hath taught me, I speak these things." "The truth which I have heard of God." "Ye have not known Him; but I know Him, and keep His sayings." "If I should say, I know Him not, I shall be a liar, like unto you."

Our Lord in these passages uses language taken from the various senses, to express the completeness of His knowledge of the great truths which He taught. Of all the forms of human knowledge, those derived directly from the testimony of the senses of seeing and hearing, or from the immediate intuitions of the mind, are the most perfect. Our Lord describes the completeness of His divine knowledge by using expressions to denote it taken from the most perfect form of human knowledge. He has seen the truths which He teaches; He has heard them from God; He speaks those things which He has been taught of God; He knows God immediately and directly, and His denial of such knowledge in this absolute form would be on His part an absence of veracity and truth.

In John vi. 61 we read:—"When Jesus knew in himself that His disciples murmured at it." John ii. 24, 25: "Jesus did not commit himself unto them, because he knew all men, and needed not that any should testify of man: for He knew what was in man." Matthew ix. 4: "And Jesus knowing their thoughts said, Wherefore think ye evil in your hearts?" Passages of this kind are very numerous in all four Evangelists.

The Evangelists assert of Christ an inherent power of discovering what was passing in the human mind. This power is described not as a special communication for a particular occasion, or as flowing from a mere suggestion made to His mind by the influence of the Spirit, but as a power habitually abiding in Him. He knew in Himself what was passing in His disciples' minds. He knew what was in man. He discovered at once what had passed through the thoughts of Simon the Pharisee. He was habitually conscious of the machinations of the Pharisees before their designs had found utterance by the lips. He discovered the conversation between Peter and the tax-gatherer. He was acquainted with the secret motives of the human mind. All this knowledge is described as not flowing to Him by suggestion, but by intuition. In this respect, the inspiration which dwelt in the person of our Lord differs from the inspiration which was possessed by either prophet or apostle.

But it has often been asserted that the Gospel of St. John differs from the other Gospels in assigning a greater degree of divine knowledge to the person of our Lord than is asserted to belong to Him by the other Evangelists, and in representing Him as more intimately acquainted with divine truth. This has been made the reason for asserting either that St. John has falsely ascribed this knowledge to our Lord, or that the Gospel was composed after the apostolic age, and has been enriched by myths and various additions. In one word, it is asserted that we have not the true Jesus in the Gospel of St. John, but one of a more divine character.

Now what is the real fact? What is the actual difference, in this respect, between St. John and the other Gospels?

The assertions of superhuman knowledge and of a divine character are undoubtedly more distinct and definite in St. John than in the other Gospels. As far as distinct assertions of such knowledge are concerned, the fact is undoubtedly correct that its existence is affirmed by St. John in terms more palpable than by the authors of the synoptic Gospels.

But the synoptic Gospels likewise affirm, in express terms, a very high form of knowledge as possessed by our Lord, differing widely from what any apostolic writer has asserted or implied respecting the nature of his own inspiration. It is a knowledge which does not differ in degree, but in kind.

But how have the authors of the synoptic Gospels described our Lord as acting? Is there any material difference between their descriptions of our Lord's mode of acting and the descriptions given in the Gospel of St. John? The mode of our Lord's acting, as described by St. John and the synoptic Gospels, is identically the same. It is impossible to affirm that, in this respect, St. John's Gospel takes a higher ground than that taken by the three first Evangelists.

The synoptic Gospels habitually describe our Lord as teaching with no derived, but with an inherent authority. He speaks like one who felt conscious that His word was entitled to a greater weight than was possessed by the highest forms of divine teaching previously existing, which He claims the right to annul or explain according to His pleasure. No less habitually they represent Him as never referring to any external source of light. The illumination with which He teaches is a light purely internal. He never, on even a single occasion, presupposes the existence of an authority superior to Himself, or that any form of divine truth could exist, however profound, with which He was not entirely competent to deal. In the same manner, the synoptic Gospels represent our Lord as never appealing to any external source of inspiration to direct Him in the performance of His actions. Whenever He performs a miracle, He performs it in such a manner that He is the only person glorified by it. His word, and His word alone, is competent to effect it. He never once refers the power by which he wrought to the Father.

The difference, therefore, which exists between St. John's Gospel and the synoptic Gospels is not that which has been frequently asserted. The Gospel of St. John affirms, in express words, the divine character of our Lord, and that the form of His knowledge of divine things differed from that which was possessed by any other messenger from God. The writers of the synoptic Gospels, although they do not make these assertions in such express terms, have, from one end of them to the other, depicted our Lord as teaching and acting like a divine person. In them He teaches and acts with a consciousness of inherent authority, which could only be justified by the assumption of the truth of the assertion in St. John. St. John's express assertions are merely affirmations, in express words, of a truth which the narratives of the synoptic Gospels presuppose. The Gospel by St. John makes numerous direct assertions of our Lord's divine character. The synoptic Gospels portray Him as acting in the very character which St. John distinctly affirms.

All these Scriptures, taken together, assert that the knowledge possessed by our Lord of divine things was direct, clear, and immediate. In the writings of the Apostles we can hardly fail to be struck with the fact, that their most elevated conceptions seem to demand on their part a great effort of the mind to raise themselves to a full conception of the Divine glories. In St. Paul's highest flights, his mind struggles with the profundities of his thoughts. This was never the case with our Lord. He displays neither struggle nor mental effort. His knowledge is always habitual, calm, self-possessed. There is no vehement struggling of the mind to raise itself to the requisite elevation. It is never dazzled by the brightness of the rays of divine light. It is the knowledge of one whose habitual society was that of Deity itself.

CHAPTER VIII.

THE NATURE OF OUR LORD'S KNOWLEDGE DERIVED FROM THE INSPIRATION OF THE SPIRIT. ITS TWO RECORDED LIMITATIONS.

WE have examined the testimony of the New Testament as to the nature of our Lord's inspiration as flowing from the union of His godhead with His manhood. But as long as human nature is finite, its knowledge must be necessarily bounded within those conditions which the Creator has Himself imposed on the human mind as the law of its conceptions. A human mind must conceive and know as a human mind. Our Lord's human nature was a created, and therefore a finite nature. Had this not been the case, our Lord would not have been truly man. But, subject to those conditions to which human conceptions must be subject, the indwelling of Deity in the human nature of our Lord communicated to it the highest form of divine knowledge (though not all the possible knowledge) which can be possessed by man.

But, in addition to the knowledge possessed by our Lord through the indwelling of Deity in His person, the Christian Scriptures assert that at His baptism He also received the highest form of inspiration which can be imparted by the Spirit, by the communication to His human nature of His influences in their richest and fullest abundance.

The synoptic Gospels agree in asserting that, after our Lord was baptized, the Spirit of God descended like a dove, and abode on Him. St. Peter, also, in his address to Cornelius, affirms that "God anointed Jesus of Nazareth with the Holy Ghost and with power." John the Baptist, also, in his public testimony given to our Lord, declares, "He, whom God hath sent, speaketh the words of God; for God giveth not the Spirit by measure unto Him." St. Luke, likewise, asserts that "our Lord, through the Holy Ghost, gave commandment to the apostles whom He had chosen." The author of the Epistle to the Hebrews tells us, that He, "through the eternal

Spirit, offered Himself without spot to God." Our Lord's designation of Christ, or Messiah, is a direct witness to the same fact.

Now all the purposes are not obvious why our Lord, uniting the divine nature with the human in His own person, should require the communication of the Spirit of God. One end for which the Spirit was imparted to Him was to bestow those influences on the Church; but this did not take place till after His crucifixion; and our Lord Himself declares that it was necessary that He should go to the Father, before the Comforter could come on the Church. This is evidently not the purpose why our Lord received the highest form of inspiration communicated by the Spirit during the period of His earthly ministry.

Another purpose why He was anointed with the Spirit was to qualify Him to offer the great atoning sacrifice to the Father. But to inquire into this is beyond our present purpose. Several of the above assertions affirm that the influence of the Spirit was imparted to Him as the great teacher of the Church. The declaration in St. Luke directly affirms this: "He, through the Spirit, gave commandment to the apostles whom He had chosen."

We might have supposed that our Lord's human nature required no other illumination than the indwelling of the Godhead in His divine person. But the passages which we have quoted expressly affirm that the human nature of our Lord received the highest form of inspiration, in addition to the knowledge communicated to it by the indwelling of Deity. It follows, therefore, that the indwelling of Deity did not necessarily communicate all possible knowledge to our Lord's human nature, of which that nature was capable. But when He had received the fulness of the Spirit, it is evident that His gifts, conferred upon Him without measure, stamp on every portion of His teaching a character which can be claimed by no inspired messenger from God.

In estimating the nature of our Lord's inspiration, we must give due weight to the fact that His human nature was a perfect manhood. It was, therefore, not omniscient, but subject to all the conditions imposed on human nature by the decree of its Creator. The human nature of our Lord was human nature in its most exalted form. But all the supernatural knowledge which it possessed must have been communicated to it by the presence of the indwelling Godhead, or by the inspiration of the Spirit. To assert that our Lord's human nature was omniscient is a practical denial of its reality.

What was the precise nature of the limitations of that knowledge we can only learn from the declarations of revelation itself. In the same manner, it is the only source of information as to the degree of enlightenment which our Lord received from the supernatural endowments of the Spirit. If we had formed our opinion on grounds of antecedent probability, we should certainly have arrived at the conclusion that there was no truth which human nature is capable of attaining, which was not communicated to Him by the presence of the Godhead. So worthless are all *à priori* reasonings on such a subject!

The Scriptures assert one limitation to this knowledge, even after He received the supernatural endowments of the Spirit, and describe one limitation to the knowledge of His human nature before His baptism. These are the only two passages in which anything is positively affirmed on the subject, and within which our knowledge is limited.

St. Luke affirms in his Gospel that, "Jesus increased in wisdom and stature, and in favour with God and man." This passage forms a portion of the only anecdote revealed in any genuine Gospel of our Lord's boyhood. St. Luke had just narrated how Joseph and Mary had found the divine child in one of the Temple schools, sitting in the midst of the doctors, both hearing them and asking them questions. The impression produced by Him was remarkable: "All that heard Him were astonished at His understanding and answers."

From these passages we may draw the following conclusions:—Our Lord, at the age of twelve, displayed an amount of understanding which greatly surprised the doctors of the Jewish school connected with the Temple. Our Lord's growth to manhood was marked by the same phenomena as those displayed by the other members of the human race. His acquisition of knowledge was progressive: He "increased in wisdom and in stature." This increase was capable of being distinctly marked. His moral and spiritual perfections likewise developed themselves gradually: He increased " in favour with God and man."

The only thing, therefore, which the Scriptures positively inform us on this subject is, that our Lord's growth in knowledge and holiness was like that of all other men—the result of a gradual progress. The Godhead dwelling in Him did not supersede this necessity of His human nature. As man, He grew in wisdom; as man, He grew in stature; as man, He grew in favour with God and man.

There is one passage in Scripture which asserts a limitation to our Lord's knowledge after His baptism. At Mark xiii. 32 we read, "But of that day and that hour knoweth no man [Gr. " none "], no, not the angels which are in heaven, neither the Son, but the Father."

The words used by St. Matthew, although they do not make the same express assertion of the ignorance of the Son respecting the day and hour of His second coming, leave abundant room for that assertion. They are, " But of that day and hour knoweth no man [Gr. " none "], no, not the angels in heaven, but my Father only."

The language of the introduction of the Book of Revelation, though not so strong as the actual language used by St. Mark, yet fully bears it out:—"The Revelation of Jesus Christ, which God gave unto Him, to show unto His servants things which must shortly come to pass; and He sent and signified it by His angel unto His servant John."

Now the assertion of St. Mark is in every point of view most important. From what we have already considered concerning the statements of the sacred writers respecting the extent of our Lord's knowledge, we should certainly never have anticipated that this thing would have been hidden from Him, especially after He had received, at His baptism, the fulness of prophetic inspiration.

L

The assertion in St. Mark has been generally pressed as an objection to the doctrine of our Lord's Deity. But it has been pressed by those who rely on verbal arguments more than on the great facts of the Christian revelation. If our Lord be really God manifest in the flesh, possessing both a divine and human nature, against that truth it can be no objection. As we have already observed, the knowledge of the most perfect man must possess limits. There is nothing in the fact of the Incarnation which renders it necessary that the Godhead must have communicated all knowledge to our Lord's human nature. If our Lord's human nature were not limited in knowledge, He would not be perfect man. The reality of His manhood is no less part of the Incarnation than the reality of His Godhead.

But the real matter of surprise is, that our Lord continued ignorant of this fact after he received the fulness of the Spirit. The declaration in St. Mark positively affirms that our Lord did not know the time of the end. Consequently, it must be inferred that our Lord's human nature only received information on matters of futurity through the inspiring Spirit; and that as it formed no portion of His appointed work to communicate futurity on this special subject, the information was not given. Our Lord has elsewhere made use of the expression, "the times and the seasons the Father hath put in His own power;" and our Lord also affirms that the will of the Son is absolutely coincident with the will of the Father.

Various have been the attempts to escape from the supposed difficulties of this passage. One is the expedient of attempting to show that the Greek word, οἶδεν, may by some possibility be made to mean, "cause to know" or "reveal." An attempt has been made to translate the passage thus:—"Of that day and hour no man causes to know, no, not the angels in heaven, neither the Son, but the Father."

No one would gravely adopt this rendering as a correct meaning of the Greek who had not some antecedent theory to maintain. The question is, Would any native Greek ever have attached such a meaning to such words in such a context? Did not St. Mark know, if he had wished to express such a meaning, how to express it with perspicuity in the Greek language? To suppose that Mark meant to assert, "Of that day and hour none makes a revelation, no, not the angels in heaven, neither the Son, but the Father," by the words in question, is to assume that his inspiration is of the lowest possible order, or, to speak more correctly, that he has given an incorrect translation of our Lord's words.

If the obvious meaning of the words, as they stand in St. Mark's Gospel, plainly contradicts the truths contained in other portions of the New Testament, the only honest recourse open to us is to maintain that the words, "neither the Son," is an interpolation. But even by taking this course we shall not escape the difficulty; for the words used by St. Matthew are little less express, "but my Father only." In the Book of Revelation, also, the revelation of the future is said to be a gift of the Father to Christ: "The revelation of Jesus Christ, which God gave to him." It may be replied, that the gift here mentioned was not the gift of the knowledge, but the gift of showing it to the Church. But this is a most unnatural meaning of the words, and one which would be only had recourse to when a particular hypothesis had to be supported. Such an interpretation the words in the fifth chapter absolutely forbid; for the sealed book of futurity is there represented, agreeably to the language of St. Matthew, as entirely in the hands of the Father, and given to the incarnate Lamb in consequence of His having accomplished the work of redemption.

But even if we could get rid of the difficulty by denying that these words were written by St. Mark, before such a measure is had recourse to, it ought to be carefully considered what effects such a principle would produce on the rules by which the sacred text must be ascertained. These rules would be entirely subverted by the assertion of an arbitrary right to strike out a text merely because it contradicts particular opinions. Such a principle is so dangerous that it ought only to be resorted to when the necessity is of the most undoubted character. If it were once established that we may deny that particular passages were not written by the authors in whose books we at present find them, merely because they contradict our views of what ought to be Christian doctrine, all certainty as to the truth of the New Testament would be destroyed.

But, in the present instance, a clear necessity for rejecting the words has not been made out. The utmost which can be said is, that, considering many of the declarations of the New Testament, we should not have expected that the human soul of our Lord was ignorant of the time of the end. But the fact that He was so contradicts none of the assertions of the Christian Scriptures respecting the Incarnation. The knowledge of the future is an attribute not of manhood, but of Godhead. Such ignorance is a proof of His perfect manhood, the reality of which is as necessary to constitute Him the objective revelation of the Father as that He possessed, in His person, the attributes of God.

This passage, then, must be admitted to have been written by St. Mark, and as such to be an assertion made by our Lord himself, that in His human nature He derived His knowledge of futurity from the inspiring Spirit, who endowed His manhood with every gift and grace which was necessary for making it the perfection of created holiness. As the knowledge in question was not communicated to Him, it was not necessary for the purposes of His divine mission: the inspiring Spirit furnished him with everything necessary for the accomplishment of His work.

We arrive at the conclusion, therefore, that the divine person of our Lord exhibits the highest form of inspiration which can be possessed by the created spirit of man. His indwelling Deity furnished Him with knowledge of God and of divine things, direct and intuitive. His teaching, therefore, exhibits divine truths in the highest form.

But, in addition to the knowledge which His human nature possessed through its union with Deity, He was endowed with the inspiration of the Spirit in a manner in which neither prophet nor apostle was endowed with it. The highest form of inspiration in an apostle was a knowledge of divine truth constant and permanent, forming a portion of his self-conscious understanding, but attended with a distinct consciousness that it had been communicated to him by a power external to himself. The inspiration of a prophet of the former dispensation formed no permanently abiding influence in the mind. It proceeded directly from without, and was always announced by the formula, "Thus saith the Lord." But even that inspiration of the Son of God which was communicated to His human nature by the inspiring Spirit was attended with no consciousness of external origin; it abode within Him as light and truth. In Him was light, and the light was the life of men.

We conclude, therefore, that our Lord's actions and teaching, and the portrait of His divine person, form the inspired element in the Gospels. If they be correctly recorded, we possess the results of inspiration in its highest form. That inspiration was the combined result of the indwelling of Deity and the communication of the Spirit in the fulness of His gifts to His human nature.

CHAPTER IX.

THE NATURE OF THE INSPIRATION OF THE APOSTLES. THE APOSTLES WITNESSES. OUR LORD'S PROMISES. THE SOURCES OF ST. PAUL'S APOSTOLIC KNOWLEDGE.

HAVING examined the declarations of the New Testament respecting the inspiration of our Lord, and ascertained its nature from its testimony, we must now consider its assertions respecting the inspiration possessed by the Apostles. The office of an apostle consisted of two branches. It was one of its functions to bear witness to the events of our Lord's ministry and the reality of His resurrection. It was another function of the apostolical office to expound the meaning of the revelation communicated in his person. It is necessary, therefore, to consider the apostolic inspiration under both these aspects.

It was essential to the office of an apostle, that he should have been an eye-witness of our Lord's ministry. This is expressly asserted by St. Peter, when the Apostles were about to fill up the vacancy occasioned by the death of the traitor Judas.

Acts i. 21, 22 : " Wherefore of these men which have companied with us all the time that the Lord Jesus went in and out among us, beginning from the baptism of John, unto that same day that He was taken up from us, must one be ordained to be a witness with us of His resurrection."

The qualifications for the apostolic office are here most distinctly stated. To qualify a person for the office of an apostle, it was necessary that he should have been an attendant on the whole of our Lord's ministry, from its commencement unto the Ascension. The words need not imply that the person to be appointed an apostle must have been present at every action performed by our Lord, but present generally during His ministry. The qualification for the apostolical office, as described by St. Peter, is taken from our Lord's description of their duties—that they were to be witnesses unto Him at Jerusalem, and Judæa, and Samaria, and unto the uttermost parts of the earth.

It was our Lord's intention, therefore, that the belief in the facts of His actions and His teaching, as well as in His resurrection from the dead, should rest on an actual human testimony. St. John accordingly affirms that a belief even in the higher doctrines of the gospel ultimately resolved itself into belief in the apostolic testimony. That testimony was founded on the evidence of their senses respecting the Word of life, "which we have seen," says he, "heard with our ears, looked upon, and our hands have handled." This human testimony of theirs was to be supported by a divine testimony—that of the Spirit of God— enabling them to work miracles in confirmation of their human testimony.

As far as the Apostles were human witnesses, the testimony of the Spirit was a divine testimony, supporting but not superseding their human one. This is too often forgotten. St. Peter expressly affirms it, "We are witnesses of these things, and so is also the Holy Ghost." This divine testimony, given in confirmation of their human testimony, consisted in endowing the Apostles with miraculous powers.

In enabling the Apostles to work miracles in attestation of the facts to which they testified, God Himself was distinctly present as a corroborating witness to the truth of the human testimony which they gave. This testimony by miracles resembled the support given to the character of the actual witnesses of certain facts by another witness of acknowledged and unquestionable credibility.

It frequently happens that witnesses depose to facts, but we require evidence of the character and credibility of the witnesses. This evidence of character is always necessary when the facts are of an extraordinary description. Many facts are of such a nature that we should only believe them when testified to by a witness of whose character for veracity we were assured. Another witness comes forward with whom we are well acquainted, and fully substantiates the character and credibility of the original witnesses.

Precisely of this nature was the power of working miracles conferred on the Apostles. The Apostles testified to facts which they asserted that they had seen and heard. These facts were of a very extraordinary nature. It was necessary that the character of the witnesses for veracity and judgment should be well established, to render them credible. To work a miracle, therefore, was to adduce God as a present witness to their veracity and credibility.

A miracle denotes the visible presence of God. If the laws of nature are the actual modes of the Divine operations, and a miracle is God ceasing to act in the ordinary mode of His operations and acting by a new instrumentality, the performance of a miracle is a special Divine attestation and recognition of that person at whose word the miracle is performed. A person endowed with the power of working miracles does not perform them himself; it is God who, at his word, ceases from one mode of His operation and acts by a new and hitherto unknown instrumentality. If, therefore, a person possesses a power of producing results by other antecedents and causes than those which we witness in

God's operations through the established laws of nature, in every exertion of that power God gives a veritable testimony to the character of that person at whose word the miraculous attestation takes place. When, therefore, miracles were performed at the word of the Apostles, it was precisely the same thing as God coming forward as a special witness to confirm the truth of the Apostles' testimony.

The human testimony of the Apostles to the great facts of Christianity and the divine testimony of the Spirit must be kept perfectly distinct. That human testimony was to be given respecting the reality of facts which they had seen and heard. Their office was to testify to actions which they had actually seen our Lord perform, and to discourses which they had heard Him utter: "That which we have seen and heard declare we unto you."

But the Divine testimony, as the author of the Epistle to the Hebrews informs us, was given in confirmation of this human testimony of the Apostles. His words are express. "How," says he, "shall we escape, if we neglect so great salvation; which at the first began to be spoken by the Lord, and was confirmed unto us by them that heard Him?" Then he mentions the divine corroborating testimony: "God also bearing witness, both with signs and wonders, and with divers miracles, and gifts of the Holy Ghost, according to His own will."

The writer of this Epistle expressly asserts the existence of a human testimony to the facts, and a Divine testimony confirming the facts. If we do not keep these elements distinct, each will lose its proper character. So St. Peter, as we have already quoted him: "We are witnesses, and so is the Holy Ghost." If we convert the human testimony into a divine testimony, we shall deny the existence of what the two sacred writers have so carefully asserted.

But the human testimony was the testimony of the Apostles as witnesses. If they testified as witnesses, whatever degree of aid they might receive from above, if they gave a testimony, the mental act involved in their testimony must have been an act of recollection.

If it had not been a distinct act of recollection, but fresh information afforded respecting those facts, or discoveries made to their minds by the Spirit of God, they would have ceased to be witnesses of what they had seen and heard: their testimony would have been simply and entirely a divine testimony.

The theory, therefore, which represents the facts and discourses recorded in the Gospels, and as the Apostles taught them in their preaching, as a pure dictation made to their minds by the Spirit, entirely destroys their testimony as the appointed witnesses to the facts of Christianity. Instead of the testimony on which Christianity rests being the eye- and ear-testimony of the Apostles to the great facts of our Lord's divine mission, and the witness of the Spirit supporting that testimony, it would make it a twofold testimony of the Spirit, first asserting the facts themselves and then confirming His own assertions by miracles. The Apostles' assertion that they testified to what they had seen with their eyes, heard with their ears, and handled with their hands, would be utterly untrue.

To constitute testimony, there must be a distinct recollection, on the part of the witness, that the facts to which he testifies were actually seen by him, and the discourses heard by him. Recollection forms the essence of testimony. The memory may be aided; but, in order that there should be testimony, the event recalled to the mind must become the subject of recollection. Without recollection, there can be no such thing as testimony.

It frequently happens that one may forget a fact which he once knew, or a discourse which he once heard, and anther person may recallh the one or the other to his mind. When this is the case, the person whose memory is refreshed must have a distinct recollection that the fact was the fact which he actually witnessed, and the discourse was the discourse which he heard, before he can give testimony respecting either the one or the other.

Whatever supernatural assistance, therefore, the Apostles received in bringing to their recollection the facts of our

Lord's ministry, or the discourses which they heard, could not have been a fresh discovery of either the one or the other to their minds, but a recalling them, if they had faded from their recollection. If they had not the fulness of certainty that the facts were those witnessed by them, and the discourses were the discourses which they had heard our Lord utter, their testimony would have been valueless.

I can only be a witness of what I have actually seen and heard. If another person tells me of a fact, and I repeat it to a third, I am no witness to that fact. My assertions add nothing to the testimony, but rest entirely on the credibility of the original witness. His assertions may be true, but my repeating them over again gives them no additional confirmation.

There are various means by which I may become acquainted with the discourse of another. It may be copied down, and I may learn it. I may have every reason for believing that it has been copied down correctly. But although I may repeat the discourse, I am no witness to the discourse. I may give the persons to whom I repeat it the evidence on which I believe it genuine; but I cannot assert, on my own authority, that that discourse was the discourse which came from the lips of the person who was said to have spoken it. No court of justice would for one moment accept such testimony. The original witnesses must be forthcoming, and declare what they have seen and heard.

Now the writers of the Christian Scriptures distinctly assert that the belief in the divine mission of our Lord rests on evidence of this description, and that Christianity demands our belief because the truth of it can be proved by such testimony. Our evidence of the validity of our Lord's divine mission rests on the fact, that we have sufficient reasons for believing that the Apostles saw certain actions performed by Him which were sufficient to prove that He was a teacher come from God. If they did not really remember those facts or discourses when they asserted their reality, they are found false witnesses of God. If they were the mere dictation of the Spirit to their minds, St. Peter's declaration which he made to the Jewish council, "We cannot but speak the things which we have seen and heard," would have to be corrected into, We cannot but speak the things which the Spirit has introduced into our minds.

There is great danger, therefore, in assuming a particular theory of inspiration, of destroying the human testimony of the Apostles as witnesses of the facts of our Lord's public ministry. It must be admitted that the Christian Scriptures contain thus far a human element; or else, in support of our particular theory of inspiration, we must be prepared to deny their most positive assertions. They are committed to the fact that the Apostles did bear an actual testimony to our Lord's acts. On its truth they claimed a right to speak with authority to the conscience. The degree in which preternatural assistance was afforded them in bearing this testimony we will consider hereafter.

Our Lord's divine person and teaching, therefore, form the divine element in the Apostles' testimony as witnesses. If that testimony has been correctly given, we are in possession of the highest results of divine inspiration in the teaching and actions and person of our Lord.

The whole question of the inspiration of the contents of the Gospels involves the inquiry — Are they correct reports of our Lord's sayings and actions?

Facts are true, if they are narrated as they actually occurred. If so narrated, they cannot possess a greater or less degree of truth as facts. As facts, they do not admit of degrees of truth: they admit of and require evidence. A fact possesses the highest degree of truth when it is correctly reported by a truthful witness. If he has ordinary intelligence, he has only to tell us what he saw. If a fact is correctly reported by a human witness, it does not acquire any greater degree of truth by being derived from a higher power.

Now ordinary men, with ordinary abilities, are endowed with all the powers necessary for narrating what they have witnessed. Peter or John were quite able to give a correct report of the facts attending a miracle which they saw our Lord perform. They possessed all the powers which were requisite for giving a true account of the Passion as they actually witnessed it. Supposing either of these Apostles to have been endowed with the ordinary powers possessed by men, if they did not give correct reports on such points, the fault must have been, not in their capacity, but in their honesty.

But if we have reports of several witnesses to the details of a considerable succession of events, we should expect these reports to vary in points of minor detail. One thing might strike one witness, and another thing another. They might report different parts of the same fact. If the events were numerous, different witnesses might witness different portions of them. Still the reports of the main facts would be accurate, and their diversity in detail would leave the credibility of the main points of the report unaffected.

But very different is the case as respects the reports of discourses. However honest the witnesses may be, even in the case of brief sayings, there is great difficulty in getting them reported accurately. Words and sayings are always open to misapprehension. A very slight variation in expression will materially affect their meaning. A person often reports them through a colouring imparted to them by his own peculiar views and feelings, without the intention of wilfully misrepresenting them. These difficulties are increased when the things requiring to be reported are not short sayings, but long discourses. Still greater is the difficulty of such reports, if the sayings and discourses have not been committed to paper till a number of years after they were uttered. They are then liable to all the defects which arise from insufficient powers of recollection. In proportion as the words actually used have faded from the recollection, the more probable is it that their true meaning will be misrepresented through the influence which the peculiar views of the writer will exert over his mind.

The reports of discourses, as given by ancient historians, are all open to grave suspicion from these causes. The practice among ancient writers was very general of introducing the speeches of eminent persons into their histories. What is the authority on which the chief portion of such speeches rest? Have we any evidence that they were ever uttered by the persons whose names they bear? The larger proportion of them were certainly not copied down when they were delivered. Many are not even pretended to have been committed to paper till years after they are alleged to have been spoken. Such speeches want all authority. We suspect them, with good reason, to have been the work of the historians themselves, who have put into the mouths of the speakers what they thought it likely they would have said, for the purpose of affording variety and interest to their readers. The larger proportion of the speeches found in ancient historians are destitute of all evidence that they were actually uttered by the persons whose names they bear.

No ordinary human memory is capable of giving a verbatim report of a discourse even a few hours after it has been uttered. A few persons have that power. We can, in ordinary cases, only have sufficient evidence that a professed discourse contains the actual words used by a particular speaker when it has been copied down as he uttered it, or when a report of the speech has been furnished by the speaker himself.

But the power of recollecting the substance, as distinct from the words, of a discourse is a faculty much more extensively diffused. This faculty is more certain in its operation exactly in proportion as the discourse is striking, or the persons hearing it feel an interest in its contents. In such cases, even the style in which it is expressed will remain in the memory for a very considerable period. Still the report even of the substance is liable to misrepresentation from the prejudices of the reporter; and the longer the period which has elapsed before it has been committed to paper, the greater is that liability.

It must be admitted that the powers of the memory in ancient times seem to have exceeded those of more recent date. This was owing to the greater exercise of the memory, through instruction having been more generally oral. When no professed reporters existed, or printing-presses were in being, the greater necessity existed for treasuring up the living utterances of men. The prevalence of artificial methods of preserving doctrines and discourses has impaired the efficacy of the natural one.

The discourses of the Gospels labour under many of these difficulties. There is no statement which implies that they were copied down at the time when they were delivered. The circumstances when some of them were uttered render the contrary absolutely certain. There is no evidence that our Lord afterwards dictated them to His followers. The persons who have recorded them distinctly state that they had a very imperfect comprehension of the meaning of many of them when they were first spoken. The length of some of them is such, that few human memories could have retained them word for word, especially those discourses which were only uttered once, as was necessarily the case with the last discourse of our Lord to the Apostles, recorded by St. John.

If, then, the principle be correct, that what man can do by himself God does not do, but what man cannot do God does, supposing that it was the intention of God that the discourses of our Lord should form a portion of the records of the Christian revelation, we should expect that, when the Apostles gave their accounts of such discourses to the Churches, supernatural assistance would be afforded to their memories sufficient to render their reports of such discourses substantially correct. We shall see hereafter that such assistance was actually provided them by our Lord, and that the phenomena presented by the discourses themselves agree with such a supposition.

But, whatever was the degree of supernatural assistance afforded in rendering the discourses, if the Apostles were to give testimony to the reality of them, it must have been not a fresh communication of the discourse to their minds, but an assistance afforded to their memories, so as to enable them to recollect that the discourse in question was the actual discourse which they heard our Lord utter. The mere repetition of a discourse which was dictated to their minds by the Spirit would have not made them witnesses of the things which Jesus taught. Without a distinct recollection of them they could not have been witnesses. The inspiration, therefore, which they received must have been an influence which strengthened their memories, but which did not supersede the necessity of their exercise.

We shall see hereafter, that the phenomena presented by the Gospels entirely agree with this supposition.

The apostolic office, therefore, involved the duty of witnessing to the great facts of the Christian revelation. On the truth of their testimony to those facts depends the entire knowledge which man at present possesses of the objective revelation of God manifested in the Incarnation. In their capacity as witnesses, the inspired element in their testimony was Christ himself.

But the apostolic office not only involved the duty of testifying to the truth of the things which they had seen and heard, and narrating the events of our Lord's ministry, life, and death; they were also the divinely appointed expositors of those things. It was intended that they should not only testify to the facts, but expound the full meaning of the Gospel revelation. As the facts of the Incarnation form the objective revelation of Christianity, so the teaching of the Apostles is a divine commentary on that revelation. To fit them for a work of this description, supernatural guidance of some kind was absolutely necessary.

Before we enter on an examination of the facts of the Gospels and Epistles, for the purpose of deducing from them a correct view of the inspiration afforded to the Apostles, it will be necessary to examine the assertions of the sacred writers themselves as to the extent of their own inspiration.

First, we will consider our Lord's promises of supernatural guidance to be afforded to the Apostles to qualify them for their work, and their recorded fulfilment.

St. John (ch. xiv. 25, 26) records that, the evening before He suffered, He made the Apostles the following distinct promises of supernatural assistance :—

"These things have I spoken unto you, being yet present with you. But the Comforter, which is the Holy Ghost, whom the Father will send in my name, He shall teach you all things, and bring all things to your remembrance, whatsoever I have said unto you."

At chapter xv. 26, 27 :—" But when the Comforter is come, whom I will send unto you from the Father, even the Spirit of truth, which proceedeth from the Father, He shall testify of me : and ye also shall bear witness, because ye have been with me from the beginning."

Chapter xvi. 12-15 :—" I have yet many things to say unto you, but ye cannot bear them now. Howbeit when He, the Spirit of truth, is come, He will guide you into all truth : for He shall not speak of Himself; but whatsoever He shall hear, that shall He speak : and He will show you things to come. He shall glorify me : for he shall receive of mine, and shall show it unto you. All things that the Father hath are mine : therefore said I, that He shall take of mine, and shall show it unto you."

St. Mark has recorded another promise of our Lord, made to the Apostles a little before His ascension :—" Go ye into all the world, and preach the gospel to every creature. He that believeth and is baptized shall be saved; but he that believeth not shall be damned. And these signs shall follow them that believe : In my name shall they cast out devils; they shall speak with new tongues; they shall take up serpents; and if they drink any deadly thing, it shall not hurt them; they shall lay hands on the sick, and they shall recover."

St. Luke gives the following account of the same promise (chapter xxiv. 48, 49) :—" And ye are witnesses of these things. And, behold, I send the promise of my Father upon you : but tarry ye in the city of Jerusalem, until ye be endued with power from on high."

Acts i. 8, he adds :—" But ye shall receive power, after that the Holy Ghost is come upon you : and ye shall be witnesses unto me both in Jerusalem, and in all Judea, and in Samaria, and unto the uttermost part of the earth."

The synoptic Gospels concur in recording another promise of supernatural guidance made by our Lord at an earlier period of His ministry :—" When they shall deliver you up, settle it in your minds not to think beforehand what ye shall speak: neither do ye premeditate; for it shall be given you in that hour what ye ought to speak : for it is not ye that speak, but the Spirit of your Father that speaketh in you."

These are the promises of supernatural assistance which our Lord actually made to the Apostles. They are promises of no vague or general character, but clear, distinct, and definite. They are restricted to particular subjects, and say not one word respecting a universal or a general infallibility.

The first of these promises is recorded in St. John :—"The Comforter, which is the Holy Ghost, whom the Father wil send in my name, He shall teach you all things, and bring all things to your remembrance, whatsoever I have said unto you."

This promise was intended to assure the Apostles that they should receive all necessary assistance to qualify them to act as witnesses to the facts of what our Lord did and taught. The Comforter is promised, to teach them all things, and bring all things to their remembrance, whatever Christ had spoken to them.

The formal promise asserts, therefore, that the Apostles should be taught all things, and have all things brought to their remembrance which Christ had spoken. It is therefore a promise of a supernatural assistance to be afforded to their memories, to enable them to recollect the sayings and discourses of our Lord. The Comforter was also to teach them all things. The two clauses of the promise have respect to the same subject : they were to be taught the meaning of what our Lord had spoken. In giving their testimony as witnesses, the supernatural guidance promised was to give them a correct view of the portion of our Lord's sayings and discourses to which they were to give their testimony.

The direct terms of the promise, therefore, assure to the Apostles supernatural guidance where our previous inquiries prove that that supernatural aid would be most required. We have seen that if the Apostles were to give a correct account of our Lord's discourses in their capacity of witnesses to Him, this work would exceed the ordinary powers of their memories. The actions of His life might be recorded correctly by their ordinary powers, or by a far lower degree of supernatural assistance.

Our Lord, therefore, makes provision for this deficiency in the express terms of the promise. He does not promise them supernatural aid to enable them to remember the facts of His life; but He does promise them such assistance to enable them to recall to their memories the discourses which He uttered. Our Lord's promise, therefore, of assistance to their natural powers is strictly proportioned to man's need of such assistance.

The promise, also, is a promise of aid to their natural powers. It is not a promise of supernatural endowments only. The memory was not to be superseded. The Comforter was to aid and assist the memory—"to bring to remembrance," "to remind them,"—not to inspire them with the knowledge of things which they had neither heard nor seen.

The second of these promises is substantially the same in meaning with those recorded by St. Mark and St. Luke: "The Spirit of truth shall testify of me; and ye also shall bear witness, because ye have been with me from the beginning."

The Spirit of truth is here promised to testify of Christ; and the Apostles are constituted witnesses of Christ, for the obvious reason, "because they had been with Him from the beginning."

From the reasons given why the Apostles should bear testimony to our Lord, the nature of their testimony is evident. It must have been to the actions of our Lord, and to the discourses which He uttered during His public ministry.

But, in addition to the testimony of the Apostles, the Spirit also was to bear witness. What was the nature of the Spirit's testimony here promised?

This is distinctly explained by St. Mark and St. Luke. They both affirm that the testimony was to be a miraculous one. "These signs," says St. Mark, "shall follow them that believe," &c. St. Luke is equally express:—"And ye are witnesses of these things. And, behold, I send the promise of my Father upon you: but tarry ye in the city of Jerusalem, until ye be endued with power from on high." "And ye shall receive power after that the Holy Ghost is come upon you; and ye shall be witnesses unto me," &c. The witness of the Apostles, therefore, was to be united with miraculous powers to be conferred upon them by the operation of the Holy Ghost.

These miraculous powers, therefore, were the testimony of the Spirit given to Christ. The Spirit did not directly bear testimony to the facts or the discourses of our Lord; that testimony, therefore, was borne by the Apostles. His testimony was to the truth of the Apostles' testimony by the exertion of miraculous power.

This exertion of miraculous power by the Spirit testified to two things—the truth of our Lord's divine mission, and to the truth of the facts and discourses of our Lord which were related by the Apostles.

The promise of our Lord, therefore, is a direct promise of miraculous power to be exerted by the Spirit, confirming what the Apostles testified to in their capacity of human witnesses.

The third promise recorded by St. John is one of a far more extensive character:—" When He, the Spirit of truth, is come, He will guide you into all the truth: for He shall not speak of Himself; but whatsoever He shall hear, that shall He speak: and He will show you things to come. He shall glorify me; for He shall receive of mine, and shall show it unto you. All things that the Father hath are mine: therefore said I, that He shall take of mine, and shall show it unto you."

The promise is a promise of such enlightenment as would make the Apostles efficient teachers of the revelation which our Lord came to communicate :—" He shall guide you into all the truth." At the time when the promise was made, the Apostles had most imperfect apprehensions as to the nature of that revelation. Had they proceeded to teach it before they received supernatural enlightenment, they would have published a very different gospel from that which our Lord came to reveal. Of many of the actions of Christ they did not understand the import. Many of His discourses they entirely misapprehended. The end and purpose of His death was, to them, hidden in complete darkness. Their blindness respecting the meaning of many of the great sayings of our Lord was most remarkable. They greatly misunderstood the relative importance of the forms of religion and of ceremonial worship, compared with its spiritual and moral realities. When He predicted His sufferings in the plainest words, the saying was hidden from them, neither understood they the things which were spoken. No less remarkable was their misapprehension of what our Lord meant when He warned them to beware of the leaven of the Pharisees. We know from the history that they actually considered that our Lord was cautioning them against purchasing bread which had been made by the hands of persons of this sect. During the whole course of our Lord's ministry, the minds of the Apostles continued deeply implicated in the entire mass of Jewish prejudices in which they had been brought up, and they were in the habit of viewing the teaching of our Lord through the colouring of those prejudices. Their views respecting the spirituality of religion, and of the worthlessness of outward ceremonialism, were most imperfect.

The extent of these prejudices may be best estimated by the declaration of our Lord, made in His last discourse: " I have many things to say unto you, but ye cannot bear them now." This assertion plainly declares the mode which our Lord was compelled to adopt in His teaching. He taught the Apostles divine truth as they were able to bear it, not as it was in itself. His teaching, therefore, was progressive. The mists of prejudice were too profound to permit the full blaze of light which our Lord came to impart to find admission into their understandings. Before they could attain to a comprehension of the truths of the Christian dispensation, it was necessary that these mists of prejudice should be cleared away.

Our Lord, therefore, as soon as He had informed the Apostles that there were many things which He came to reveal, but which He had not discovered to them because they were unable to bear them, assures them that a time was coming when these truths should be imparted to their minds:—
" When the Spirit of truth is come, He shall guide you into

all the truth." Our version has most incorrectly rendered our Lord's declaration as though He promised the Apostles guidance into all truth. Such a meaning cannot possibly attach to the expression, εἰς τὴν ἀλήθειαν πᾶσαν, which can only mean, distinctly and definitely, not all truth, but all the special truths which Christ came to reveal. The Spirit was to unfold to their minds whatever He should hear or receive of Him. He was especially to teach them those truths which were to glorify His person: "He shall glorify me; for He shall receive of mine, and shall show it unto you." The things which were Christ's were the great revelation of the Father: "All that the Father hath are mine: therefore said I, He shall receive of mine, and shall show it unto you." He would disclose to them the great subjects of the Christian revelation in their full proportions, and qualify them to be the communicators of the meaning of the revelation of the Father made in the person of the incarnate Son.

In addition to the promise of guidance into all the truth which He came to reveal, He also assures the Apostles that the influence of the Spirit on their minds would disclose to them events of the distant future.

In this declaration, therefore, our Lord makes an express promise of supernatural enlightenment to the Apostles in the great subjects of Christian truth. It is also by far the most extensive promise of supernatural inspiration anywhere contained in the pages of the New Testament.

But the inspiration promised is not a mere vague or general inspiration conferring a universal infallibility; it is an inspiration specially restricted to the great truths of the Christian revelation only. The truth into which supernatural guidance is promised is all the truth of that revelation. The promise, therefore, is carefully guarded against being supposed to imply inspiration on any other subject than those which Christ came specially to reveal. It conveys to the Apostles no promise of supernatural guidance into any truths of natural science, or chronology, or history. It does not even assure them that they would be preserved from errors in conduct. The promise is rigidly confined to a supernatural guidance into the meaning and import of the Christian revelation.

The words, "He shall receive of mine, and shall show it unto you," are remarkable. By these words the idea that the inspiration was to be extended to any general department of knowledge is precluded. The things which the Spirit was to receive and to impart to the Apostles' minds were the things which were Christ's, not the things which were man's. Whenever they passed into regions beyond the things which were Christ's, no supernatural inspiration is promised. This reservation ought to be carefully attended to and meditated on by those who propound theories as to the extent of the inspiration of the Christian Scriptures. We shall show hereafter that the facts of the New Testament are in strict accordance with this promise of our Lord.

But while the promise is thus carefully guarded, it is express that the Apostles should receive full instruction in the truths, nature, and character of the Christian revelation. It even informs us of the manner in which that inspiration was to be communicated.

The mode of the Divine teaching was to consist of a guidance into all the truth. The use of this expression implies, that the enlightenment was not to be sudden, but gradual. Guidance is a gradual process. It is an advance by successive steps. The enlargement, therefore, which their views were to receive, although it was to be due to a supernatural influence, was to follow the ordinary laws of the development of the human mind. In the natural progress of the mind, its enlightenment is a slow growth. With the Apostles, their enlightenment was likewise to be a growth, but a growth at an accelerated ratio.

It is most important to observe that, in the communication of inspiration, it was the Divine purpose that the ordinary laws of the mind should be infringed upon as little as possible. We are not justified in assuming that God varies from the usual law of His government more than the necessities of the case require.

In conformity with this view of the nature of our Lord's

promise the history informs us that the promise was fulfilled. We learn from the Acts, that the Apostles were not suddenly, but gradually enlightened in Christian truth. They continued ignorant of that great truth the calling of the Gentiles, for a considerable period after they had received the gift of the Holy Spirit. Their prolonged ignorance on a subject of such importance is one which we should not have contemplated, and forms an impressive warning to us not to form our opinions of inspiration on antecedent grounds of probability, but on the facts of the New Testament Scriptures and on the assertions of their authors. Had we formed our opinions on abstract reasons, nothing would appear to have been antecedently more improbable than that the Apostles should have been allowed to remain ignorant of the great truth "that God is no respecter of persons, but that in every nation he that feareth Him, and worketh righteousness, is accepted of Him."

The last promise of supernatural assistance is of a more definite description. Our Lord warns the Apostles that the time was at hand when they would have to suffer persecution for His cause, and they would be brought before kings and rulers for His name's sake. When this should come to pass, He directs them not to prepare an elaborate defence. He promises them that, under such circumstances, the Holy Spirit should inspire them with what they ought to say; "For it is not ye who speak, but the Spirit of your Father which speaketh in you."

We have, then, five most distinct and definite promises, made by our Lord to the Apostles, of supernatural assistance and inspiration.

1. Our Lord promised the Apostles the aid of His Spirit to teach them and refresh their memories, so as to enable them to give a faithful testimony to the subject-matter of His teaching.

2. He constituted them witnesses of what He had done and taught, and promised them the witness of the Spirit by the exertion of miraculous power to confirm their human testimony to the great facts of our Lord's life, death, and resurrection.

3. He promised them His Holy Spirit to reveal to their

minds the full nature of the truths intended to be communicated by the Christian revelation.

4. He promised them that the same Spirit should reveal to them certain events connected with futurity.

5. He promised that in times of persecution, when they should be called upon to make a legal defence before kings and governors, they should receive supernatural guidance as to the proper topics of that defence.

These promises thus made to the Apostles were doubtless intended to be applicable, within their proper limits, to the other inspired persons who were authorized to publish the Christian revelation.

The original Apostles, then, attained their first knowledge of Christian truth by being actual eye- and ear-witnesses of our Lord's acts and teaching. Their views as to the nature of the Christian revelation were subsequently, but gradually, enlarged by the supernatural gifts of the Spirit bestowed on them after our Lord's ascension. The nature of these gifts we will consider presently.

But in marked contrast to this mode of instruction in Christian truth was the method which it pleased God to adopt for the enlightenment of St. Paul, who, as an apostle, was destined not to preach the Gospel within the limits of the Jewish church, but to carry the divine light throughout the length and breadth of the Gentile world.

St. Paul had heard none of our Lord's discourses while He was on earth: he had witnessed none of the facts of His life. Prior to his conversion, he was most probably a stranger to our Lord's person. The mental training which he had received differed widely from that of the original twelve. Theirs had been the training of ordinary Jews. St. Paul superadded to the most enlarged forms of Jewish training an acquaintance with Gentile literature. The only point in common between St. Paul and the original twelve was, that both had seen the divine person of our Lord after He was risen from the dead. We must now examine St. Paul's own assertions as to the mode in which he was instructed in the truths of the Christian revelation.

We need not dwell on the great appearance of our Lord to the Apostle, which changed him from a persecutor of the church into a preacher of the word. He himself expressly tells us that the object of this appearance was to constitute him a minister and a witness of this appearance of our Lord, and of any similar future manifestation.

In the course of the writings of St. Paul, we possess numerous assertions that his entire knowledge of the facts of the gospel, and of the truths of the Christian revelation, was derived from no human source of information, but was communicated to him by direct inspiration.

In Galatians i. 11-20, the Apostle gives us the following account of the mode of his instruction in gospel truth:— "But I certify you, brethren, that the gospel which was preached of me is not after man. For I neither received it of man, neither was I taught it, but by the revelation of Jesus Christ. For ye have heard of my conversation in time past in the Jews' religion, how that beyond measure I persecuted the church of God, and wasted it: and profited in the Jews' religion above many my equals in mine own nation, being more exceedingly zealous of the traditions of my fathers. But when it pleased God, who separated me from my mother's womb, and called me by His grace, to reveal His Son in me, that I might preach Him among the heathen; immediately I conferred not with flesh and blood: neither went I up to Jerusalem to them which were apostles before me; but I went into Arabia, and returned again unto Damascus. Then after three years I went up to Jerusalem to see Peter, and abode with him fifteen days. But other of the apostles saw I none, save James, the Lord's brother. Now the things which I write unto you, behold, before God, I lie not." Chap. ii. 1-11: "Then fourteen years after I went up again to Jerusalem with Barnabas, and took Titus with me also. And I went up by revelation, and communicated unto them that gospel which I preach among the Gentiles, but privately to them which were of reputation, lest by any means I should run, or had run, in vain. But neither Titus, who was with me, being a Greek, was compelled to be circumcised: and that because of false brethren unawares brought in, who came in privily to spy out our liberty which we have in Christ Jesus, that they might bring us into bondage: to whom we gave place by subjection, no, not for an hour; that the truth of the gospel might continue with you. But of these who seemed to be somewhat, (whatsoever they were, it maketh no matter to me: God accepteth no man's person:) for they who seemed to be somewhat in conference added nothing to me: but contrariwise, when they saw that the gospel of the uncircumcision was committed unto me, as the gospel of the circumcision was unto Peter; (for he that wrought effectually in Peter to the apostleship of the circumcision, the same was mighty in me toward the Gentiles:) and when James, Cephas, and John, who seemed to be pillars, perceived the grace that was given unto me, they gave to me and Barnabas the right hands of fellowship; that we should go unto the heathen, and they unto the circumcision. Only they would that we should remember the poor; the same which I also was forward to do. But when Peter was come to Antioch, I withstood him to the face, because he was to be blamed."

St. Paul here declares that his knowledge of the gospel, and his possession of the apostolical office, were derived from no human authority whatever: "His Gospel was not after man. He was not taught it by men, but by the revelation of Jesus Christ." Here we have the most direct assertion of the divine character of the revelations communicated to him. Previously to his conversion, he had been educated and had always lived in the practice of the strictest Judaism. As soon as he was called to a knowledge of the gospel, and to be a minister of its truth, he was instructed in its truths by no human teacher. He abstained from going to Jerusalem; so that he could have had no instruction from the original Apostles. On the contrary, he took a journey into Arabia, a country where it would have been hardly possible to have obtained instruction in the truths of Christianity, had such instruction been necessary. On his return to Damascus, he at once preached the gospel which he had attempted to destroy. Three years after his conversion, he paid Peter a visit of only fifteen days' duration, during which visit he saw no other apostle but James. During so short a visit it would have been impossible that he could have obtained any deep instruction in Christian truth. After having employed fourteen years in preaching the gospel, he again revisited Jerusalem. This time he went to that city in consequence of an express divine revelation. During this visit he explained the great truths, which he was in the habit of preaching among the heathen, secretly to the leading members of the Jewish church. He adopted this course lest it should be supposed that his authority as an apostle stood in need of any confirmation. The chiefs of the Jewish church neither attempted to confer on him authority nor knowledge. They fully recognized his apostolical commission, and the truth of that gospel which he had preached among the Gentiles. They made no attempt to fetter him, but only solicited him in his labours among the wealthy heathen to remember the Jewish churches which were comparatively poor—a thing which he was disposed to have done without solicitation. So far from having received any knowledge of gospel truth from the original Apostles, he felt that his knowledge of Christianity was so complete and perfect, that when Peter came to Antioch, and was weakly guilty of conduct compromising the truth, he openly rebuked him, and stated the great truths of the gospel in opposition to him.

St. Paul, therefore, directly asserts that the facts of the gospel as he delivered them to the churches, and the doctrines which he taught as the great truths of Christianity, were not learned by him through any ordinary operation of the human mind, but were communicated to him by inspiration.

We shall treat of the inspiration of St. Paul when we consider the degree of supernatural assistance under the influence of which the writers of the Epistles wrote and taught, and the nature of the inspiration which the facts of the Epistles themselves presuppose.

CHAPTER X.

THE SPIRITUAL GIFTS—THEIR CHARACTER.

BEFORE we enter on the examination of the nature and degree of the inspiration afforded to the Apostles, as witnessed by the Gospels and Epistles, it will be necessary to inquire what light the New Testament affords as to the nature of the spiritual gifts with which they were endowed, for the purpose of unfolding the Christian revelation, and of bearing testimony to its truths to the world. St. Luke, in the Acts, in giving the history of the descent of the Spirit on the Apostles, most unequivocally asserts that the events of the day of Pentecost were the fulfilment of our Lord's parting promises to His Apostles.

We will therefore adduce the chief statements in the New Testament as to the nature of the supernatural gifts of the Spirit.

1 Cor. i. 4–7 : "I thank my God always on your behalf, for the grace of God which is given you by Jesus Christ; that in every thing ye are enriched by Him, in all utterance, and in all knowledge; even as the testimony of Christ was confirmed in you: so that ye come behind in no gift; waiting for the coming of our Lord Jesus Christ."

1 Cor. xii. 4–11 : "Now there are diversities of gifts, but the same Spirit. And there are differences of administrations, but the same Lord. And there are diversities of operations, but it is the same God which worketh all in all. But the manifestation of the Spirit is given to every man to profit withal. For to one is given by the Spirit the word of wisdom; to another the word of knowledge by the same Spirit; to another faith by the same Spirit; to another the gifts of healing by the same Spirit; to another the working of miracles; to another prophecy; to another discerning of spirits; to another divers kinds of tongues; to another the interpretation of tongues: but all these worketh that one and the selfsame Spirit, dividing to every man severally as He will."

Ver. 28-31: "And God hath set some in the church, first apostles, secondarily prophets, thirdly teachers, after that miracles, then gifts of healings, helps, governments, diversities of tongues. Are all apostles? are all prophets? are all teachers? are all workers of miracles? have all the gifts of healing? do all speak with tongues? do all interpret? But covet earnestly the best gifts: and yet shew I unto you a more excellent way."

1 Cor. xiii. 1-3: "Though I speak with the tongues of men and of angels, and have not charity, I am become as sounding brass or a tinkling cymbal. And though I have the gift of prophecy, and understand all mysteries, and all knowledge, and though I have all faith, so that I could remove mountains, and have not charity, I am nothing. And though I bestow all my goods to feed the poor, and though I give my body to be burned, and have not charity, it profiteth me nothing." Ver. 8-10: "Charity never faileth: but whether there be prophecies, they shall fail; whether there be tongues, they shall cease; whether there be knowledge, it shall vanish away. For we know in part, and we prophesy in part. But when that which is perfect is come, then that which is in part shall be done away."

1 Cor. xiv: "Follow after charity, and desire spiritual gifts, but rather that ye may prophesy. For he that speaketh in an unknown tongue speaketh not unto men, but unto God: for no man understandeth him; howbeit in the spirit he speaketh mysteries. But he that prophesieth speaketh unto men to edification, and exhortation, and comfort. He that speaketh in an unknown tongue edifieth himself; but he that prophesieth edifieth the church. I would that ye all spake with tongues, but rather that ye prophesied: for greater is he that prophesieth than he that speaketh with tongues, except he interpret, that the church may receive edifying. Now, brethren, if I come unto you speaking with tongues, what shall I profit you, except I shall speak to you either by revelation, or by knowledge, or by prophesying, or by doctrine? And even things without life giving sound, whether pipe or harp, except they give a distinction in the sounds, how shall

it be known what is piped or harped? For if the trumpet give an uncertain sound, who shall prepare himself to the battle? So likewise ye, except ye utter by the tongue words easy to be understood, how shall it be known what is spoken? for ye shall speak into the air. There are, it may be, so many kinds of voices in the world, and none of them is without signification. Therefore if I know not the meaning of the voice, I shall be unto him that speaketh a barbarian, and he that speaketh shall be a barbarian unto me. Even so ye, forasmuch as ye are zealous of spiritual gifts, seek that ye may excel to the edifying of the church. Wherefore let him that speaketh in an unknown tongue pray that he may interpret. For if I pray in an unknown tongue, my spirit prayeth, but my understanding is unfruitful. What is it then? I will pray with the spirit, and I will pray with the understanding also: I will sing with the spirit, and I will sing with the understanding also. Else when thou shalt bless with the spirit, how shall he that occupieth the room of the unlearned say Amen at thy giving of thanks, seeing he understandeth not what thou sayest? For thou verily givest thanks well, but the other is not edified. I thank my God, I speak with tongues more than ye all: yet in the church I had rather speak five words with my understanding, that by my voice I might teach others also, than ten thousand words in an unknown tongue. Brethren, be not children in understanding: howbeit in malice be ye children, but in understanding be men. In the law it is written, With men of other tongues and other lips will I speak unto this people; and yet for all that will they not hear me, saith the Lord. Wherefore tongues are for a sign, not to them that believe, but to them that believe not: but prophesying serveth not for them that believe not, but for them which believe. If therefore the whole church be come together into one place, and all speak with tongues, and there come in those that are unlearned or unbelievers, will they not say that ye are mad? But if all prophesy, and there come in one that believeth not, or one unlearned, he is convinced of all, he is judged of all: and thus are the secrets of his heart made manifest; and so falling down on his face he will worship God, and report that God is in you of a truth. How is it then, brethren? when ye come together, every one of you hath a psalm, hath a doctrine, hath a tongue, hath a revelation, hath an interpretation. Let all things be done unto edifying. If any man speak in an unknown tongue, let it be by two, or at the most by three, and that by course; and let one interpret. But if there be no interpreter, let him keep silence in the church; and let him speak to himself, and to God. Let the prophets speak two or three, and let the other judge. If any thing be revealed to another that sitteth by, let the first hold his peace. For ye may all prophesy one by one, that all may learn, and all may be comforted. And the spirits of the prophets are subject to the prophets. For God is not the author of confusion, but of peace, as in all churches of the saints. . . . . . . If any man think himself to be a prophet, or spiritual, let him acknowledge that the things that I write unto you are the commandments of the Lord. But if any man be ignorant, let him be ignorant. Wherefore, brethren, covet to prophesy, and forbid not to speak with tongues. Let all things be done decently and in order."

Eph. iv. 7, 8: "But unto every one of us is given grace according to the measure of the gift of Christ. Wherefore he saith, When he ascended up on high, he led captivity captive, and gave gifts unto men." Ver. 11–13: "And he gave some, apostles; and some, prophets; and some, evangelists; and some, pastors and teachers; for the perfecting of the saints, for the work of the ministry, for the edifying of the body of Christ: till we all come in the unity of the faith, and of the knowledge of the Son of God, unto a perfect man, unto the measure of the stature of the fulness of Christ."

In this passage to the Ephesians, St. Paul distinctly informs us that the communication of these gifts was the result of our Lord's ascension: "Wherefore He saith, When He ascended up on high, He led captivity captive, and gave gifts unto men." Our Lord, in like manner, declared that it was necessary that He should go to the Father, in order that the Spirit, in His supernatural influences, might be communicated to the minds of the Apostles. The possession of those gifts, therefore, constituted the inspiration of the Apostles. They were the fulfilment of our Lord's promises of supernatural guidance made to them before His departure, which we have just considered. We will therefore first distinctly state what we learn from the New Testament was the nature of those gifts, and then give the reasons on which these conclusions are founded.

I. The gifts of the Spirit were the fulfilment of our Lord's promises of supernatural inspiration intended for the full discovery of gospel truth and the establishment of the Church.

II. That the gifts are nine in number: 1, the word of wisdom; 2, the word of knowledge; 3, faith; 4, gifts of healing; 5, the working of miracles; 6, prophecy; 7, the discerning of spirits; 8, the gift of tongues; 9, the gift of interpretation.

III. That the list given by the Apostle of the spiritual offices corresponds with these gifts, and that each separate gift qualified the possessor for the spiritual office. These are nine in number: 1, the apostle; 2, the prophet; 3, the teacher; 4, the worker of miracles; 5, the possessor of the gifts of healing; 6, the helper; 7, the possessor of the gift of government; 8, the speaker with tongues; 9, the interpreter.

IV. Many of these gifts, after having been once communicated, were attached in a permanent form to the mind of the possessor, and were subject to the control of his will, in the same manner as any other mental faculty in its ordinary operation.

V. The gifts were restricted in their operation to a particular subject-matter: they did not extend their influence beyond the subject-matter which formed the special function of each gift, or confer a general infallibility on the possessor.

VI. These gifts were conferred on different persons in different degrees.

I. The gifts of the Spirit were a direct fulfilment of our Lord's promise of miraculous inspiration.

The passage we have already quoted from the Ephesians is a direct assertion of this truth. The Apostle declares that they were communicated as the result of our Lord's ascension. They were given for the express purpose for the perfecting of the saints, for the work of the ministry, for the edifying of the body of Christ. They therefore qualified the Apostles for their functions as the teachers of the truths of the gospel and the builders up and establishers of the Church. In inferior degrees their influence was not confined to the Apostles merely, but portions of them were largely bestowed on different members of the Church, for the purpose of qualifying them for their appointed work. To this fact the most ample testimony is given both in the Acts of the Apostles and the writings of St. Paul. They were not intended to be permanent: they were designed to continue only "till we all come unto the unity of the faith, and of the knowledge of the Son of God, unto a perfect man, unto the measure of the stature of the fulness of Christ." St. Luke records, in the Gospel, that our Lord directed the Apostles to continue at Jerusalem until they were endowed with power from on high. Our Lord assures them that He would send the promise of the Father upon them. In the Acts, he represents our Lord as promising them that they should receive power after that the Holy Spirit was come upon them, and that they should be His witnesses in Jerusalem, and in Judea, and in Samaria, and unto the uttermost parts of the earth.

Having recorded the promise, he is no less particular to report to us what was the fulfilment of the promise. He accordingly narrates the communication of the Spirit in His miraculous influences to the Apostles and other primitive believers, on the day of Pentecost, as that fulfilment. He represents St. Peter, in his discourse following that event, as distinctly asserting that this outpouring of the Spirit was the supernatural enlightenment promised by God in the Old Testament dispensation to be communicated to men in gospel times.

But St. Luke does not describe the supernatural enlightenment afforded as confined solely to the Apostles. They were its chief depositories, and possessed the largest number of the spiritual gifts united in their persons, and the gifts themselves in the highest degree; but these were in different degrees very extensively communicated to believers. Accordingly, St. Peter describes the extent of the spiritual enlightenment, in the words of the Old Testament prophets, as neither limited to person, age, nor sex. "This is that which was spoken by the prophet Joel, And it shall come to pass in the last days, saith God, I will pour out of my Spirit upon all flesh; and your sons and your daughters shall prophesy, and your young men shall see visions, and your old men shall dream dreams: and on my servants and on my handmaidens I will pour out in those days of my Spirit; and they shall prophesy."

From this passage it is evident that the communication of the gift of supernatural inspiration was not intended to be confined to the Apostles, but that it was one which was communicated in various degrees to large numbers of believers. The supernatural gifts were bestowed in reference to different offices held in the Church, and different functions to be performed by different believers. Each person on whom the gift was bestowed was supernaturally qualified by it for his work in the Christian Church.

The assertions of St. Paul directly bear out this view. It is evident, from his Epistles, that the supernatural gifts were widely diffused. He thanked God that the Corinthian church were "enriched by God in all utterance and in all knowledge, even as the testimony of God is confirmed in you, so that ye come behind in no gift."

The gifts as conferred on believers had the effect of enriching them in all utterance and in all knowledge, and in confirming in them the testimony of God. A supernatural gift must have conferred on the person possessing it an inspiration within the sphere and influence of that gift.

But, although widely diffused, they were not conferred in the same degree or in the same abundance on all. To this St. Paul gives his direct testimony: "He gave some apostles, and some prophets, and some evangelists, and some pastors and teachers." To the same effect he writes to the Corinthians: "There are diversities of gifts, but it is the same Spirit; and there are diversities of administrations, but it is the same Lord; and there are diversities of operations, but it is the same God who worketh all in all." "To one is given by the Spirit the word of wisdom; to another the word of knowledge by the same Spirit; to another faith by the same Spirit; to another the gifts of healing by the same Spirit; to another the working of miracles; to another prophecy; to another discerning of spirits; to another divers kinds of tongues; to another the interpretation of tongues: but all these worketh that one and the selfsame Spirit, dividing to every man severally as He will."

The Apostle here most expressly asserts that the gifts, as bestowed on members of the Church generally, while bestowed in great abundance, were not all communicated to the same individual: "they were divided to every man severally as the Spirit willed." The Apostle's assertions are no less positive that the gifts possessed a difference of function. "There are," says he, "differences of administrations, but the same Lord; and there are differences of operations, but it is the same God who worketh all in all." One had the gift of healing, another that of discerning of spirits, another that of prophecy. The gifts, therefore, were powers imparted to the mind, each of which possessed a distinct and separate function.

Nor were they all of equal importance. They resembled the different members of the human body. One member of the body is more important than another, but all are necessary. Certain gifts specially qualified a man for the office of an Apostle in the Church; others qualified for inferior offices.

Nor were they given in equal degrees. The Apostles, as being qualified to fill all offices in the Church, would possess the whole of the gifts; but yet inferior men might possess a particular gift in a higher form than they. St. Paul was ignorant of a future event which was revealed to Agabus.

The history of the Acts contains frequent allusions to the wide extent in which these gifts were imparted to believers.

II. & III. It will be observed that the two lists of the spiritual gifts, as given by the Apostle, are each nine in number. The second list contains only eight names; but the gift of diversities of tongues is immediately divided into its two branches—the gift of tongues and that of interpretation.

As then in each list the gifts are nine in number, it is a legitimate inference that the gifts in the two lists must correspond. Five of them actually correspond in name. The remaining four will not be difficult of identification. In the second list the gifts are specified, not in their simple nature as gifts, but as qualifications for certain offices in the Church.

The five gifts in each list which actually agree in name are the two miraculous gifts—viz. the gifts of healing and the gift of working of miracles—the gift of prophecy, the gift of tongues, and that of interpretation.

The four other gifts admit of identification. The office of apostle corresponds with the gift of wisdom; that of teacher, with the gift of knowledge; that of governor, with the gift of discerning of spirits; that of helper, with the gift of faith.

Now although some of these gifts are closely allied together, the Apostle asserts that they were distinct and separate gifts of the Spirit. The gift of wisdom was distinct from the gift of knowledge: a person might have possessed the one, and not possessed the other. They must therefore have had separate functions, and different subject-matter on which they were exercised. No less positive also are his assertions that the gift of working miracles was distinct from the gift of healing. In these cases, therefore, the subject-matter and the functions of these gifts must have been distinct likewise. Several of these gifts were frequently united in the same person; but the union did not interfere with their fundamental distinctness as separate gifts or endowments. All were united in the persons of the Apostles. But it was a common case for individuals in the Church only to possess a single gift, even when the gifts were so closely allied as the gift of tongues was with that of interpretation. The Spirit divided to every man severally as He willed.

CHAPTER XI.

THE SPIRITUAL GIFTS THE CHIEF SOURCE OF APOSTOLIC INSPIRATION—THE NATURE OF THE INSPIRATION IMPARTED BY EACH GIFT.

THE nature of some of the supernatural gifts is unfolded with considerable detail in the New Testament. Respecting others our information is less precise. The five respecting which our information is the most full are the gifts of tongues, interpretation, prophecy, wisdom, knowledge, and the two miraculous gifts. And first, the gift of tongues.

In Acts ii. St. Luke writes, "There appeared unto them cloven tongues like as of fire, and it sat upon each of them. And they were all filled with the Holy Ghost, and began to speak with other tongues, as the Spirit gave them utterance." "Now when this was noised abroad, the multitude came together, and were confounded, because that every man heard them speak in his own language. And they were all amazed and marvelled, saying one to another, Behold, are not all these which speak Galileans? And how hear we every man in our own tongue, wherein we were born? Parthians, and Medes, and Elamites, and the dwellers in Mesopotamia, and in Judæa and Cappadocia, in Pontus, and Asia, Phrygia, and Pamphylia, in Egypt, and in the parts of Libya about Cyrene, and strangers of Rome, Jews and proselytes, Cretes and Arabians, we do hear them speak in our tongues the wonderful works of God. And they were all amazed, and were in doubt, saying one to another, What meaneth this? Others mocking said, These men are full of new wine."

Now three opinions are possible as to the nature of the gift of tongues. First, it was a power of speaking languages previously unknown, for the purpose of enabling him who was endowed with it to speak in a language which he had never previously learned. Second, it was a power of giving utterance to spiritual truths and feelings previously unknown: in a word, it was a spiritual utterance, and not an ordinary language. Third, it was a union of a spoken language combined with a spiritual utterance. The assertions of St. Luke, in the Acts, favour the first of these views; those of St. Paul, in the Corinthians, the second. The gift was, therefore, probably a union of both.

It seems hardly possible to put any fair construction on the assertions of the author of the Acts of the Apostles which does not, at least, include the fact that St. Luke meant to assert that languages distinct and intelligible were spoken on the occasion. Neander and others have made the attempt, but they are obliged to put a forced construction on the language employed by St. Luke. In what manner the miracle was wrought is another question. Some have supposed, not that the Apostles spoke, but that the hearers heard what they uttered, in all these languages. But this is merely a variation of the mode of the miracle. According to St. Luke's report of the transaction, at the news of what had taken place, a multitude came together. They were penetrated with astonishment. The reason of their surprise is expressly given—that every man heard them speak in his own language. The historian uses no expression which can be made to mean that the surprise was occasioned by their hearing utterance given to a new spiritual language which the hearers did not understand. They heard them speak in their own διάλεκτος (dialect). The spectators say, We hear them speak in the tongue wherein we were born. A list of the places of which the hearers were natives follows. It will be readily admitted that the languages of many of the places mentioned were not distinct languages, but dialects. This is quite consistent with the use of the word employed by St. Luke. Scoffers, who did not understand the languages, not unnaturally ascribed the phenomenon to the effect of drunkenness.

Now it is a certain fact, if the gift of tongues is viewed as a gift bestowed to enable its possessor to preach Christian truth in languages which he was previously unacquainted with, that at no period of the world's history was such a gift so little needed as in the apostolic age. The chief labours of the Apostles and primitive missionaries were confined to the great cities of the Roman empire. In most of these cities the knowledge of Greek and Latin would have been sufficient to enable them to execute their divine commission. Paul and Barnabas do not seem to have been endowed with any such gift for the purposes of preaching: it is implied in the history that they did not understand the language of Lystra, and that the intention of sacrificing to them took them by surprise. It is also certain that, in the age next after, the apostolic missionaries had no endowment of speaking languages which they had never learned. But there is no necessity for assuming that the gift which was bestowed on the day of Pentecost, if it involved the power of speaking intelligible languages, was given to enable the possessor to preach the gospel in a tongue which he had not learned, or that it may not have included along with it the phenomena mentioned by St. Paul.

St. Paul expressly describes the gift of tongues as intended for a sign to them who believed not. In this point of view it might have involved a miraculous power of speaking languages, without its being intended that it should form a permanent gift in the Church for the purpose of preaching.

But the assertions of the Apostle to the Corinthians present this gift under a very different aspect. We gather from the Apostle's description of that gift the following facts:—A person who spoke in a tongue, and had not the gift of interpretation, spoke not to himself, but unto God. It did not follow that he was intelligible to himself or others, although in the spirit he might speak mysteries. Although he did not speak intelligibly to himself, he could edify himself by the use of the tongue; but he produced no edification to the Church. The prophetic gift was a far higher one than the gift of tongues. The only way in which the Church received edifying by the use of the gift was when it was accompanied by the gift of interpretation. As there must be a distinction of sounds in musical instruments to make their utterances intelligible, so, unless the tongue gave utterance to things easy to be understood, it was no better than speaking into the air. A person, therefore, endowed with the gift of tongues was to pray to have superadded to it the gift of interpretation. If a person with this gift, but without the gift of interpretation, prayed in a tongue, his spirit prayed, but his understanding was barren. Similarly useless was the gift to the Church; for neither prayer nor praise offered in this way could draw forth an Amen on the part of the congregation. The other is not edified: he understands not what the speaker in the tongue says. St. Paul would prefer to speak five words with his understanding, for the purpose of edification, than ten thousand words in a tongue. Tongues, as a miracle, were intended to be a sign to unbelievers. But if the whole Christian assembly possessed and exercised this gift, instead of its being a sign to unbelievers, by its indiscriminate use the Church would incur the charge of being under the influence of madness. Such were the phenomena.

The first point which draws our attention in this description is, that the person speaking in a tongue, without the gift of interpretation, spoke not unto himself, but unto God. This fact is very difficult to reconcile with the use of an ordinary human language. If it was a language, it must have been one of the meaning of which the speaker was no less ignorant than the hearer. But the Apostle adds shortly after, that he who spoke in a tongue edified himself; and further adds, that in the spirit he spoke mysteries. The utterance, therefore, whatever it was, must have been accompanied with the emission of feelings which were attended with edification to the person giving utterance to them. The person using the tongue really gave utterance to prayer or praise when its meaning could be distinctly ascertained. These phenomena are consistent with the gift's consisting in the kindling of deep spiritual emotions in the soul, which could not be expressed in the form of intelligible words without the aid of one possessed of the gift of interpretation. In conformity with this view of the nature of the gift, the Apostle writes to the Romans, "The Spirit also helpeth our infirmities; for we know not what we should pray for as we ought; but the Spirit itself maketh intercession for us, *with groanings which cannot be uttered*" (ἀλαλήτοις στεναγμοῖς).

The tongue, therefore, without the gift of interpretation, might convey no meaning even to the person using it. If its use was attended with edification to his mind, that edification must have been produced by the arousing of deep spiritual emotions, with which the use of the tongue was accompanied, and of which the utterance must have been the expression.

Although, therefore, the gift of tongues might have involved the use of languages, it seems also to have been united with unconscious utterances of deep spiritual feeling implanted in the heart by a supernatural influence.

The importance of such a gift may be duly estimated, when we consider the dead state of feelings as to all spiritual things into which the ancient world had sunk. Before Christianity could create new conceptions in the mind, it must create new emotions in the heart. The conceptions would have been meaningless without the emotions. The existence of the emotions in man's inmost spirit, after a time, rendered the conceptions intelligible in his understanding. This gift was apparently one most extensively bestowed on the Christian Church. If it formed the ground on which the spiritual conception of religious truth rested, we at once see the necessity for the gift: it formed the groundwork of the possibility of the communication of the Christian revelation. No obstacle which modern missionaries have to encounter is greater than the want of suitable conceptions to express spiritual ideas in the nations among whom they preach. This difficulty is constantly encountered in making translations of the Scriptures, and in finding suitable expressions for the translation of spiritual ideas. But, as a sign to the unbeliever, the gift of tongues must not only have been displayed in the power of giving utterance to deep inward spiritual feelings, but probably, as on the day of Pentecost, in occasionally giving utterances in actual languages: " we do hear them speak in our tongues the wonderful works of God."

Such a gift, if used indiscriminately by the whole Church, would be in danger of producing the most disastrous consequences on the minds of unbelievers, for whose benefit it was specially intended. The Apostle therefore gives directions that it should never be used when there was no one present with the gift of interpretation, and then only by two or at most three persons at a single sitting of the Church.

The nature of the gift of interpretation must be determined by the view which we take of the gift of tongues. If the gift of tongues involved the use of a language, the gift of interpretation must have involved the power of translating that language into another which was understood by the congregation. If the gift of tongues involved the power of giving utterance to spiritual feelings by corresponding sounds, the gift of interpretation must have been the power of representing those spiritual feelings in terms cognizable by the ordinary understanding. It is evident from the Apostle's assertions, that the gift of tongues was frequently possessed without the gift of interpretation. In this case it must have presented the extraordinary phenomenon of the person who made the utterance being unable to represent it to others in intelligible language. No less remarkable would it have been if it were a spoken language, and the person using it wholly unconscious of its meaning. Frequently both gifts were united in the same person: it is then difficult to conceive what could be the inducement to speak in a foreign language, when the person speaking had it in his power to speak in an intelligible one. The Apostle distinctly asserts that the gift of tongues, like all the other spiritual gifts, was under the control of the will of the person who possessed it.

But the three gifts directly connected with the inspiration under the influence of which the Christian Scriptures have been composed, are the gift of wisdom, the gift of knowledge, and the gift of prophecy.

We can hardly be mistaken in considering that the two lists of spiritual endowments are the same gifts under different names. The gift of wisdom, therefore, must be the gift conferring the inspiration peculiar to the office of an apostle, and which distinguished him from all the other inspired teachers in the Church. This gift, therefore, occupies the first rank.

The gift of prophecy, common to both lists, is expressly placed by the Apostle as second in importance among the spiritual gifts. He assigns teachers the third rank; and to this office the gift of knowledge is the appropriate endowment.

Although, however, the peculiar apostolic gift was the gift of wisdom, yet we know that the Apostles possessed the prophetic gift. As the highest authority in the Church, they would naturally possess the inferior gifts to qualify them for the direction of every function in the Church. They would therefore fill the office of teacher as well as that of apostle, and would consequently possess the corresponding gift of knowledge. The three gifts, therefore, of wisdom, knowledge, and prophecy would form the main element of the apostolic inspiration, as far as they were the teachers of the truths of the Christian revelation.

The gift of wisdom is the highest of the supernatural gifts. As the office of an apostle was a special function in the Church, there must have been a special gift qualifying for the discharge of that function.

The separation of the gifts, both as gifts and functions, is most distinctly asserted by the Apostle. Had he not most distinctly asserted that separation of function, we should have considered that the gifts of wisdom and of knowledge were the same gift under a different aspect. We should have formed the same conclusion respecting the gifts of miracles and the gifts of healing. The Apostle not only asserts the distinctness in the functions of these gifts, but also that one of these gifts could be possessed by one person, without its being necessary that he should possess the other.

The word wisdom, or $\sigma o\phi ía$, when applied in the New Testament to divine things, is uniformly used to denote the highest form of the knowledge of divine truth. In the same manner when applied in philosophical language to human things, it denotes the highest possible form of human knowledge and philosophy. In the language of St. Paul, wisdom is used to express the profoundest truths of Christianity. He speaks of Christ as "the power of God, and the wisdom of God." He speaks of "the depths of the wisdom of God." He uses this expression in connexion with the profoundest of gospel truths. "Christ is made unto us wisdom, righteousness, sanctification, and redemption." "We speak wisdom among them who are perfect." "We speak the wisdom of God in a mystery, even the hidden wisdom which God ordained before the world unto our glory." In the whole context of this passage, the Apostle describes the gospel revelation as the manifestation of the highest form of divine wisdom. "Whom we preach, warning every man, and teaching every man in all wisdom." "In whom are hid all the treasures of wisdom and knowledge." In the Epistle to the Ephesians, he calls the deep truths of the gospel "the manifold wisdom of God." The term mystery is used by the Apostle to denote this high form of apostolic wisdom: "though I understand all mysteries and all knowledge." The mysteries of the gospel are, in fact, those truths specially revealed to the Apostles under the Christian dispensation. "And to make all men know what is the fellowship of the mystery which from the beginning of the world was hid in God, who created all things by Jesus Christ; to the intent that unto the principalities and powers in heavenly places might be known by the church the manifold wisdom of God." Here the Apostle distinctly identifies the mysteries of the gospel with the highest form of revealed wisdom. But St. Peter, in his Second Epistle, describes the gift of wisdom as the gift peculiarly apostolic: "even as our beloved brother, Paul, according to the wisdom given unto him, hath written unto you; as also in all his Epistles, speaking in them of these things, in which are many things hard to be understood." Here St. Peter expressly asserts that St. Paul wrote his Epistles under the influence of the special gift of wisdom with which he was endowed. He also describes the higher truths contained in St. Paul's Epistles as the result of the influence of this gift.

The gift of wisdom, therefore, is the supernatural endowment which formed the peculiar gift of apostolic men, by which the deep truths of the Christian revelation were discovered and imparted to their minds.

We will examine fully the precise extent and degree of the inspiration imparted by this gift, when we examine the nature of the inspiration under the influence of which the Epistles were composed.

The gift of prophecy holds the second rank among the spiritual gifts. It is frequently mentioned in common with the gift of tongues. It was a gift extensively bestowed on the Church. It was not unfrequently imparted even to females. It occasionally afforded glimpses into futurity; but its proper function was to qualify the prophet to address the Christian assembly on the subject of Christian truth.

In the Epistle to the Corinthians we learn that the gift of prophecy was specially adapted for edification; but it also operated greatly for the conversion of unbelievers. This was effected by affording the unbeliever a clear view of the state of his own heart through the prophetic utterance. By means of these disclosures the unbeliever was convinced of all, he was judged of all, and forced to confess that of a truth God was present in the Christian Church. In the congregation itself, the influence of the gift enabled the prophet to speak to edification, and exhortation, and comfort. The Apostle describes it as a very high spiritual gift. High gift as it was, it admitted of being abused no less than the gift of tongues. Several prophets in the Corinthian church attempted to address the assembly at the same time, and thereby created confusion. To remedy this the Apostle directs that only two, or at most three, prophets should speak at a single church-meeting. But it was also possible that false prophetical gifts should be obtruded on the Church instead of true ones. The Apostle, therefore, directs that no prophet was to speak in the assembly unless there was a prophet present who possessed the gift of discerning of spirits, who was to act as judge as to the nature of the prophetic utterance. The owner of the gift was not urged on by violent and ungovernable impulse; the gift was possessed in complete subordination to the supremacy of the rational will: "the spirits of the prophets were subject to the prophets." Being of the highest importance for the edifying of the Church, the

Apostle exhorts all Christians earnestly to desire its possession.

We learn from this description of the gift, that although the prophet was occasionally inspired to utter predictions of the future, this was not his proper function. It is a great mistake, therefore, to view the utterance of predictions as affording the chief exercise of the prophetic gift. If his proper function had been that of revealing the future, the prophetic gift would not have received the high commendation of St. Paul. A constant revelation of the future would be no blessing to man: the knowledge of it is mercifully withheld from him. His ignorance respecting what will happen forms part of his necessary moral discipline. To reveal the future is no part of the scheme of Divine Providence. The Apostle's commendation of the gift is founded on its edifying nature to the Church.

The gift seems to have consisted of two branches—an ordinary gift and one of a special character. When the prophet exercised the special gift, he had a consciousness of an immediate suggestion made by the Spirit to his mind: he was then under the influence of conscious inspiration. But in the usual form of the gift, the prophet does not seem to have been able to discern between the mode of its action and that of his other endowments.

A distinction of this kind is the only way of making some of the Apostle's directions intelligible. When a prophet, who was sitting by, received a direct suggestion, if another prophet was speaking, as soon as he was informed that that prophet had received a Divine communication, he was to sit down and make way for the other prophet to communicate his inspired message. We must suppose that the prophet who was speaking must have been exercising some ordinary form of his gift, or giving an account of some suggestion which he had received previously to coming to the assembly; for if he was equally under the influence of a direct suggestion with the other, there could be no reason why he should be silent before he had delivered his inspired message. This would be explained if the ordinary form of the gift was exercised without a sense of direct suggestion. Its ordinary form seems to have endowed the prophet with the qualifications needful for the work of preaching.

The prophetic gift, then, appears to be an extension of the same gift as possessed by the Old Testament Church. It differed, however, in one very important particular. In the exercise of the gift the Old Testament prophets were frequently hurried along by an overwhelming vehemence of impulse. In the higher dispensation of the gospel, the prophetic influence was always subject to the control of the rational will. That will always retained its entire supremacy.

The prophetic gift as possessed by the Christian Church, though affording occasional glimpses into futurity, had for its especial function to communicate to the mind a deep perception of the nature of spiritual and moral truth, so as to apply it powerfully to the heart and conscience. It consisted in a deep perception of truth as truth, and a corresponding insight into the nature and character of the human mind, so as to enable the prophet to apply it suitably to the state and condition of the persons addressed. This was the ordinary form of the gift. In its extraordinary form the prophet was favoured with a direct consciousness of suggestion, and a particular truth was communicated to his mind by direct and immediate revelation.

If the gift of wisdom constituted the highest form of apostolical inspiration, the gift of knowledge must have consisted in a lower form of supernatural enlightenment. Judging from St. Paul's use of the expression, the gift of knowledge, as a supernatural gift, must have related to matters of a practical description, to truths which have a direct bearing on the human heart. If it was the gift of the teacher, it must have involved the knowledge of such truths as enabled him adequately to discharge his functions. But it would form no portion of the ordinary functions of a teacher to communicate fresh revelations from Heaven. His proper and legitimate province must have been to expound the revelation already communicated. Accordingly we find that the word knowledge is generally used in the New Testament to denote that form of truth which is practical. It means truth in that form which is calculated to produce an immediate effect on the heart. The Apostle writes, " that I may know Him, and the power of His resurrection;" "that ye may know the love of Christ." In both these passages a divine knowledge is spoken of in a practical form. "Though I understand all mysteries and all knowledge;" "whether there be knowledge, it shall vanish away." Here the term mysteries evidently denotes the higher truths of the gospel—the proper subject-matter of the apostolic gift of wisdom. By knowledge, therefore, must be intended an acquaintance with the lower forms of Christian truth.

The term knowledge is used in the New Testament in a more unrestricted sense for an intellectual acquaintance with truth generally. St. Paul writes, " Knowledge puffeth up; but charity edifieth." But even here the Apostle uses the term to denote such an enlarged acquaintance with Christian truth as would raise a man above prejudices respecting meats and drinks and outward ordinances. But in the sense in which we are now speaking of it it had a special subject-matter, so as to be a spiritual gift imparted to the mind, and it did not extend over a vague generality of subjects. As a supernatural gift, when its functions could be supplied by ordinary human means, it would vanish away. As a gift qualifying the possessor to fill the office of teacher, it must have consisted in a general acquaintance with revealed truth, especially in its practical bearing on the human heart. We can see the necessity of such a supernatural gift in the infancy of the Church, when it contained within it few men of trained intellect; and therefore we can estimate the reason which the Apostle gives for the cessation of those gifts at the proper time: " When that which is perfect is come, that which is in part shall be done away. Whether there be prophecies, they shall fail; whether there be tongues, they shall cease; whether there be knowledge, it shall vanish away." When the Christian revelation was fully communicated, and the Church firmly rooted in the world, the occasion for supernatural gifts would cease, and they would consequently be withdrawn.

The three gifts of wisdom, prophecy, and knowledge, when united in the same person, would constitute the highest form of that inspiration which was required for the purpose of communicating the great truths of the gospel revelation.

Immediately after these three gifts the Apostle places, as next in importance, the two miraculous gifts. By the first three gifts the Christian revelation was communicated; by the two miraculous gifts it was attested as coming from God.

It is most remarkable that in both lists the Apostle has described them as distinct gifts. In the first list he has most clearly asserted their distinct functions, and the possibility that one could be possessed without the other. Had it not been for this distinctness of the Apostle's assertions, we should have concluded that they were separate forms of the same gift. The nature of the distinction we can only learn from the facts of the New Testament; it is nowhere expressly stated.

The Apostle uses the expression, "the gifts of healings," always in the plural number; we may therefore conclude that the gift had distinct branches.

The gift of miracles is described by the expression, ἐνεργήματα δυναμέων (inworkings of powers). In the second list it is designated by the expression δυνάμεις (powers). With respect to this gift, the same expression is used by the Evangelist to denote the view taken by Herod of our Lord's miracles, on the supposition that he was John the Baptist risen from the dead—αἱ δυνάμεις ἐν αὐτῷ ἐνεργοῦσι (the powers energize in him). The gift of miracles, therefore, enabled the possessor to work miracles analogous to those wrought by our Lord. They must have been of such a nature as to afford adequate proofs of a divine mission. They were inworkings of power—acts essentially and properly miraculous.

The second miraculous gift is called χαρίσματα ἰαμάτων (gifts of curings). The term implies that it was a gift of a lower nature, more analogous to the ordinary operations by which cures are effected by the use of human means.

Most of the great miracles of the New Testament consisted in cures wrought on the human body. Some of our Lord's were exceptions, and consisted in operations wrought on outward nature. But the essence of the difference in the two gifts cannot consist in this distinction. The higher form of miraculous power must have been frequently exerted in cures wrought by our Lord. We cannot conceive of a higher form of miracle than the cure of a person born blind, or a person deaf and dumb, or devoid of a limb, or lame, or in raising the dead by a word. Such actions must belong to the highest exertions of miraculous power.

It is evident that there is a distinction in character between the miracles recorded in the New Testament. Some, according to human apprehension, are more unquestionably miraculous than others. The exertion of power may be the same in each; but the one class of acts is more nearly allied to effects coming within the range of the operation of ordinary means than the other. In this must have consisted the distinction between the two miraculous gifts.

There is obviously a wide distinction between the raising of the dead, the cure of a man born blind, or the restoration of a lost limb, and the expulsion of a demon, the cure of an ordinary disease which is curable by human art, or the anointing a sick man with oil in the name of the Lord and his slow and gradual recovery. The power exerted in each case may be divine; but in the former class of actions their miraculous nature is far more evident than in the latter. These latter approach much more nearly to ordinary acts of Providence. The former class of miracles would be clear and indubitable proofs of the reality of a divine commission, and constitute the divine attestation on which the evidences of Christianity, as a divine revelation, rest. The other class may be miraculous, but are capable of being referred to human causes.

We conclude, therefore, that the first miraculous gift must have consisted in the exercise of a power which was wholly and essentially divine. The gift of healings consisted in a lower exercise of such power, combined with the use of human agencies. The general nature of such gifts would be fairly expressed in St. James's precept:—"Is any sick among you? let him call for the elders of the church; and let them pray over him, anointing him with oil in the name of the Lord: and the prayer of faith shall save the sick, and the Lord shall raise him up; and if he have committed sins, they shall be forgiven him."

This act is not one which could be appealed to as a proof of miraculous inspiration; but it must have been a power unspeakably important to the Christian missionary, in awakening attention, and in securing for him a favourable reception. The importance of such a power we can fully estimate when we consider the beneficial effect, in promoting the missionary's labours, with which medical skill is attended in modern missions. By conferring the greatest of human benefits, it secures attention to the missionary when he speaks of divine and spiritual truths. We need not wonder that, in the age of the first planting of Christianity, such a power was supplied by a supernatural gift. Some of the other spiritual gifts were obviously intended to supply the lack of training and education in the Church. A power analogous to that possessed by the modern educated physician might, with equal propriety, be afforded, not merely for the purpose of attesting the divine origin of Christianity, but for exerting a benevolent influence favourable to the propagation of the Christian faith. This gift appears to have continued in the Church after the higher gift of miracles had ceased. The reason for such continuance is obvious. The higher gift of miracles was the direct testimony of the Spirit, confirming the truth of the Apostles' testimony to the Christian revelation as coming from God. The lower gift was intended to afford facilities for the propagation of Christianity among the unconverted.

As, then, the gifts of wisdom, prophecy, and knowledge were the instruments for communicating the subject-matter of the Christian revelation, so the gift of miracles formed its divine attestation, and the gift of healing formed the great means to assist its propagation in the world.

The gift of the power of discerning of spirits was one which was suited for the purpose of qualifying the possessor to exercise the office of government in the Church. The gift and the function mutually correspond. No power would more fit a man for exercising the office of government than the power of discerning of spirits.

Such a power was particularly needed in the primitive Church. A large portion of its members was collected from the lower classes of society. The natural endowments of such a class would have been particularly unsuited for the exercise of authority. Circumstances of difficulty would arise, requiring the exercise of particular discretion on the part of the officers of the Church. Among these would be the employment of proper persons, well qualified for the work of preaching to the heathen, for the careful guarding against imposition in the management of the Church funds (to which, we know, on the testimony of pagan writers, that the Christians were liable), and for the maintenance of proper relations with the civil authorities. In addition to difficulties calling for the exercise of peculiar discretion in the rulers of the Church, the entrance of Christianity into the world occasioned so mighty a stir in the inmost spirit of man, that a deep power of insight was required on their part to discern what was genuine from what was false. There must have been frequent occasion to " try the spirits whether they were of God," because, together with what was genuine and holy, " many false prophets had gone out into the world." The spirit of delusion was at this time extremely prevalent, manifesting itself in extravagances in every direction. The supernatural gift of discerning of spirits would therefore be an endowment exactly suited to the wants of the Church, and one exactly corresponding to the office of government mentioned by the apostle in his second list. It was an endowment both possessed and exercised by the Apostles.

There remains but one more gift in each list—the gift of faith in the one list, and the office of helper in the other.

Respecting the nature of the office, we derive only a few hints in the New Testament. Apostolic men were accompanied in their labours by a number of assistants. Luke, Timothy, Silas, and several others accompanied St. Paul in that capacity. He also describes Aquila and Priscilla as his helpers in Christ Jesus, who, for his life, laid down their necks. To such persons we at once discern that a high degree of faith would be a necessary endowment.

A supernatural gift of faith is mentioned (1 Cor. xiii. 2): "Though I have all faith, so that I could remove mountains, and have not charity, it profiteth me nothing." The Apostle, in this chapter, is speaking of the gifts, not in the usual form in which they existed, but in their highest possible conception. He speaks "of the tongues of men and of angels," of understanding "all mysteries and all knowledge," of having "all faith, so that I could remove mountains," of bestowing all his goods to feed the poor, and giving his body to be burned. The gift of faith here spoken of, therefore, represents that gift in its highest possible form. The allusion is to our Lord's discourse after cursing the barren fig tree: "If you say to this mountain, Be thou removed, and be thou cast into the sea, it shall be done." But the gift of faith was not the same as the gift of working miracles. Faith was required in the performer of a miracle, before it could be wrought. But, as there were two distinct miraculous gifts, these gifts must have imparted the necessary faith to enable them to be called into successful operation. Our Lord, in His discourses, invariably draws the attention of the hearer, by means of the outward subject, to a spiritual reality. When He speaks of faith, such as would remove mountains, He means faith capable of conquering difficulties equally insurmountable. The gift of faith, therefore, would develope itself into an endowment of supernatural courage.

Such an endowment would be particularly necessary to the assistants of apostolical men in their labours. Aquila and Priscilla had been called to lay down their own necks for Paul. The frequent exposure of the missionaries to great personal dangers in sudden tumults must have required the endowment not only of moral but physical courage. To these tumults, which must have constantly placed their lives in jeopardy, they were frequently exposed. The supernatural gift of faith, therefore, was a special endowment to qualify the possessor to be the assistant of men in their apostolical labours, and would have been peculiarly necessary to one filling the office of an evangelist: it would consist in such a confidence in the Divine support and protection as would produce the human virtues of courage, firmness, and presence of mind.

Such, then, as far as can be gathered from the New Testament, were the supernatural gifts of the Spirit, the bestowing of which was the fulfilment of our Lord's promises made to the Apostles. These gifts, in their fulness, constituted the apostolic inspiration. But each gift must have afforded an inspiration within its respective bounds and functions. As these gifts were extended largely among believers, a degree of inspiration, which appertained to the respective gifts, must have received a similar extension. The inspiration of the Apostles differed from that of others, in that they possessed the gifts themselves in larger measure, possessed one gift which was preeminently apostolic, and united the whole of the gifts in their own persons. While the three gifts which formed the chief instruments for communicating the Christian revelation were the gifts of wisdom, prophecy, and knowledge, the two gifts of miracles, the gift of faith, the gift of tongues and of interpretation contributed to its establishment, and the gift of discerning of spirits ministered to the good government of the Church.

IV. The greater part of these gifts, when once communicated, were permanently attached to the mind of the possessor, and were subject to the control of the rational will, in their exercise, in the same manner as any other mental faculty.

From this rule two of these gifts must be excepted, the two gifts of miraculous power. Anything miraculous in their operation must have depended on a distinct exertion of a divine energy. A person possessing the gift, therefore, before he attempted to work a miracle, would await a distinct intimation of the Divine pleasure. One of these gifts involved the actual attestation by the Spirit to the truth of the Christian revelation. Such an exertion of power could not have been dependent on the volition of any human will: no person possessed of such a gift would attempt to call it into exercise but at the suggestion of God Himself.

The gift of prophecy and of tongues, as their phenomena are described by St. Paul, afford distinct proof that these gifts were exercised in subordination to the rational will. Each prophet could control his own gift in its exercise. "The spirits of the prophets," says the Apostle, "are subject to the prophets." They were not impelled by ungovernable impulse. In this point of view, the prophetic gift presented phenomena strikingly contrasted with the pretended utterances of heathen oracles or prophetic inspirations. Whatever these oracles or inspirations were, or however they were produced, the descriptions which we possess of them have one common feature. The influence affecting the person pretending to inspiration appeared to place him entirely beyond the control of his own will. In all heathen inspiration, the rational will was entirely dethroned from its supremacy. The terms used to describe these pretended heathen inspirations are all expressions which denote madness. The person supposed to be inspired is always represented as fanatically raving. The maddening influence of the god destroys the exercise of all rational self-control. This deposition of the will from its supremacy was usually attended with violent bodily contortions. Of a similar description are the accounts of the phenomena of various religious excitements in modern times. In these the human soul, its reason and its will, have passed under the empire and dominion of another. Phenomena of this description have often been exhibited in times of great religious excitement. They have been the almost invariable accompaniments of all pretensions to inspiration. But widely different were the manifestations of the gift of prophecy, as following the effusion of the Holy Spirit: "He is not the author of confusion, but of peace." Whatever phenomena of the kind of which we have been speaking took place in the apostolic Church, the Apostle asserts that they did not flow from the gift which the Spirit imparted, but from the human abuse of it. He gives special directions for the purpose of repressing these abuses. As the whole passage throws great light as to the manner in which the exercise of these gifts was subject to the control of the rational will, we will paraphrase it.

"The Spirit of God is not the author of confusion, but of peace. The confusion which has taken place flows from the human abuse of these gifts; but of that confusion God is not the author. If a tongue is used in your assembly, let only two, or at most three, use it at one sitting of the Church; and let there be always one at hand who is able to interpret. If there be no one present with the gift, let no tongue be used. Let the possessor of the gift be content with speaking unto himself and unto God. Let no more than two or three prophets use their gift at one meeting of the Church; and for the purpose of preventing every spurious kind of prophetic utterance, let one who possesses the gift of discerning of spirits, in addition to his prophetic gift, sit in judgment on the nature of the matter uttered. Should anything be specially communicated to any prophet's mind, let the prophet who is engaged in addressing the assembly be silent, as soon as he shall be informed that another prophet has received a special communication. I wish you all to have the opportunity of exercising your gifts, but it must not be done by a multitude attempting to speak at the same time. If this practice is continued, the heathen will pronounce you mad. I wish you all to speak in turn. You will then all have the opportunity of speaking, learning, and being comforted. There is no difficulty about the matter. The spirits of the prophets are under the prophets' own control. Now if any man thinks that he has the prophetic gift, he will best prove the existence of the true prophetic spirit by at once acknowledging that the things which I write unto you are the commandments of the Lord. If any man, after these instructions of mine, continue in these courses, he has no true prophetic spirit. Let him be ignorant."

It seems hardly possible that words could have been framed to convey more clearly the fact that these spiritual gifts were, in their exercise, subject to the control of the possessor's will, than those used by the Apostle. Every direction which he gives for regulating the manner in which the gifts were to be exercised is founded on that supposition. Nothing more strongly shows the purpose of God not to interfere with the ordinary laws of the mind more than was necessary in communicating divine inspiration, than His having bestowed the supernatural gifts in such a manner that they could be exercised in strict subordination to the will of the possessor.

If the supernatural gifts were subject to the control of the will in their exercise, they must have existed in the form of permanent endowments in the mind. A faculty which is under the control of the will cannot depend upon a fluctuating influence: it must have become a portion of the mind itself. The spiritual gifts, therefore, must have been powers not originally possessed by the mind, but which, when once conferred, became a permanent portion of its consciousness.

It follows, from the direction given by the Apostle that one possessing the power of discerning spirits was to sit as judge during the prophetic utterance, either that it was possible for a person to suppose that he was possessed of the prophetic gift, or had a special inspiration, when he had not, or else that he must have been a deliberate impostor. This fact proves that the prophetic influence was not always attended in the mind with a clear consciousness of its divine origin at the moment of utterance, but, on the contrary, acted like the other mental faculties. Occasionally a conscious presence of inspiration from above must have actually existed. The Apostle expressly asserts that there were times when a prophet was distinctly conscious that he had received a revelation.

We infer from this fact, that there must have been an ordinary and an extraordinary exercise of the gift. In the ordinary one, the prophet could not have perceived any material difference, when he was exercising the gift, from the usual state of his consciousness. But there were times when the prophet was conscious that he had a distinct suggestion made to his mind. In the one case the gift must have been subject to the ordinary laws of human thought; in the other case it could not have been subject to them. The special suggestion could not enter the prophet's mind at the bidding of his will. Still the laws of the human mind were so far observed, that the will could dictate when utterance should be given to the suggestion.

Nothing in the description of the prophetic gift is more striking than the calmness with which that gift acted on the mind of the person possessing it. None of the faculties of the soul were overborne by it. There was no violence attending it, no bodily contortion, no hurrying of the prophet's mind by uncontrollable impulse, no dethronement of the supremacy of the rational will. This forms the high glory of the New Testament inspiration: it stands out strongly contrasted with the same influence in the elder dispensation. In the Old Testament, we read of the mind's being hurried away from the power of conscious self-control by the prophetic influence. Jeremiah declares that the word of the Lord which was in him was like a fire which consumed him. He would have resisted its impulses, but was unable. The influence even seized on unwilling minds. Powerful effects on man's bodily frame were not unfrequently its result. Saul stripped himself naked under its influence. But in the case of the New Testament gift, if the prophets were not calm, it was no result of the gift itself: the individual mind of the prophet was still delivering the sacred truth, with which it was deeply penetrated. As in providence, so in revelation, God wills man to be a fellow worker with Himself. The individual mind itself, and even its peculiarities, are used as the channel for the conveyance of divine truth. The rational will of man constitutes his personality. The object of Christianity is to restore that will to absolute freedom. Its supremacy, therefore, was neither invaded nor interrupted in the communication of revelation.

We shall show the nature of the gifts of wisdom and knowledge, and the extent in which they formed endowments permanently attached to the minds of the possessors, when we examine the nature and degree of the inspiration under the influence of which the Epistles were composed.

CHAPTER XII.

THE LIMITS OF THE INSPIRATION CONFERRED BY THE SUPERNATURAL GIFTS.

THE spiritual gifts were restricted in their operation to the peculiar subject-matter with which the gifts were connected. They did not extend their influence beyond the sphere of that subject-matter. While they conveyed supernatural guidance within the influence of the gift, they did not confer a general infallibility. They also admitted of being abused, like the other faculties of the mind.

The fact that the spiritual gifts were restricted in their operation to the definite subject-matter connected with the gifts is not only obvious from the reason of the thing, but it is definitely asserted by the Apostle. He distinctly affirms that each gift was a separate gift, having distinct and definite functions. He declares that the Spirit divided them to each individual severally in conformity with His own will.

It is evident that if these gifts could be separately possessed by individuals, they must have had distinct and definite functions. But this is not a mere matter of inference. The Apostle compares the different gifts, in their operations, to the different members and functions of the human body. Now the members of the body are all restricted in their functions and operations. The eye has its own distinct function and operation, and invades that of no other member. The ear has its distinct function. The feet have their functions. In the same manner every member of the body possesses its distinct function. To these members of the body the Apostle compares the spiritual gifts. The spiritual gifts, therefore, must have had distinct functions, and distinct subject-matter on which they operated. The eye cannot do the work of the ear, nor the ear that of the nose, nor the feet that of the hands. In the same manner, the gift of tongues did not convey the gift of interpretation. The gift of prophecy did not convey the power of discerning of spirits. The gift of knowledge did not involve that of faith, nor the gift of faith that of wisdom.

Each gift must therefore have been limited, in the enlightenment which it conveyed, to the special subject-matter immediately connected with the gift itself. If several gifts were united in the same person, the enlightenment which they afforded would be confined within the range of the functions of the combined gifts. Such is the case with the united action of the members of the human body, to which the action of the gifts is compared. Not only would not one gift invade the functions of another, but several united gifts would not confer supernatural knowledge on any point which lay beyond the range of the separate gifts. The gift of wisdom, confined as it was to the special subjects of a divine revelation, would not enlighten the possessor on the principles of natural philosophy. The gift of discerning of spirits would afford no insight into the truths of geology. The three united gifts of wisdom, knowledge, and prophecy would give a person no supernatural knowledge on perplexing questions of chronology. The discovery of such truths belongs to human science. Such truths, therefore, could have no light thrown upon them by gifts specially limited in their functions to supernatural knowledge.

The fact that the gifts had each a separate function, and a distinct subject-matter on which that function was exercised, cannot be too carefully observed, because most of the difficulties connected with inspiration have proceeded from extending unduly the range of the supernatural gifts to subject-matters wholly unconnected with them. It has been taken for granted that, whenever we assert that a man is inspired, we must assume his general infallibility. Nothing, however, can be more fallacious than such an assumption. St. Paul expressly asserts that the gifts had each a distinct range. It is absurd to suppose that they could convey infallibility beyond the range of their respective functions, or, when several gifts were possessed by a single person, beyond the range of their united influence. It would be just as reasonable to confound between the functions of the members of the human body, or to assert that the human body possessed powers beyond the range of its united functions.

If, then, the divine information conveyed by a special gift was confined within the range of that gift, whenever a person possessing that gift wandered within the range of the subject-matter of another gift, he would be entirely devoid of any supernatural light on that subject. It would be the same thing as if we were to attempt to supply by the use of the eye the functions of the ear. The ear was not intended to give us information on the subject of light. In the same manner, the gift of interpretation gave no information on a matter which pertained to the gift of discerning of spirits. On the subject-matter connected with this last gift, its possessor would have no other light than that afforded by his natural powers, if he invaded the province of the interpreter. The eye is a correct judge in matters of colour, but a very untrustworthy informant in matters of taste or smell. In a similar manner, a person possessed of the gift of tongues, but not of interpretation, would have been a very incorrect judge whether the meaning of an utterance had been properly expounded.

It is highly probable that persons who possessed the higher gifts were likewise endowed with many of the lower. The Apostles were certainly endowed with the inferior gifts. It would be no difficult matter to prove that St. Paul possessed them in their entireness. But although they possessed them all, they were not all endowed with equal degrees of the same gift. Still the general result is plain. The inspiration supplied by the gifts could not have extended beyond the inspiration furnished by their united powers. It afforded no general enlightenment extending to every subject-matter on which the human mind could exercise itself. An apostle would be as ignorant on questions of geography as any other man who was left to the use of his natural powers. It is a most remarkable fact that the supernatural gifts admitted of abuse in their exercise, in the same manner as any ordinary human faculty. If we viewed the question on mere grounds of antecedent probability, we should certainly have concluded that, if a supernatural gift had been bestowed, a power to secure the right use of that gift would have been communicated along with the gift itself. But this supposition is expressly negatived by the testimony of St. Paul. Nothing can be more clear from his assertions in his Epistles, than that the supernatural gifts were as much open to abuse as the ordinary faculties. This fact furnishes the strongest possible proof that the inspiration supplied by the gifts was strictly limited to their respective functions, and was not a mere indefinite and general inspiration.

The degree in which the gifts were actually abused in the church at Corinth is most remarkable. The use made of the gift of tongues and prophecy caused the church to incur the danger of being converted into a Babel of confusion. The desire of display in the exercise of the gifts was extreme. "Every one of you," says St. Paul, "hath a psalm, hath a doctrine, hath a tongue, hath a revelation, hath an interpretation." The most unseemly results must have followed. One could not have believed, on anything less than apostolic testimony, that one possessing so high a gift as that of prophecy could have been guilty of a disorderly use of it. But his observations, and the precepts which he gives to regulate its exercise, necessarily presuppose that a high state of disorder existed in the church even in reference to this very gift. If, therefore, the possession of the gift did not confer the right use of the gift, who will venture to argue that it could have conferred a general infallibility beyond its proper subject-matter?

But the possession of the gifts did not prevent the existence of other evils in the Corinthian church. This church was largely endowed with gifts. St. Paul blessed God "that they were enriched in all utterance, and in all knowledge, so that they came behind in no gift;" yet in the celebration of our Lord's Supper one was hungry, and another was drunken. The same church was animated by a vehement party-spirit. A numerous party set St. Paul's apostolical authority at defiance. Their morality was far from pure. Had not the Apostle interfered, a person who married his father's wife would have been retained in church-communion. There were persons in the church who not only indulged most freely in various philosophical speculations, but who denied the reality of a bodily resurrection. This church, then, largely endowed as it was, had evidently no pretentions to the possession of a universally infallible guidance : the guidance did not extend beyond the range of the gifts. Probably the same error prevailed among them as has prevailed in modern times, and many possessed with special gifts extended the influence of those gifts beyond the range of their proper functions. Those possessed of the inferior gifts must have been greatly exalted, and refused to submit to the proper influence of the superior, in the same manner as it frequently happens that those who possess some inferior mental endowment are so puffed up by it as to refuse their legitimate influence to mental endowments of a far more exalted character. Hence would originate the resistance even to apostolical authority by a numerous party in this church. Endowed with some of the inferior gifts, they would view themselves as no less inspired than the Apostle himself. This is the only principle on which we can explain the resistance to apostolical authority, which we learn from the Epistles of St. Paul was so frequent in the primitive Church. It will also enable us to understand how it was possible that doctrines different from those taught by the Apostle obtained currency. Had it been an admitted truth in the primitive Church that inspiration was solely confined to the Apostles, the state of things to which St. Paul so frequently alludes in his Epistles would have been impossible; but if the authority of other supposed inspired teachers could be quoted, it becomes intelligible enough.

The same gifts also differed in the degree in which they were imparted to different persons. This is implied in the words of St. Peter to have been the case even in the great apostolical gift of wisdom :—" our beloved brother Paul also according to the wisdom given unto him hath written unto you; as also in all his epistles, speaking in them of these things; in which are some things hard to be understood."

In this assertion of St. Peter it is plainly implied that even this gift admitted of degrees in the mode in which it was imparted. St. Paul's wisdom was of the highest order. It was given unto him to be able to apprehend and explain divine truths which were hard to be understood. It implies that some apostolic writers were not possessed of so high a power. We can discover in each of the great apostolic writers a different mode of contemplating and surveying truth. If St. Paul's wisdom led him to describe the deeper portions of the truth, St. James's wisdom led him to treat of that truth in its practical form and in its outward manifestations. The gift of prophecy, also, evidently admitted of degrees as to the extent in which it was imparted. Various orders of minds had, through the instrumentality of the gifts, to be illumined with the heavenly light. The illumination afforded by inspiration was not supplied in conformity with the requirements of some abstract idea of humanity, but in accordance with the wants and necessities of living men.

It is further evident that the spiritual gifts did not confer a general infallibility, but that they were confined to their distinct functions, from the fact that they afforded no guarantee as to the correctness of the conduct of the possessor. The spiritual gifts possessed by the Apostles did not render them infallible, or afford them a Divine guidance in the ordinary actions of life, even in matters directly connected with their ministry. The Apostles were inspired to teach the Christian faith; they were not inspired to act the Christian faith.

The conduct of an inspired teacher may have been often liable to have doctrinal inferences deduced from it. It not unfrequently would bear a close relation to the truth which he taught; but even to such points, the history makes it plain that neither the apostolic inspiration nor the apostolic gifts extended.

The nature of the supernatural direction which the Apostles received through the prophetic gift, as to the places where they should preach the gospel, is worthy of our attention. It was an influence only occasionally exerted. The intimations in the history are distinct, that in ordinary circumstances they were left to the guidance of their own minds. We will adduce a few examples.

Philip had a supernatural direction to preach the gospel to the Ethiopian eunuch. St. Peter received a Divine injunction to preach the gospel to Cornelius. St. Paul saw, in a vision, a man of Macedonia saying, "Come over into Macedonia and help us." From this St. Luke tells us that they gathered that the Lord had called them to preach the gospel unto them. The warning, however, was not given in the form of a direct command: the call to preach the gospel was an inference from the vision. St. Paul's first apostolical journey is expressly affirmed to have been undertaken by a special suggestion of the Divine Spirit. St. Paul also informs us, that his journey to Jerusalem for the purpose of deciding the question about circumcision was undertaken by him in consequence of a revelation made to that effect. On several occasions, the historian informs us that, after the Apostle had formed a plan of ministerial labour, he was hindered from carrying it into execution by a special suggestion made by the Spirit to his mind: "Now when they had gone throughout Phrygia and the region of Galatia, and were forbidden of the Holy Ghost to preach the word in Asia, after they were come to Mysia, they assayed to go into Bithynia; but the Spirit suffered them not."

But no less distinct are the historian's assertions that on ordinary occasions St. Paul was guided in forming his plans of apostolical labour by the suggestion of human prudence. The passage which we have just referred to is a singular illustration of this fact. They went through Phrygia and the region of Galatia. Respecting neither of these journeys does the historian imply that they had any special suggestion made to their minds. They proposed to travel into Asia: this they were forbidden to do. They then came to Mysia: no special suggestion is recorded. They proposed to go into Bithynia: here they were hindered by the influence of the Spirit.

Many of St. Paul's journeys are expressly asserted to have

been suggested to his mind by considerations of human prudence. "And when there was an assault made both of the Gentiles, and also of the Jews with their rulers, to use them despitefully, and to stone them, they were ware of it, and fled unto Lystra and Derbe, cities of Lycaonia, and unto the region that lieth round about: and there they preached the gospel." Their departure from Lystra and Antioch is expressly declared to have been occasioned by persecutions which they encountered in those cities. The danger of persecution induced the brethren to send away Paul and Silas from Thessalonica to Berœa. From Berœa "the brethren sent Paul *as it were* to the sea; but Silas and Timotheus abode there still. And they that conducted Paul brought him to Athens." In these cases we have no Divine direction asserted or implied, but various human motives stated as the cause of the Apostle's journeys. At Ephesus the historian records that the Apostle expressly stated that he was directed in his journeys by no other light than that of God's ordinary providence: " But he bade them farewell, saying, I must by all means keep this feast that cometh in Jerusalem; but I will return again unto you, if God will." This is not the language of a man who felt that his journeys were always directed by a supernatural guidance.

But we have St. Paul's own express testimony on this subject. He informs us that more than once he purposed in his mind to visit Corinth. After having formed this purpose, he altered his resolution from prudential considerations: "to spare you, I came not as yet unto Corinth." He tells the Ephesian elders that he knew that those among whom he had gone preaching the gospel should see his face no more. He writes to the Romans, that he designed to take a journey into Spain, and to visit them on his road. In the Epistles written during his imprisonment at Rome, he declares his intention, if set at liberty, to visit the churches in Asia Minor. He even writes to Philemon to prepare him a lodging, so confident was he of speedily undertaking this journey. He must, therefore, have entirely abandoned his intention of going to Spain after his visit to Rome, and must then have fully purposed to visit those very churches which, at his last departure from them, he had told that they would see his face no more. Such is not the conduct nor the language of a man who felt that all his movements were directed by a supernatural direction.

The state of the case is therefore clear. Some of the Apostle's great journeys were commanded or directed by the Spirit; the details of those journeys were left to the direction of ordinary human prudence. Sometimes, when the Apostle's judgment suggested what would have been contrary to the interests of the gospel, he was specially restrained by the influence of the Spirit; at other times his human judgment was left free and unfettered.

Nor is it less evident that in the course of his journeys no supernatural provision was made to supply his wants, nor any supernatural guidance afforded him to obtain a supply by ordinary means. His maintenance was generally due to the labours of his own hands: when the supplies afforded by those labours were insufficient, he was aided by funds contributed by his converts. He himself tells us that he was thrice shipwrecked; "a night and a day I have been in the deep; in journeyings often, in perils of waters, in perils of robbers, in perils by mine own countrymen, in perils by the heathen, in perils in the city, in perils in the wilderness, in perils in the sea, in perils among false brethren; in weariness and painfulness, in watchings often, in hunger and thirst, in fastings often, in cold and nakedness."

From this passage it is evident that the Apostle was exposed to a double set of dangers and sufferings—those which would beset the zealous missionary, arising from furious opponents, and those which would be the lot of the ordinary traveller. From neither of these had he such a supernatural guidance as to ensure his exemption from difficulties and dangers. His condition required the exercise of prudence. As a missionary, he was in danger from his zealous opponents the Jews, he was exposed to the fierce attacks of the heathen mob, he was in peril from the machinations of professed Christians who were false brethren. As a traveller, he was exposed to all the dangers to which journeys in difficult and dangerous regions are liable, both by land and sea: he was in peril from robbers; he was in danger of hunger and thirst; he was exposed to cold and nakedness. The apostle neither expected nor experienced any alteration in the laws of nature for his special protection. He received no supernatural guidance to warn him of his dangers. He was possessed of no inspiration to tell him where, in inhospitable regions, he could get needful supplies of food or clothing. He boldly trusted himself to the ordinary laws of God's providence, and to the power of prudent foresight with which he was gifted, and found them sufficient for his need. All such things lay entirely beyond the illumination afforded by the supernatural gifts with which even an apostle was endowed.

But it is most remarkable that in the important matter of practice the supernatural gifts even of apostles afforded them no special illumination, nor secured their infallibility. The great truths which they were inspired to teach fully acted on their minds: they were influenced by them like other men; but their inspiration did not secure them from errors in conduct. The only infallible representation in practice of the truths taught by him was the divine person of our Lord Himself.

This want of supernatural guidance in practice is the more remarkable, because it was possible by errors in practice to compromise even the truths which an apostle taught. The union between truth in a theoretical point of view, and truth practically exhibited, is of a very intimate description. An inspired person might deny practically what he taught theoretically. To do so was attended with danger to the faith. We have the express testimony of St. Paul that even an apostle could be guilty of this inconsistency. St. Peter had been the instrument, in the hands of Providence, through whom the doors of the Christian Church were thrown open to the Gentiles. He was informed, by express revelation, that outward distinctions between Jew and Gentile were entirely abolished—that the hearts of both alike were to be purified by faith, and that from henceforth no man was to be esteemed common or unclean. At the council assembled for the purpose of determining the position which the Gentiles were to occupy in the Church, he gave the full weight of his authority to the truth that the Gentiles were freed from all obligation to keep the law of Moses. Shortly after, he paid a visit to the church at Antioch, and, in direct contradiction to his own opinions expressed at the council, after having at first freely eaten and conversed with the Gentiles, when certain Jewish Christians made their appearance, he openly retired from the society of the Gentiles and refused to eat with them.

This act of Peter was of a very important character. He said nothing with his mouth in contravention of his former teaching. But what Peter did was most important, and formed a practical teaching in the eyes of many; it even induced an apostolical man like Barnabas to join him in the act of dissimulation.

We shall be able better to estimate the importance of St. Peter's conduct, when we consider that at this time Judaism formed as strong a ground of separation from those who were not Jews as the castes in India do at the present day among themselves and from those who are men of no caste. Although the theoretical grounds of the distinction may have been different, yet the distinction was equally real, and subversive of the great truth which it was the end of Christianity to teach —that the whole human race alike, without distinction of kindred, tongue, or nation, of barbarian, Scythian, bond or free, are redeemed to God, and through faith united into one Church by the blood of the Lamb.

But St. Peter's withdrawing himself from the company of the Gentiles did not simply affect a caste-question, important as that was both doctrinally and practically. It led to inferences directly contrary to other great truths of the gospel.

St. Paul had maintained that it was a fundamental article of Christian truth, that man is justified by faith, without the deeds of the law. If St. Peter's conduct was justifiable, it involved consequences which were subversive of that doctrine.

But whatever consequences might be deduced from the conduct of St. Peter, it was certain to act as a stumbling-block to those weaker brethren in the Church, the strength of whose prejudices rendered it difficult for them to receive the truth of the complete equality of Jew and Gentile. To such it could only operate as a temptation to attach a high importance to institutions which the gospel had utterly abolished.

So dangerous, therefore, was St. Peter's conduct, that St. Paul felt it his duty to rebuke him, though an older man and a senior apostle, openly before the Church. In doing so, he directly charged him with compromising the most important of Christian truths by his compliance with Jewish prejudices.

This conduct of St. Peter at Antioch, and St. Paul's open rebuke of him, require the most careful consideration in estimating the nature of apostolic inspiration. According to the views entertained by many respecting the nature of inspiration, it would be in the highest degree improbable that one apostle should have rebuked another for being guilty of compromising Christian truth. The fact proves to demonstration that the inspiration even of apostles must have been the result of the action of distinct functions, each limited in its exercise to a definite subject-matter.

It has been often observed, in treating of this subject, that St. Peter was guilty of a sinful act of weakness. He was so undoubtedly; and he was guilty of a sinful weakness which directly compromised Christian truth, and led, by a fair inference, to a doctrinal error. It is most important that this should be kept carefully in view in estimating the nature of inspiration. St. Paul therefore uses, respecting the conduct of St. Peter, the strong expression, "that he walked not uprightly according to the truth of the gospel," and that he compelled "the Gentiles to live as do the Jews." St. Paul considered that the inference which might be deduced from

St. Peter's conduct was, that the law of Moses was necessary to salvation, and that faith alone in the Redeemer was not sufficient; and that if St. Peter was looked upon as inspired in his conduct equally as in his teaching, erroneous views of Christianity were deducible from his conduct.

If we were to form our views of the nature of apostolic inspiration on mere grounds of antecedent probability, and not on the facts of the New Testament, we should not unreasonably have assumed that the special apostolic gifts would not have been so rigidly limited to actual teaching, but that they would have secured the possessor from those errors in conduct from which doctrinal errors were fairly deducible. But the facts of the New Testament contradict such a theory, however apparently probable, exactly in the same way as the facts of creation contradict numerous theories as to the mode in which God must have acted as Creator and Preserver of the universe. Nothing can be a more emphatic warning against having recourse to such theories in ascertaining the nature of the inspiration with which the New Testament has been composed.

The danger arising from St. Peter's conduct is more strongly impressed upon us when we consider the character of the Jewish Christians. The doctrine of the equality of Jew and Gentile in God's Church was to them peculiarly distasteful—one which they could with the utmost difficulty receive. They must have viewed the assertion of it as almost disproving a pretension to divine inspiration. To persons with such prejudices, the conduct of St. Peter must have been a sore temptation: it must have seemed like a direct confirmation of their views by the senior Apostle.

It is evident, from the nature of the views and prejudices entertained by them, that Jewish Christians who were present would be only too ready to catch at anything, coming from such an authority, which could be urged as giving a support to their opinions. Numbers, beyond question, considered St. Paul as a renegade. He had been their persecutor; and they were not unlikely to argue that, like all persecutors and violent men, having abandoned his original faith, he had now adopted views no less extreme in the opposite direction. When they saw Peter withdraw from holding intercourse with the Gentiles, they would naturally say, "The throwing open of all the privileges which are the just inheritance of the seed of Abraham is nothing but an invention of that renegade and pretended apostle Paul. Men with our spiritual gifts have had no such revelation made to them. We actually saw the apostolic Peter leave the company of such pretended Christians, and decline to eat with them who refuse to enter the kingdom of God through the gate of circumcision. Paul has been pretending that the only needful qualification for the enjoyment of all the blessings of the kingdom of heaven is faith alone. It is plain that St. Peter holds no such opinion. He thinks all who have not the seal of the covenant polluted. With such persons he will not even eat. He must think them spurious Christians—an inferior caste. The so-called doctrine of justification by faith is only an invention of that apostate Paul, who, after having ravaged the Church of God, is now attempting to destroy all the privileges which are the heirloom of the children of Abraham. Peter's actions prove plainly enough that he has only shown a little weakness in yielding to the pressure put upon him: it is evident that his real opinion is, that the only gateway into the kingdom God is through our rites and ordinances."

Had the gifts of the Spirit guaranteed St. Peter's conduct, such reasoning would have been irresistible. Unless we clearly understand the real nature of the spiritual gifts, that they each possessed a definite function, and were each exerted on a distinct subject-matter, the argument will still possess no small degree of plausibility. But the gifts of the Spirit only exerted their influence within the distinct subject-matter appertaining to the gift, and left the person possessing them subject to ordinary human influences, beyond the range of the special function. The apostolic gift of wisdom, even when united with the gift of knowledge and the prophetic gift, afforded only a supernatural guidance as to truth in its direct statement. The gifts afforded no such guidance in matters of practice. In practice, apostles were on a level with other holy men; they were capable of being led away by sinful infirmities. While Peter is teaching the great truths of the Christian religion, the guidance of the supernatural gifts with which he is invested will prevent him from saying anything contrary to truth. In action he is without such guidance. St. Paul's rebuke of St. Peter is equivalent to saying, "You must be guided by what Peter preaches, not by what Peter does." The error of the Jewish Christians consisted in supposing that inspiration conferred universal infallibility.

In giving us this narrative of St. Peter's sinful compliance with Jewish prejudices, St. Paul sets before us the limit beyond which the infallibility of the Apostles did not extend. Their infallibility was specific, not general. The definite subject of their inspiration was the teaching of the truths of the Christian revelation, and the giving directions for the regulation of the Church. When they went beyond their proper functions, they spoke as men. Their human judgments are to be regarded as the judgments of those "who had received mercy of the Lord to be faithful," but must not be treated as divine oracles.

The Jewish converts, therefore, in inferring apostolic truth from apostolic practice, mistook the limits of inspiration. Those who in modern times infer their general inspiration from their particular inspiration are not the imitators of St. Paul, but of his Jewish adversaries.

We are not without proof that Paul and Barnabas were subject to similar infirmities. In their case, however, their errors in conduct only proved that they were subject to human weaknesses, and possessed on such subjects no infallible guidance to direct them. They did not compromise Christian truth.

The facts, as they are narrated by St. Luke, are well known. Paul and Barnabas had formed the plan of a fresh missionary journey. Barnabas had made up his mind that he would take as his assistant his nephew, John Mark, who had deserted them on their former journey. Of this desertion Paul retained so lively a recollection that he had made up his mind that he should not accompany them in the mission. The sequel is best told in the language of St. Luke:—"the contention was so sharp between them, that they departed asunder one from the other: and so Barnabas took Mark, and sailed unto Cyprus; and Paul chose Silas and departed, being recommended by the brethren unto the grace of God. And he went through Syria and Cilicia, confirming the churches."

It has been often remarked that this brief statement of St. Luke affords melancholy proof of infirmity in the best of men. This is true; but our concern with it is to ascertain what inferences are deducible from it as to the nature of apostolical inspiration.

The assertions of St. Luke make it plain that neither Paul nor Barnabas were assisted by supernatural guidance, even in the organization of a mission. They evidently had no expectations of receiving Divine direction on such a subject. The whole passage which we have quoted describes them as acting under the suggestions of mere human feelings. Their separation was the result of a personal disagreement. Had they possessed any acknowledged way of seeking the Lord's pleasure on such subjects, they would doubtless have had recourse to it for the purpose of settling their disagreement. But they had no authority to which they could appeal. They were firm men, and their disagreement ended in the breaking up of their common mission.

It is needless to determine which was in the wrong; probably both were. St. Paul's subsequent reconciliation with Mark, and his desire to employ him in the ministry, look like an admission that on this occasion he was influenced by a hasty judgment. The ties of relationship seem to have influenced Barnabas. Both were apostolical men. Both are called apostles. A dispute arises between them on a point directly connected with their vocation as preachers of the gospel. Neither would yield to the other. They felt that they had no supernatural direction to which they could appeal. It was a subject lying beyond the influence of their inspiration. Their contention was sharp. Their only solution was separation.

It has been often remarked, in connexion with this disagreement, that Divine Providence overruled the contention of these holy men for good, in the sending out two missions instead of one. Such a double mission arose out of their contention; but who can certainly tell us whether the progress of Christianity would have been more promoted by their conjoint or by their separate mission? Divine Providence overrules all existing evil for good. But our inquiry is, What is the bearing of this contention on the nature of apostolic inspiration?

The answer which must be returned is, that the narrative in question affords the strongest proof that the conduct of apostles was not overruled by the inspiring Spirit. The regulation of the mode of prosecuting their missions was, with occasional exceptions, left to their ordinary human judgments. On such subjects they could form different opinions as to what was right. They could engage in a sharp contention, when they disagreed about their missionary work. They had no supernatural guidance, to which they could have recourse to settle the points at issue between them: their mode of solving them was the same as that which other men are compelled to have recourse to under similar circumstances; it was separation.

There are other cases in which it is doubtful whether St. Paul did not fall into error on matters of practice in connexion with his ministry. Eager supporters of the theory of the infallibility of the Apostles have endeavoured to prove that St. Paul was in the right on these points. Whichever way that question may be determined, a consideration of the facts presented by the history will throw great light on the nature of the apostolic inspiration. (We have already shown that the gifts of the Spirit were of such a nature as to leave his character as a teacher of divine truth entirely independent of all such considerations.)

The means which St. Paul employed, on his last visit to

Jerusalem, for the conciliation of the Jewish Christians, in conformity with the advice of St. James and the elders, were unquestionably open to inferences by which persons with a Judaizing bias might have confirmed themselves in their errors, if the actions of the Apostle had been equally the result of inspiration with his teaching. Acting in conformity with the advice of St. James and the elders, for the purpose of conciliating his opponents and preventing a tumult, he joined several Jews in the discharge of a Nazarite vow. The whole history leads us to the conclusion that in such cases apostles were wholly unconscious of any supernatural assistance to which they could appeal for direction. The following is the historian's account of the transaction :—

"And the day following Paul went in with us unto James; and all the elders were present. And when he had saluted them, he declared particularly what things God had wrought among the Gentiles by his ministry. And when they had heard it, they glorified the Lord, and said unto him, Thou seest, brother, how many thousands [Greek, "ten thousands"] of Jews there are which believe; and they are all zealous of the law: and they are informed of thee, that thou teachest all the Jews which are among the Gentiles to forsake Moses, saying that they ought not to circumcise their children, neither to walk after the customs. What is it therefore? the multitude must needs come together; for they will hear that thou art come. Do therefore this that we say to thee: We have four men which have a vow on them; them take, and purify thyself with them, and be at charges with them, that they may shave their heads, and all may know that those things whereof they were informed concerning thee are nothing; but thou thyself also walkest orderly, and keepest the law. As touching the Gentiles which believe, we have written and concluded that they observe no such thing, save only that they keep themselves from things offered to idols, and from blood, and from things strangled, and from fornication. Then Paul took the men, and the next day purifying himself with them entered into the Temple, to signify the accomplishment of the days of purification, until that an offering should be offered for every one of them. And when the seven days were almost ended, the Jews which were of Asia, when they saw him in the Temple, stirred up all the people, and laid hands on him."

St. Paul had taught everywhere, not only that the observance of the Jewish law was no longer necessary for salvation, but that the rites of that law, now that the reality which they typified was come, were in themselves of no spiritual value to either Jew or Gentile. He had taught that the whole of the Temple worship and ceremonies had been fulfilled in Christ, and, being thus accomplished in Him, they were now weak and beggarly elements. He had not objected that men who were born and educated in Judaism might continue the observance of their national customs, provided that they neither taught nor held that they were essential to salvation.

This was the precise point at issue between St. Paul and the Judaizing Christians. He did not oppose the observance of their customs as harmless institutions; but he strongly affirmed that if it was maintained that they had an essential spiritual value, it was a denial of the great truths of the gospel revelation.

Great numbers of Jewish Christians were unable to receive this teaching. They not only clung to their rites as national institutions, but, at least a large party among them, believed and taught that they ought to be incorporated with Christianity. This was the party who followed the Apostle closely in all his missionary labours, and endeavoured, in opposition to him, to scatter the seeds of their doctrines in nearly every church which he had planted. To this party he gave the sternest opposition, and declared that he would afford them "place by subjection, no, not for a single hour."

When St. Paul presented himself to the elders of the Jewish church, they inform him of the greatness of the numbers of the believing Jews—many ten thousands, as they say,—and that they were all zealous for the law. Their zeal for the law differed probably considerably in different sections of the church. Among these many thousands of believing Jews, some would hold to the law more or less as a matter of national custom; others would hold that it was essential to salvation. Both parties, however, agreed in zealously supporting its observance.

Various reports of what the Apostle had taught among the Gentiles had reached the ears of both parties in the Jewish Church, and had produced a very unfavourable impression respecting him. Some of these reports exceeded the truth. They had been informed that the Apostle had gone the length of teaching the Jews who were living among the Gentiles to forsake Moses, by not circumcising their children, nor observing the customs. By these and similar reports the Apostle's name had become odious to both parties in the Jewish church, as a subverter of their national faith and privileges.

St. James and the elders apprehended that the news of the Apostle's arrival would create a tumult. The language used by St. Luke implies that they apprehended that it would not be confined to unbelieving Jews, but that there was a danger that the prejudices of a portion of the Jewish Christians would lead them to take part in it. "The multitude," say they, "must needs come together; for they will hear that thou art come." The multitude which they have just referred to, and the only multitude mentioned in the passage, is the many thousands of professed Jewish believers who were all zealous for the law, and who were stated to be prejudiced against the Apostle from the reports which had reached them respecting his teaching.

St. James and the elders therefore formed a plan which they hoped would obviate the danger. St. Paul had been in the habit among the Jews of living as a Jew, that he might gain the Jews. He had adopted their mode of living, as far as he could honestly, for the purpose of conciliating them. There were four Christian Jews who had taken on them the Nazarite's vow. Being poor, they were under some difficulty about the expense of the offerings which they had to offer on its termination. It was esteemed a no small act of piety among the Jews to assist such persons with the requisite pecuniary supplies. King Agrippa had acquired a considerable reputation for zeal by doing so. St. James and the elders advise St. Paul to join these men in the performance of their vow, and to bear the expense of the requisite sacrifices.

They evidently expected by this device to afford palpable proof that the charge which the Jewish Christians had heard, that the Apostle taught the foreign Jews to forsake Moses, was a calumny, and thus to allay the danger of a tumultuous assembly, and to remove the prejudices of the more enlightened portion of the members of the Jewish church. The Apostle complied with the advice which was offered to him. While he was in the Temple performing the injunctions of the law, the Jews fell upon him. What had been planned for the purpose of conciliation became the immediate occasion of the outbreak of the tumult which it was intended to allay.

It is doubtful to what extent the act which we have been considering was, or was not, a compromise of the great principles of the gospel. The Apostle himself, doubtless, viewed it it as a condescension to the prejudices of weaker brethren. Acting on the principle of conciliation, he had formerly circumcised Timothy, whom he designed to be an assistant in his labours. The Jews would not otherwise have associated with him. Conformity to the ordinary customs of Jewish life is an intelligible principle of action, and, if entered upon for the purpose of inducing Jews to attend to Christian teaching more readily, compromised no great principle.

But the engaging in the performance of a Nazarite vow was a very different thing from the circumcising of Timothy, or conforming to the customs of ordinary Jewish life. The vow of the Nazarite was a vow purely voluntary. A man might lead the life of a consistent Jew without making this vow: the law neither required nor commanded it. Our Lord, who came to fulfil all righteousness, and, therefore, who submitted to all the legal ordinances of the Jewish Church, never made this vow. At its termination, it involved the necessity of offering a sacrifice. If not an act of supererogation, it was an act which a Jew was free to do or to leave undone.

If the Apostle did not offer a sacrifice himself, the part which he undertook to perform rendered it necessary that he should defray the expenses of those who offered them. St. Paul himself unquestionably held that the offering of the one great sacrifice on Calvary had for ever rendered all other sacrifices useless. Whatever might be the case with the other Jewish rites, it is difficult to conceive how the Apostle could view the offering of a sacrifice in any other light than as an invasion of the solitary dignity of the great sacrifice on the cross. Sacrifices could have been no longer typical.

The act was therefore liable to misconstruction, and was certainly open to a doctrinal inference adverse to the sole efficacy of the one great offering once for all offered on the cross, and to the great doctrine of the new covenant that all Christians are priests, able to offer the acceptable offering of prayer and praise to God through the one great High Priest of the Christian calling. There must have been numbers of the Apostle's enemies who would be quite ready to put such an interpretation on it. Many a Judaizer could hardly help feeling a secret exultation when he heard that the great maintainer of the doctrine of justification by faith alone was going into the Temple to announce to the priests the duties which he had undertaken. He would say in his heart, "That Paul is bold enough among the Gentiles; but when brought under the influence of the leaders of the Jewish church, he does not dare to maintain his views. Nay, he does more; he is not content to live like an ordinary Jew, but he actually undertakes to perform vows which the strict letter of God's law does not require, and to assist at the offering of sacrifices which he has been teaching among the Gentiles have lost all value and efficacy."

To persons who would entertain feelings of this description (and they could not have been few), the act of the Apostle could hardly help proving a stumbling-block.

But, for our present purpose, we have no occasion to determine the degree in which the act of the Apostle was a stumbling-block in the way of Judaizers. Every word used by the historian implies most distinctly that neither St. James and the elders in giving the advice, nor St. Paul in complying with it, acted under the influence of supernatural guidance. Every fact recorded contradicts such a supposition.

If St. Paul received supernatural guidance on the subject, he would have had no need of the advice of St. James and the elders. They would, in fact, have hardly ventured to advise him on a subject on which they knew him to possess distinct illumination from above. St. Paul himself has informed us that, on subjects upon which he possessed the light of inspiration, he never had recourse for guidance to any human authority. He did not even go up to Jerusalem for the purpose of learning from the original witnesses the chief facts of our Lord's ministry. What he learned from the revelation of Jesus Christ he would not learn from man. Had the Apostle been conscious that he was on this occasion under the influence of divine inspiration, he would not have advised with St. James and the elders as to what was fitting to be done.

Nor do St. James and the elders claim any inspiration on the subject. If they did, they must have known that St. Paul's inspiration was equal to their own. It is inconceivable that one inspired person should advise another inspired person on points upon which the one knew that the other was under the influence of supernatural guidance.

They gave the reason on account of which they tendered their advice—their fear of a tumult, and the consequent danger to St. Paul's person. They hoped that, by complying with the advice, the tumult would be averted.

The very steps which they took to avert this danger from the Apostle became the immediate occasion of the seizure of his person and his four years' imprisonment by the Roman government. It is incredible that they adopted such a course by the suggestion of the inspiring Spirit.

It is evident, therefore, that even on points of this description, so intimately bearing on their apostolic character, apostles received no supernatural guidance from above. It was a subject which lay entirely beyond the range of the supernatural gifts with which they were endowed; and beyond the functions of those gifts they possessed no supernatural enlightenment.

But there are other subjects on which an infallible guidance has been claimed for inspired men, without any authority either from the facts or the assertions of the Scriptures to sustain such claim.

There are certain well-known difficulties respecting the chronology of the Old Testament as it is commonly received, and certain chronological statements made by St. Paul. Various solutions have been proposed for the purpose of reconciling the one with the other, as if the inspiration of the Apostle as a teacher of divine truth could be at all affected by questions of chronology.

To adduce a single example. In his discourse at Antioch, St. Luke reports St. Paul to have said, "He gave them judges by the space of 450 years, until Samuel the prophet." It has been supposed necessary, for the purpose of maintaining the Apostle's inspiration, that a theory should be invented whereby this statement should be reconciled with the supposed chronology of the Book of Judges.

Difficulties connected with such questions never would have existed unless theories of inspiration had been invented which neither the facts of the New Testament warrant nor its assertions justify. Where is the promise of our Lord to be found which asserts that He would make the Apostles adepts in the knowledge of chronology? By which of the supernatural gifts was such knowledge imparted? Questions of chronology have nothing to do with the salvation of man, or with the great truths of the Christian revelation. Not one single truth connected with the well-being of man, for time or for eternity, can be affected by determining the question whether the Judges bore rule for 450 or 4500 years. Whatever number of years may have elapsed between the call of Abraham and the deliverance from Egypt may be a curious question, interesting to chronologists, but does not affect one truth of Christianity recorded in the gospel. It is a low view to take of the purposes of revelation, to think that Christ came, or the supernatural gifts of the Spirit were imparted, to teach us truths of this description. The Apostles, in their days of ignorance, imagined that it was within the purpose of our Lord's mission to give men warnings against the yeast used by the Pharisees: to think that Christianity can be affected by questions of chronology is only one degree removed from such perversity.

The object for which Christ appeared to St. Paul was not to impart to him a new system of chronology, but to make him a witness of His resurrection, and to enlighten his mind on truths connected with the everlasting well-being of mankind. The supernatural gifts of the Spirit were communicated, not for the purpose of solving dubious points of history, but to open the mind of the Apostles to the end and design of the Incarnation; to reveal to them the great truths of the Christian revelation; to bring to the minds of the Apostles whatever Christ had said unto them, and to afford a miraculous attestation to the truth of their testimony. What right have we to assume that, because St. Paul was put in trust with the gospel, and supernaturally assisted in the discharge of that trust, so that when he treated of gospel truth his assertions were to be received, not as the "word of men, but of God"—or because, when He gave commands for the regulation of the churches, "the things which he wrote unto them were the Lord's;" that he was inspired with a supernatural knowledge of chronology or history, without the smallest support for such an assumption in one single assertion in the New Testament? His Old Testament chronology might have been that which he had learned in the school of Gamaliel. If he had learned a system of chronology there, there is nothing in his assertions respecting his own inspiration, or in the promises of our Lord, which requires us to believe that the defects of Gamaliel's chronology would be corrected by inspiration.

It has been asked, If St. Paul gives a false chronology, how can we know that any of his assertions on any of the great subjects of the Christian revelation are to be relied on? The answer is very simple: Because the one subject lies within the functions of the supernatural gifts with which he was endowed, and the other beyond their limits. To take a human example: we might as well inquire, if an eminent lawyer occasionally administers medicine to the members of his family, how we can be certain, if he is wrong in his prescriptions, that he is right in his legal opinions.

We have now considered the nature of the spiritual gifts, as far as they constitute apostolic inspiration. We have arrived at the conclusion that they each conveyed a separate and distinct knowledge to the mind of the possessor. Within the range of their operation, they conferred infallibility; beyond the range of their respective functions, they conveyed no supernatural knowledge, not even on subjects very closely connected with the proper functions of inspiration. The spiritual gifts were strictly limited to the conveyance of such knowledge as formed the proper subject-matter of a divine revelation, and conferred no general infallibility on subjects connected with revelation and not forming an integral portion of its contents.

We must now consider the last promise of supernatural guidance made by our Lord, and the meaning which general promises of this description are intended to convey.

Our Lord repeatedly warned His disciples that they would derive no outward human advantages by following Him, but would have to suffer persecution, perhaps to give their lives, for His cause. On the special occasion when He made the promise which we are going to consider, He told them that they should be brought before kings and rulers for His name's sake. When this should happen, He directs them not anxiously to premeditate what they should say; "for," says He, "it is not ye who speak, but the Spirit of your Father that speaketh in you." Now it is a most important question, In what way are all such general promises to be understood? There are many such general promises in Scripture. To take a single example. Our Lord made the following promise to the Apostles, and through them to the Church, in relation to prayer offered in His name:—" Whatsoever ye shall ask in my name, that will I do." Are we to interpret such a promise on principles of common sense, or in conformity with strict and absolute verbalism? Construed literally, the promise is of a most absolute description. Does the promise mean that there is not a single petition, offered in Christ's name, which, in consequence of the promise, our Lord is not bound to grant, however short-sighted or ill-timed the request may be? If we insist on interpreting the promises of the New Testament to the letter, and not according to their spirit, the literal meaning of the words would pledge our Lord to grant every petition offered in His name, without reference to the subject-matter of the request. Common sense, however, suggests the obvious restrictions to which all general promises are liable: they must not be tied up in strict literal formulæ.

The case before us is similar. Our version, in representing our Lord as warning the Apostles not to think beforehand on the subject of their defence, has committed the same error as when it makes our Lord teach us to take no thought about the morrow. In both cases, not thinking beforehand, but taking anxious thought is the thing prohibited. Our Lord's words forbid His disciples from taking anxious thought as to the subject of their defence, because His Spirit would afford them all needful supernatural guidance. The words of the promise, construed rigidly, are of the most strict and absolute description: "for it is not ye that speak, but the Spirit of your Father which speaketh in you." How are we to understand such a promise? Does it necessarily mean that every word uttered on such an occasion, by one to whom the promise was made, would be directly and positively dictated to his mind by the Holy Spirit?—or is it only meant to convey the assurance that all the needful topics for making the defence would be suggested? The promises of answers to prayer are equally absolute; and yet they must be interpreted as implying very important limitations. This promise was meant to convey the assurance of all necessary assistance, just as the promises of answers to prayer were intended to assure us that all things really good for us would be vouchsafed in answer to our petitions. There can be no reason for pressing the one to the extreme of literalism, which is not equally applicable to the other.

The facts of the history will best explain the sense in which one of the writers, who has recorded the promise, understood it. St. Luke has recorded the promise, and in the Acts of the Apostles he has reported the defence of St. Stephen. He could not have considered the defence otherwise than as a fulfilment of the promise. It is impossible to conceive a case to which our Lord's promise was more applicable than that of the protomartyr Stephen, when answering for his life before the Jewish council. St. Luke tells us that he was filled with the Holy Ghost. We may therefore consider the defence as a Divine commentary on the promise. That defence is singularly adapted to meet the charge against him. The charge was, that he had blasphemed Moses and God. To this charge the defence is an effectual answer. Every part of it implies a profound respect, on the part of the speaker, for the person and the divine commission of the Jewish lawgiver, and proves the falsehood of the charge of blasphemy. But in the midst of the defence occurs the following passage:—" So Jacob went down into Egypt, and died, he and our fathers, and were carried over into Sychem, and laid in the sepulchre that Abraham bought with a sum of money of the sons of Emmor * the father of Sychem."

The facts, as stated in Genesis, are as follows:—Abraham bought the cave of Macpelah for a burying-place of Ephron. In this cave Jacob was buried by Joseph according to Jacob's express commandment. Joseph died, and was put in a coffin in Egypt. Of the burial of the other patriarchs the Old Testament is silent. Joseph, however, took an oath of his brethren, that when the time of their deliverance from Egypt

---

* The usual meaning of the Greek τοῦ Συχίμ is "the son of Sychem." If, however, there was only one man of this name, and he was well known both to the hearers and the speaker, it might mean "the father of Sychem," as in our version. If it was an hereditary name, alternating, like Greek names, between father and son, each Emmor would be both father and son of a Sychem, and each Sychem father and son of an Emmor.

arrived, they would carry his bones with them into the land of promise. Moses took the bones of Joseph with him; but nothing whatever is stated as to the bones of the patriarchs. We learn from the Book of Joshua (chap. xxiv. 32) that Joseph's bones were finally deposited at Sychem, in a parcel of ground which Jacob had bought of the sons of Emmor, the father of Sychem. The plot of ground, as we read in Genesis, had been specially given by Jacob to Joseph.

Now, to avoid the historical difficulty presented by the disagreement of St. Stephen's speech with the historical facts as found in the Old Testament, it has been proposed to understand the burial at Sychem as applying only to the patriarchs, whose bones, according to tradition, were deposited there along with the bones of Joseph. But, according to the fair construction of the passage, Jacob and the patriarchs are both asserted to have been buried at Sychem. But even supposing it to be a possible interpretation of the passage that the patriarchs only were buried at Sychem, the great difficulty still remains. No ingenuity can extract from the passage any other meaning than that Abraham bought the parcel of ground at Sychem of the sons of Emmor, whereas the Book of Genesis expressly declares that Abraham's purchase was a transaction entirely different—the purchase of the cave of Macpelah of the sons of Heth,—and that Jacob effected the purchase of a piece of ground of the sons of Emmor, which is nowhere stated to have been intended for a sepulchre. Ingenuity has done her utmost to get rid of this difficulty. It has been proposed, against the authority of the manuscripts, to strike out the word Abraham; but then the passage will be ungrammatical. The next device is most unsatisfactory: it is nothing less than that of interpreting the word Abraham to mean the son of Abraham, i.e. Jacob, which is simply to assume the point at issue. Another device is, in defiance of the authority of the manuscripts, to leave out the word Abraham, and, in the face of all correct Greek, to render the word which our translators have correctly rendered "bought" "was bought." Such an attempt to solve a difficulty needs no comment.

But another mode of solving the difficulty has been invoked, the readiest of all possible methods of solution—the assumption of the point at issue, and the assertion, without an atom of evidence from the Book of Genesis, or the pretext of the existence of a tradition to that effect, that Abraham bought two sepulchres, one the cave at Macpelah and the other the field at Sychem. It has been said, "It has never been shown, nor ever can be, that Abraham did not purchase a plot of ground at Sychem, where Joseph and the patriarchs were buried." It is usually admitted to be very difficult to prove a negative; but surely those who assert that Abraham purchased two sepulchres, one at Macpelah and another at Sychem, are bound to give some proof of the fact. St. Stephen asserts that he purchased, not only a piece of land at Sychem, but the sepulchre where the patriarchs were buried. Those persons who, on any emergency, are ready to double over our Lord's miracles, or the events of His ministry, with the repetition of precisely the same words and circumstances, will find little difficulty in the fact that a man should purchase two sepulchres in his lifetime, the second of which was not used for a burial-place till several hundred years after the purchase. It has been asserted, because Abraham built an altar there, he must have purchased some land. Was there no unoccupied land at this time in Canaan? The narrative in Genesis leads us to believe that it existed there in great abundance. If Abraham had already purchased a piece of land to erect an altar, it is highly improbable that Jacob, on his return from Padan Aram, would have purchased another piece of land for the same purpose in the same place, instead of erecting his altar on the land already purchased by Abraham.

Writers of this description can use very strong language respecting persons who find it difficult to admit their right to assume everything, at their pleasure, which will help their theories of inspiration out of a difficulty. Dr. Wordsworth, in his notes on the Greek Testament, writes:—"The allegations in question, when reduced to their plain meaning, involve the assumption that the Holy Ghost, speaking by St. Stephen (who was 'full of the Holy Ghost'), forgot what He had written in the Book of Genesis, and that His memory is now to be refreshed by biblical commentators of the nineteenth century!"

After writing this passage, Dr. Wordsworth proceeds, as might have been anticipated, to read his opponents a solemn lecture on the duty of humility. We say, " Physician, heal thyself."

If it were sufficiently reverential so to speak of God's Spirit, the language here employed might be amply retorted on the writer; but we forbear. Let us suppose the facts to be exactly such as Dr. Wordsworth states them. According to him, the history in Genesis and the speech of St. Stephen are the *ipsissima verba* uttered by the Divine Spirit, without one single human element in them; they are, in fact, the utterance of one and the same historian. It then becomes a most important question whether the style of the history and the speech is fully worthy of a divine author. Does it as much transcend the style of men as the Divine works transcend the human? Have the history and the speech that perspicuity of expression which they would have had, if they had been the work of an accomplished and educated human writer? As matter of fact, nine hundred and ninety-nine out of every thousand of the readers of St. Stephen's speech have always identified the purchase of the sepulchre mentioned by him with the purchase by Abraham of the cave of Macpelah. Allowing, therefore, all which Dr. Wordsworth says, the only result of his unsupported assumptions is to charge the omniscient Spirit with a very imperfect use of human language.

Unless we assume some of these solutions, which are of a most questionable utility, the defence of St. Stephen contains a statement of an historical fact at issue with the Book of Genesis. How then are we to view the case? What is the nature of the promise? Did our Lord fail His first martyr in his hour of need? Those only will be in danger of thinking so, who, for the purpose of avoiding that danger, will have recourse to one of the above solutions, and insist on construing to the letter our Lord's promise of supernatural assistance.

But why should this promise be construed to the letter, and not the promises in answer to prayer or several of our Lord's precepts in the sermon on the mount? Does any rational interpreter think it necessary to understand our Lord's precept, " I say unto you that ye resist not evil," as a command forbidding a Christian to offer resistance when he is attacked by a robber or a murderer? St. Stephen's defence, as recorded in the Acts, effectually answers the charge of blasphemy. Thus far the promise of all needful assistance in making the defence was redeemed. As far as the defence was concerned, it was an entirely unimportant point whether Abraham or Jacob bought the cave at Sychem. The most corrupt court of law on earth could not have taken notice of such a point. It had not the remotest bearing on the charge of blasphemy. The object of St. Stephen's speech is not to prove his own divine inspiration, or even to prove the divine origin of Christianity, but to answer a specific charge. He therefore goes over the chief points in the Jewish history, expressing, as he goes along, profound reverence for the fathers of the Jewish Church and for Moses in particular. The promise we are considering is one entirely special in its nature: it assures the Apostles of Divine aid when they should judicially answer before the rulers of this world for their obedience to the commands of Christ. As interpreted by the history, it must therefore have been intended as an assurance to the Apostles, that when they answered for their lives before the rulers of this world, they should be supernaturally guided into all the necessary topics for making their defence. They were not anxiously to premeditate what they should say. They were to be void of all fear. Their cause was the cause of God. The Spirit of God should impart to them what they ought to say. Had Stephen taken false ground in making his defence—had Paul, when he stood before Felix, Festus, or Agrippa, addressed to them arguments which were not to the point—had he failed in answering Tertullus—had either he or Stephen got confused or nervous on so trying an occasion, both might be said to have been deserted by their Master, and His promise consequently would have failed.

CHAPTER XIII.

THE GENERAL CHARACTER OF THE GOSPELS, AND THE NATURE OF THEIR INSPIRATION. THEIR INSPIRATION NOT VERBAL.

We must now proceed to inquire into the nature of the inspiration presented by the historical books of the New Testament, and to test our theories respecting the nature of such inspiration by the facts presented by the histories themselves, and then proceed to extend the same inquiries to the Epistles.

We have already proved that our Lord possessed the highest form of inspiration in His divine person. What he taught was the truth as it exists in God, as far as finite conceptions and human language can represent it to the mind of man. His actions were the actions of God manifest in the flesh. The actions and sayings of our Lord, therefore, are the divine element in the Gospels.

The Gospels contain the records of those sayings and actions. If our Lord's divine person embodies inspiration in its highest form, nothing more is required for our possessing the results of such inspiration than that our Lord's sayings and actions should have been transmitted to us as they actually occurred. A second communication by inspiration will not render the words and actions of incarnate Deity more divine. It follows, on the principles which we have established respecting the nature of the gospel revelation as made in our Lord's person, that if the report of our Lord's sayings and actions contained in the Gospels is a true report, any amount of inspiration possessed by the persons who have reported them would add neither to their truth nor to their divine authority. The inspiration which He possessed was already the highest possible form of inspiration; additional inspiration, therefore, could do nothing more than insure the correctness of the report. If correctly reported, by whatever means that report was composed, the actions and sayings of our Lord would present us with the results of the inspiration of God manifest in the flesh.

The whole question respecting the inspiration of the Gospels, therefore, resolves itself into the determination of the amount of supernatural assistance necessary to be afforded to the writers to enable them to give a true account of the actions and sayings of our Lord. If the writers of the Gospels were eye-witnesses of the actions of our Lord, a large proportion of those actions could not but have been recorded correctly, if the writers of the Gospels composed them honestly: they could not but have known what they had actually seen.

If they delayed the composition of their histories till a considerable period after the events had occurred, still a large number of the events were of so striking a character that they would be indelibly engraven on their memories; they would therefore require supernatural aid to recall to their recollection only such things as they had forgotten.

If the writers of the Gospels were not eye-witnesses, but derived the accounts in their narratives from those who were such, supposing they carefully recorded what was reported by such eye-witnesses, we are in possession of the results of the highest form of inspiration.

If the writers of the Gospels, not being eye-witnesses, derived the accounts which they have embodied in the Gospels from the oral testimony of the Apostles as delivered to particular churches, and they have carefully ascertained that that oral testimony was actually delivered, the records of the Gospels present us with the results of the highest form of inspiration.

We have already stated that a higher degree of supernatural assistance would be required to enable the writers of the Gospels to give a correct record of the discourses than of the actions of our Lord. But if our Lord's promise that the "Holy Spirit should teach the Apostles all things, and bring all things to their remembrance whatever He had spoken to them," was fulfilled, abundant provision was made for putting us in possession of the divine teaching of our

Lord. The deficiencies of human memory would be supplemented by the influence of the Spirit through the prophetic gift.

All the grounds of antecedent certainty which we possess lead us to the conclusion that God would not give man supernatural assistance to effect what he is able to do without such assistance, or, where such assistance was needed, that He would impart a larger degree of assistance than the necessity of the case required. No fact or assertion of the New Testament contradicts, but many support this probability.

The Gospels present the reader with a succession of very remarkable phenomena, to which no parallel can be found in any similar productions. The whole of existing literature may be searched, and no such peculiar phenomena will be found in any four biographies of the same individual, composed by four different writers. Their resemblances and dissimilarities are of a character absolutely unique. They chiefly record the history of the last three years of our Lord's life. Only one records an anecdote of His early years. The synoptic Gospels are almost entirely filled with details of His ministry in Galilee; the fourth, with that in Judea. The synoptic Gospels contain a large amount of matter in common. The verbal similarity and dissimilarity in this common matter can hardly be accounted for on any ordinary principle. Ingenious men have propounded vast numbers of theories with a view of explaining it. Sometimes we find the agreement perfect: precisely the same words are employed in reporting the same action or the same discourse. At other times facts are introduced in the one account which are omitted in the other. Sometimes a particular respecting the history which is omitted by one evangelist is supplied by another, by which the shorter narrative becomes more intelligible. At another time a fresh sentence is introduced into a discourse, which another evangelist has omitted in his report of it. Then a sentence in a discourse as recorded by one evangelist is transposed in another. Sometimes the introduction of a word by one evangelist helps to make the statement of another clear, which would be obscure without it.

Sometimes one evangelist reports one portion of an action, while another reports another portion of it. Besides statements of fact and discourses which the Gospels contain in common, there are facts and discourses which are narrated only by separate evangelists. The whole Gospel of St. John, with few exceptions, is of this description.

Now all these phenomena as presented in the Gospels are of the utmost importance in estimating the degree of supernatural assistance which was afforded to the writers.

To the attentive reader of the Gospels the inquiry can hardly fail to present itself, Is each Gospel a distinct and separate history, composed without either of the writers communicating with the others, or deriving any assistance from the others' labours? Had either of the writers seen or copied from another Gospel, or had they the intention to supply omissions or defects in that Gospel?

Happily our present inquiry does not compel us to settle either of these questions. They have been discussed in every possible form, and received every possible solution; but as some one of the views which have been proposed must be true, we have only to observe the consequences to the theory of inspiration which follow from any or all of them. The question for us to determine is, How do the different proposed solutions bear on existing theories as to the nature and extent of inspiration? Do, or do not, the facts presuppose the existence of a human element of considerable extent in the composition of the Gospels? We will endeavour to answer that question.

Let us suppose the Gospels to be four distinct and independent histories, written by the authors without the smallest concert with one another. The four Gospels undoubtedly present all the peculiar phenomena to which we have referred. How are they to be accounted for? A person holding the theory of verbal inspiration explains the phenomena by asserting that each Gospel has been dictated, word for word as it stands, by the Holy Spirit. According to this view, the four Gospels are not the work of four independent human minds, giving their distinct and independent testimony to facts and discourses, but of one Divine mind. If such be the case, how are the remarkable peculiarities which we have mentioned to be accounted for? whence come the variations in the narratives? whence the variations in professed reports of the same discourse? How, on the assumption of one single Divine authorship, do we account for the transposition of sentences? how for one part of a fact being reported in one Gospel, and another in another? If the whole be the simple dictation of one inspiring Spirit, why have we four distinct versions of the same facts and the same discourses? The supporters of the theory, when hard pressed, generally plead that some of these things are to be accounted for by assuming that some small human peculiarities have been permitted to exist in them. But what then becomes of the theory? Its difficulties are so great that it is impossible to carry it out consistently, when it is applied to the Gospels, even by its strongest supporters. It is utterly inconsistent with the marks of diversity of authorship which the Gospels unquestionably present. Many difficulties would have been avoided, if only one Gospel had been written. But if there had been only one Gospel, or one author of the four Gospels, we should have lost all independent testimony to the facts of the evangelical history. We should get one witness only, and that witness not a human one, as the Apostles declare that they were appointed to be, but a Divine one, who has already borne testimony by the exertion of miraculous power.

But what view of authorship does a careful perusal of the four Gospels present to the reader? Would he ever guess, if he were ignorant of all theories on the subject, that the four Gospels were really the work of one Author, who had employed four different amanuenses to copy down what He had dictated? Every appearance presented by them would be entirely at issue with such a supposition. It is by no means difficult to say how four lives of the same person would be characterized, presenting the mark of difference and distinct authorship which are presented by the Gospels, if they were composed by one and the same individual. If they were a work simply human, the evidences which they afford of the presence of four distinct authors would be considered indubitable. The only way of evading the force of that evidence would be to ascribe their diversities to a distinct purpose, on the part of the writer, to make these pass as the works of four distinct and independent witnesses.

But difficulties meet those who maintain the theory of verbal inspiration in every part of the evangelical narratives. That theory requires its supporters to eliminate from them every mark of individuality, and to weave the narratives into a consistent whole. But how incongruous do they seem when forced together into a harmony! They have no appearance of a structure of similar materials, erected by the same architect, but of a building patched up by several. The different styles of architecture will not agree together: they as ill assort as the Grecian and the Gothic in the same building. The Gospel by St. John possesses a character quite distinct from that possessed by the other three; and although woven into a narrative with them, it presents no signs of amalgamation. The Gospel by St. Mark displays a power of graphic painting in its narratives, which is almost entirely wanting in that of St. Matthew. Frequently the plain marks appear in one evangelist of superior means of information, compared with those possessed by another. One narrative, again, has the evident traces of the presence of an eye-witness, in which the other narrative is deficient. St. Mark is particularly rich in touches of this description. How are such phenomena to be accounted for on the assumption of the truth of the theory of verbal inspiration? Did the Holy Spirit imitate the phenomena which the testimony of actual witnesses usually presents? Did He inspire one evangelist to introduce these traits into his narrative, and another to omit them? We ask distinctly, Do we not find in the four Gospels as positive indications of the free exercise of the powers of the human mind as in any four narratives of the same events, extending over an equal period of time?

No doubt the Gospels present difficulties, whether we assume that they were written independently of each other, or that the writer of some one Gospel had read the narrative of another, or that they have for their foundation a common narrative. But with these difficulties we are not concerned. We have only to assume the existence of the facts as they appear in the pages of the Evangelists, and inquire how they bear on particular theories of inspiration.

Let us suppose the Evangelists to have written quite independently of each other. How comes the verbal agreement? The only solution which can be given of such verbal agreement is that they received supernatural assistance, or used a common document, or copied from each other. But if they either copied or derived the common words by dictation from above, whence come the variations of expression in the very midst of sentences nearly alike? In these variations their distinctive human characters appear. This human element is also distinctly to be traced in what they have recorded or omitted in their common narratives. The utmost difficulties, as will be seen hereafter, result from supposing that either Evangelist had read the narrative of the other. Every possible assumption has been made on that subject. One writer has assumed that Matthew copied from Mark; another that Mark copied from Matthew. Others have assumed a similar copying on the part of St. Luke. There have not been wanting those who have affirmed that the other Evangelists borrowed from him; others have affirmed that St. John had both read and that he meant to supply the deficiencies of his predecessors. Whichever theory we assume as true, either that the Evangelists are independent witnesses, or that they borrowed from each other, or that they meant to supplement each other, or that they derived their narratives from the same document or from several previously existing documents (and some one of these views must be the correct one), all are alike incompatible with the theory that they wrote under the influence of verbal inspiration.

But if, in accounting for the phenomena presented by the Gospels, we assume that one writer had used the Gospel of another, and borrowed from it some portion of its contents, this assumption is entirely subversive of the theory in question. Many writers of eminence have held that Mark's is an epitome of Matthew's Gospel, but enlarged in some of its details. Now we are not called upon to determine whether the phenomena presented either by St. Matthew or St. Mark justify such an assumption. But, supposing such a theory to be correct, is it consistent with the existence of an inspiration like verbal inspiration in St. Mark's Gospel? It is a usual thing for human authors to borrow one of another; but when they do so without acknowledgment, the act is generally looked upon with considerable suspicion. But, on the assumption that the writers of the Gospels composed them by the aid of verbal or any cognate inspiration, what are we to say of an author, who is the mouth-piece of the Spirit of God, actually borrowing and copying from another who is acting in the same capacity? Such an act would be as much like a contradiction as anything which we can possibly conceive. On what principles would such an author venture on making alterations or additions in the work of a writer whom he considered to be recording what was dictated to him by the Holy Spirit? Why should such a writer copy at all, and not record what the Spirit dictated to him? If he had done anything but copy *verbatim*, he must have thought that he could improve on the Spirit's work! Could he conceive any account which he read in a book thus composed imperfect? If the writer of a Gospel thought that he could improve on a Gospel which he had perused, he never could have believed such Gospel to have been verbally inspired. We know from St. Luke's testimony that he had perused memoranda of our Lord's life, and that he thought he could improve upon them. The theory that one Evangelist copied from another, or from any existing document, is subversive of the idea that either was verbally inspired. We can understand how an Evangelist, giving a human testimony to facts, and receiving such Divine assistance as was requisite to enable him truthfully to narrate the facts or record the discourses, if he himself had not been actually present when an event occurred which he wished to record, or when a particular discourse was delivered, should make diligent inquiry of persons who had been eye- and ear-witnesses of the events in question. It is also quite intelligible how an inspired person, who only received Divine assistance when necessary, could make use of memoranda which may have contained brief accounts of the testimony of apostles or other eye-witnesses. But by direct copying of an actual Gospel, or epitomizing one, no additional testimony whatever would be afforded. To publish a Gospel which was a direct copy or epitome of another Gospel, without any acknowledgment of the source whence the materials were derived, would be to present oneself as a fresh witness, without having any testimony to give to the facts in question : it would be simply to repeat what the preceding witness had deposed to. To assert that such a proceeding on the part of a writer of a Gospel has actually taken place seems hardly consistent with believing in his honesty, much less in his inspiration.

The Gospel by St. Mark presents all the peculiar phenomena which usually belong to narratives derived from direct ocular testimony. They are traits in the highest degree difficult for a forger to imitate. It is an undoubted fact that this Gospel is far more distinguished by such marks than the Gospel of St. Matthew. How is this difference to be accounted for, on the supposition that both Gospels have been alike dictated by the Holy Spirit? How, in fact, is it possible, in such a case, to account for the marks of ocular human testimony at all?

But it has been extensively held that some of the writers of the Gospels had read those previously published, and that they designed to supplement them by the publication of their own. This has been very generally held respecting St. John's Gospel. That Gospel presents many phenomena which appear to favour that supposition. It has been generally believed that, previously to the publication of this Gospel, St. John had read the three other Evangelists, and that he intended by his Gospel to supply those parts of them in which he esteemed their narratives deficient. This opinion may be almost said to have been a primitive tradition of the Church. The contents of the Gospel of St. John are remarkably different from those of the other three. St. John details few facts which have been mentioned by the other Evangelists. When he does so, it is always with a view to the discourse which follows. The discourses also found in this Gospel differ in a remarkable manner from those contained in the synoptic Gospels.

It is not too much to assert that St. John's is by far the most spiritual Gospel. Had it not been for his testimony, we should certainly have been ignorant of the profound depth of our Lord's teaching. It records the higher mysteries of the kingdom of heaven in direct terms, whereas the other Evangelists only furnish us with indirect hints of those truths. It is true that there are difficulties presented by the contents of this Gospel in the way of believing that St. John had previously read the other three. Still, on any supposition, the phenomena presented by this Gospel can only be explained by supposing that the author was well acquainted with the contents of the synoptic Gospels, or the general oral teaching on which they had been founded, and that by the publication of this Gospel he intended to supply the higher element of divine truth which was taught by our Lord, in which these Gospels, or the oral teaching out of which they were composed, was deficient.

Now, if this be the case, is it possible that St. John could have held that the three Gospels, or the teaching out of which they were derived, had been communicated to the Church by that species of inspiration designated verbal inspiration? If they were pure dictations of the Spirit, free from every species of human element, would he have ventured to criticise them? Could it possibly appear to him that he could supply anything deficient in their teaching, if that teaching was not in any sense the work of the respective authors, but the pure dictation of the divine Spirit? How is it possible to talk of deficiencies existing in those Gospels, except on the supposition that the writers were in some degree left to the exercise of their own judgments? If a human writer undertakes to supplement another writer's work, it is plain that he thinks the work more or less imperfect, and that he can improve it. If a biography of a particular person has already been published, and another person, who knows of its existence, undertakes to set forth a new one, it is plain that he is of opinion he can improve on the original biography, or else that he must be influenced by the *cacoëthes scribendi*.

Now, as it is an indisputable matter of fact that the discourses and events narrated in the synoptic Gospels differ in a remarkable manner from those detailed in the Gospel of St. John, this difference requires to be accounted for. The variation is of such a nature as to imply that it is not the result of accident, but of design. We must arrive at the conclusion that the apostle was aware of the general nature of the facts and discourses which had been reported by eye- and ear-witnesses to the Church, and that he considered that they involved omission in connexion with the higher forms of truth which he was able to supply. But if he thought that there was any defect in the previously existing details of our Lord's life and teaching, what becomes of the theory of verbal inspiration? Would a writer who believed himself verbally inspired deliberately set himself to correct defects in writers whom he believed no less verbally inspired than himself?

Perhaps it may be replied that, as gospel truth was only slowly developed as such truth was able to be borne, the mind of the Church was not able to bear for a long time anything higher than the teaching of the synoptic Gospels, and that the Gospel of St. John was written as soon as the Church was fitted to receive it. Such a view would imply that the Gospel by St. John is an improvement on the synoptic Gospels, in the same manner as the New is on the Old Testament. But, as the Gospels are professed histories of our Lord's ministry, the cases are not parallel. To fulfil their character as witnesses, it was necessary that the writers should report what they had seen and heard, and give us a fair sample of our Lord's actions and teaching. The New differs from the Old Testament in a totally different manner: it is a higher, brighter, clearer, and more glorious revelation.

But this supposition fails in a still more important particular; it is not founded on fact. There is no doubt that the Gospel of St. John was composed late in the apostolic age. St. Paul had composed his Epistles, and gone to his rest, before the Gospel of St. John was given to the world.

It is not true, therefore, that the Church could not have borne St. John's Gospel at an earlier time. The Church, for which the Epistle to the Romans was good spiritual food, would evidently have been edified by the Gospel of St. John; but this Epistle was written before even St. Luke's Gospel was published. The contents of the Gospel of St. John would have been highly edifying to that state of the Church's mind for which the Epistles to the Ephesians, Philippians, and Colossians were intended.

If, then, St. John considered that he could publish a Gospel which would improve on the hitherto existing accounts of our Lord's life and discourses, it is evident that the inspiration with the aid of which the Gospels have been composed cannot be verbal inspiration, but must be, at least, an inspiration which admits of difference of degree. St. John must have been possessed of a higher form of inspiration than was possessed by the authors of the synoptic Gospels. He must have believed that there were higher truths respecting our Lord's life, and that more spiritual discourses were uttered by him, which he had it in his power to communicate. If St. John meant to supplement the other Gospels, it may be consistent with the possession of verbal inspiration by St. John, but it is only compatible with the existence of a human element of some sort in the Gospels of Matthew, Mark, and Luke.

CHAPTER XIV.

EXAMINATION OF PARALLEL PASSAGES IN THE GOSPELS, WITH A VIEW TO DETERMINE THE NATURE OF THE INSPIRATION BY THE AID OF WHICH THEY WERE COMPOSED.

WE will now proceed to test the theory of verbal inspiration and its kindred theories, not by considerations taken from the general structure of the Gospels, but from the various specific facts contained in them, by comparing together their different narratives of the events of our Lord's life and their accounts of His discourses.

If this theory were a true account of the influence under which the Gospels were composed, there are some peculiar passages in them in which we should certainly expect to see it exemplified.

One of the passages to which we should expect to find the theory of verbal inspiration or some one of its kindred theories applicable, if anywhere in the New Testament, would be the report of the words in which the Evangelists state that our Lord instituted the Eucharist. That rite was intended for celebration in all ages in the Church: it was designed to be a visible institution, accompanied with a certain amount of form in its celebration, having been ordained for the perpetual memory of Christ's death. We should naturally, therefore, expect the very words used by our Lord when instituting the Supper to have been reported by the Evangelists. St. Matthew, Mark, Luke, and St. Paul have each given an account of the transaction: each account contains variations.

St. Matthew's account of the institution of the bread is given in the following words:—" And as they were eating, Jesus took bread, and blessed it, and brake it, and gave it to the disciples, and said, Take, eat; this is my body."

The words reported by St. Mark are identical with those reported by St. Matthew.

St. Luke's is as follows :—" And He took bread, and gave thanks, and brake it, and gave unto them, saying, This is my body which is given for you: this do in remembrance of me."

St. Paul's account of the institution, which he declares he received directly by revelation from our Lord, is as follows :— "The Lord Jesus the same night in which He was betrayed took bread; and when He had given thanks, He brake it, and said, Take, eat; this is my body which is broken for you: this do in remembrance of me."

But the difference in the words declared by them to have been used by our Lord in the institution of the cup is far more remarkable. St. Matthew represents our Lord to have said—

"And He took the cup, and gave thanks, and gave it to them, saying, Drink ye all of it; for this is my blood of the new testament, which is shed for many for the remission of sins."

St. Mark, " And He took the cup; and when He had given thanks, He gave it to them: and they all drank of it. And He said unto them, This is my blood of the new testament, which is shed for many."

St. Luke, " Likewise also the cup after supper, saying, This cup is the new testament in my blood, which is shed for you."

St. Paul, " After the same manner also He took the cup, when He had supped, saying, This cup is the new testament in my blood : this do ye, as oft as ye drink it, in remembrance of me."

Now it is to be observed, that these different accounts present only one agreement in the words stated to have been used by our Lord as the actual words of institution, that between St. Matthew and St. Mark in those said to have been used in the institution of the bread. But it is most remarkable, that, in each Evangelist, the words which the four different reports ascribe to our Lord are introduced with the formula, " He spake and said," or, " saying," and yet contain a considerable difference as to the actual words employed. The diversity of the words stated in the four accounts as having been used in the institution of the cup is far more striking than those used in the institution of the bread. Our Lord could not have used all these formularies; and if He did, the natural construction of the words used by the Evangelists requires, on the theory that they recorded them under the influence of verbal inspiration, that each account should be the account of the very words used at the institution. When the words used are, " He said," " saying," in so short a formula and on so solemn an occasion, we should expect that those recorded would have been neither more nor less than the exact words actually used. But by no possible contrivance can the words which St. Paul asserts our Lord to have used, in the institution of the cup, be reconciled with those reported to have been used by Him in Matthew and Mark. St. Matthew and St. Mark report the words to have been, " This is my blood of the new testament, which is shed for many." St. Paul reports the words to have been, " This cup is the new testament in my blood." St. Matthew and St. Mark omit the direction to drink it in remembrance of Him, which St. Paul inserts; neither do the words reported, as used by St. Matthew and St. Mark, precisely agree together. It will hardly be pretended, by the most zealous harmonizer, that our Lord repeated all these varieties of expression in the course of the distribution of the elements to the disciples.

Now St. Paul expressly tells us that the account which he has handed down of the institution of the Supper was actually received by him from no human source of information, but from the Lord: "Now I received of the Lord that which also I delivered unto you." Human memory, therefore, was not concerned in the report which he gave. It follows that St. Paul's report contains the *ipsissima verba* used by our Lord at the institution. In accordance with this declaration, the account of the institution of the supper delivered by St. Paul is the fullest and most exact. From him alone we learn that the institution of the cup was separated by an interval from the institution of the bread: he states that it took place after they had supped. If we had only St. Matthew and St. Mark's accounts, we should have certainly come to the conclusion that the cup was instituted during the supper, immediately after the institution of the bread.

It is also most remarkable, that St. Paul and St. Luke's accounts agree. Now on the assumption that the history of the Acts of the Apostles is a true history, this is exactly what might have been expected. The evangelist is there asserted to have been St. Paul's intimate companion and friend. Now St. Paul's account of the institution of the Eucharist is an incidental account, given, not in a formal history, but in a letter. Had St. Paul composed a Gospel, the agreement between these accounts would have been nothing remarkable. The history is effectually confirmed by the letter. But although St. Luke's account is just what we might have expected, bearing evident marks of having been derived from St. Paul, yet there are verbal differences between the two accounts of a very instructive character, illustrating the nature of the inspiration afforded to St. Luke. In the account of the institution of the bread, St. Luke adds to St. Paul's the words, "and gave unto them." He leaves out the words, "Take, eat." Instead of "broken for you," he substitutes "given for you." In his account of the institution of the cup, he adds the words, "which is shed for you;" and he omits the words, "this do ye, as oft as ye drink it, in remembrance of me."

Now although these variations make no substantial difference in the sense, they are just such differences as might have been expected in the narrative of one who, to arrive at certain information, employed the means which St. Luke states, in the preface to his Gospel, that he employed. St. Luke tells us that, not being an eye-witness himself, he obtained his knowledge of the facts which he relates from the testimony of competent witnesses, and he was at pains to obtain a true account of those facts from such witnesses. He knew St. Paul had had the true facts of the institution of the Eucharist communicated to him by direct revelation.

When about to write this portion of his history, he would naturally ask St. Paul to furnish him with an account of the institution of the Lord's Supper. He has accordingly reported the apostle's account of the institution. The variations in words are just those which might have taken place, if St. Luke had asked St. Paul to narrate the account to him as he received it from the Lord, and then had gone and copied down what he remembered the apostle to have said.

Now although St. Luke's and St. Paul's agree substantially, their agreement is not verbal. The promise, therefore, of our Lord, that the Spirit should bring to their remembrance the words which He had spoken to the Apostles, must not be tied down rigidly to the letter: it is sufficiently redeemed if the Apostles were enabled to record the sense. "The letter killeth; but the spirit giveth life." Christianity is not a religion of rigid forms, but of actualities.

It follows, as a necessary consequence, from this comparison of the fourfold account of the words recorded to have been spoken by our Lord at the institution of the Eucharist, that the theory of verbal inspiration entirely fails for the purpose of giving a correct account of the phenomena presented by the evangelists. According to that theory, the Holy Ghost would have dictated to the evangelists the whole account: there was no human element in it whatever. He must have known the words used by our Lord; and if He had dictated the words to each evangelist, He would have dictated the right ones. But the words actually used present considerable variations; it is impossible, therefore, to ascribe those variations to the dictation of the Spirit. All four accounts report the substantial truth; but substantial truth is not the present question. Sufficient inspiration, therefore, was afforded to the Apostles to secure the report of substantial truth, but not of verbal truth. The only theory consistent with the facts as they stand before us is, that the sacred writers had their memories supernaturally assisted so as to enable them certainly to report the sense of what our Lord uttered, but no further. The assistance afforded was an assistance consistent with their character as witnesses. The knowledge of the identical words used to express that sense was not necessary for the purposes of the Christian revelation, and therefore was not imparted.

We have a similar example of verbal disagreement in a parable uttered by our Lord, and recorded by St. Matthew, St. Mark, and St. Luke. When our Lord after His last journey had arrived at Jerusalem, He uttered the parable of the vineyard. We will first direct attention to a small verbal discrepancy in that parable, at its close, which is utterly inconsistent with the theory of verbal inspiration. St. Matthew represents our Lord to have said, " and taking him, they cast him out of the vineyard, and slew him."

St. Mark represents our Lord to have said, " and taking him, they slew him, and cast him out of the vineyard." The arrangement of the Greek words in St. Luke is ambiguous; but taking them in their most natural sense, they support St. Matthew's account of the order in which they were uttered. They are, Καὶ ἐκβαλόντες αὐτὸν ἔξω τοῦ ἀμπελῶνος, ἀπέκτειναν.

Now it will be readily conceded that the variation is small. This is the precise reason why we have adduced it. Small inaccuracies and great are alike to Omniscience. Though the variation is a small one, it is a variation utterly irreconcilable on the assumption that the Gospels were composed under the influence of verbal inspiration. No conceivable ingenuity can make our Lord to have uttered both expressions. He either represented the son as killed inside the vineyard or outside it; but He could not have used both forms of words. He must either have said that he was killed and then the body was cast out, or that he was cast out and then killed. In relation to the meaning of the parable, the variation is utterly unimportant; it only assumes weight when particular theories as to the mode in which Scripture must have been inspired are assumed, without the smallest authority from those Scriptures themselves, on the mere rationalizing ground that, if any conceivable error or incongruity exists in any of their minor details, they cannot be the word of God.

Those who lay down such principles are the parents of scepticism and infidelity; they throw wide open the gates of the citadel for the unbeliever to enter and make wild havoc. It may be said with truth of such unwise defenders of the inspiration of the Christian Scriptures, "They know not what they do."

There is also a variation in the verbal expressions of the Evangelists as to the number of the servants who were sent to the husbandmen. St. Matthew says, "He sent his servants unto the husbandmen, that they might receive the fruits of it. And the husbandmen took his servants, and beat one, and killed another, and stoned another. Again he sent other servants, more than the first; and they did unto them likewise."

St. Mark's report is, "And at the season he sent to the husbandmen a servant, that he might receive from the husbandmen of the fruit of the vineyard. And they caught him, and beat him, and sent him away empty. And again he sent unto them another servant; and at him they cast stones, and wounded him in the head, and sent him away shamefully handled. And again he sent another; and him they killed, and many others; beating some, and killing some."

St. Luke says, "And at the season he sent a servant to the husbandmen, that they should give him of the fruit of the vineyard: but the husbandmen beat him, and sent him away empty. And again he sent another servant: and they beat him also, and entreated him shamefully, and sent him away empty. And again he sent a third: and they wounded him also, and cast him out."

St. Mark and St. Luke agree in reporting that our Lord mentioned in the parable the distinct mission of three separate servants. St. Mark adds to the account, that the owner of the vineyard sent also others, some of whom were beaten, and some killed. St. Matthew represents our Lord to have mentioned two distinct missions of several servants in a body: out of the first body, one was beaten, another killed, and another stoned; the second and larger party suffered in like manner.

Now such variations in the details of a parable are only important when people will propound a particular theory of inspiration, and assert that, if God gave a revelation of His will, that particular mode of inspiration must be the mode employed by Him in communicating the revelation. St. Mark's or St. Luke's report most probably contains the actual words uttered by our Lord; but if these reports contain these words, it is evident that the report of St. Matthew cannot. The report of St. Matthew has all the appearance of a general statement of the sense of what our Lord uttered; it, in fact, sums up in one account the results of the mission of the three servants. Now although this variation in the report of the parable has not the smallest influence on the sense, they prove that all three Evangelists could not have received the parable by direct verbal inspiration. Matthew's account at least is a summary, and not the real words uttered. The variation is only important as showing that the theory of verbal inspiration is incompatible with the facts of the New Testament. If the parable was received by each of the Evangelists by direct dictation of the Spirit, no such variation would have been found; we should have had the words themselves. It is impossible that our Lord could have uttered both forms: to suppose that He did so is to rush headlong into absurdity.

We have another remarkable instance in the reports of the words asserted to have been uttered by our Lord during His agony in the garden. St. Matthew records the words as follows:

"And He went a little farther, and fell on his face, and prayed, saying, O my Father, if it be possible, let this cup pass from me: nevertheless not as I will, but as Thou wilt. . . . . He went away again the second time, and prayed, saying, O my Father, if this cup may not pass away from me, except I drink it, Thy will be done. . . . . . And he left them, and went away again, and prayed the third time, saying the same words."

St. Mark reports as follows :—"And He went forward a little, and fell on the ground, and prayed that, if it were possible, the hour might pass from Him. And He said, Abba,

Father, all things are possible unto Thee; take away this cup from me: nevertheless not what I will, but what Thou wilt. . . . And again He went away, and prayed, and spake the same words." St. Mark gives no report of the words of the third prayer. St. Luke says:—"And He was withdrawn from them about a stone's cast, and kneeled down, and prayed, saying, Father, if Thou be willing, remove this cup from me: nevertheless not my will, but Thine, be done. And there appeared an angel unto Him from heaven, strengthening Him. And being in an agony He prayed more earnestly: and His sweat was as it were great drops of blood falling down to the ground."

We observe the following variations in the reports of the words used, which in each Evangelist are introduced with the words, "He prayed, saying," or, "And He said." St. Matthew makes our Lord to say, in the first prayer, "O my Father, if it be possible, let this cup pass from me." St. Mark reports the words to have been, "Abba, Father, all things are possible unto Thee; take away this cup from me." St. Luke, "Father, if Thou be willing, remove this cup from me." St. Luke varies the words, "not what I will, but what Thou wilt," into "not my will, but Thine, be done." The words used in the second prayer, according to St. Matthew, varied considerably from those used in the first prayer: they do not contain a request that the cup may pass from Him; they express an increased submission to the Father's will. St. Mark's report, according to our translation, represents the words used on both occasions to have been the same; but to translate them as our translators have done makes the discrepancy even greater than it actually is. All that the words necessarily imply is, that they were to the same effect. They were, in a certain sense, to the same effect; but there is a fresh element introduced into the second prayer, as recorded by St. Matthew, showing an increased submission to the Father's will, which St. Mark's report of them fails to record. St. Mark's expression entirely overlooks the existence of this fresh element in the prayer. St. Matthew asserts that the repetition of the same words took place at the third prayer, and not at the second. In St. Luke the whole three prayers are summed up as one continuous act, or rather, if the appearance of the angel from heaven and the bloody sweat took place during the first prayer, the mention of the second and third prayers is altogether omitted.

Now, if in any place in the Evangelists, supposing they wrote under the influence of an inspiration resembling verbal inspiration, we should certainly expect to find the unmistakable presence of such inspiration in their report of words so sacred as those used by our Lord in prayer to His Father during His agony in the garden. But, although each reports the words which are ascribed to our Lord with the expression, " He prayed, saying," yet even in a case like this we find no literal verbal agreement. We find the evident presence of a human element in the reports given, and not one uniform Divine testimony. It is plain that the Evangelists do not mean to imply that our Lord used the whole of these forms. He might have used some of them in the precise words. If we have the true meaning of our Lord's words, we have all that is necessary for the purposes of a divine revelation. But although our knowledge of the meaning, and not of the very words used by our Lord, is quite consistent with the fact that the writers of the Gospels possessed an inspiration sufficient for the purpose of giving us such an account of our Lord's actions and sayings as God intended us to possess, it is utterly inconsistent with the theory that that inspiration must have been verbal inspiration. If such passages had been written by express dictation, without the presence of any human element whatever, the Gospels must have contained the very words uttered by our Lord.

We have observed that the second prayer of our Lord, as given by St. Matthew, implies that a portion of the mental struggle was passed and a more perfect fulness of submission to the Divine will attained. St. Mark simply says that the second prayer was to the same effect. St. Matthew says that the third prayer was to the same effect as the second. The obvious inference is that St. Matthew's source of information was more perfect than St. Mark's. Can it be pretended that variations of this description were actually dictated to the Evangelists by the Holy Spirit in the identical words in which we read them. All that is requisite is, that the Evangelists were aided by the Spirit to give the true meaning of our Lord's words in all cases where their natural memories would have failed them, or their natural faculties were insufficient.

We now come to the well-known inscription on the cross. To the ordinary reader of the narratives of the Evangelists, their accounts of the inscription present four variations.

St. Matthew writes:—"And they set up over His head His accusation written, This is Jesus the King of the Jews."

St. Mark—" And the superscription of His accusation was written over, The King of the Jews."

St. Luke, strictly translated, writes—" And an inscription was written over Him in letters of Hebrew, Greek, and Latin, The King of the Jews, this."

St. John—" Pilate wrote a title, and put it on the cross, and it was written, Jesus the Nazarene, the King of the Jews."

Now it is doubtful, if we consider the number of verbal disagreements presented by the Evangelists, whether it will repay any one for examining the various ingenious attempts which have been made by the supporters of the theory of verbal inspiration, and its kindred theories, to reduce these various reports to verbal harmony. These disagreements are so numerous and of so undeniable a character that a large expenditure of labour on any one of them is quite thrown away while the others remain. We shall notice only one attempt to reconcile them—that of Mr. Elliott, in his letters to Dean Alford.

It has often been observed that, as the inscription is stated to have been written in Hebrew, Greek, and Latin, there may have been the same substantial inscription, with three different verbal variations in each of the languages mentioned. The old mode of reconciling the difficulty was, that Matthew, writing for Jews, had copied the Hebrew inscription; Mark the Latin one, which it was supposed would be the shorter; and St. John, who wrote after the destruction of Jerusalem, and for the benefit of Gentiles, the Greek one. The persons who offered this solution of the difficulty took it for granted, as most persons naturally would, that four different forms of inscriptions were reported by the Evangelists. What then was to be done with the inscription in St. Luke? Ingenuity propounded its answer:—St. Luke had reduced two of the inscriptions into one, although the only natural meaning of the words used by him asserts that what St. Luke has reported were the words of a positive inscription. Mr. Elliott, however, has come to the rescue and corrected all such blundering. Millions have read St. Matthew and never doubted that the language used by him was intended to assert that he had reported a positive inscription over the cross. Mr. Elliott has discovered that St. Matthew intended to report no inscription at all: it is the mere $αἰτία$, or the charge on which our Lord was condemned—the sum and substance of the three inscriptions—which St. Matthew gives. Unfortunately, St. Matthew is pledged to the assertion that the $αἰτία$, or charge, which he reports, was an actually written charge: "they set over His head His charge written." He most plainly implies that this written charge was over the cross, and that the written $αἰτία$, or charge, over our Lord's head was, "This is Jesus the King of the Jews." No reader of St. Matthew, who had not some particular theory to maintain, would have even guessed that St. Matthew did not intend to report an inscription over the cross, actually written there, but the special charge on which our Lord was condemned, which, in actual words, was not in writing over the cross at all.

The worth of this reasoning may be tested by a somewhat similar case. It is well known that when the Long Parliament overthrew one of the statues of King Charles I., they caused the following words to be engraven on the pedestal:— "Exit tyrannus ultimus regum" (Away goes the tyrant, the last of the kings). Now, supposing an historian had described this fact in the following language —"They placed on the pedestal the charge against Charles, and the ground of the abolition of royalty, in a written inscription, 'Charles was a tyrant;

kingship is ended," would any reader of English ever have
imagined that the writer meant by these words to convey
the mere sense of what was engraven on the pedestal, and
not to assert that the words were actually written there? To
such devices do ingenious men have recourse when they wish
to bolster up a theory to which they stand committed. Such
devices are more likely to urge the waverer into unbelief, than
to convince the gainsayer.

But the explanation in question is burdened with many
other difficulties. It is obliged to represent that St. John, who
wrote after the destruction of Jerusalem, and for the benefit
of Gentiles, reported not the Greek, but the Hebrew inscription; and that St. Matthew, who wrote the earliest of the
evangelists, and for the benefit of Jews, has reported no
inscription at all, but a charge of his own composition, which
none of his readers who might have been actual witnesses of
the crucifixion had ever seen in actual writing over the
cross. One sacred writer calls what was written over the
cross ἐπιγραφή, and another τίτλος. Pilate is stated to have
written it. If so, he no doubt wrote the Latin one with his
own hand, and probably the Greek; he would most probably
employ his usual interpreter to translate the Hebrew. What
right have we to assume that his interpreter, instead of translating what Pilate had written, would venture on alterations?
Before any advantage can be gained by those who wish to
maintain the theory of verbal inspiration by such criticisms,
they must rewrite the Gospels and alter their entire structure. The statements of the evangelists as to the inscription
over the cross are obviously subversive of the theory of
verbal inspiration. The degree in which they are adverse
to that theory may be estimated by the shifts to which its
supporters are driven to evade the plain meaning of language. The history of the cure of the demoniac at Gadara
is another similar example. St. Matthew's account is as
follows:—

"And when He was come to the other side into the country of the Gergesenes, there met Him two possessed with
devils, coming out of the tombs, exceeding fierce, so that no

man might pass by that way. And, behold, they cried out, saying, What have we to do with Thee, Jesus, Thou Son of God? art Thou come hither to torment us before the time? And there was a good way off from them an herd of many swine feeding. So the devils besought Him, saying, If Thou cast us out, suffer us to go away into the herd of swine. And He said unto them, Go. And when they were come out, they went into the herd of swine: and, behold, the whole herd of swine ran violently down a steep place into the sea, and perished in the waters."

St. Mark: "And they came over unto the other side of the sea, into the country of the Gadarenes. And when He was come out of the ship, immediately there met Him out of the tombs a man with an unclean spirit, who had his dwelling among the tombs; and no man could bind him, no, not with chains: because that he had been often bound with fetters and chains, and the chains had been plucked asunder by him, and the fetters broken in pieces: neither could any man tame him. And always, night and day, he was in the mountains, and in the tombs, crying, and cutting himself with stones. But when he saw Jesus afar off, he ran and worshipped Him, and cried with a loud voice, and said, What have I to do with Thee, Jesus, Thou Son of the most high God? I adjure Thee by God, that Thou torment me not. For He said unto him, Come out of the man, thou unclean spirit. And He asked him, What is thy name? And he answered, saying, My name is Legion: for we are many. And he besought Him much that He would not send them away out of the country. Now there was there nigh unto the mountains a great herd of swine feeding. And all the devils besought Him, saying, Send us into the swine, that we may enter into them. And forthwith Jesus gave them leave. And the unclean spirits went out, and entered into the swine: and the herd ran violently down a steep place into the sea, (they were about two thousand;) and were choked in the sea."

We do not quote St. Luke's account, because it presents few additional particulars.

Now both Mark and Luke speak only of one demoniac

throughout; St. Matthew speaks of two. The miracle of curing the blind man at Jericho is similarly doubled by St. Matthew; but as there are several most remarkable circumstances connected with that miracle, we shall examine it in its proper place. It is quite beyond our purpose to inquire what is the best mode of reconciling difficulties of this description; but we are concerned with them for the purpose of ascertaining, even supposing they admit of the most satisfactory reconciliation, what theory they suggest respecting the nature of the inspiration of the New Testament.

Let it be supposed that two demoniacs were cured; and St. Mark and St. Luke have particularized one only, and that, too, in terms which would lead their readers to apprehend that there was no other, even while in all other respects they narrate the miracle itself with the greatest fulness. Or it may be that a single demoniac only was cured, and that St. Matthew had a less authentic source of information, or that the number of spirits possessing the man occasioned the multiplication of the miracle. As a matter of testimony, this narration does not affect the certainty of the fact that a miracle was performed. But, taking the narratives as they stand, what theory do they necessarily suggest respecting the degree of the inspiration with which they were written? Can we consider that all three evangelists were alike verbally inspired? Did each evangelist receive the narrative from express dictation?—or do not these narratives contain indubitable evidence of the presence of a human element along with the divine one? If we suppose two demoniacs were cured, then St. Matthew's account is the more accurate of the three; if one only, superior accuracy will belong to the accounts of Mark and Luke. But if there is no human element in these reports, but both are express dictations of the Spirit of God, how can we talk of greater or less degrees of accuracy as to facts, in what must be the account of those facts given by the Spirit of God?

But the two narratives have another striking contrast. The narrative of St. Matthew states the bare facts of the miracle, and nothing more; that of St. Mark is most graphic as to the details. A person who had not witnessed the miracle might easily have written the narrative of St. Matthew. There is no reason for supposing that all the apostles were constantly in attendance on our Lord's person. The narrative of St. Mark has all the appearance of the most graphic picture drawn by an eye-witness. We remark the following points in it:—*The man met our Lord immediately on His coming out of the ship. He comes from the tombs. There he had been long living. His fierceness was such that no man could tame him, or bind him with chains. As soon as he sees Jesus afar off, he runs to Him and worships Him. He cries with a loud voice.* Then follows the report of the dialogue between our Lord and the demoniac. He beseeches Him *much* not to send them away. Jesus *immediately* gives them leave to enter the swine. The herd, when the devils have entered them, rush *violently*. The numbers of the destroyed swine are actually given.

Now here is the most marked difference in the mode of narration—the one narrative having the strongest appearance of being that of an eye-witness, the other narrative having but small traces of being written from express ocular testimony. This same difference, however it may be accounted for, pervades several other narratives in St. Matthew's Gospel. Is it explicable on the supposition of a Hebrew original, and that what we possess is only a translation? For this difference there must be a cause. If the theory of verbal inspiration be correct, both passages are the work of one and the same author, without any intermixture of a human element. According to that theory, the Spirit must have dictated to Mark the graphic narrative, and to St. Matthew the mere details, only making him the more accurate narrator by mentioning two demoniacs instead of one. But such a course is certainly one which nothing but the most extreme necessity can justify us in ascribing to the omniscient Spirit of God; and, even viewed thus, relative accuracy in two accounts which have equally the Divine Spirit for their author is out of the question.

If the Gospels contain a human testimony, all these difficulties vanish; they only arise by destroying the character of the Apostles as witnesses of what they heard and saw, and resolving the whole testimony as to the gospel facts into the testimony of the Divine Spirit. The existence of such strong marks of ocular testimony, and of such descriptive power, in St. Mark, are quite consistent with the old tradition that he derived much of his information from St. Peter, who was in constant and close attendance on our Lord's person, but not with the theory which makes the evangelist the mere mouthpiece of the Holy Spirit. A man with St. Peter's peculiar temperament would naturally be a graphic describer of what he actually witnessed. The scene of the miracle must have been almost terrifically grand and impressive as it is painted by St. Mark. The whole of these narratives may be consistent with the assumption of there being various degrees of inspiration, or with supernatural guidance united with a human element of some sort; but they are inconsistent with the assumption that their authors wrote under the influence of verbal inspiration, and positively imply the presence of a human testimony and of different styles of composition.

No less impossible is it to reconcile the different accounts of the miracle at Jericho with any theory of verbal inspiration. St. Matthew's account is as follows:—" And as they departed from Jericho, a great multitude followed Him. And, behold, two blind men sitting by the way side, when they heard that Jesus passed by, cried out, saying, Have mercy on us, O Lord, Thou son of David. And the multitude rebuked them, because they should hold their peace: but they cried the more, saying, Have mercy on us, O Lord, thou son of David. And Jesus stood still, and called them, and said, What will ye that I shall do unto you? They say unto Him, Lord, that our eyes may be opened. So Jesus had compassion on them, and touched their eyes: and immediately their eyes received sight, and they followed Him."

St. Mark: "And they came to Jericho: and as He went out of Jericho with His disciples and a great number of people, blind Bartimæus, the son of Timæus, sat by the highway side begging. And when he heard that it was Jesus of Nazareth, he began to cry out, and say, Jesus, thou son of David, have mercy on me. And many charged him that he should hold his peace: but he cried the more a great deal, Thou son of David, have mercy on me. And Jesus stood still, and commanded him to be called. And they call the blind man, saying unto him, Be of good comfort, rise; He calleth thee. And he, casting away his garment, rose, and came to Jesus. And Jesus answered and said unto him, What wilt thou that I should do unto thee? The blind man said unto Him, Lord, that I might receive my sight. And Jesus said unto him, Go thy way; thy faith hath made thee whole. And immediately he received his sight, and followed Jesus in the way."

St. Luke: "And it came to pass, that as He was come nigh unto Jericho, a certain blind man sat by the way side begging: and hearing the multitude pass by, he asked what it meant," &c., nearly in the words of St. Mark. After the performance of the miracle, St. Luke resumes :—" And Jesus entered, and passed through Jericho." Then follows the story of Zacchæus.

Now the difficulties in these narratives are, that St. Mark represents our Lord to have cured Bartimæus as He went out of Jericho; St. Luke makes Him to have cured a blind man as He went into Jericho; and St. Matthew represents Him to have cured two blind men as He went out of Jericho. To reconcile these difficulties, it has been supposed that the miracle was doubled, one blind man being cured as our Lord entered Jericho, and another as He went out of it; and that St. Matthew, who represents two blind men to have been cured as He *went out* of Jericho, has united the two accounts into one.

The difficulties with which this mode of reconciliation are attended are hopeless. St. Mark states expressly that the miracle was performed as they went out of Jericho, and St. Luke's narrative is no less express that the miracle was performed as they were entering it. How could the cure of a blind man performed as our Lord was entering a city, and another on the road as He was going out of it, be reported by any historian as the cure of two blind men wrought as He was going out of the same city? The cause of verbal inspiration will gain but little from such a solution: as much as it will gain, the credibility of the Scriptures will lose. It is far better to explain the difficulty by the presence of a human element, than to assert that both narratives, if this was their intended meaning, were alike dictated by the Holy Spirit.

But the expedient of considering the miracle performed at the entrance into Jericho, and repeated on going out of it, is a very doubtful one. We are then forced to suppose that there was a blind man sitting at the entrance of the city begging, and another in the opposite direction, leading out of it; that they each uttered the same cry, in the same words; that the multitude on each occasion charge them to be silent, and that, too, after our Lord had, in answer to the prayer, performed the miracle just before; that, notwithstanding the rebuke of the multitude, each blind man persisted in his prayer in the same words; that on each occasion our Lord stood still and commanded the blind man to be called; that our Lord makes the same inquiry of each, receives precisely the same answer, confers the benefit in the same language, and is followed in the way by each.

Now, we ask, can any person read these narratives and assert that they do not denote the usual phenomena of human testimony, which usually presents variations in small and unimportant particulars? The points of disagreement are of minor importance; they do not affect the great fact that a blind man was cured somewhere near Jericho. Mark's narrative bears the strongest indications of being derived from an actual witness. Every minor point is brought out just as such a witness would have narrated it, even to the blind man's arising and throwing aside his garment in his haste to get to our Lord. Such circumstances, so naturally introduced, do more to prove truthfulness than the most exact verbal agreement with other accounts.

The same view is presented by the narrative of the two thieves reviling our Lord on the cross. St. Matthew says, "The thieves also which were crucified with Him cast the same in His teeth."

St. Mark, " And they that were crucified with Him reviled Him."

St. Luke, " And one of the malefactors which were hanged railed on Him, saying, If Thou be the Christ, save thyself and us. But the other, answering, rebuked him."

To reconcile this difference, it has been affirmed that both reviled our Lord at first, but afterwards one of them repented, confessed our Lord, and rebuked his fellow. It may be so; but neither narrative drops a single hint that such was the fact. The reader of each separate narrative would certainly be of opinion that the contrary was the case. The only question which we are called on to consider is, Is the present form of the narratives consistent with the supposition that each separate narrative was actually dictated to the writer by the Spirit of God?—or do the narratives clearly imply the presence of human testimony?

It is well known that the greatest possible difficulty exists in forming a direct narrative of the events of our Lord's passion out of the four narratives of the Evangelists. We cannot ascertain with certainty from them the precise order of the different events, nor is it always easy to make different events recorded by separate writers agree with one another. We may almost say that the views of the order of the events prior to the crucifixion are almost as numerous as the writers who undertake to treat of them. The difficulties on this point presented by the four Gospels are so generally felt and acknowledged, that it will be superfluous to make long extracts from them: an example or two will be sufficient. St. John represents our Lord to have been scourged at some time early during the proceedings before Pilate, evidently with the purpose, on Pilate's part, of inducing the Jews to consent to His release; and he makes no mention of any subsequent scourging. St. Luke omits the mention of the scourging altogether, but leaves ample room for St. John's statement, by representing Pilate as proposing to the Jews that he should chastise Him and release Him. But the natural meaning which a reader, who knew nothing of the statement of St. John, would assign to the narratives of St. Matthew and St. Mark is, that the scourging was inflicted in the usual Roman manner, as a preliminary to the crucifixion, and after sentence was actually passed. Some commentators maintain that the scourging is misplaced by St. Matthew and St. Mark; Others, that it was repeated twice, of which no hint is found in either Gospel, and that the mention of the second scourging is omitted by St. John. The historical fact of the scourging is affirmed by three Evangelists, and implied by the fourth: they differ as to the time of its infliction. If inflicted in private, we can see how such difference might naturally arise, if the writers of the Gospels are delivering the results of human testimony. St. John might have known the actual fact: he had superior means of information. He was acquainted with persons in authority. St. Matthew and St. Mark, knowing that He had been scourged, might have concluded that it took place at the usual time. Now what do the phenomena suggest as to the authorship? Are the four Gospels the result of one author, or of many? Do they contain the witness of distinct individuals to the facts, or the one testimony of the omniscient Spirit?

St. John's Gospel contains a passage which has all the appearance of being a continuous narration of the actual official condemnation of our Lord by Pilate. The Jews have just intimidated Pilate by intimating to him that the course which he was pursuing with respect to our Lord showed that he was no friend of Cæsar. The passage is as follows:—
"When Pilate therefore heard that saying, he brought Jesus forth, and sat down in the judgment seat in a place that is called the Pavement, but in the Hebrew, Gabbatha. And it was the preparation of the passover, and about the sixth hour: and he saith unto the Jews, Behold your King! But they cried out, Away with Him, away with Him, crucify Him. Pilate saith unto them, Shall I crucify your King? The chief priests answered, We have no king but Cæsar. Then delivered he Him therefore unto them to be crucified. And they took Jesus, and led Him away."

Now it is not our intention to express an opinion as to the correct method of harmonizing this portion of the Gospel narrative; but, to the ordinary reader, this passage presents all the appearance of being a continuous narrative of facts, certainly without any long break occurring in them. Pilate has all the appearance of having taken his place on the judgment seat for the purpose of giving a judicial sentence. But Greswell, in his Harmony, has thought it necessary to break this passage into pieces. Between its different sentences he has introduced not only a great deal of matter from the other Evangelists, but also the long account by St. Luke of the sending of our Lord to Herod. This event could not well have occupied less than an hour. Between another of these clauses he thinks it necessary to introduce the communication to Pilate of his wife's dream. Now, whatever we may think of this manner of dealing with the passage of St. John, it is beyond denial that the forming the four accounts into a continuous whole presents great difficulties to the harmonizer.

St. John's Gospel also contains an account of a private examination of our Lord by Pilate, given in very considerable detail. In the course of this examination, in answer to Pilate's question, "Art thou the king of the Jews?" our Lord confesses himself a king, after explaining distinctly to Pilate that He claimed that title in no sense implying that He was a temporal sovereign. Pilate accepts the explanation, and pronounces our Lord not guilty of the charge adduced by the Jews. The accounts of the other Evangelists would lead the reader to draw the inference that, in answer to the charge of pretending to be the king of the Jews, our Lord made the direct reply, "Thou sayest it," thereby confessing the charge, without giving to Pilate any explanation of the sense in which He confessed Himself to be a king.

Now, in explanation, some commentators make our Lord to have answered Pilate's question, "Art thou the king of the Jews?" in public, before the private examination. Others represent Him to have answered it after that examination. Others think that the confession of our Lord, as it is recorded by St. Matthew and St. Mark, was not made at all in the words mentioned by them, but that theirs is a more general account of what passed at the private examination, which St. John has given more in detail.

The whole of the narrative, both of the events before Annas and Caiaphas and before Pilate, presents similar difficulties.

Now it forms no portion of our present inquiry to discover the missing links which would reconcile passages of this description, but to ascertain what theory of inspiration such narratives imply. Would any reader, who had no previously formed opinions on the subject, ever rise from the perusal of these narratives with the opinion that they were written under the influence of verbal inspiration? He would see the plain, indubitable marks of human testimony. He would consider that he was reading the accounts of various witnesses. Faithful witnesses, in recording the events of a most exciting day, and events in which their feelings were most deeply interested, would naturally testify, some to one event to which their attention had been particularly drawn, and some to another. One witness might have seen one portion of an event, another might have seen and testified to the other portion only. There is no necessity for supposing that every witness was present during the whole proceedings; and if he were, he might often be prevented by the crowd from witnessing every portion of them; or the intensity of his feelings may have caused him to observe one thing, and not to observe another. The cries uttered by the Jews were, no doubt, various. One person might have heard and reported one cry, and another another cry. Variations in different accounts as to time and place might easily arise among eye-witnesses in the midst of a scene so deeply exciting. The whole of these considerations, put together, are fully sufficient to account for great variations and even occasional discrepancies in the narratives. Such variations would not in the smallest degree affect the credit of the testimony as to the great facts. But while such considerations are amply sufficient to account for the variations and the discrepancies, they account for them only on one supposition, that the narratives before us are the results of credible human testimony. They are consistent with the fact that our Lord constituted the Apostles His witnesses of the great facts of the gospel history; they are inconsistent with the assumption that those facts, in the form we read them in the four gospels, were actually dictated to the writers by One possessing omniscience.

The same remarks are even in a greater degree true of the four narratives of the events of the Resurrection. Perhaps there is hardly a reader in existence who has not observed the difficulties of weaving those narratives into a consistent whole, and of harmonizing their different assertions. Innumerable attempts have been made to harmonize these accounts; but the harshness of the resulting narratives forbids us to suppose that the harmonizers themselves are well satisfied with their performances. If we take the four histories as the separate accounts of different witnesses, testifying to what they had actually seen or had heard reported on good authority by persons who had actually witnessed the events, the fact of the resurrection of our Lord is established on evidence such as no other human fact possesses. But if we think it necessary, before that great fact can be believed, that we should be able to give a harmony of the Evangelical narratives, we shall be in danger of a long and dreary wandering in the dismal regions of unbelief. If, instead of assuming theories of antecedent probability as to what the New Testament ought to be, we simply ascertain from the facts themselves what they declare on the subject, they will furnish us with the answer :—We are the faithful reports of persons who were constituted by our Lord witnesses of His resurrection, who have testified to what our eyes have seen, what our ears have heard, and what our hands have handled.

It is well known that the Gospel of St. John is at apparent disagreement with the synoptic Gospels, as to whether the night on which our Lord celebrated His passover was the night of the actual passover. The reader of St. John's Gospel would naturally conclude that the night in question was passover-eve; the readers of the synoptic Gospels would as naturally infer that it was on the very Paschal night. A few quotations will show the nature of the disagreement.

St. Matthew, xxvi.: Our Lord says to the Apostles, "Ye know that after two days is the feast of the passover." "Now the first day of the feast of unleavened bread the disciples came to Jesus, saying unto Him, Where wilt Thou that we prepare for Thee to eat the passover?" "And they made ready the passover." St. Mark, xiv.: "And the first day of unleavened bread, when they killed the passover, His disciples said unto Him, Where wilt Thou that we go and prepare that Thou mayest eat the passover?" "And they made ready the passover." St. Luke, xxii.: "Then came the day of unleavened bread, when the passover must be killed." "And He said unto them, With desire I have desired to eat this passover with you before I suffer." Now all these expressions imply that our Lord celebrated the Jewish passover with the disciples on the regular Paschal night; and had we no other information, they would have left no doubt of it on the mind of the ordinary reader.

St. John, however, has the following assertions. Chap. xiii.: "Now before the feast of the passover, when Jesus knew that His hour was come. . . . He riseth from supper." "For some of them thought, because Judas had the bag, that Jesus had said unto him, Buy those things that we have need of against the feast." Chap. xviii.: "They themselves went not into the judgment hall, lest they should be defiled; but that they might eat the passover." Chap. xix.: "And it was the preparation of the passover, and about the sixth hour."

Now it is self-evident that a discrepancy exists in the words of these statements, a discrepancy which might admit of reconciliation if we knew the whole of the facts. It is not our business to attempt that reconciliation. Our concern is simply with the mode of statement adopted in the different narratives of the Evangelists, and to inquire whether those statements, as we now read them, were dictated to each several Evangelist by the omniscient Spirit. Whatever mode of reconciling the synoptic Gospels with St. John may be the true one, still the reader of the synoptic Gospels would draw the conclusion that the night on which our Lord celebrated the passover was the night of the regular Jewish passover. St. John's assertion is distinct that the day on which our Lord was condemned by Pilate was about the sixth hour on passover-eve, and, consequently, that the night when He ate His passover could not have been the night of the regular Jewish passover. We must assume a theory, therefore, which will assign this discrepancy or want of perspicuity in expression, or by whatever name we choose to designate the fact in question, to some human element existing in the minds of the writers of the Gospels, and not to the agency of the Spirit of God.

Of a similar description is the twofold statement in St. Matthew and the Acts respecting the mode of the death of Judas. St. Matthew's statement is, " He departed, and went and hanged himself." This contains no allusion whatever to any other cause of death; it simply asserts that he committed suicide by hanging or strangulation. St. Peter, in the Acts of the Apostles, says, " And falling headlong," or, more correctly, on his face, " he burst asunder in the midst, and all his bowels gushed out. And it was known to all the dwellers at Jerusalem."

Now there is no doubt that, to persons who knew the exact mode of Judas's death, those two accounts would present nothing which was irreconcilable; but, to those who do not know the actual state of the facts, there is no connecting link which will explain the difficulty. As each account now stands, it is an imperfect narrative, and we have no means left us of constructing a perfect one. To the reader of St. Matthew, Judas appears to have perished simply by suicide and strangulation. To the reader of St. Luke it appears no less evident that the immediate cause of his death was a fall, which caused him to burst asunder, and his bowels to gush out. Now all this is quite consistent, if the accounts have been derived from the testimony of human witnesses, one of whom has reported one side of this transaction, and the other the other, and that the connecting link has perished. The theory of verbal inspiration requires us to assume that the Spirit of God dictated to St. Matthew one part of this transaction, and to St. Luke another, and omitted the connecting link between them. The necessity must be of the clearest description before we can be justified in making such assumptions, and ascribing such a mode of dictation to the Spirit of God.

A similar result follows from the different arrangements adopted by St. Matthew and St. Luke in the narrative of the Temptation. Here no one will hesitate for a single moment to adopt the order of the events as given by St. Matthew: St. Luke's order cannot be the correct one. But when the reader unhesitatingly assumes that St. Matthew's order is the correct order, and that St. Luke has narrated the second temptation out of place, do we not also necessarily assume the presence of a human element which is the cause of this difference of arrangement? It has been said, no divine truth is at all compromised by the arrangement adopted by St. Luke. This is perfectly true; but the admission gives no account of the influence which led St. Luke to adopt this arrangement.

We have a similar example in the account given by St. Matthew and St. Luke of the healing of the centurion's servant. St. Matthew writes:—" There came unto Him a centurion, beseeching him, and saying, Lord, my servant lieth at home sick of the palsy, grievously tormented. And Jesus saith unto him, I will come and heal him. The centurion answered and said, Lord, I am not worthy that Thou shouldest come under my roof," &c. "And Jesus said unto the centurion, Go thy way; and as thou hast believed, so be it done unto thee."

St. Luke writes:—" And a certain centurion's servant, who was dear unto him, was sick, and ready to die. And when he heard of Jesus, he sent unto Him the elders of the Jews. . . . And when they came to Jesus, they besought Him instantly, saying, That he was worthy for whom He should do this: for he loveth our nation, and he hath built us a synagogue. Then Jesus went with them. And when He was now not far from the house, the centurion sent friends to Him, saying unto Him, Lord, trouble not Thyself: for I am not worthy that Thou shouldest enter under my roof: wherefore neither thought I myself worthy to come unto Thee," &c., &c.

St. Matthew's account represents the centurion to have come in person; and he is represented as the speaker, and our

Lord as speaking to him, in the whole narrative. St. Luke's account represents that the centurion sent the elders of the Jewish synagogue first; and when he found our Lord was actually coming to his house, he sent friends expressly to say that his sense of unworthiness had induced him to send the elders of the Jews, and not to come himself. Two different modes of reconciliation have been adopted: the one is, that he first sent friends to our Lord, and finally came himself; the other is a method highly useful in getting over all difficulties—that what a person does by another he does by himself. The first method will not solve the difficulty; and if the truth of the latter mode of solution be admitted, still we have two different accounts of the same transaction, one of which asserts that the centurion came in person, and the other that he presented his request through others. This mode of expression is quite consistent with the presence of a human element, but not with the assumption of nothing but a divine one.

The comparison of the accounts given by St. Matthew and St. Mark of the cure of the woman with an issue of blood will throw considerable light on the principles for which we are contending. Matthew (ix.) writes:—

"And, behold, a woman, which was diseased with an issue of blood twelve years, came behind Him, and touched the hem of His garment: for she said within herself, If I may but touch His garment, I shall be whole. But Jesus turned Him about, and when He saw her, He said, Daughter, be of good comfort; thy faith hath made thee whole. And the woman was made whole from that hour." Mark, v. :—" And Jesus went with him; and much people followed Him, and thronged Him. And a certain woman, which had an issue of blood twelve years, and had suffered many things of many physicians, and had spent all that she had, and was nothing bettered, but rather grew worse, when she had heard of Jesus, came in the press behind, and touched His garment. For she said, If I may touch but His clothes, I shall be whole. And straightway the fountain of her blood was dried up; and she felt in her body that she was healed of that plague. And

Jesus, immediately knowing in Himself that virtue had gone out of Him, turned Him about in the press, and said, Who touched my clothes? And His disciples said unto Him, Thou seest the multitude thronging Thee, and sayest Thou, Who touched me? And He looked round about to see her that had done this thing. But the woman fearing and trembling, knowing what was done in her, came and fell down before Him, and told Him all the truth. And He said unto her, Daughter, thy faith hath made thee whole; go in peace, and be whole of thy plague."

We do not give St. Luke's account; for the only additional fact mentioned by him is, that the person who almost expostulated with our Lord was Peter.

Now the narrative of St. Matthew is a bare account of the facts, and not of the entire facts. His object seems to have been simply to record the reality of the miracle. He has done so with a brevity which would have left us entirely in the dark as to the character of the woman's faith. We should have had no idea from him that the faith was imperfect, that our Lord compelled the woman to make confession of the cure, or that the blessing was not pronounced on her till after she was compelled publicly to declare the reality of the great work wrought in her. St. Matthew's narrative contains no mark of descriptive power, and no evident trace of the presence of an eye-witness. But how is all this altered when we read the description of St. Mark! From him we learn that the woman tried to obtain the cure secretly. He informs us that she made an attempt to evade the observation of our Lord, and that our Lord forced her to confess the fact. From him we learn that the woman's faith was imperfect, and that she evidently thought that some secret power resided in our Lord's clothes; and that she was not dismissed with our Lord's blessing until she had been subjected to His rebuke.

How graphic is St. Mark's description! how strongly do we discover the presence of an eye-witness to the transaction! The people thronged our Lord on the occasion. The woman had spent her all on physicians, in attempting to get cured. How did the evangelist know this? She was forced to make full confession of the facts of her case. She had got no better, but worse, under the physicians' treatment. Her secret thoughts are described. The miracle takes place *immediately*; she has an inward feeling of its reality. Our Lord recognizes the reality of the miracle *instantly*. He *turns Him about*, and inquires, " Who touched me ? " The disciples expostulate. *He follows the woman with His eye. The woman falls before Him, with fear and trembling*, and confesses everything. Then the blessing is pronounced.

Now these different phenomena in the two narratives must have some cause. In an ordinary narrative we should at once assume that the writer of St. Mark's Gospel had a greater degree of graphic power of description, and possessed access to ocular testimony to a greater extent, than the writer of St. Matthew's Gospel. At any rate, the phenomena in question are inconsistent with the assumption that both narratives were dictated by the same person. Difference of authorship is the conclusion which the human mind forms from this remarkable difference of phenomena.

But this narrative also affords us a remarkable instance of the mode in which human language and conceptions are used by writers under the influence of inspiration, nay, even by our Lord himself. We have already observed that " it follows from the fact that the Creator never works by a double instrumentality, that an inspired writer, if he has occasion to mention matters connected with scientific truth, may use popular language and popular conceptions on such subjects, even when they involve an incorrect scientific theory." The expression used by the Evangelist, and asserted by St. Luke to have been also used by our Lord, is a very remarkable example of this mode of speaking. Our version has made the difference between the literal meaning of the words and scientific truth greater, by rendering the word $\delta \upsilon \nu a\mu\iota\varsigma$ in this solitary case "virtue," instead of " power" as it has correctly done in the very numerous other passages where it occurs. The woman was not cured by an unconscious virtue residing in our Lord's clothes, but by the direct and conscious energy of the power of His divine nature. The power which effected the cure was the same power as that by which He has created and still upholds the universe—a power the result of the spontaneous energy of His will. But the literal meaning of the words used to express this imply a particular theory as to the mode in which that power was exerted: "I perceive that power has gone out of me." It was surely no purpose of our Lord to teach the mode in which the infinite power of the Almighty is exerted. The mode in which the Creator energizes, either in the creation of a world or in the cure of a disease, is quite beyond the reach of finite conceptions. What our Lord meant to assert was, that He himself was the sole and only source of the cure, that He knew that the cure had been effected, and that the attempt of the woman to escape His observation was useless. In expressing this, He adopted the mode of conception of those by whom He was surrounded. They thought that power issued from His person. It was no part of His mission to teach that power is not a force or kind of abstract essence issuing from its possessor, but is the result of the energy of his being. The language used may have been scientifically incorrect, but infinitely better for our Lord's purpose than words involving the highest degree of scientific exactness, which, if they had been used, would have involved an amount of explanation, to render them comprehensible to the multitude, which must wholly have withdrawn their attention, and that of the woman, from the truths which our Lord was enforcing. In the same way our Lord did not ask the question, "Who touched me?" from ignorance of the person who had done so, but to draw attention to the fact that a great miracle had been wrought in proof of His divine mission.

The history of the cure of the demoniac child, as given by St. Matthew and St. Mark, is equally inconsistent with a belief that both narratives were written under the influence of verbal inspiration. In St. Matthew (chap. xvii.) we read:—

"And when they were come to the multitude, there came to Him a certain man, kneeling down to Him, and saying, Lord, have mercy on my son: for he is lunatick, and sore vexed: for ofttimes he falleth into the fire, and oft into the water. And I brought him to Thy disciples, and they could not cure him. Then Jesus answered and said, O faithless and perverse generation, how long shall I be with you? how long shall I suffer you? bring him hither to me. And Jesus rebuked the devil; and he departed out of him: and the child was cured from that very hour."

But St. Mark's account of the same event (in chap. ix.) is: "And when He came to His disciples, He saw a great multitude about them, and the scribes questioning with them. And straightway all the people, when they beheld Him, were greatly amazed, and running to Him saluted Him. And He asked the scribes, What question ye with them? And one of the multitude answered and said, Master, I have brought unto Thee my son, which hath a dumb spirit; and wheresoever he taketh him, he teareth him: and he foameth, and gnasheth with his teeth, and pineth away: and I spake to Thy disciples that they should cast him out, and they could not. He answereth him, and saith, O faithless generation, how long shall I be with you? how long shall I suffer you? bring him unto me. And they brought him unto Him: and when He saw him, straightway the spirit tare him; and he fell on the ground, and wallowed foaming. And He asked his father, How long is it ago since this came unto him? And he said, Of a child. And ofttimes it hath cast him into the fire, and into the waters, to destroy him: but if Thou canst do anything, have compassion on us, and help us. Jesus said unto him, If thou canst believe, all things are possible to him that believeth. And straightway the father of the child cried out, and said with tears, Lord, I believe; help thou mine unbelief. When Jesus saw that the people came running together, He rebuked the foul spirit, saying unto him, Thou dumb and deaf spirit, I charge thee, come out of him, and enter no more into him. And the spirit cried, and rent him sore, and came out of him: and he was as one dead; insomuch that many said, He is dead. But Jesus took him by the hand, and lifted him up; and he arose."

St. Luke's narrative presents no special features beyond that of St. Mark.

The whole of this description by St. Mark is a most graphic painting: it contains about it a terrible reality, which none but an eye-witness could have drawn. Its power does not consist merely in its detached parts, but in its continuous whole. We have the terrible convulsions of the child, the despair of the father, and the calmness of our Lord, represented before our eyes with a vivid reality almost reaching the sublime. Every word of St. Mark is instinct with life. The whole representation impresses the mind of the reader with the idea that the narrator had contemplated the scene which he is describing with wonder and with awe. The description, after the unclean spirit has resigned his prey, is drawn from the very life. No words can do justice to the power of the narrative. St. Matthew's account, on the other hand, is a description of the same facts, with only one graphic touch—that the parent of the child came to our Lord kneeling. With this exception, the painting and the scenery is all wanting. There are no fierce convulsions, no father's struggle, no running multitude, no child extended on the ground as dead. We have the fact of the miracle adduced as proof that Jesus was the Messiah, and little beside the fact.

Now, if to every effect there is a cause, a reason must exist for this remarkable difference between the two Evangelists. To what are we to attribute it? If we assert that both narratives were dictated, as they now stand, by the same Author, will that supposition account for the difference of the manner in which the story is narrated? It may be said that it did not form part of St. Matthew's plan, and did form a portion of St. Mark's plan, to give this graphic narrative. But this leaves the difference in great measure unaccounted for; and what it does account for, it assigns to a human origin. If we had no theory to maintain, we should have no difficulty in assigning, as the ground of the distinction, the possession by St. Mark of more graphic powers of description and of better sources of ocular information than those possessed by St. Matthew.

But although St. Mark's narratives usually possess this

superior graphic character, compared with those of St. Matthew, we have an exception in the history of the Syrophenician woman.

St. Matthew, xv. : "Then Jesus went thence, and departed into the coasts of Tyre and Sidon. And, behold, a woman of Canaan came out of the same coasts, and cried unto him, saying, Have mercy on me, O Lord, thou son of David; my daughter is grievously vexed with a devil. But He answered her not a word. And His disciples came and besought Him, saying, Send her away; for she crieth after us. But He answered and said, I am not sent but unto the lost sheep of the house of Israel. Then came she and worshipped Him, saying, Lord, help me. But He answered and said, It is not meet to take the children's bread, and to cast it to dogs. And she said, Truth, Lord: yet the dogs eat of the crumbs which fall from their masters' table. Then Jesus answered and said unto her, O woman, great is thy faith: be it unto thee even as thou wilt. And her daughter was made whole from that very hour."

St. Mark, vii. : "And from thence He arose, and went into the borders of Tyre and Sidon, and entered into an house, and would have no man know it: but He could not be hid. For a certain woman, whose young daughter had an unclean spirit, heard of Him, and came and fell at His feet: the woman was a Greek, a Syrophenician by nation; and she besought Him that He would cast forth the devil out of her daughter. But Jesus said unto her, Let the children first be filled: for it is not meet to take the children's bread, and to cast it unto the dogs. And she answered and said unto Him, Yes, Lord: yet the dogs under the table eat of the children's crumbs. And He said unto her, For this saying go thy way; the devil is gone out of thy daughter. And when she was come to her house, she found the devil gone out, and her daughter laid upon the bed."

Now neither of these accounts is in itself complete. St. Matthew's account implies that the whole transaction took place in public. The disciples say, "Send her away; for she crieth after us." St. Mark's narrative no less distinctly implies that the whole took place within the walls of a house. Some portion of the events mentioned must have taken place within the house; but the fair reading of each narrative, separately, implies that the whole of the transaction took place either inside or outside the house, and not part inside and part outside. St. Mark also furnishes us with full particulars respecting the woman's origin, and states the additional fact that her daughter was young. From him also we learn that our Lord uttered the words, "Let the children first be filled;" and he also gives us the additional fact, that, after the performance of the miracle, the woman found the child, on her return, reclining on a bed.

But, in all the other circumstances, the narrative of St. Matthew is far richer, especially in depicting the greatness of the woman's humility and faith. "She besought Him that He would cast forth the devil out of her daughter," is the representative in St. Mark for St. Matthew's more graphic description—"She cried unto Him, saying, Have mercy on me, O Lord, thou son of David; my daughter is grievously vexed with a devil." But for St. Matthew, we should have missed the fact altogether, that the Gentile woman actually recognized our Lord as the Messiah. The intercession of the disciples is, by St. Mark, entirely omitted. So also St. Mark omits the particularly affecting incident, that when our Lord answered the disciples that He was not sent but unto the lost sheep of the house of Israel, she came and worshipped Him, saying, "Lord, help me." This is a sort of circumstance which, judging from his usual style, we should certainly have expected St. Mark to have mentioned, if he had been aware of it. The final commendation of the woman's faith, and its glorious triumph, is represented by St. Mark in the expression, "For this saying go thy way; the devil is gone out of thy daughter;" but by St. Matthew, "O woman, great is thy faith: be it unto thee even as thou wilt." St. Mark's report is here evidently the shadow of St. Matthew's great reality.

Now what does the careful examination of these two passages suggest? Obviously, that St. Mark possessed a few peculiar circumstances which St. Matthew had not; but who would hesitate in arriving at the conclusion that the account in Matthew is the actual dialogue which took place between our Lord and the woman, of which St. Mark's report is the imperfect outline or almost the echo? The facts are before us; and whatever account we may give of the origin of these facts, as they are respectively depicted by St. Matthew and St. Mark, they never would suggest to any reader that each separate account was dictated in the form in which it now stands to each evangelist by the Spirit, and that all which the evangelists have had to do with the report was to copy down the words so dictated to them. If we take the parallel narratives which we have examined, and observe the undeniably different phenomena which these narratives present in the pages of St. Matthew and St. Mark, and then assume that the same Author dictated both, and assert that to doubt this is inconsistent with the belief that the New Testament was given by Divine inspiration, we assume a position destructive of all certainty, and which is the high road to unbelief.

In the records of the last week of our Lord's ministry, we find several minor discrepancies in the evangelical narratives, as, for example, whether our Lord cleared the Temple on the day on which He entered Jerusalem in triumph, or whether the Apostles observed the withering of the barren fig tree immediately on its being cursed or on the next day. The expedient of supposing that our Lord cleared the Temple on two successive days, and that the same circumstances recurred on each occasion, or that the Apostles noticed the withering of the fig tree immediately after it was cursed and on the following morning, and that our Lord, on each occasion, repeated the very same observations to them, is most unsatisfactory. Small disagreements like these are what almost always exist when honest independent witnesses give their testimony to the events of daily life. If we refuse to believe testimony till all such minor variations are removed or accounted for, the range of fact over which our belief will extend will be contained within very narrow limits.

But it must not be overlooked, that the existence of such variations proves that the testimony is human testimony. As the descrepancies which occur in the Evangelists do not in the smallest degree affect one point of Christian truth, there was no necessity that the memories of the writers of the Gospels should, on such subjects, be refreshed by the aid of supernatural influences. Had such supernatural assistance been afforded to the Evangelists in every inconsiderable matter, the Gospels would not present the appearance which they actually do, and which it was intended that they should present, of being the recorded testimony of actual human witnesses of facts.

But the state of the Gospel narratives is only consistent with one of two assumptions respecting the manner in which they have been composed: they are either the works of witnesses delivering a human testimony, and narrating the facts in their own peculiar style, aided by supernatural assistance afforded to their memories when such assistance was required for the purposes of Divine revelation; or those phenomena, on the strength of which, in any ordinary history, we should arrive at such a conclusion, are imitations of such peculiarities of human testimony and human style by the inspiring Spirit of God. This latter alternative few will be prepared to adopt.

We must now notice one passage in St. Matthew's Gospel which can only be accounted for in accordance with the preceding views. It is well known that, in St. Matthew's genealogy of our Lord, it is stated, Joram begat Uzziah. In this place of the genealogy, the names of three kings are passed over in silence. The Book of Kings distinctly asserts that Joram begat Ahaziah, and Ahaziah begat Joash, and Joash begat Amaziah, and Amaziah begat Uzziah. Now various attempts have been made to explain this omission; but with them we are not concerned: we are only concerned with the omission. St. Matthew's Gospel adds, "So all the generations from Abraham to David are fourteen generations; and from David until the carrying away into Babylon are fourteen generations; and from the carrying away into Babylon unto Christ are fourteen generations."

Now, whether the Evangelist composed this genealogy for himself, or whether he derived it from Jewish sources, may admit of question; but there can be no doubt that the passage last cited is the composition of the Evangelist. This is proved by his mentioning the words, "from the carrying away into Babylon unto Christ;" for the word Christ would appear in no Jewish register. The three periods of fourteen generations can only be made up by omitting the three kings in question from the genealogy; and even then it is not easy to effect it. Now it has been given as a reason for the omission, and for St. Matthew's summing up the genealogy in three sets of fourteen generations, that the Jews delighted in round numbers. This may probably be the solution; but then it distinctly asserts the presence of a human element and human considerations in the composition of the genealogy and in Matthew's subsequent summary. The statement, then, that the number of the generations between Abraham and Christ consisted of three sets of fourteen generations, and that the first name in each of these orders of fourteen generations was coincident with three very remarkable periods of Jewish history, can only be made out by the omission of three names which the Book of Kings asserts to belong to the list. We wish to ask the supporters of the theory of verbal inspiration how they account for the statement of St. Matthew that there were fourteen generations between David and the captivity, when the narrative of the Book of Kings makes it plain that there were at least seventeen? or the supporters of any kindred theory, whether they consider that the statement was communicated to St. Matthew by direct inspiration, or whether it did not owe its origin to a partiality which the Evangelist entertained, in common with his countrymen, for round numbers?

CHAPTER XV.
THE SILENCES OF THE GOSPELS PROOFS OF THEIR INSPIRATION.

But the Gospels are not only remarkable for what they have narrated, but also for what they have omitted to relate. The silences of the Gospels have the most important bearing on the question of the nature of their inspiration. These silences are of a most remarkable character. It would be impossible to select any four biographies which contain similar omissions to those presented by our Evangelists. It is evident that there must have been a vast multitude of facts connected with our Lord's life and ministry, well known to His early followers, all mention of which is entirely omitted in the Gospels. St. John informs us, that "many other signs truly did Jesus in the presence of His disciples, which are not written in this book; but these are written that ye may believe that Jesus is the Christ, the Son of God, and that, believing, ye may have life through His name." Here the principle of selection is not only affirmed, but the ground on which the selection was made is recorded. The purpose which St. John states that he had in view was to afford Christians sufficient reason for believing "that Jesus was the Christ; and that, by believing, they might have life through His name." This passage, however, only refers to the signs which Jesus did. The concluding verse of the Gospel asserts the existence of a very extensive mass of materials: "And there are also many other things which Jesus did, the which, if they should be written every one, I suppose that even the world itself could not contain the books that should be written."

This last assertion is, of course, an hyperbole of no ordinary character. We leave the discussion of such hyperboles to those who maintain that the Christian Scriptures are dictated by verbal inspiration. An hyperbole can hardly be referred to the Spirit of God, but must owe its origin to a human element existing in the writer's mind. The writer of the Gospel did not mean to assert that the world could not contain the books which would be written, but to affirm the extent of the materials out of which the actual selection had been made. The principle of selection is here expressly affirmed, not only with respect to the miracles, but with respect to the general facts of the Gospel history. The writer affirms that he knew much more than he has actually told—a truth which the contents of the Gospels render evident.

Now how were the Apostles guided in making this selection? We cannot well over-estimate the importance of the selection being made rightly. It was necessary that the Gospels should contain such a view of our Lord's character, His teaching, and His actions as would convey to their readers those great truths which the Incarnation was intended to reveal. It is impossible, therefore, to over-estimate the importance of the silences of the Gospels. Had the record contained either too much or too little, our knowledge of the manifestation of the Godhead would have been imperfect.

Unless, therefore, the Apostles had some guidance as to what things connected with our Lord's actions, His ministry, and person they should record, and what portion they should omit, Christianity would not have conveyed the truths of a divine revelation as it was intended that they should be imparted to man. The fact that a selection has been made presupposes the possibility that important things, which our Lord did or said, may not have been handed down to us. It was necessary, therefore, that the sayings and actions reported should be such as would convey a fair idea of the whole, at least as far as it was the Divine purpose that subsequent ages should be acquainted with them. If the existing records therefore, have failed to give us a fair sample of the life, actions, sayings, and sufferings of our Lord, Christianity has in a proportionate degree failed as a divine revelation.

Were, then, the human judgments of the Apostles adequate to enable them to make such a selection? What hindered them from recording things which were not necessary, or omitting things which were? The extent of the matter which they have omitted is evidently very large, and some of the subjects on which they have left us in complete darkness are of the profoundest human interest. We know, from their own testimony, that our Lord's sayings and actions were most imperfectly apprehended by them before His resurrection. At that time, therefore, their ordinary human judgments would have been inadequate guides to enable them to select those actions and sayings of our Lord which required to be recorded, and to omit those things which ought not to have been recorded, to give us a right knowledge of the Christian revelation. The only way in which their judgments could have become trustworthy in matters of such importance would have been by the fulfilment of their Master's promise, that the Spirit should "guide them into all the truth."

Now it is quite evident that a great number of circumstances, which all ordinary human writers would have recorded, have been wholly omitted by the authors of the Gospels; and that the knowledge of a great number of facts, which men ardently crave to know, must have been within the reach of the Apostles and their followers, if they had taken the trouble to ascertain them. The omission cannot be accounted for on the ground of ignorance. The number of anecdotes with which our Lord's brethren must have been acquainted, respecting the first thirty years of His life, must have been very large; why, then, have none of these anecdotes been recorded, if the writers of the Gospels composed their narratives with the feelings of ordinary human historians?

The silences of the Gospels are as remarkable as their utterances. In their silences they differ from every other human writer who has composed a biography. Precisely those very portions of our Lord's life which every other human writer has never failed to record, when the materials were within his reach, are left by them unrecorded. Could they have been ignorant of them? They have not pleaded ignorance as the reason of their omissions. Were, then, the Evangelists not men of ordinary human feelings or ordinary human curiosity? Had the subjects which they have passed over in silence no interest in their breasts, as they have to those of other men? Their writings give us the most distinct proof that they were men of similar feelings, ideas, and conceptions as ourselves. Yet on many subjects, on which they must have felt the profoundest interest, they preserve a silence absolutely unbroken.

How is this silence to be accounted for? The person from whom many narratives in St. Mark's Gospel were derived must have felt the deepest interest in numbers of anecdotes respecting our Lord's history, the knowledge of which he could easily have obtained, and which he, with his graphic power, would have felt the deepest interest in depicting. Whence this silence? Why has a writer omitted to report the very things in which his genius must have particularly delighted? Why has he omitted to report the very things which all men wish to know? The fact suggests the theory: if the Evangelists have not recorded things which all other men similarly situated would have recorded, they must have been hindered from doing so by a preternatural influence exerted on their minds. On some subjects their silence is most surprising, and, one might say, to ordinary human curiosity most provoking. In every subsequent age of the Church, the profoundest intellects have been busy in their speculations, and occupied themselves with incessant attempts to dissipate the profundity of the gloom. We shall notice a few instances of their silence, in which they have followed a course which no other human author has ever pursued.

The Evangelists have not given us one single description, no, not even the smallest delineation, of the outlines of our Lord's person. Respecting our Lord's countenance, form, or the expression of His face, not one word has escaped from the pen of either of them. This is the more remarkable because, from the second century downwards, perhaps not a year has passed in which attempts have not been made to delineate His supposed features. This, at any rate, demonstrates how congenial it is to the feelings of the human heart to attempt to perpetuate them. Christendom is full of such supposed likenesses; but the painter is forced to draw upon the resources of his own imagination, and utterly fails to find a solitary outline in the pages of the Evangelists to direct him. The interest which the human mind would have felt in some sketch of his personal appearance is of the profoundest description: the temple of incarnate Deity was there. Was not the impression of our Lord's face one full of divine and heavenly dignity? or did not that divine form make any impression on the cold hearts of the Apostles? When He was removed from their bodily eyes, had they no endearing recollections of the mild love which must have beamed forth from that heavenly countenance? They were not men of hard or stern insensibility, for they have occasionally distinctly alluded to our Lord's glances. "The Lord turned and looked upon Peter." "He looked round about to see her that had done this thing." "Jesus, beholding him, loved him." "He looked round about Him with indignation, being grieved at the hardness of their hearts." The persons who have handed down these touches could not have been insensible to our Lord's human glances. The beloved disciple describes His person as He appeared to him in awful majesty, the King of kings, and Lord of lords; but he, who reclined on his Master's breast at supper, has not one solitary hint to give us of his recollections of His human person. Had the beloved disciple, had the warm-hearted Peter, no fond recollections of the human countenance of their departed Lord? How do the natural affections of the heart prompt us to desire to know the expression of the face of Him who wept at the sorrows of the family at Bethany, and who yet denounced the Pharisees! Has ever human biographer, who intimately knew the features and deeply loved the character of the subject of his biography, wholly denied to others all knowledge of that form which he loved and reverenced, and which moved every affection of his heart? But the writers of the Gospels have not given us the smallest hint of the personal appearance of Him whom they must have viewed as incarnate God. Wherefore? We answer, because such a delineation of the features of His human countenance formed

U

no portion of the revelation of God to man. Though they knew Christ after the flesh, yet when they wrote their Gospels they knew Him as such no more. Would that subsequent ages of the Church had deeply meditated on this most impressive silence of the Evangelists!

With one solitary exception, the writers of the Gospels have not given a single anecdote respecting the boyhood or the youth of their divine Master. The deep interest felt by mankind in anecdotes of this description is a fact respecting which no doubt can be entertained. The writers of the spurious Gospels have borne witness to this interest by the number of grotesque stories of this description of which the narratives of some of them are chiefly composed. But the visit to the passover, at twelve years of age, forms the whole which the Evangelists have let us know of the first thirty years of our Lord's life. Did they know nothing more? Had Mary, with whom they certainly held communication, who actually abode with one of them from the time when her dying Son commended her to His beloved disciple's care, nothing to narrate as to the wonders of His boyhood, His growth in knowledge, the heavenliness of His temper, or the dutiful obedience which she had experienced at His hands? Had His brethren or His sisters no anecdotes to narrate respecting His conversation, His mode of life, how He spent His time, or how He associated with others of the same age? Did not He, who was incarnate Deity, differ from other children? The solitary anecdote recorded informs us that He did. How did He spend His youth? How did He spend His early manhood? How much time in each day was devoted to communion with His Father? Was He not present at the bed of the dying Joseph? Did He maintain His mother by His labours? How did He associate with His mother's friends? What impression did His perfect manhood, unsullied by one single imperfection, make on those whom He met in the daily intercourse of life? Had such questions no interest for the Evangelists, as they have for us? Could they live with those who could have answered them, and never put them? Let each reader ask his own heart what he certainly would have done. Did John never make one such inquiry of Mary, while she abode under the shadow of his roof? Did St. Luke, who has furnished the one solitary anecdote, neither inquire into or care for further information? Notwithstanding the undying human interest which such narratives would have possessed, with this solitary exception, the silence of the writers of the Gospels is as unbroken as the grave. What human historian has not given us some anecdote of his hero in boyhood, or early youth, or ripening manhood? Had some words of our Lord's early wisdom been recorded, they would have possessed the profoundest interest. How we should have wished to have been able to trace the youth and development of our Lord's human mind throughout every stage! How edifying should we have thought even a brief description of some of our Lord's gracious deeds! One ray of light only penetrates the thick darkness in which the whole is enveloped. Shall not these things be revealed for our edification? Will Mary continue obstinately mute? Such things, though they have the profoundest human interest, yet form no portion of the revelation of God to man. One anecdote is recorded—one, to show us that the minds of the Evangelists have not, through indifference, omitted to record more; but one only, to teach us that, however deeply such narratives strike cords in the human bosom, they have nothing to do with the great purpose of the Christian revelation—the giving men life through His name.

But there are several other points on which the determination of the writers of the Gospels not to gratify ordinary curiosity, or to enter into points of curious speculation, is most remarkable, and, on ordinary human principles, most unaccountable. There were persons whom they have designated brethren and sisters of our Lord. Who these were, and the precise degree of their relationship, has been the subject of the fiercest controversy; and matters of profound Christian truth have been considered to be involved in the solution of the problem. But the Evangelists decline to give us positive information. The language used by them favours the opinion that they were the actual children of Joseph and

Mary. It is not absolutely inconsistent with the supposition that they were our Lord's cousins. Learned doctors have written libraries to prove the perpetual virginity of Mary. One sentence of the Evangelist would have saved the weary labour. What the Evangelists will not determine, or what they pass over in silence, can involve no mysterious truth of divine revelation.

St. John narrates the miracle of the resurrection of Lazarus: it proves that Jesus was the Christ. The history implies that Lazarus lived a considerable period after his resurrection. The Apostles must certainly have conversed with a man who had been brought again from the unseen world. Did none of them ask him what dying actually was, or what were the feelings which burst on his mind on his issuing from the body in the world of spirits? Did they not inquire, or could he not tell them, anything about the condition of a disembodied soul? A few words from him, on these or similar subjects, might have saved volumes of metaphysical speculation. Men could hardly converse with one who had been brought again from the dark chambers of the unseen world, without asking him something about its unknown scenes. What were his employments there? What was the condition of a disembodied spirit while waiting for the resurrection? Did he know anything which was passing on earth? Had he possession of full consciousness while he was separate from the body? What is the difference between Hades and heaven? What was the precise nature of the unseen world? What were the employments of a glorified spirit? A few words from him on such subjects would have been more valuable than whole libraries of so-called Christian speculation. We cannot tell whether Lazarus could have answered such questions; but if St. John had even told us whether he was or was not able to solve such points, he would have added greatly to the certainty of our knowledge on many subjects of the most curious speculation respecting the spiritual world. But St. John not only gives us no information on these most interesting subjects; he even refuses to inform us whether Lazarus could or could not answer them. Human curiosity has been busying itself ever since with vain attempts to penetrate the darkness which St. John refuses to dispel. If the tomes of speculation and reasoning on points on which the Gospels are determinately silent could be obliterated, the science of theology might be reduced within reasonable limits.

If we read a large number of religious books, we shall be generally guided to the most impressive silences of the Evangelists by observing the places where those writers are most diffusive. Many examples will occur in the history of our Lord's passion. Deep religious mysteries have been elaborated from hints, or less than hints, of the Evangelists. Who would not wish he knew more about the real nature of our Lord's agony in the garden? There is no subject in Christian theology with which speculation has been more busy. What was the precise cause and extent of His sufferings there? Did He there endure the sins of the whole world? Did His human soul suffer the entire hiding of the light of His Father's countenance? Why the need of the strengthening angel? What was the precise cause of His bitter cry on the cross? and what the nature of His desertion by His Father which it implied? What was the amount of suffering necessary for making the atonement? Could not the Evangelists and Apostles have solved some of these questions? or were they without interest to their insatiate hearts? Christian divines have determined what Evangelists and Apostles have veiled in silence. The Evangelical narratives tell us of our Lord's agony; they furnish us with the prayer used by our Lord; they describe His rejection, His mocking, His scourging, His death; they give us the exclamations which He uttered on the cross. The Apostles, in their comments on these divine facts, tell us that they were the means by which man was reconciled to God; but they tell us no more. They have left to more adventurous speculators to rend asunder the veil which hides from our view the profound mysteries of God, which they themselves have only dared slightly and reverently to raise.

Apostles keep silence on subjects of the deepest interest to the human heart: what is the cause of this? Attempts have been made in every direction to supply that information which Apostles and Evangelists refuse to give. Nor has Christian speculation been less active on points of minor importance. Our Lord spent forty days on earth after His resurrection; where was He during the intervals of His appearances to the Apostles? The Apostles handled His raised body; why have they not told us the difference, in its physical condition, between it and the body which was crucified? Saints left their graves on the morning of the resurrection; who were they? Some have guessed their names. What was the precise cause of our Lord's death?—was it from a broken heart? Profound mysteries have been elaborated from the assumption that it was so. These and kindred truths the mind of man intensely wishes to know. Many think that they can disclose to open day the dark truths which Evangelists and Apostles have veiled in silence. They can tell that it required an infinite suffering to redeem a human soul. Matthew, Mark, Luke, and John refuse, by one word of explanation, to cast one ray of light to dispel the gloom; nor do the writers of apostolic Epistles, by one direct assertion, disclose the secrets of the unseen. Wherefore, then, this silence on subjects of the profoundest interest to the human bosom? Not because the Evangelists or Apostles were cold to the feelings which animate the human heart, but because they knew, by the influence of the restraining Spirit, that the subjects on which they must have been deliberately silent formed no portion of the revelation of God to man.

We might notice many other silences in the Gospels and the Epistles; but we have stated enough to point out the great outlines of the subject. With respect to the latter, we shall only observe that the great Apostle who learned Christian truth, not from man, but by revelation from Jesus Christ, has scarcely dared to uplift the veil from mysteries which his more adventurous disciples have rudely torn for the purpose of throwing open the heavenly temple to human gaze. They possess a line to sound the depths of infinity, which the line even of an Apostle is unable to fathom. The silences of the sacred writers read most solemn lessons both to theologians and unbelievers: they warn the one not attempt to pry into truths on which Apostles and Evangelists, with the fullest information, have deliberately been silent; they ask the other to consider whether these silences can be accounted for on the supposition of the purely human origin of the Gospels.

The silences which we have noticed are of such a nature that it is absolutely impossible that writers with ample information at their hands, and at the same time animated with the feelings of our common nature, could have preserved, had they not been restrained by an influence from above. Is it in man, if animated by devout love, after conversing with Him for three years, to have been silent about our Lord's person? Could those who associated with Him—who were familiar with the mild radiance of His character, who must have caught glimpses of the rays of incarnate Deity dwelling in His person, who beheld Him expire on the cross, who afterwards believed that He was seated on the throne of God—have habitually associated with those among whom He must have passed His youth and early manhood, and only put to them one solitary question as to the events of the first thirty years of His life? Could any human being live for a day with one whom he believed to have returned from the unseen world, and not ask Him a single question on the nature of that world which is declared to be man's long home? Every feeling of the human heart denies the possibility. Man has been endeavouring to get information on these subjects ever since, with the deepest earnestness. Where certain knowledge has been refused him by Apostles and Evangelists, he has, by the feeble light of conjecture, laboured to dispel the gloom.

With respect to these silences of the Gospels there are but two alternatives; either the writers have been hindered from breaking them by a supernatural influence exerted on their minds, or the facts are not real. If the facts are not real, they must have been invented by the Evangelists themselves; or if the Evangelists honestly composed their histories, the original facts must have been added to and embellished by our Lord's early followers.

A modern writer * has embraced the latter of these alternatives. He informs us that large portions of the Gospels are legendary. It is difficult, after reading his pages, to arrive at any definite opinion as to what portion of them he would eliminate as mythic, and what portion of them he considers to have been actually set forth by the persons whose names they bear. One can hardly see any principle adopted by him, but the exercise of his " verifying faculty" or, to speak plainly, the pleasure of his sovereign will. The principle adopted seems to be a very simple one—" Whatever suits my previous conceptions I will adopt; whatever contravenes them I will reject." But a large legendary element is directly asserted. We readily adopt the alternative which this writer presents us with. Either the contents of the Gospels are the veritable facts, or they have received a colouring from the inventive power of the writers whose names they bear, or they are legendary. If the facts are true facts, if Matthew, Mark, and John actually witnessed the actions of our Lord's life, or if they drew their reports from those who had, whence these silences? If they have invented (and E. Renan has not been slow to accuse the latter of invention on a large scale), we again ask, whence these silences? If their accounts are legendary, we emphatically demand whence these silences? The Gospels exist: the silences must be accounted for. If fiction has had much to do with developing the original story into the form in which we read it in our present Gospels, it matters little who is the author of the fiction. True witnesses, actuated by simple human feelings, must have broken the silences. Inventors of fiction or myth, or by whatever name we choose to designate it, when they invented the facts, would certainly have had ample information to communicate on the subjects of the silences. Fiction, or legend, or poetic creation might easily have depicted our Lord's human features, or given us myriads of anecdotes of His boyhood and youth. Have not the painters been at work on His features ever since? Would not the same powerful tendencies in human

* See Renan, ' Vie de Jésus,' Introduction.

nature, which would have compelled witnesses to break these silences, have impelled inventors to supply their deficiencies of knowledge by the imagination? Are they not the precise points on which fiction loves to dwell? Does not all existing literature testify to the fact, that the authors of legendary biographies abound in narratives of this description? Is the writer of a fiction or a novel ever at a loss to paint the person of his hero? Fiction is fuller of such descriptions than reality *. We summon Renan himself to bear witness that, wherever facts are wanting, the aid of the inventive faculty is all-powerful to supply them. Let no writer of biographies be daunted; if our records do not contain the facts, there is a superior verity—the height of an idea! It will supply the biographer with all which he can require. If, then, these silences could not have been maintained by actual witnesses, if they would certainly have been broken by writers of fiction and of legend,—as those concerned in the composition of the Gospels, whether setters forth of truth or of fiction, have left those silences utterly unbroken,—it follows that their existence can only be accounted for by the agency of the inspiring Spirit restraining the minds of the Evangelists from recording what was not intended to form a portion of the Christian revelation. We have already learned from the history that a similar restraining influence was exerted, when necessary, over the Apostles in their travels.

* The following passage from Renan's Introduction, p. xlviii, is a curious exemplification of his ideas of historical veracity :—" Les détails ne sont pas vrais à la lettre ; mais ils sont vrais d'une vérité supérieure ; ils sont plus vrais que la nue vérité, en ce sens qu'ils sont la vérité rendue expressive et parlante, élevée à la hauteur d'une idée."

CHAPTER XVI.

THE VIEW WHICH THE FACTS OF THE GOSPELS WOULD SUGGEST TO A CAREFUL READER, WHO HAD NOT PREVIOUSLY PERUSED THEM, RESPECTING THEIR ORIGIN AND THE MODE OF THEIR INSPIRATION.

LET us suppose the Gospels to be put into the hands of a reader who had never previously perused them, and what is commonly called the mythic theory, or some kindred theory, suggested to him as giving an account of the probable origin of their contents. Would the leading phenomena, as he reads them in the Gospels, allow him to arrive at the conclusion that that theory afforded a probable account of their origin?

By the term mythic theory we intend not only the theory which views the entire contents of our Gospels as mythic, but any of its numerous and possible modifications. We will suppose that the Evangelists themselves invented the myths, or, being themselves perfectly honest, that they have simply reported such as were current in the Church, or modified them in conformity with their own views. We will suppose that these myths may contain a considerable admixture of truth, but that in course of time the original facts have become encrusted with mythic additions now difficult of disentanglement; that the additions have grown by passing from hand to hand, or have been deliberately introduced by the Evangelists, or by those who have modified the original narratives; that the original Jesus of the Gospels made no miraculous pretensions, or at least not till He was impelled into them by others; that whatever remains of His original teaching is to be found in the synoptic Gospels, and that the Gospel of St. John is the superaddition of a later age and a different order of thought. But the number of the different modifications of the mythic theory is legion; we may therefore be excused from enumerating more of them.

Such a reader would observe that the Gospels contain one feature in common with mythic stories—a miraculous narrative; but he would also observe that the miracles of the

Gospel differ in their entire complexion from every other miraculous narrative in existence. Taking the circumstances of the case into account, if the Gospel narrative is what it professes to be, there is not a single miracle ascribed to our Lord inconsistent with probability. The miracles are all sober, grave, dignified, and have not the smallest appearance of being after-thoughts superadded to the facts. But myths are simple creations of the popular mind; they grow out of and harmonize with its tastes; they are the mere reflexions of its ideas and its feelings. If the miracles of the Gospel are myths, they must be exact representations of the popular taste when those myths were invented. There never was a state of the human mind of which the Gospel miracles are the popular embodiment. Let every existing myth be summoned to give its evidence. What testifies the whole mass of Oriental fable, from China to Arabia? What is witnessed by Greek and Roman mythology? What testimony is borne by Scandinavian legends? What says the whole mass of mediæval miracle and superstition, which even had the benefit of the Gospel miracles on which to model its stories? The answer which they will all unanimously return is, The feelings and ideas out of which we grow are strangers and aliens to the miracles of the Gospel. The nature of the tastes of that period is best shown by the miracles of the Apocryphal Gospels.

But if the Gospels were largely mythic, he would conclude that they must have been the reports of several sets of myths springing up in the bosom of the Christian community, or of these myths modified to suit the views of the authors of the Gospels.

But, if myths, he would naturally inquire, would not the authors of them have revelled in giving full details on those subjects on which the Evangelists are profoundly silent? Would they not have certainly abounded in the grotesque, the romantic, and the monstrous? Would they not have laid open the unseen world, where invention can revel without danger of being checked by facts? Would no myth have been invented respecting our Lord's boyhood? How could long discourses have been preserved ro transmitted in a mythic story? If the history of Whitfield or Wesley had been preserved in a mythic or legendary form, what evidence should we have had that their discourses were their veritable utterances, forty or fifty years afterwards? Would there not have been as many versions of their sermons as sects into which their followers might have divided? Is such morality ever found in myths? Myths must be propagated by the agency of considerable numbers of men. Has the morality of the discourses ever been the realized morality of a community, so that it could be idealized in the form of myths? What was the original germ of the morality in these discourses, and what the mythic additions? The morality of the Evangelists was never the morality of large bodies of men who were in that state of mental development in which the generation of myths is possible.

But there is the singular verbal agreement and disagreement both in the narratives of the facts and in the discourses which the Evangelists present; how is this to be accounted for? Let him suppose, first, that the Evangelists have faithfully detailed the narratives which, whether mythic or otherwise, were floating about on the surface of the Christian society. It is evident, in that case, that several such myths must have existed. If they were transmitted by one society, this might be given as the reason for the verbal agreements in our three different accounts of the same events or of the same discourse; but if this were adduced as the reason for the agreement, how can it account for the disagreements, for the transposition of sentences, for their singular omissions and insertions? If they are the faithful accounts of myths as transmitted by different societies or bodies of men, then, although the variations may be accounted for, the existence of the large amount of common words and sentences in the Gospels is utterly incredible. He would consider that the existence of these phenomena is utterly incompatible with the present narratives of the Evangelists having grown up in a mythic form. But might not the Evangelists, when they reduced the myths into the present narratives, have been the authors of these singular variations? He would naturally consider, On what principle could they have made the variations? What end had they in view? What could have induced them to make some of the changes? Did they consult about the matter in order that they might have the appearance of three independent histories? If so, they must have been devoid of ordinary understanding to have retained so much of the common matter, or the same words and phrases.

But it has been suggested that Matthew is the collector of the discourses, and Mark of the stories, as they floated about in the original Christian society; and that the original Gospel of Matthew contained nothing but discourses, and that of Mark nothing but facts; and that the additions of the facts in one, and the discourses in the other, were made by other hands. He would naturally desire to be informed on what principles have the facts been inserted into the one, and the discourses into the other? If Mark's original facts, as they were depicted in his Gospel, were described in all their graphic reality, what stupid compiler has made Matthew's so jejune and dry? Who, with Matthew's grand discourses before him, would have deliberately composed those of Mark? Why has Matthew, the great compiler of parables, omitted the greatest of all parables, that of the prodigal son, and left it and others to be recorded by St. Luke? But if, as it has been assumed, Matthew's be the representation of the original mythic story, and Mark and Luke have copied and modified it to suit their views, whence come the long discourses in Matthew? What is the source of the apparently most capricious variations in Mark and Luke? Some of the changes are very minute; what purpose could they possibly serve? for instance, why did Luke change Matthew's third temptation into his own second, and place it in a most unnatural position? Or what could have induced Mark to say that our Lord uttered the same words in the second prayer at Gethsemane, when he had Matthew before him asserting that this took place in the third prayer? or if Mark's be the original story, what could have induced the compiler of Matthew to make so capricious an alteration? But many have stated that

Matthew's Gospel is the original mythic or legendary Gospel. In that case the mythic Matthew reports the dry facts, and Mark and Luke the pictorial additions in the common narratives. He would observe, however, that, with singular perversity, this was reversed in the story of the Syrophenician woman. But if the ground were varied, and he were told that Mark is the original mythic Gospel, and Matthew the improved version of it, then he would be struck with the fact that Matthew's Gospel contains the facts which wear the most mythical appearance in the whole history—as the opening portion of it, and the dream of Pilate's wife. He would certainly conclude that the facts are not explicable by the theory.

But supposing it were suggested that the three Gospels are distinct, and give us three accounts of the mythic story as it was believed in and developed by three or more independent Christian societies, with some additions of the authors' own, he would then observe that the fundamental groundwork of the three narratives consists of an account common to all three Evangelists. The common narrative must, therefore, contain the facts or the myth, as they were believed in by the original Christian society before it became divided. The parts which are not common must be subsequent mythic additions, made after the original society had divided itself into three or more distinct societies, or they must be inventions of the Evangelists: if, therefore, any fragments of the original teaching of Jesus exist, it must be found in the common narrative.

But supposing he were also informed that the historic Jesus was purely a moral teacher, and made no pretensions to miraculous power; and that all the miraculous portions of the Gospels must be of mythic origin, and have grown up around the original story. He would observe that the miraculous element pervaded the common narrative quite as much as the subsequent additions. If, therefore, Jesus did not profess to perform miracles, those portions of the common narrative which contain accounts of miracles must be of mythic origin, and must be struck out as forming no portion of the original history. He would therefore naturally ask, after all that was evidently mythic had been removed from the Gospels, whether the substratum of truth remaining was sufficiently large for a religion to be erected upon it, which in a comparatively short period overspread the civilized world? He would answer that there is no instance on record of a religion being successfully propagated, resting on a mere basis of moral teaching, least of all of such a moral teaching as that exhibited in the Gospels. He would ask, At what period of the world's history has such a morality been realized in practice among considerable numbers of men? Such morality must have been realized in some bosom before it could have been promulgated. He would hardly fail of arriving at the conclusion, that, after the Gospels had been thus effectually weeded of every mythic element, a residuum would remain which, if it formed the original history and teaching of Jesus, would be more incredible than all the miracles of the Gospel taken together.

But if he were informed that it was utterly incredible that a miracle ever had been performed, and that Jesus had fallen in with the tendencies of the times, and had lent Himself to the performance of miracles which were not real, he would at once assume it as certain that the moral teaching of the Gospels never originated in such a character. No impiety is greater than the working of a pretended miracle: to do so successfully always involves a previous rehearsal. Most of the miracles of the Gospel could have left no doubt as to whether they were, or were not, performed by the aid of supernatural power on the part of Him professing to perform them.

But he would observe that, when the additions were made to the common narrative, the original society must have broken up into several distinct societies; by these the mythic additions to the common narrative were produced. But, while these additions were being made, a considerable interval must have elapsed; and consequently the laws of mythic development require that the common narrative should have undergone a far greater variation during this interval than it presents in our present Gospels. The variations also would have been of a very different character from those which we actually find there. But, on the supposition in question, not only did these myth- and legend-generating societies conspire together to preserve the thread of the original story nearly in the words of the primitive myths and legends, but each of these different societies went on creating myths and legends of the same character and formed in the same mould. All these myths and legends must have been sober, none extravagant or grotesque. Each society must have made additions to the conceptions of its Jesus formed in reference to the same ideal. Not one of them ever thought of investing Him with the more specious and heroic attributes, the admiration of which is deeply implanted in the human bosom. He would naturally expect to be informed how it came to pass that each of these myth-generating societies preserved the character of its Jesus free from a single blemish, whatever additions they might make to it, or with whatever attributes they invested it. Amidst the continual accessions of new mythic facts, new mythic discourses, and new mythic parables, the same consistency, whether in theology, morals, or character, reigns throughout. That three or more separate societies, each generating myths, should concur in filling up the Saviour's portrait to the ideal of perfection, he would consider more incredible than all recorded miracles.

But he would observe that these societies had accomplished a feat yet more wonderful. While engaged in the process of developing myths, they have not only preserved the great ideal features of the Saviour's character, but the same peculiarities of expression, uniformly and consistently. A cunning forger finds this extremely difficult; how then is it to be effected in societies developing myths? There is one peculiarity of expression which the Jesus of the Gospels invariably uses when speaking of God. He never uses the expression "Our Father" as common to Himself and other men : He has used the expression "my Father and your Father;" but never once is the expression "Our Father" represented as having passed from His lips as applicable to himself. Now the uniform use of these expressions is very natural, if the Gospel discourses are not myths but veritable utterances of our Lord, and if He professed to be the Son of God in a sense in which no human being is; but it is utterly inconsistent with the supposition that He taught that His disciples were the sons of God in the same sense as Himself, or with His alleged great discovery of the real relationship of man to God, in which the peculiarity of His teaching has been asserted to consist*. If such was the actual teaching of our Lord, it would follow that all such passages in the Gospels, with the context, where the expressions "my Father" and "your Father" are found, must be mythic additions, representing ideas contrary to His original teaching; and further, that not only must the myth-generating societies have developed such myths contrary to the original conception of the character of Jesus, but also continued to develope myths of the same character, with the strictest propriety of expression, so that the words "our Father" have not once even by accident been placed in the mouth of Jesus by these developers of myths. Societies of men developing myths cannot maintain minute proprieties of expression continued through long periods of time.

But if Matthew, Mark, and Luke, when they published their versions of the myths, altered the original expression of "our Father" into "my Father and your Father," then it is evident, not only that they must have agreed together to make this substitution in the mythic narratives as they existed in the different Christian societies, but that they must have held the views respecting our Lord's person which are explicitly stated in the Gospel of St. John, which explicit statement the supporters of the mythic theory are never weary of adducing as affording conclusive proof that the Gospel of St. John is of later date than the synoptic Gospels.

Such a reader would inevitably come to the conclusion that no miracle narrated in the Gospels is so incredible as the peculiar phenomena which they present, if they largely consist of myths or of facts incrusted with myths developed by the original Christian societies, or even if they are such myths modified by the persons who have reduced them to the form in which we now read them in the pages of the Evangelists. The general possibility of the mythic origin of Christianity we shall consider hereafter.

* See Renan.

We will now make the contrary supposition, that such a reader was informed that the peculiar phenomena which strike him on perusing the Gospels can be fully accounted for, on the assumption that they have been composed by men under the guidance of verbal inspiration. What inferences would he draw as to the nature of their inspiration from the phenomena in question?

Careful perusal would at once convince him that he had in his hands four histories, which profess to be reports of the same series of miraculous events. But would the perusal of these books lead him to the conclusion that they were four accounts of the same events set forth by one and the same author, or that they were the works of four distinct authors? The whole aspect of the Evangelists would lead him to the conclusion, which he would consider incontrovertible, that he had before him the works of four distinct and independent minds. It would be impossible to persuade him that the Gospels were composed by a single person only, unless with the intention to impose on his readers by imitating all the phenomena which prove the presence of four distinct personalities. But he would find the evidences of the honesty of the writers so strong that, if he adopted this for a moment as a possible supposition, he would soon abandon it, and arrive at the conclusion that, if there is any certainty in the principles on which the authorship of books is determined, these books bear the most certain indications that they were composed by four authors, and not by one only.

But would he not find some phenomena in the Gospels very difficult to account for on any ordinary human principle, whether he assumed that they had been written quite independently of each other or that one author had borrowed from another? The first thing which would certainly strike him would be the long discourses. We would observe that the writers are pledged to the fact that all the discourses contain the veritable substance of what was uttered by our Lord, nearly in the same words. Every indication intimates that the discourses were not copied down from our Lord's mouth. We are expressly told that the hearers had but an imperfect comprehension of many of them when they were uttered. What means had the original witnesses of accurately committing these discourses to writing?

But, on comparing the Gospels together, another striking phenomenon would present itself. They frequently contain three different reports of the same discourse, but with a few striking variations. The nature of these variations has been already explained. He would naturally inquire, How have these most singular variations originated? Is it the fact that the discourses have been copied from each other? Then how come the variations? The variations are so peculiar, that he would certainly come to the conclusion that, if one Evangelist copied from the other, they must have made the variations for the express purpose of avoiding the suspicion of having copied. What, then, are we to think of three independent writers who have given us three reports of the same discourse, the greater portion of which verbally agrees, but with verbal differences such as have been already referred to, if the discourses were not copied down at the time, with these verbal differences as the result of copying, and if the facts presented by them render it impossible that they should have been copied from each other?

The following circumstance will help such a reader to the solution. We read in the Gospels that, a little before their Master left the disciples, He promised them that when He was gone to His Father He would send them the Spirit of truth, to bring to their remembrance whatever He had said unto them. Now if this promise was actually fulfilled, it afforded an assistance exactly proportioned to the necessities of the case. The discourses not having been copied down at the time of their delivery, it would enable the Apostles to do what otherwise their human memories would have been unable to effect—to give faithful and correct reports of the discourses of our Lord, which, without this assistance, would have been impossible. But if the fulfilment of this promise will account for the recording of the discourses, how will it account for the small variations which they contain?

On reflection, he will observe that the promise is not a promise that the discourses should be absolutely dictated to the Apostles; it is a promise of assistance exactly proportioned to the necessity. Our Lord tells the Apostles that the Spirit would refresh their memories; there was therefore combined a divine and a human element. The Apostles remembered; the Spirit supplemented the deficiencies of their memories. The small variations, omissions, and transpositions, therefore, may be traced to the human element subsisting in the Apostles' memories.

But when he examined the narratives of facts in the Evangelists as distinct from the discourses, what conclusions would they inevitably suggest? He could not fail to observe in the narratives of the same discourses greater agreement than in the reports of the same facts. The variations in the discourses consist of a few words only: the discourses never contain divergent statements; they contain no contradictions in moral or doctrinal teaching, but form an harmonious whole: the short passages inserted by one Evangelist are easily brought into agreement with the discourse as reported by the other. But the facts present all the variations which we have already noticed; they have all the phenomena which the testimony of independent witnesses usually presents, and are extremely difficult to weave into a perfectly consistent narrative. Now, if the narratives of the Evangelists are four distinct biographies, composed by four different writers by the use of nothing but the ordinary human faculties, he would naturally expect to find much greater variations in discourses which different persons had heard, and which they afterwards endeavoured to commit to writing, than in different accounts of the same fact which the reporters had actually witnessed. How can a difference so contrary to all human probability be accounted for? On recurring to the promise of our Lord which we have already noticed, he would find that while the promise is distinct that supernatural aid should be imparted to recall to the Apostles' memories whatever Christ had said to them, it contains no such promise of recalling to their memories the precise facts as they had actually witnessed them: it is a promise exactly proportioned to the necessities of the case.

But while this would aid him to account for the superior accuracy of the discourses compared with the facts, there would be another phenomenon equally striking—the large amount of verbal agreement in the report of the same events by the different Evangelists. He would consider this verbal agreement to be so great, that it would be impossible to exist in the narratives of four independent writers, unless they had some common source of information out of which that verbal agreement could arise. In describing the same event, the same words never suggest themselves to any considerable extent to four independent writers, unless they possess some common source of information. He would feel himself compelled to assume the existence of this common source of information, and would think it highly probable that the Apostles, before they separated at the time of St. Stephen's martyrdom, composed various brief memoranda of such events as they respectively witnessed for mutual use, which must be the source of the verbal agreements in the narratives of common events contained in the Gospels, and that their divergencies arise from their never having been woven by the Apostles into a consistent whole, and from our Gospels containing reports of their more enlarged testimony respecting the same facts, supplemented by additional reports derived from other eye-witnesses.

But what conclusion would such a reader deduce from the narratives of the facts presented by the Evangelists, respecting the theory that they were dictated to the authors by verbal inspiration? Would he be able to believe that what he was reading was a fourfold account of the same facts composed by the same author? He would say, "I see the indubitable marks of different styles of writing—marks which cannot be mistaken. I observe that one of the writers narrates a bare event, while another pictures that event in all the reality of life." It is evident also that, in narrating the same facts, one has recorded one portion of a fact, while another has recorded another portion of it. Occasionally one fact recorded by one

Evangelist, which has been omitted by another, makes the narrative of the other intelligible, whereas, without the knowledge of that fact, the other narrative would have been liable to misapprehension. He would also observe that, in minor points of detail, there were small variations in the narratives, which, with the information furnished by the Gospels, do not seem capable of being brought into verbal agreement without offering violence to the natural meaning of the passages. He would consider the narratives of the Crucifixion and of the Resurrection remarkable examples of this, and that they bear evident marks of having been derived from the accounts given of that exciting scene by several witnesses of it. While he would observe that all the great points of the narratives were supported by the most ample testimony, he would see that it is hardly possible to reduce the four accounts into a history, setting forth the precise order of the events as they occurred, in the words used by the Evangelists.

Now, what would be the general conclusion which these striking facts would suggest? He would be of opinion that the accounts of the facts, as detailed by the Evangelists, are precisely such as independent witnesses would have given of events of an exciting nature in which they had been deeply interested. He would observe that, while all the main facts were testified to with substantial accuracy, the minor details would present considerable divergency, but a divergency of that kind which always attaches to the testimony of various witnesses, especially in cases where their feelings were deeply interested. He would conclude, therefore, that whatever assistance might have been afforded to the authors of the Gospels, that assistance was certainly not that of verbal inspiration.

But further, such a reader would not fail to observe that the histories themselves presuppose that there were a large number of facts connected with our Lord's life, and His public ministry, which the writers of the Gospels have either taken a very general view of, or passed over in the most absolute silence.

The reader would find it difficult to account, on any ordinary human principles, for these silences of the Evangelists. But he would observe that when their Master promised them supernatural assistance to aid the memories of the Apostles, He also assured them that they should receive guidance into the entire meaning of His revelation. Such guidance, if actually afforded, may explain the reason why the writers of the Gospels have related the facts which they have recorded, and omitted others, and how it comes to pass that they have all pursued a course directly contrary to that which would have been pursued by any other writers of a similar biography, and unanimously refused all information on points which touch the deepest sympathies and the liveliest feelings of the human heart.

Such a view as that which has been taken could hardly fail of being suggested to the mind of a reader of the Gospels, who had no theory to maintain respecting the nature and degree of the inspiration with which they had been composed. The facts and phenomena presented to him would certainly never lead him to guess that they were composed by persons under the influence of verbal inspiration. If that theory were suggested to him as a probable account of the origin of the Gospels, he would pronounce it utterly irreconcilable with the facts.

But if the facts, as they are exhibited in the Gospels, will not suggest the theory of verbal inspiration, if the facts, instead of suggesting such a theory, have every appearance of contradicting that theory, on what principle do we assume its truth? The narratives of the facts contained in the Gospels have all the phenomena which are exhibited by similar narratives by independent witnesses in courts of justice. We find that the very points on which such witnesses are particularly liable to variation, such as the particulars of time and place, numbers, and arrangement of events, the omission or insertion of minute particulars, are precisely those which constitute the variations in the narratives of the Evangelists. As, in particularly exciting scenes, the hurried state of the mind of ordinary witnesses leads to the greatest amount of minor variation in details, so it is with the

Evangelists. If, then, the facts, as recorded in the Evangelists, present all the phenomena of human testimony, why should he assume an explanation which is entirely at issue with those phenomena, and which the utmost amount of human ingenuity cannot reconcile with them?

Nothing but the most overwhelming necessity can justify us in making such an assumption. But does such necessity exist? If it does, on what is it founded? Have we any positive assertions of the writers themselves, that they wrote under the influence of verbal inspiration, of so distinct a character that, if we were to assume that they wrote under the influence of any other form of inspiration, it would be to question their veracity? We examine the writings themselves, and find no such thing asserted, either expressly or by implication. If, then, neither the facts reported by the writers nor the assertions made by them require the assumption of such a theory, what renders the assumption necessary? It may be said, it lies in the antecedent necessities of the case: Divine inspiration must have been so given. We have shown that the alleged grounds of such necessity are utterly fallacious. We may think it probable that Divine revelation would have been communicated by means of such an influence; we may think that it was most desirable that it should be so communicated; yet neither our views of its probability, nor our sense of its convenience, will justify us in assuming that it has been so communicated, in the face of the facts leading to a directly contrary conclusion. Nothing but an express assertion of the books themselves, or a direct promise of our Lord, would justify us in making an assumption which the entire evidence of the facts themselves seems expressly to contradict.

But such promise or assertion can nowhere be found. On the contrary, our Lord declared that the Apostles should bear witness, because they had been with Him from the beginning. They themselves declare that they could not but bear testimony to the things which they had seen and heard. When there was danger that their testimony would be defective, our Lord promised them supernatural aid. When their ordinary powers were sufficient, no promise of supernatural assistance is recorded. Our Lord also promised them to enlarge their comprehension of those truths which they had not understood during His personal ministry, and to lead them into the knowledge of all the truths which He came to reveal. He also promised them that they should be endowed with miraculous powers, by which the Spirit Himself would bear witness to the truth of their testimony. He also promised them supernatural guidance as to what they should say in their defence when called upon to answer for their conduct before the authorities of the world, for propagating His religion, and that the Spirit should reveal to them some events connected with the future. But other promise there is none.

Now these are promises of supernatural assistance sufficiently large for the purpose of enabling the Apostles to communicate the Christian revelation to mankind, but they contain no hint that they were to be endowed with a gift like verbal inspiration. If there is no promise of our Lord that He would endow the Apostles with such a gift—if there is only a promise of supernatural guidance into the knowledge of the truths of the Christian revelation—if the writers of the Gospels make no claim to the possession of such a gift—if the facts and phenomena of the Gospels do not only not require the assumption of this theory, but present appearances irreconcilably at issue with it, what right have we to assume such a theory against the evidence of the facts, without any warrant from Christ or the Apostles, without any grounds of antecedent certainty, merely because it suits our views that the Gospels ought to have been written under its influence? The assumption of such a theory is not the result of humbly receiving the teaching of God, but of a rationalizing principle in man.

Human authors, when they compose a biography and state the sources whence the facts in the biography are derived, are usually allowed the full benefit of their assertions. We are informed by Boswell that he copied down most of his reports of Johnson's sayings and conversations shortly after he had uttered them, and that whenever he omitted to do so, his reports have suffered in consequence; and we accept his assertion as to the mode in which his work was composed. Why should the assertions of St. Luke, as to the sources whence he derived the contents of his Gospel, be disregarded? St. Luke has given us a formal account of the sources whence he drew the contents of his Gospel, and of his reasons for writing it.

Luke i. 1–4: "Forasmuch as many have taken in hand to set forth in order a declaration of those things which are most surely believed among us, even as they delivered them unto us, which from the beginning were eyewitnesses, and ministers of the word; it seemed good to me also, having had perfect understanding of all things from the very first, to write unto thee in order, most excellent Theophilus, that thou mightest know the certainty of those things, wherein thou hast been instructed."

St. Luke, in this passage, makes the following assertions:— Many persons had composed memoranda of the things most surely believed amongst Christians, as they had been reported to them by eyewitnesses and ministers of the word, previously to the time when St. Luke wrote his Gospel. By the expression, "a declaration of the things which are most surely believed among us," &c., St. Luke evidently means the oral testimony of the original eyewitnesses to the leading facts of the evangelical history, and not mere statements of doctrinal truth delivered by the Apostles. They were memoranda, more or less extensive, of real facts, such as could be reported by eyewitnesses. The expression, $\pi\alpha\rho\acute{\epsilon}\delta o\sigma\alpha\nu$, denotes the fact of such transmission. Of these memoranda St. Luke neither expresses approbation nor the contrary, but implies their general correctness as far as they went. He merely asserts that many persons had undertaken to set forth such memoranda, and expresses his intention of setting an account of the same autoptic testimony before his reader in a more regular form. He implies that his work would be one of greater accuracy and better arrangement; for he states that the object which he had in view was, that Theophilus might know the CERTAINTY of the things in which he had been instructed—an expression which evidently implies the writer's opinion that the existing memoranda did not exist in a form well suited to convey that certainty.

The instruction which Theophilus had received had been chiefly oral, as is implied in the use of the word $κατηχήθης$ to denote that instruction. St. Luke declares that he designed to reduce the memoranda and facts into an orderly arrangement ($καθεξῆς\ γράψαι$). We may infer, therefore, that many of these memoranda followed no orderly arrangement with respect to the time and place of the events reported. St. Luke then proceeds distinctly to inform us from what sources he derived his information on the subject of the evangelical history. He says, "having had perfect knowledge of all things from the very first." The Greek, $παρηκολουθηκότι\ ἀκριβῶς$, has a larger meaning than our version suggests: it is intended to convey the idea that the Evangelist had accurately traced out the facts which he reports with pains and labours, and had ascertained their correctness by careful inquiry. There is a kind of implication that this had been neglected to be done by the authors of the existing memoranda. It can hardly be doubted that, in prosecuting this inquiry, St. Luke made use of such existing memoranda of autoptic testimony as fell in his way.

Now every reader observes that St. Luke says not one word about supernatural assistance. He neither asserts his inspiration nor disclaims it. But, on the principles which we have already established when we considered the apostolic gifts, there would be no occasion for him to do so. He was St. Paul's companion in travel and special friend, and we may, without danger, conclude that those spiritual gifts which were bestowed in such large measure on the Corinthian church were not denied to any of his companions. The possession of these gifts would be matter of notoriety, and would no more require a distinct mention than the possession by him of his natural faculties. We may therefore conclude that St. Luke had the assistance of whatever spiritual gift he was endowed with; and therefore we can scarcely err in arriving at the conclusion that the gift of prophecy would be among them, considering the extent in which it was imparted. But, while he says nothing about his supernatural gifts, he expressly tells us that the facts which he intended to publish were such as he had diligently traced up to the testimony of eyewitnesses, and that he had spared neither pains nor labour thus to trace them. The spiritual gifts, therefore, did not supersede the necessity of laborious inquiry.

But while St. Luke's assertions are quite consistent with the consciousness of supernatural assistance, they are utterly inconsistent with that assistance being of the nature of verbal inspiration. If St. Luke was conscious of an inspiration of this kind, on what principle could he have inquired into the reports of facts as they had been narrated by eyewitnesses? Had he not a far more direct and certain source of information in the communication of the facts to his mind by the Spirit of God? Is it possible to believe that, if St. Luke had the facts dictated to him by the Spirit, he would proceed to test the truth of the facts which the Spirit had assured him of by the testimony of witnesses? Did St. Paul call in human testimony to corroborate what he had received by Divine inspiration? St. Paul expressly tells us that those subjects which he derived from inspiration, he never sought to confirm by the authority of man. Had St. Luke been conscious of possessing verbal inspiration, instead of spending his time in ascertaining the truth of facts from those who saw them or reporting discourses from the testimony of those who heard them, he would have had nothing else to do but to take his pen and write what was dictated to him by the Spirit of God.

St. Luke had abundant means of ascertaining the facts by ordinary human methods. There is every reason for believing that Cæsarea was the chief place of his residence during the two years of St. Paul's imprisonment; for we know that he accompanied the Apostle on his last journey to Jerusalem, and on his leaving Cæsarea for Rome. The interval would have afforded St. Luke ample opportunity for doing what he asserts himself to have done, viz. to have made the most minute inquiry about the facts of the Gospel history from the various persons who had been eye- and earwitnesses of it. His means of communicating with different parts of Judæa, where most of such witnesses must have resided, would have been easy. He had been already in frequent communication with apostolic men. St. Paul's long imprisonment at Cæsarea would naturally bring many of them to that place; for St. Luke records that free access was permitted to the Apostle's friends. The facts, therefore, were easily within reach. When St. Luke wanted the report of a discourse or of a parable, he could easily apply to such apostles as resided in Judæa, or other persons who were present at their delivery, who possessed the requisite supernatural assistance to refresh their memories, and even copy them down at their mouths. He could compare all the information thus obtained with the written memoranda in his possession. He, consequently, had every facility of ascertaining the "certainty" of the facts of the evangelical history, and composing a true account of such facts for the instruction of the Church. We have already remarked that he evidently consulted St. Paul on the institution of the Eucharist—on which that Apostle expressly informs us he received his information directly "from the Lord."

But what have become of the memoranda mentioned by St. Luke? Had their authors supernatural assistance in their composition? We can only answer that some of the spiritual gifts, such as the gift of prophecy, are proved both by the statements of St. Paul and St. Luke to have been extensively communicated. St. Luke describes the memoranda as in conformity with autoptic testimony. If they were the accounts of eyewitnesses, and recorded actions and words actually done and spoken by our Lord, they must have contained the results of the highest form of inspiration, viz. that inherent in the person of God manifest in the flesh. But, having the defects which St. Luke's preface leads us to suppose that they had, nothing is more probable than that their use would be gradually superseded by the more methodical arrangements of the evangelical history as we now read it in the pages of the four Gospels, and that they would be suffered to perish. The recovery of but one of them would throw a flood of light on some of the remarkable phenomena presented by the Evangelists.

From this investigation, therefore, we arrive at the general conclusion that supernatural aid was afforded to the Evangelists in proportion as such aid was required by them. Their ordinary memories were assisted to enable them to give correct reports of the discourses of our Lord. Their judgments were supernaturally directed as to what portion of the facts which they were acquainted with they should record, and what portion they should leave unrecorded.

Where human faculties were sufficient to effect the work, supernatural assistance was not given. Where human faculties were insufficient, they received the spiritual gift which met the necessities of the case and qualified them for being able witnesses to the facts of the evangelical history. The great Worker has proportioned the means which He employs to the ends which He purposes to effectuate, alike in creation, providence, and redemption.

CHAPTER XVII.

THE GRADUAL ENLIGHTENMENT OF THE APOSTLES IN THE GREAT TRUTHS OF THE CHRISTIAN REVELATION.

HAVING considered the facts of the Gospels as they throw light on the question of their inspiration, we must now proceed to examine the assertions of the Apostles as to the nature of their own inspiration, and the facts presented by the history and the Epistles as far as they throw light on existing theories. The specific portion of apostolic inspiration to which we are now to direct our inquiries is the degree of supernatural enlightenment which the Apostles received to qualify them to be the expounders of the meaning of the Christian revelation and the teachers of the Christian Church. The necessary supernatural guidance was promised them by our Lord, when He told them that He had many things to say unto them, but they could not bear them then; "howbeit when

He, the Spirit of truth, is come, He will guide you into all the truth: for He shall not speak of Himself; but whatsoever He shall hear, that shall He speak: and He will show you things to come. He shall glorify me: for He shall receive of mine, and shall show it unto you."

We have already shown that this promise of our Lord was intended to assure the Apostles that they should receive such a degree of supernatural enlightenment as would qualify them to be the expounders of the full meaning of the revelation which He came to communicate in His divine person. This function the Apostles discharged in their written and oral teaching.

St. Paul speaks of his written and oral teaching as possessing an equal authority. The nature of the case forbids us to assume that his written teaching had any different degree of inspiration from his oral teaching. We shall presently examine his assertions respecting the nature of his teaching. We shall find that those assertions have a greater reference to his oral than to his written teaching.

The full apostolical inspiration, as it affected the Apostles' knowledge of Christian truth, and its accurate communication, was imparted, as we have already seen, by the first three supernatural gifts of the Spirit—the gift of wisdom, of prophecy, and of knowledge. The gift of wisdom, which was the gift preeminently apostolical, communicated to their minds an acquaintance with the highest forms of Christian truth; the gift of knowledge imparted to them an acquaintance with Christian truth in its practical form; the gift of prophecy enabled them to state those truths in intelligible language, and to apply them to the heart. It could communicate to them a power of spiritual insight, and also impart to them supernatural guidance on all requisite occasions, and afford them occasional glimpses into futurity. Special suggestions seem to have been made to the minds of inspired writers through the instrumentality of this gift. The other gifts would enable them to discharge special functions in the Church; but the action of these three would constitute their inspiration as the authorized teachers of Christian truth.

We have already observed that our Lord's promise that the Spirit would guide them into all the truth implies that their enlightenment would not be a sudden, but a gradual process. The promise of our Lord received its fulfilment, on the day of Pentecost, to such a degree as to qualify the Apostles for preaching the gospel to the Jewish people. But the testimony of the history of the Acts of the Apostles is express that the enlightenment which was imparted by the Spirit to the minds of the Apostles at His first effusion was not sudden and complete, but gradual. Till the conversion of Cornelius, the minds of the Apostles remained ignorant of one great truth connected with their Master's kingdom. Their ignorance of this truth must have involved a partial view of other great truths of the Christian dispensation.

It is important to observe that, in making a gradual communication of truth to the minds of the Apostles, the Divine Spirit has shown His purpose to interfere as little as possible with the existing laws of the human mind. In communicating inspiration, He has preserved the analogy of the mode in which God acts in creation and providence. Man grows in his ordinary knowledge, not suddenly, but by successive stages. In strict conformity with this rule of the Divine acting, with the single exception of St. Paul, the Spirit of God communicated even supernatural truth to the minds of the Apostles.

The ignorance of the Apostles, even after their enlightenment by the Spirit, that the Gospel was to be preached in the Gentile world, is a fact attended with very important consequences. We should have been slow to believe that their supernatural enlightenment by the Spirit did not extend to this subject, if it had not been so expressly stated by St. Luke. The careful consideration of this ignorance and its consequences will throw much light on the nature of apostolic inspiration.

This ignorance of the Apostles that the Gentiles were to form a portion of the kingdom of God is the more remarkable because the direction to preach the Gospel in the most distant regions of the earth had formed an integral portion of the apostolical commission. Not only is their ignorance on this subject one which we should not have anticipated, but it must have greatly modified their views on other points of Christian truth. The Apostles most probably held that, if the Gentiles were ever to become partakers of the kingdom of God, their only mode of obtaining entrance into it would be through the gate of circumcision.

Yet our Lord had not only intimated to the Apostles, He had distinctly told them before His ascension, that His kingdom was to embrace the Gentile nations. Nothing can be apparently more distinct than His parting commands. The Apostles could not even recur to the terms of their own apostolical commission without that truth being brought before their minds. That commission, as recorded by St. Matthew, is as follows:—

"Go ye therefore, and teach all nations, baptizing them in the name of the Father, and of the Son, and of the Holy Ghost: teaching them to observe all things whatsoever I have commanded you: and, lo, I am with you alway, even unto the end of the world."

St. Mark's words are even, if possible, more express:—"Go ye into all the world, and preach the gospel to every creature. He that believeth and is baptized shall be saved; but he that believeth not shall be damned."

St. Luke also records that our Lord informed the Apostles that repentance and remission of sins should be preached in His name among all nations, beginning at Jerusalem. In the Acts, he tells us that our Lord, immediately before His ascension, distinctly informed the Apostles where they were to testify of Him:—"Ye shall be witnesses unto me, both in Jerusalem, and in all Judæa, and in Samaria, and unto the uttermost parts of the earth."

Directions of this kind seem to us of the utmost possible plainness. We should have supposed that the Apostles could never have recurred to the terms of their commission without the great truth flashing on their minds. What meaning could they have attached to the words, that they were to go into all the world, and preach the gospel to every creature? What could they have thought our Lord meant when He directed them to make disciples of all nations? How could such plain directions be misapprehended?

But not only did the Apostles misunderstand our Lord's words, but the first illumination imparted to their minds by the Spirit was not sufficient to dispel the darkness. This is the more remarkable because we find St. Peter, in his earliest addresses, repeatedly referring to the very words of the apostolical commission. "We are witnesses," says he, "of these things." "He appeared not unto all the people, but unto witnesses chosen before of God, even to us, who did eat and drink with Him after He rose from the dead; and He commanded us to preach unto the people." It is most remarkable that St. Peter should refer to these words, and yet that the latter portion of our Lord's command should have been entirely misunderstood by him, and that his prejudices should have been so strong that they were not overcome by the enlightenment of the Spirit which he had received. He evidently considered that the whole benefits of the kingdom of God were still limited to the people of the old theocracy, and had, as yet, no idea that his Master was the great Shepherd of the Gentile nations. According to this narrow view of the Gospel dispensation, he taught, " Him hath God exalted to be a Prince and a Saviour, to give repentance," not to mankind generally, but "*unto Israel*, and forgiveness of sins."

We learn, from the express declarations of St. Luke, that till the time of the conversion of Cornelius St. Peter's Jewish prejudices were so deeply seated that he would not have entered the house of a Gentile for the purpose of preaching the gospel to those who inhabited it: he thought its inhabitants common and unclean. These prejudices had to be dissipated by an express revelation.

After that vision, St. Peter speaks of a truth which to us seems of a most obvious character as a fresh discovery, of which he had been previously ignorant. He speaks like a man to whom its discovery occasioned deep surprise. " Of a truth," says he to Cornelius, " I perceive that God is no respecter of persons; but in every nation he that feareth Him, and worketh righteousness, is accepted of Him." St.

Peter, previously to this revelation, must have viewed God as a respecter of persons, and must have considered that fearing God and working righteousness would be unavailing to procure acceptance, unless a man became a member of the Jewish church. Nothing appears to us more surprising than that, up to this period, the Apostle should still have remained ignorant of this great truth.

We see, therefore, that the Apostles' ignorance respecting the calling of the Gentiles could have been no isolated ignorance, confined to that one particular fact; it must have exerted an influence upon the views entertained by them on other great points of Christian truth: it even affected the views entertained by St. Peter as to whether fearing God and working righteousness were sufficient to obtain acceptance with Him.

To form a clear conception of the effect of their ignorance on this subject, we must consider what St. Paul asserts as to the important bearing which the knowledge of the calling of the Gentiles had on the most important points of Christian truth.

Eph. ii., St. Paul writes:—" Wherefore remember, that ye being in time past Gentiles in the flesh, who are called Uncircumcision by that which is called the Circumcision in the flesh made by hands; that at that time ye were without Christ, being aliens from the commonwealth of Israel, and strangers from the covenants of promise, having no hope, and without God in the world: but now in Christ Jesus ye who sometimes were far off are made nigh by the blood of Christ. For He is our peace, who hath made both one, and hath broken down the middle wall of partition between us; having abolished in His flesh the enmity, even the law of commandments contained in ordinances; for to make in Himself of twain one new man, so making peace; and that He might reconcile both unto God in one body by the cross, having slain the enmity thereby: and came and preached peace to you which were afar off, and to them that were nigh. For through Him we both have access by one Spirit unto the Father."

The Apostle here declares that a knowledge of several of

the great truths of the gospel is dependent on the calling of the Gentiles into the Church of Christ. The clear comprehension of the spirituality of the Christian religion, and the knowledge of the worthlessness of serving God by a religion of rites and ordinances, is closely connected with this truth. Several other great truths of the gospel can only be half understood without it: for instance, the nature of the sacrifice of Christ as efficacious alike for all men; and that all alike, both Jew and Gentile, have, through the cross, communion with the Father by the Spirit. A person ignorant of the calling of the Gentiles could not have been aware of the pure spirituality of the Divine worship, nor of the extent or perfection of the Divine love. It was impossible for such a person to appreciate the profundity of the great truth taught by our Lord, "The hour cometh, when ye shall neither in this mountain, nor yet at Jerusalem, worship the Father." "God is a Spirit; and they that worship Him must worship Him in spirit and in truth."

To the same effect St. Paul writes (Col. iii. 11)—"Where there is neither Greek nor Jew, circumcision nor uncircumcision, Barbarian, Scythian, bond, nor free: but Christ is all, and in all."

A person ignorant, therefore, of the calling of the Gentiles could have had but partial views of the universal headship of Christ.

In Col. i. 26, 27, the Apostle writes respecting the calling of the Gentiles, "Even the mystery which hath been hid from ages and from generations, but now is made manifest to His saints: to whom God would make known what is the riches of the glory of this mystery among the Gentiles; which is Christ in you, the hope of glory." The Apostle here uses two expressions respecting the calling of the Gentiles, each sufficient to prove the importance of that truth in the scheme of Divine revelation: it is "the mystery which hath been hid from ages and from generations;" it is "the riches of the glory of this mystery among the Gentiles; which is Christ in you, the hope of glory."

Now of these truths the Apostles were ignorant previously to the conversion of Cornelius. Their views of gospel truth were bound up within the narrow range of Judaism. The world-wide range of Christianity, the purely spiritual nature of the religion, the offering of Christ's blood for every member of the human family, the free communion of every sanctified soul with God through the Spirit, and the universality of their Master's kingdom must have been either unknown to them or most imperfectly comprehended. They must have viewed all the benefits of redemption as restricted to the family of Abraham.

When St. Peter, therefore, was divinely directed to open the doors of the Church to the Gentile world, the Apostles and the Church must have received the greatest amount of supernatural enlightenment which had been imparted since the day of Pentecost. The stages of enlightenment through which the minds of the Apostles passed are, therefore, distinctly set before us in the history. They were first enlightened sufficiently to preach the gospel to the Jews only, and were afterwards instructed in its nature as a universal dispensation adapted to the wants of men.

But their ignorance of this great truth must have exerted a considerable influence on the nature of their previous teaching. On many points connected with the calling of the Gentiles they could not have kept absolute silence. Their general views of Christian truth must have been influenced by the consideration that the great bulk of mankind were outcasts from the promises of the gospel. We are hardly capable of grasping the precise state of a mind to whom the announcement, that "in every nation he that fears God and works righteousness is accepted of Him," was the discovery of a profound mystery. That truth is obvious now; but it is a truth which even the minds of Apostles could not embrace previously to St. Peter's vision.

Much of their ordinary teaching to the Jewish converts must have been affected by this ignorance. What could they have taught about the value of existing Jewish rites? What could they have said respecting the efficacy of the whole sacrificial worship daily going on before their eyes in the Jewish Temple? Was it to receive a commemorative and

Christian meaning? What was its connexion with the great Sacrifice of the cross? Some of these questions must have received a solution from them of some kind. St. Luke tells us that "a great company of the priests became obedient unto the faith." What did the Apostles direct them to do respecting their duties in the Temple, in connexion with its ritual? Did they allow them still to offer the sacrifices, and to sprinkle the altar with the blood of victims, after the great High Priest had appeared for ever, in the presence of God, with His own blood? St. Luke is silent as to the nature of their teaching on these subjects. We only know from him that the Apostles still continued frequenters of the Temple worship.

But, as the illumination which was imparted to the Apostles was a gradual one between the first communication of the Spirit and the conversion of Cornelius, we have no right to assume that the illumination which was imparted to them by this last event at once opened to their minds a full and complete view of the higher mysteries of the gospel. An increasing degree of knowledge seems to have been imparted to their minds when the providence of God opened to them fresh spheres of labour. For the first preaching of the gospel to the Gentiles a very different instrument was prepared, in the person of St. Paul. The original Apostles, for a considerable time longer, confined their labours to the conversion of the Jewish people, although the providence of God had provided that St. Peter should be the instrument to break down that middle wall of partition which had hitherto separated Jew from Gentile.

The language of St. Paul on this subject is remarkable:—
"And when James, Cephas, and John, who seemed to be pillars, perceived the grace that was given unto me, they gave to me and Barnabas the right hands of fellowship, that we should go unto the heathen, and they unto the circumcision." This language certainly implies that the three pillars of the Jewish church did not at that time take an active part in preaching the gospel to the Gentiles. They did not consider it as their proper sphere of labour till a later period of their lives. They only gave to Paul and Barnabas *the right hands*

of fellowship, that they should go to the heathen. They approved of their work, but did not personally engage in it.

We have few data for determining the stages of enlightenment which their minds underwent after the conversion of Cornelius. St. Paul determines the period when the great truth of the calling of the Gentiles, and all its attendant consequences, had been fully revealed to the whole inspired body of the Christian Church. He assures us that such was the case when he wrote the Epistle to the Ephesians. "The mystery of Christ," says he, "which in other ages was not made known unto the sons of men, as it is *now revealed unto His holy apostles and prophets by the Spirit; that the Gentiles should be fellowheirs, and of the same body, and partakers of his promise in Christ by the gospel.*"

This passage distinctly affirms that this great truth had been fully communicated to the whole inspired body when St. Paul wrote this Epistle: it implies that it had even been revealed for a considerable time.

But both St. Paul's Epistles and the Acts of the Apostles afford grounds for believing that this revelation was not fully made to the whole of the inspired body for some considerable time after the conversion of Cornelius,—probably not till after the time of St. Paul's last journey to Jerusalem.

There was in existence a large body of Jewish Christians who disputed this truth: they were unable to bear it. The inspired teachers of the Jewish church could not, therefore, have distinctly stated this truth as an integral portion of Christian doctrine; or professed believers holding these opinions must have set themselves against their authority, and created a schism.

We find that a Jewish party everywhere followed St. Paul in his preaching among the Gentiles, and endeavoured to propagate among the churches which he planted the belief that, in addition to faith in Christ, the observance of the Mosaic ordinances was essential to salvation. Their object was to encumber Christianity with a mass of ritualism. Everything in the Epistles implies that such persons were not unbelievers, but professedly Christian Jews, who rejected the authority of the alleged revelation which St. Paul asserted that he had received—that the privileges of the kingdom of God were not dependent on the observance of any outward rite or ordinance, but could be obtained by faith alone.

According to the testimony of the Epistle to the Corinthians, St. Paul's opponents quoted against him the authority of some Christian teacher: "Every one of you saith, I am of Paul; and I of Apollos; and I of Cephas; and I of Christ." From the Epistle to the Galatians we learn that Judaizers professed to preach a gospel, though a different one from that preached by St. Paul. It follows, therefore, that they could not have been unconverted, but professedly Christian Jews. St. Paul also tells us that they were brethren who came down from James who tempted St. Peter to his great act of hypocrisy of openly withdrawing from the society of the Gentiles.

It is evident that these persons were in communion with the church at Jerusalem. They must have quoted authority of some kind: on what could their views have been founded? James, at the council, had given his opinion that the Gentile Christians were only to be required to observe the four precepts. He seems to have considered that the Jewish Christians would still continue in the observance of the Mosaic rites. St. Peter had gone still further: he not only declared that God made no difference between Jew and Gentile, purifying the hearts of both alike by faith, but he even pronounced that the Mosaic ritual was a burden which neither they nor their fathers were able to bear. Still it would seem to be impossible that the doctrines which St. Paul taught could have been openly proclaimed by the inspired teachers of the Jewish church. Persons with the opinions in question would have separated from such a communion. Such a schism subsequently took place. This is confirmed by the following fact.

At the time of St. Paul's last journey to Jerusalem, St. James and the elders told him that there were many (ten-) thousands of Jews who believed, who were all zealous for the law. These had heard certain reports of St. Paul's teaching among the Gentiles, which had exasperated them against him. They apprehended danger to the Apostle's person, and advised him to take the course for conciliating them which we have already considered.

Now how do we account for the existence of this state of things in the Jewish church? Whether we consider that the danger would arise to St. Paul's person from Christian or from unconverted Jews, the fact is undeniable, that there were many thousands of Jews in communion with the Jewish church, all zealous for the law, and who were deeply prejudiced against St. Paul, so that from this prejudice there was the probability of a tumult which would endanger his life. The Jews zealous for the law, who were highly prejudiced against St. Paul, were evidently members of the Jewish church.

Had the inspired teachers of the Jewish church then preached the gospel in such terms as we read in St. Paul's Epistles? Had they announced the great truth that there is neither circumcision nor uncircumcision, but that both Jew and Gentile are one in Christ? Had they taught that legal observances were weak and beggarly elements, only to be justified in their observance because they were valueless? It is evident that the thousands of believing Jews were animated by no feelings of animosity towards St. James and the elders. These do not dread a tumult on their own account, but because of St. Paul. Wherefore this difference in feeling? Could the great truths respecting the calling of the Gentiles, and all the important consequences flowing from them, as we read them in St. Paul's Epistles, have been proclaimed in the ears of the Jewish Christians? If they had been so, the conclusion would seem to be inevitable, either that they would have yielded to the inspired authority of the teachers of the Church, or that St. James and the elders would have incurred the same hatred at their hands as that which was incurred by St. Paul.

But as St. James and the elders entertain no sense of danger for themselves, it is evident that they could not have offended the prejudices of the Jewish Christians in a similar manner to St. Paul. St. Paul had consented to the observance of the

Jewish rites by native Jews as national institutions which possessed in themselves no intrinsic value. But those Jewish Christians who could come together and endanger a tumult must have had very different views of the value of those rites from regarding them as national customs retained for a temporary purpose: they must have viewed them as things deeply important, and of the highest obligation.

The only explanation which can be given of this circumstance is, that the prophets and teachers of the Jewish church could not yet have habitually proclaimed as an integral portion of their teaching the great truth that all men are equal before God in Christ. They must have avoided touching on such topics in their public teaching, and have dwelt on such truths of the gospel as did not involve them: they must have taught those Christian truths which did not give offence to the prejudices of the Jews, and carefully avoided points of controversy. On this principle, the peculiarities of the Epistle of St. James are easily explicable. The great mysteries of Christianity, as they are treated of by St. Paul, in this Epistle are passed over in silence; we may take this Epistle, therefore, as a fair exemplification of Christianity as it was taught by the inspired teachers of the Jewish church. There is nothing in the Epistle to wound the prejudices of a Jewish Christian.

But if, as St. Paul asserts, the great truth had been disclosed in all its fulness, when he wrote the Epistle to the Ephesians, to all persons possessed of the gift of inspiration, this revelation must have been completed in the interval between his imprisonment at Jerusalem and the termination of his imprisonment at Rome.

The mind of the Jewish church, at this period, must have resembled that of the Apostles prior to our Lord's ascension. The Spirit must have had many things to say unto them; but, like the Apostles, they could not bear them then. They were dealt with in a similar manner, in the earlier portion of the dispensation of the Spirit, to that in which our Lord dealt with the Apostles: the truth was discovered to them as they were able to bear it. But a time was rapidly approaching when it would be no longer the Divine purpose to bear with the prejudices of the Jewish people. What they could not endure in the way of teaching, they were forced to endure by a terrible providence. As that day approached, the revelation of gospel truth, in its full proportions, was no longer withheld. At last the Jewish vineyard was laid completely waste; it could be neither pruned nor digged. No longer could a single rite of its religion be celebrated according to the injunctions of the law. The day arrived which St. Stephen had foreseen. Jesus of Nazareth destroyed the holy place, the Temple, and the city, and for ever rendered the celebration of the Mosaic worship impossible. The Church separated from the Synagogue. No sacrifice on Mount Moriah could any longer be set up as a rival to the great Sacrifice on the cross.

The contents of the Epistle of St. James form a marked contrast to those of the Epistles of St. Paul, and they are a remarkable illustration of Christianity as it was taught in the Jewish church. We therefore subjoin a summary of it. There is not even a solitary allusion to the fact that the Gentiles formed part of the Church of God. Its topics are:—
The trial of faith ought to be a subject for rejoicing. God is a liberal giver in answer to prayer. The necessity of faith, if prayer is to be answered. The instability of riches. Temptation to evil cannot come from God, but is resolvable into the free will of man. God is the author of all good. The necessity of manifesting the reality of religion by outward actions. The danger of self-deceit. Solemn warnings to the rich. The nature of the law. The worthlessness of faith which does not exert a corresponding influence on the conduct. The duty of governing the tongue. The danger of lust: solemn denunciations of its indulgence. The sin of evil-speaking. The folly of calculating on tomorrow. Denunciations of the rich oppressor. The duty of patient waiting for the coming of the Lord. Several precepts for the steady performance of duty. It is worthy of particular observation, that in this Epistle the place of Christian assembly is still designated as the synagogue, and not the church.

It is impossible that the most careless reader of this Epistle can help being struck by the contrast between its contents and those of an Epistle of St. Paul. If it was composed early, its peculiarities are accounted for. Its contents are evenly strongly contrasted with those of the Epistles of St. Peter, who had been the instrument of opening the door of faith to the Gentiles, and which were certainly written late in the Apostle's life. The peculiarities of the Epistle of St. James have often been attempted to be accounted for by asserting that the circumstances in reference to which he wrote only led him to treat on the topics included in the Epistle. This is, no doubt, the real account of the matter. But it should be observed that the topics of the Epistle are those which might be addressed to Jewish Christians without wounding their religious and national prejudices. Such Christians required instruction in far higher and more glorious truths, to bring them to the measure of the stature of the fulness of Christ. But it was necessary to feed them with milk, and not with meat, until the appointed hour of God's providence arrived, when that which had long been decaying and waxing old was ready to vanish away. As their views were gradually enlarged by the Spirit, the original Apostles betook themselves to larger spheres of labour.

The inspiration possessed by the Apostles in the earlier period of their ministry prevented them from teaching, as Christian truths, doctrines not possessed of that character. It illuminated their minds with that amount of Christian truth which was suitable for enabling them to preach the gospel to the Jewish people. It enlarged their views of Christian truth, and dispelled their prejudices gradually. It was only after a training of this description that their minds attained unto the measure of the stature of the fulness of Christ. To the fulness of that knowledge it ultimately led them. The nature of that full inspiration we must now consider.

CHAPTER XVIII.

THE NATURE AND EXTENT OF FULL APOSTOLIC INSPIRATION.

In estimating the full effects produced on an apostle's mind by the influence of the great gifts of the Spirit, we must inquire into St. Paul's assertions as to the nature of his own inspiration, and the mode and extent in which it existed in his mind.

In St. Paul's case, enlightenment was not a gradual process, like that of the other Apostles. He was an instrument who had undergone a very different previous preparation for his work from that of the original Apostles. He himself expressly declares that his entire knowledge of Christian truth was derived directly from a miraculous revelation, and from that alone.

An examination of the assertions of St. Paul respecting the extent of his own inspiration, and the mode in which divine truth existed in his mind, will give us a distinct conception of the nature of the supernatural gift of wisdom, which communicated the highest form of apostolical inspiration.

According to the Apostle's assertions, his knowledge of divine truth embraced a comprehensive view of all the great outlines of the Christian revelation. It formed a system of truth which, while it had been divinely taught him by the influence of the Spirit, was yet constantly present to his mind, and clearly and definitely comprehended by his understanding. To form a clear view on this subject, we must examine his assertions in detail.

The first passage which we adduce as pointing out the nature of the Apostle's inspiration is 2 Cor. xii. 2-4: "I knew a man in Christ above fourteen years ago, (whether in the body, I cannot tell; or whether out of the body, I cannot tell: God knoweth;) such an one caught up to the third heaven. And I knew such a man, (whether in the body, or out of the body, I cannot tell: God knoweth ;) how that he was caught up into paradise, and heard unspeakable words, which it is not lawful for a man to utter" (ἄρρητα ῥήματα ἃ οὐκ ἐξὸν ἀνθρώπῳ λαλῆσαι).

This latter clause must mean that some of the revelations which the Apostle received were of such a nature that they could not be conceived of in ordinary human conceptions, and therefore could not be expressed in language. If they could be expressed in language, they could not have been unspeakable (ἄρρητα). The Apostle does not mean by the expression, "which it is not lawful for a man to utter" (ἃ οὐκ ἐξὸν ἀνθρώπῳ λαλῆσαι), to assert that he could utter them but was forbidden to do so, but that it was not possible for man to speak them in conceptions which would be intelligible to others.

Comparing this passage with the Apostle's assertions to the Galatians which we have already considered, we learn that he must have received supernatural communications respecting two kinds of truth; of these, one was distinctly intelligible, which he not only could utter, but which it was his great duty to utter and to proclaim. We shall find him asserting, in numerous other portions of his Epistles, that his great revelations of Christian truth were of this description. The second was that species of supernatural communications referred to in the above passage: these he expressly declares to have consisted of unspeakable things, which are not lawful for a man to utter; they must have been communications, therefore, addressed to the higher forms of the Apostle's consciousness, but incapable of being expressed in comprehensible human language.

During the time of their delivery, St. Paul asserts that he was in a state of unconsciousness as to locality: his mind was incapable of asserting whether he was in the body or out of it.

Whether, therefore, we consider that the truths thus communicated were unutterable because the Apostle was forbidden to disclose them, or because they did not admit of being expressed in intelligible language, we must arrive at the same conclusion, that they were designed for the Apostle alone, and that they were not intended to form a portion of the Christian revelation. All attempts to explain their nature must therefore be mere idle curiosity.

But the Apostle is no less positive in his assertions that his great revelations of Christian truth were of a wholly different character, and were communicated to him in an intelligible form. Not only did they consist of truths which were utterable, but which he felt it his high duty and privilege to proclaim. They might ascend into regions beyond the utmost powers of human thought; but, as far as they were revealed, they were distinctly cognizable by the human understanding.

One of the most remarkable assertions of the Apostle respecting the nature of these truths is 1 Cor. ii. 6–16: "Howbeit we speak wisdom among them that are perfect: yet not the wisdom of this world, nor of the princes of this world, that come to nought: but we speak the wisdom of God in a mystery, even the hidden wisdom, which God ordained before the world unto our glory: which none of the princes of this world knew: for had they known it, they would not have crucified the Lord of glory. But, as it is written, The things which eye saw not, and ear heard not, and which came not up upon heart of man, the things which God hath prepared for them that love Him, to us God revealed through His Spirit*: for the Spirit searcheth all things, yea, the deep things of God. For what man knoweth the things of a man, save the spirit of man which is in him? even so the things of God knoweth no man, but the Spirit of God. Now we have received, not the spirit of the world, but the spirit which is of God; that we might know the things that are freely given to us of God. Which things also we speak, not in the words which man's wisdom teacheth, but which the Holy Ghost teacheth; comparing spiritual things with spiritual. But the natural man receiveth not the things of the Spirit of God: for they are foolishness unto him; neither can he know them, because they are spiritually discerned. But he that is spiritual judgeth all

* See Alford *in loco*. The authorized version is evidently wrong.

things, yet he himself is judged of no man. For who hath known the mind of the Lord, that he may instruct Him? But we have the mind of Christ."

We first observe that the Apostle designates the subject of his preaching by the term "wisdom." This expression he elsewhere uses to denote the highest spiritual gift, which formed the special endowment for the office of an apostle. We therefore conclude that in this passage he is speaking of the highest forms of revealed truth. In this passage the Apostle makes the following declarations respecting the nature of his own inspiration:—

1. He asserts that the truths thus revealed were cognizable by his understanding. The term wisdom ($\sigma o \phi i a$) implies the highest order of human thought, but in a distinctly intelligible form. He tells us that "he spoke these truths;" they found utterance in language through him.

Now truths which are capable of being spoken by man must exist in the understanding in an intelligible form; as such, they stand contrasted with "unspeakable words, which it is not lawful for a man to utter." Truths capable of utterance must be capable of existing in the mind in the form of distinct conceptions.

2. The Apostle also distinctly asserts that these truths were of such a nature that he was capable of exerting his rational powers upon them. He spoke these words, "comparing spiritual things with spiritual." Wherever a comparison between truth takes place, the powers of rational judgment must be exerted. To enable the human mind to exercise judgment or comparison, the thoughts on which judgment or comparison takes place must be comprehensible by the understanding. It is impossible to pronounce a judgment respecting two thoughts, of which the human mind cannot form a distinct conception.

3. But the wisdom which the Apostle preached formed a distinct subject of divine revelation to his mind: he derived it from no human source. He tells us that it was once "a hidden wisdom, which God ordained before the world unto our glory." He then informs us that, although hidden in

former ages, " God has revealed them unto us by His Spirit." He then gives the reason of the possibility of the disclosure of such deep counsels of the Divine mind, that "the Spirit searcheth all things, even the deep things of God." He further tells us that this wisdom was communicated " to him in words which the Holy Ghost taught him," and that the Spirit's acquaintance with the deep things of God is as perfect and accurate as man's acquaintance with the secrets of his own mind. " For who knoweth the things of a man, save the spirit of man which is in him? even so the things of God knoweth no man, but the Spirit of God." The Apostle in these words implies that the great truths which formed the subject of the special gospel revelation are as much above the reach of man's ordinary powers to have discovered, as the things belonging to man, and his mental processes, would be beyond the powers of any inferior order of creation. Words could not have been used more suited to express the reality of the Apostle's conviction that the truths which he taught had originated in no human source of knowledge, but were introduced into his mind through the agency of the Divine Spirit.

4. But as the subject of the Apostle's preaching was a high form of divine knowledge, it differed entirely from ordinary human wisdom as developed by the action of man's natural powers: this wisdom the Apostle affirms to be the wisdom of God, and not the wisdom of man. " The hidden wisdom," says he, " which none of the princes of this world knew; for had they known it, they would not have crucified the Lord of glory." It was a wisdom consisting of such things as eye had not seen, nor ear had heard, which had not come into the heart of man—the things which God had prepared for them that love Him. These words, also, in the strongest manner assert the preternatural source and origin of his knowledge.

5. The wisdom which the Apostle preached would not be discovered to be wisdom by men of earthly minds and appetites. They, viewing things according to their low and degraded standard, might consider it not as a high and divine wisdom, but as mere folly. The reason of this was obvious:

z

it was a wisdom which required a divine sense for its appreciation. The reason why worldly men did not appreciate the gospel revelation as wisdom is given by the Apostle. "The natural [or mere animal] man (ψυχικὸς ἄνθρωπος) receiveth not the things of the Spirit of God; for they are foolishness unto him: neither can he know them, because they are spiritually discerned."

6. To enable the truths of God to be appreciated, man must be raised above the mere wants and affections of his animal nature; he must acquire a sense which is capable of discerning and appreciating spiritual things. In the same manner as the eye is an incorrect judge of sound, and the ear of light, so the mere affections of man's animal nature are incorrect judges of the things and affections of the Spirit of God, and of God's mode of acting in the spiritual world. What man with his animal faculties may pronounce foolishness might be seen by proper spiritual powers of discernment to be the wisdom of God, worthy of the Divine character and perfections.

7. The Apostle had learned these truths by having received the Spirit which is of God. By His influences he had received spiritual senses, spiritual faculties, and a spiritual apprehension; so that "he knew the things which were freely given to him of God." By means of this illumination, the "spiritually minded man was the adequate judge of all spiritual things." None but a spiritually minded man could sit in judgment on spiritual subjects. The great truths of the Christian revelation were the mind of Christ.

We infer, therefore, that truths of this kind must have been distinctly cognizable by the Apostle's understanding, and were capable of being reasoned on by him: as such they must have formed a permanent portion of his mental consciousness.

We next adduce 2 Corinthians, xi. 5, 6: "For I suppose I was not a whit behind the very chiefest apostles. But though I be rude in speech, yet not in knowledge; but we have been throughly made manifest among you in all things."

This passage contains a distinct assertion, on the part of the Apostle, that the knowledge of Christian truth was possessed by his mind, not in a transitory, but in a permanent form. He compares his knowledge of Christian truth with his powers of language: in speech he was rude, but not in knowledge. His knowledge of Christian truth was capable of a most favourable comparison with his powers of utterance. As the one must have been a permanent endowment, so must the other have formed a portion of his general consciousness.

Had the Apostle been speaking of any branch of scientific truth, he could hardly have spoken of it as more under the control of his mental powers than he has spoken of his acquaintance with the subjects of divine revelation. If a man of science were to say, "My acquaintance with this particular branch of philosophy is far deeper than my powers of speaking," we could hardly fail to understand his meaning. Such an expression would most clearly imply that his knowledge existed as a permanent mental endowment. Imperfect, however, as the Apostle says his powers as a speaker were, he yet asserts that he was thoroughly made manifest unto them in all things. The truths, therefore, as capable of a distinct enunciation in language, must have existed in an intelligible form in the understanding.

The conclusions respecting the nature of the Apostle's knowledge which these two passages suggest are in strict conformity with what we have already learned respecting the nature of the supernatural gifts, and with the exercise of them being in subjection to the supremacy of the rational will.

Eph. iii. 1-11, contains a very important declaration of the Apostle as to the nature and extent of apostolic inspiration:—" For this cause I Paul, the prisoner of Jesus Christ for you Gentiles, if ye have heard of the dispensation of the grace of God which is given me to you-ward: how that by revelation He made known unto me the mystery; (as I wrote afore in few words; whereby, when ye read, ye may understand my knowledge in the mystery of Christ) which in other ages was not made known unto the sons of men, as it is now revealed unto His holy apostles and prophets by the Spirit. . . . . . Unto me, who am less than the least of all saints, is this grace given, that I should preach among the Gentiles the unsearchable riches of Christ; and to make all men see what is the fellowship of the mystery, which from the beginning of the world hath been hid in God, who created all things by Jesus Christ: to the intent that now unto the principalities and powers in heavenly places might be known by the church the manifold wisdom of God, according to the eternal purpose which He purposed in Christ Jesus our Lord."

The Apostle, in this passage, makes several most distinct assertions respecting the nature of his own inspiration.

1. The knowledge which he possessed of Christian truth was not the result of human teaching, but was a communication from God. He expressly declares that it was made known to him by revelation.

The word "revelation" ($\dot{a}\pi o\kappa\dot{a}\lambda v\psi\iota s$) bears a distinct reference to the word "mystery" ($\mu v\sigma\tau\acute{\eta}\rho\iota o\nu$): "how that by revelation He made known unto me the mystery," which might be fairly represented in English by the words, "how that by uncovering He made known to me the hidden truth." The thing made known was a revelation or disclosing of divine truth: it had been, before it was disclosed, a mystery or hidden truth. The mysteries of the ancient world were truths hidden from the great bulk of mankind, and disclosed to the select few. The mystery, therefore, which had been hid in former ages became a revelation when discovered to the mind of the Apostle. The Apostle does not use the term mystery to designate the incomprehensible nature of the truth, but to express the fact that it was truth once hidden in the Divine counsels, but now made known by revelation.

2. The subject-matter disclosed to the Apostle was the mystery or hidden truth "which, from the beginning of the world, had been hid in God." If, therefore, it had been from the beginning of the world hid in God, it consisted of truths which had not previously been discovered by any former revelation of God. But a revelation had been previously

made of the Divine perfections by the natural universe. Respecting this revelation the Apostle writes to the Romans that "the invisible things of God from the creation of the world are clearly seen, being understood by the things that are made, even His eternal power and Godhead." Things, therefore, discoverable by the light of nature formed no part of the mystery which had been hid in God from the foundation of the world; they were therefore no portion of the disclosures made to St. Paul by revelation. The mystery which was made known by revelation did not consist of any knowledge of God communicated through the created universe, but was strictly limited to the great truths connected with Christian truth. St. Paul designates them as "the mystery of Christ," or the great truths manifested in and by the Incarnation. It follows, therefore, that St. Paul in this passage has distinctly determined the limit of the knowledge which was communicated to him by revelation, and, by consequence, of his own inspiration—that it was confined to the special subject-matter of the Christian revelation. He had no revelation made to him on subjects which had not been "hid in God from the foundation of the world." But there was another class of divine truths which had not been thus hidden; for the Apostle writes (Rom. i. 20), "The invisible things of Him from the creation of the world are clearly seen, being understood by the things that are made, even His eternal power and Godhead." Such subjects, therefore, formed no portion of the Apostle's revelations.

3. The Apostle distinctly states the manner in which this body of revealed truth existed in his own mind. "As I wrote before," says he, "in few words, whereby when ye read ye may understand my knowledge in the mystery of Christ."

The Apostle here tells us that, by reading the previous part of the Epistle, the extent of his knowledge in the mystery of Christ might be made the subject of estimation. It would have been hardly possible to employ words more suited to assert the fact that the Apostle's knowledge of Christian truth must have existed in his mind in a permanent form, like his other knowledge, than the words used by him. The reader would be able to estimate the extent of that knowledge by reading what he had written : we have only to make a substitution in his language to see that this is the only meaning which it can naturally convey. Let us suppose him to have said, " I have written in the former part of my letter on the science of astronomy. By reading what I have written on that subject, you may understand my acquaintance with that science." Had he written thus, we could not have doubted that he was speaking of truths permanently existing in his mind, and clearly comprehended by it.

It follows, therefore, that the gift of wisdom, with which the Apostle was endowed, was a permanently abiding gift, communicating to his mental consciousness a clear knowledge of the great truths of the Christian revelation in a distinct and intelligible form.

4. The Apostle further asserts that his revealed knowledge embraced an acquaintance with the profoundest Christian truth: "as I have written before in few words, whereby when ye read ye may understand my knowledge in the mystery of Christ."

The Apostle here assures us that the perusal of the former portion of the Epistle will convince us of the depth of his knowledge of the great Christian truths. What, then, are the topics which he has dwelt on ? God's blessing the Church with all spiritual blessings in Christ. His choice of the Church, in His eternal purposes, to be holy and without blame in love. The great doctrine of redemption by Christ. The sealing of Christians by the Spirit. God's purpose to bring them to an everlasting inheritance—to the praise of His glory. The quickening of those who were dead in sins to a new spiritual life in Christ. The whole plan of man's redemption and salvation by faith. The bearing of all these great truths on the calling of the Gentiles into the Church of Christ, and the presenting of the whole Church blameless to the Father through sanctification of the Spirit ; and the free access and communion which the whole Church of the redeemed, without distinction of race or outward privilege, enjoys with the Father.

These were the subjects which the Apostle wrote on in the former part of the Epistle. They form the great mystery which had in former ages been hid in God, and was now revealed to St. Paul. Such deep truths, therefore, form the proper subject-matter of the apostolical gift of wisdom, and point out the profundity of those truths which it communicated in a clear and intelligible form in the Apostle's mind.

5. The Apostle informs us that these disclosures not only consist of truths in former ages unknown to men, but that by means of this great revelation of the gospel, in conformity with an eternal purpose existing in the Divine mind, "now unto the principalities and powers in heavenly places is made known by the Church the manifold wisdom of God." The disclosures made in the Christian revelation were not only a burst of light respecting the Divine character to men, but to the angels in heaven.

St. Paul writes to the same effect in the Epistle to the Colossians, i. 25-28: "Whereof I am made a minister, according to the dispensation of God which is given to me for you, to fulfil the word of God; even the mystery which hath been hid from ages and from generations, but now is made manifest to His saints: to whom God would make known what is the riches of the glory of this mystery among the Gentiles; which is Christ in you, the hope of glory: whom we preach."

This statement of the Apostle corroborates all the deductions which we have made from the former passage. He here speaks of the mystery which has been hidden from ages and generations, but which is now made manifest unto the saints. That mystery, he says, "is Christ in you, the hope of glory." The mystery has a riches of glory: St. Paul was intrusted with the publication of it.

It follows, therefore, first, in conformity with the usage of St. Paul, that the expression "the mystery" denotes the great truths of the gospel revelation, including the Divine person of our Lord himself. Secondly, that this mystery became the subject of revelation, and that, when revealed, it contained such displays of the Divine character and perfections that St. Paul designates its discovery "the riches of glory." Thirdly, that although the mystery was now a revealed truth, it had been hidden in times preceding the gospel dispensation. Fourthly, that as the truths contained in it had been hidden from all preceding times, the great mystery revealed by the gospel could not have contained truths revealed by the natural universe; for the apostle has elsewhere distinctly stated that the material universe contains a distinct discovery of those truths. Fifthly, that the hidden mystery was revealed intelligibly by the gospel dispensation: "Christ, whom we preach," says he, "is now made manifest." Sixthly, that this mystery formed the subject of the revelation made to St. Paul, which was therefore limited to the communication of the great truths of the Christian revelation, being the mystery hid in bygone ages, now made manifest to the saints—the great truths of the Incarnation.

St. Paul, in 1 Corinthians, xiii., unites together three gifts: "Though I have the gift of prophecy, and understand all mysteries, and all knowledge." He is speaking in this passage of the supernatural gifts of the Spirit. Now the only supernatural gift of the Spirit to which the "understanding of all mysteries" can belong is the gift of wisdom. This gift, therefore, being the one preeminently apostolical, as we have seen, is the one through which the higher forms of Christian truth—the great mystery or truth of the gospel, once hidden, but now revealed—were communicated.

To the same effect the Apostle writes, Titus i. 1-3 :—" Paul, a servant of God, and an apostle of Jesus Christ, according to the faith of God's elect, and the acknowledging of the truth which is after godliness; in hope of eternal life, which God, that cannot lie, promised before the world began; but hath in due times manifested His word through preaching, which is committed unto me according to the commandment of God our Saviour." "The truth which is after godliness" must mean the great disclosures of the Christian revelation. The

Apostle speaks of it as synonymous with "the faith of God's elect." This truth contains the hope of eternal life. It was promised before the times of the ages (called in our version "before the world began"). The Apostle then asserts that in times suitable to the Divine purposes God has made manifest this great revelation through preaching, with which preaching St. Paul himself was intrusted. In this passage the same truths are asserted as in the former ones.

As the gift of wisdom communicated Christian truth in its highest forms to the minds of the Apostles, the gift of knowledge imparted that truth in its practical bearings. As it was the special gift qualifying the possessor for the office of teacher in the Church, it was a gift more widely diffused than the apostolical gift of wisdom. The Apostle even assigns it a rank inferior to the gift of prophecy. It helped to form the complete idea of apostolical inspiration.

We read (Phil. iii. 8-10) :—"Yea doubtless, and I count all things but loss for the excellency of the knowledge of Christ Jesus my Lord : for whom I have suffered the loss of all things, and do count them but dung, that I may win Christ, and be found in Him, not having mine own righteousness, which is of the law, but that which is through the faith of Christ, the righteousness which is of God by faith : that I may know Him, and the power of His resurrection, and the fellowship of His sufferings, being made conformable unto His death."

The Apostle here evidently speaks of his knowledge of Christian truth in its practical form. He is speaking of a knowledge of Christianity extending its powerful influences to the heart. The clear comprehension of the higher truths formed the means by which the experimental enjoyment of them was attained. He speaks of "counting all things but loss for the excellency of the *knowledge* of Christ Jesus," and then describes it as the end of his efforts "to *know* Him and the power of His resurrection." The language employed by him, even in the case of this gift, implies a form of permanently abiding knowledge in the mind of the possessor.

We have already considered the nature of the prophetic gift. By means of it the Apostle received special suggestions respecting divine truth, and was enabled to communicate the results of the other gifts in suitable and intelligible language. The Apostle's writings also supply us with two examples in which the prophetic Spirit imparted to him a revelation of the distant future (2 Thess. ii., and 1 Tim. iv.) It also appears to have been the gift through which a restraining influence was exerted over the mind, hindering the inspired person from bringing forward truths or stating facts which, although true in themselves, formed no portion of the Christian revelation.

To complete the full idea of the Apostle's inspiration, we must add the supernatural assistance imparted by the other spiritual gifts. He would possess the two miraculous gifts, the gift of discerning of spirits, that of faith, of tongues, and of interpretation. Each of these would convey an inspiration within its respective limits.

We must not forget that each of these gifts admitted of degrees in the fulness in which it was possessed. This was even the case with the gift of wisdom. St. Peter's express testimony affirms this: he tells us that St. Paul wrote some things hard to be understood, " according to the wisdom given to him." St. Paul, therefore, possessed a very high form of this gift: it enabled him to treat of the profoundest doctrines of the Gospel dispensation. It does not follow that every apostolical man had the same degree of the gift, but, as St. Paul himself affirms, that each of the gifts was imparted in measure and degree in conformity with the pleasure of the Spirit, " who divided to every man severally as He would." In conformity with this assertion, St. Peter tells us that St. Paul's high form of the apostolical gift was " according to the wisdom given to him." Another apostle's gift might not have developed itself in the knowledge of things hard to be understood, but in some other form. We have already seen, by the history of the Acts of the Apostles, that the prophetic gift sometimes imparted to an apostle a less insight into the future than it did to an ordinary prophet.

We possess a few statements of the Apostle as to the general effect which his inspiration exerted on his teaching. In 1 Thess. ii. 13, we read:—"For this cause also thank we God without ceasing, because, when ye received the word of God which ye heard of us, ye received it not as the word of men, but as it is in truth, the word of God, which effectually worketh also in you that believe."

This passage contains two distinct statements: first, that the Apostle's oral teaching was of the same authority as his written teaching; and secondly, that there is a sense in which both were to be received as the word of God.

This passage is express in its assertion of the full inspired authority of his oral teaching. It has reference to his oral teaching alone. At the time when he visited Thessalonica he had written nothing. Whatever divine authority he ascribes in this passage to his teaching, he asserts it of his oral teaching. We may safely infer that the same authority must have extended to his written teaching; for his Epistles are, in fact, his oral teaching expressed in writing. Similar references to his oral teaching abound in his other Epistles.

But what is the degree of divine authority which it ascribes to his teaching, whether oral or written? He commends the Thessalonians for not receiving it as the word of man, but as it was in truth, the word of God. What, then, is the meaning which he intended to convey by saying that his teaching was "the word of God"?

The Apostle's assertion is evidently made of himself, in his capacity of a teacher of the Christian revelation. He does not mean to assert that whatever he said was to be received as the word of God, but that it was to be viewed as such when he communicated the great message with which he was charged —the truth of the gospel.

In the first portion of the passage, the expression "the word of God which ye have heard of us" obviously means the alleged revelation which the Apostle asserted to have been communicated to him by God. He commends the Thessalonians for receiving his alleged revelation as delivered by him, which he calls "the word of God which ye have heard of us," as it was in truth—not a cunning revelation of human craftiness, but really a divine revelation.

Our translators have involved the Apostle's meaning in some little obscurity by rendering the two words παραλαβόντες and ἐδέξασθε by the same English word "receive," whereas it is evident that the Apostle intended to express an entire distinction of meaning between them. By ἐδέξασθε he meant to express the actual embracing of the subjects of his preaching by the Thessalonians as positively true. By παραλαβόντες he merely meant to denote that they had heard from him the announcement of what professed to be a divine revelation. The one word denotes the objective proclamation of it, the other the subjective reception of it, as true.

We have already considered the sense in which a preternatural revelation can be God's word, the channel through which the divine truths must be communicated, and the limitations to which they must be subject in passing through the finite mind. In calling his teaching the word of·God, the Apostle, therefore, means to affirm that the truths which he taught were communicated to his mind by supernatural revelation, and that he possessed such supernatural guidance as enabled him to communicate the truths which had been imparted to him correctly to others.

But the passage determines nothing as to the mode in which the Divine communication was made to the mind of the Apostle, or the degree in which a human element might be employed by God in connexion with that revelation. The Apostle designates the subject of his teaching as the word of God, because the great truths of the Christian revelation were imparted to him by God by the aid of supernatural inspiration. As we have already seen, the words cannot mean that the expressions contained in a revelation are the word of God in the same sense in which the expressions contained in a human book are the word of man. They are called "God's word," because they represent the truth and mind of God.

Another similar assertion is made by the Apostle, 1 Cor. xiv. 37 :—" If any man think himself to be a prophet, or spiritual, let him acknowledge that the things that I write unto you are the commandments of the Lord," or, as the Greek says, " are the Lord's." " But if any man be ignorant, let him be ignorant."

The Apostle is here giving special directions for regulating the mode of exercising the spiritual gifts, and for the maintaining due order in the church. His object was to repress the abuses which had arisen in connexion with the gifts of tongues and prophecy. In opposition to these abuses, St. Paul declares that any person professing to be a prophet or spiritually-minded man would afford the best proof that he was what he professed to be, by at once assenting to the fact that the directions which he had been writing to the church were the Lord's, stamped with his authority.

We have therefore the Apostle's declaration that when he gave directions to the Church, and expressed his authoritative judgment, the directions as delivered by him are equivalent to commandments of the Lord. Some directions given by him, he distinctly tells us, do not possess this authority. Directions, to possess this authority, must have respect not to mere private matters, but to the ordering of the Church. In giving orders about the collections for the saints, the Apostle is careful to state that that direction is not given by Divine authority. 2 Cor. viii. 7, 8 : " Therefore, as ye abound in every thing, in faith, and utterance, and knowledge, and in all diligence, and in your love to us, see that ye abound in this grace also. I speak not by commandment, but by occasion of the forwardness of others, and to prove the sincerity of your love." On another occasion, the Apostle observes that he gives a direction as "one who had obtained mercy of the Lord to be faithful."

A few other directions of the Apostle must be excepted, which he has left to the discrimination of common sense, as when he directs Timothy to bring his cloak, or not to drink water, but wine. To the same purpose is his direction to Philemon to prepare him a lodging, and his request to receive with brotherly affection his slave Onesimus, where the Apostle expressly declares that, " although he might be bold in Christ to enjoin what was convenient, yet for love's sake he used entreaty, being such an one as Paul the aged, and now also a prisoner of Jesus Christ."

In 2 Cor. xi. 17, the Apostle writes, " That which I speak, I speak it not after the Lord, but as it were foolishly, in this confidence of boasting."

To assert that this or similar passages were dictated to the Apostle by the Spirit, after his own express declaration that he did not write them after the Lord, is expressly to contradict the testimony of an inspired man.

But in the same Epistle the Apostle no less clearly expresses his consciousness of writing under the influence of inspiration. "I told you," says he, "before, and foretell you, as if I were present, the second time; and being absent now I write to them which heretofore have sinned, and to all other, that, if I come again, I will not spare: since ye seek a proof of Christ speaking in me, which to you-ward is not weak, but is mighty in you" (2 Cor. xiii. 2, 3).

St. Paul frequently describes himself as holding the office of " an ambassador for Christ." A few points in which the illustration was intended to hold will throw light on our subject. An ambassador represents the person of him who sends him. He receives the instructions of his principal: he is bound to act in conformity with them. He communicates to others the will and pleasure of the person which he represents. As long as his language is in conformity with his instructions, the words uttered by him may be viewed as the declarations of the power for whom he acts. He may neither use the words nor the style of expression of his instructions; all that is required is, that his assertions and declarations should fully represent the meaning of them. The instructions of the Apostles were their knowledge of Christian truth communicated by inspiration to their minds. Such was the position which St. Paul asserts that he occupied in communicating the revelation of Jesus Christ. The Apostle, therefore, describes his inspiration by the expression, "Christ speaking in him." All that such an expression proves is that, as an ambassador for Christ, the Apostle's declarations possessed

Divine authority whenever they represented the instructions which he had received from Christ.

In Gal. iv. 14, the Apostle writes, "Ye received me as an angel of God, even as Christ Jesus." The Apostle had no wish to be received as the Saviour; what he claimed was to be received as His ambassador, and as the interpreter of His will. In this passage he speaks only of his oral teaching, and consequently asserts its equal inspiration with his written teaching.

We must now consider the Apostle's assertion, 2 Tim. iii. 14-17:—"But continue thou in the things which thou hast learned and hast been assured of, knowing of whom thou hast learned them; and that from a child thou hast known the holy scriptures, which are able to make thee wise unto salvation through faith which is in Christ Jesus. All scripture is given by inspiration of God, and is profitable for doctrine, for reproof, for correction, for instruction in righteousness: that the man of God may be perfect, throughly furnished unto all good works."

This passage is written of the Scriptures of the Old Testament, being the only Scriptures which Timothy knew from a child. Whatever inspiration it claims for the Old Testament Scriptures may safely be assumed as belonging to the New.

The great question is, What is the correct translation of the passage πᾶσα γραφὴ θεόπνευστος καὶ ὠφέλιμος? Were these words intended to convey the meaning "all scripture is given by inspiration of God, and is profitable," or, "all scripture given by inspiration of God is also profitable"?

High authorities may be adduced in favour of either rendering. As there is no absolute certainty which is the correct translation, numerous attempts have been made to determine the meaning by arguments as to the sense which the context requires. Weighty arguments can be adduced on both sides.

No well-informed person who has considered the subject, however much he may prefer the translation, "all scripture is given by inspiration of God," will be prepared to affirm that the passage cannot be translated, "all scripture given by inspiration from God is also profitable." It cannot be denied that numerous instances of a similar construction are to be found in the New Testament. Nor is it possible to affirm that powerful arguments in support of this translation may not be deduced from the context.

It must be admitted, therefore, that the passage is one of those whose meaning cannot be determined with actual certainty, and therefore cannot be quoted in evidence on either side of the argument.

There are several other passages in the New Testament which, owing to the doubtfulness either of the reading or the translation, are in a similar position. It is impossible to determine with actual certainty whether, in Heb. ix., the word διαθήκη means "covenant" or "testament." No well-informed person would, at the present day, quote the passage, " Feed the church of God, which He hath purchased with His own blood," as conclusive on the doctrine of the Trinity. The expression " church of the Lord " can vindicate a high claim to be esteemed that really written by St. Luke.

The doubtful meaning of such passages renders it impossible to quote them in controversy. Any person who is at all acquainted with the state of the evidence as to the translation must admit that this passage is one of a similar description.

But even admitting that the Apostle wrote " all scripture is given by inspiration," it is worth while to inquire whether the passage asserts that the New Testament is written under the influence of verbal inspiration and denies the existence in it of any human element.

Now, what meaning must be attached to the words πᾶσα γραφή? Does it mean the book generally, or every sentence or separate word in the book? Does it include the whole form of thought, and every expression in the style? Unless we are prepared to assert that it must have this meaning, it will be useless to adduce it in proof of the theory of verbal inspiration.

But we have direct proof that, by the use of this expression, the Apostle did not intend to assert that each of the books of Scripture was composed by the aid of inspiration at all analogous to verbal inspiration.

It is evident that these words were written of the Scriptures of the Old Testament. The peculiar phenomena presented by the Book of Job render it utterly impossible that the Apostle could have attached this meaning to them. To ascribe such a kind of inspiration to the various portions of the Book of Job is directly to contradict the assertions of the book itself. In this book, God is introduced as directly asserting that Job's friends had not spoken of Him that which was right. Although Job's general view of God's providence was correct, he had given utterance to many expressions respecting the Almighty highly presumptuous. The things, therefore, which the several speakers uttered in this book, according to its own assertions, were not dictated to them by the omniscient Spirit of God.

The author of the book may have been directed to record these speeches for the edification of the Church. This is a wholly different thing from saying that the discourses themselves, containing such representations of the Divine character, were dictated to their authors by supernatural inspiration.

It follows, therefore, that the assertion, "all scripture is given by inspiration of God," cannot be meant to declare that every expression in them was dictated by the Spirit of God, and is therefore infallibly true. The declaration of the Apostle must be capable of reconciliation with the phenomena presented by the Book of Job and abundance of similar phenomena in the Old Testament, and is therefore quite consistent with the presence of a human element existing in the Scriptures by the side of the divine one.

CHAPTER XIX.

THE HUMAN ELEMENT IN APOSTOLIC INSPIRATION.

WE have considered the declarations of St. Paul respecting the nature and extent of the divine element involved in his inspiration. We must now examine what traces his writings afford us of the presence of a human element. The first human element which we shall notice is the presence of his individuality.

Throughout the writings of the Apostles we discover the most certain proofs of the existence of their individuality. This is particularly the case with St. Paul. Perhaps of no man who ever lived, whose life we know from so concise a biography as that written by St. Luke, and whose writings are so brief as St. Paul's Epistles, have such marks of individuality been impressed both on the biography and on the writings. The Apostle is depicted in them as he lived and moved. This individuality forms the human element in the Epistles.

The supernatural communication of truth was made to the mind of the Apostle in such a manner that it did not overthrow or even interfere with this individuality: it left it whole and entire. The man Paul still existed. The revelations encircled the individual; the individual was encased in them: he was neither swallowed up nor absorbed by them. What Paul was before his conversion, he continued after his conversion, with altered views, different aims, with impulses receiving a new direction, with feelings and affections kindled into a brighter flame, and directed to a holier object. In every portion of his actions and his writings we see Paul, the energetic man, the self-sacrificing man, the much-enduring man, the man of tender feelings, the man of deep determination, the man of mighty intellect and of consummate judgment. His individuality is as clearly discernible from those of Peter, James, and John, as the individuality of Luther from Melancthon, or that of Whitfield from Wesley.

We discover no less distinctly the individuality of the other sacred writers: it is preserved throughout their writings. Who would ever be in danger of confounding between St. Peter, St. Paul, St. James, and St. John? Their great characteristics are as distinct as those of any four writers who ever lived. Great as were the endowments of St. Paul and St. John beyond those of the other Apostles, and high as were the regions of the spiritual world into which they soared, who would ever be in danger of failing to discern in their writings their distinctive characters? Every line of St. John is filled with self-conscious calmness; every line of St. Paul is replete with self-conscious power. The feelings and affections of the one resemble the mild sunshine of a genial spring; those of the other burn with the fervour of the summer's sun, and occasionally resemble the upheavings of the mighty deep. The Peter of the Epistles is the Peter of the Gospels, only refined, purified, and chastened. Unmistakeably does every line written by St. James differ from St. Paul, St. John, and St. Peter. He is sententious, brief, practical. Whatever influence inspiration exerted over the mind of an apostle, it in no case superseded his individuality: it enlarged and improved it; it carried it forward to its true idea. The inspiration was attached to the man, not the man to the inspiration. If it penetrated his individuality, it quickened it; it did not overwhelm it. The natural faculties and modes of thought were not set aside; they still existed in their most active vigour. The knowledge communicated by inspiration formed part of the individual self: the personality was not swallowed up in the knowledge.

It follows, therefore, that a distinct human element is retained in the highest form of the inspiration even of an apostle: the divine treasure is placed in an earthen vessel. While communicating the great truths of revelation, an individual human mind is exhibited before us in all its feelings, in all its affections, in all its struggles, and, what is stranger still, in all its peculiarities. We read St. Paul, and say at once, such is the peculiar manner of the Apostle. We find him treating some great question. An expression which he employs suggests a fresh idea to his mind; he pursues that idea to its consequences: parenthesis is interwoven within parenthesis; surely the original thought must have faded away from his view: but to the original subject he returns, as though nothing had interrupted the course of his reasoning.

To adduce an example. The Apostle has begun to entreat his readers to walk in a manner worthy of their Christian calling. In doing so, he mentions the grace of God displayed in the gospel. His pen is suddenly arrested and unable to reach its destined purpose. The great revelation of gospel truth—the calling of the Gentiles to the full possession of Christian privileges, a purpose which was kept secret in bygone ages in the counsels of the Most High—the unsearchable riches of Christ—the discovery of the Divine glories to higher intelligences than those of men by the gospel revelation—burst on his mind. He bows his knees to the Father of our Lord Jesus Christ in earnest prayer that the fullest comprehension of those truths, and the richest experimental enjoyment of them, might, in accordance with the greatness of the Divine glory, be vouchsafed to those whom he loved. He then adores the Author of boundless good, who is able to do exceeding abundantly above their highest aspirations to satisfy His people's wants. Then the prisoner of the Lord returns calmly to entreat the Ephesian church to walk as became their Christian calling, in all lowliness and meekness, in long-suffering, forbearing one another in love.

Instances of the same individuality of character are scattered about in numerous places in his writings. In one place we find the Apostle heaping climax upon climax, while his struggling mind seems vainly to be endeavouring to give utterance to the profundity of his thoughts. In another place the course of his reasonings is interrupted by the outbursting of the expression of fervent feelings of sympathy for his unbelieving countrymen. Elsewhere the injured man struggling with his emotions rises before us: his emotions are profound—too profound to find utterance in words. On another occasion he has received intelligence that dangers have beset his converts' faith; the tempter is trying them : perhaps they have believed in vain. The heathen world around him is dark and threatening : without were fightings; within were fears. Titus arrives with good news : a burst of joy and light flashes on the Apostle's soul. In his extremity of danger, those who should have been his support in the hour of trial have forsaken him in his greatest need ; but the Lord stands by him : may the sin of their desertion not be laid to their charge. His holy services and disinterested labours —working with his own hands for his maintenance, to enable him to communicate to others the riches of spiritual treasures —have been requited by the spiritual father having been almost disowned by those children whom he had begotten. "I will gladly spend and be spent for you," says he, "though the more earnestly I love you, the less I be loved." He is mild and gentle as a nurse cherisheth her children. For his brethren according to the flesh, he almost wishes himself anathema from Christ; "but the seducers of you, my converts, from the truth of the gospel, I would that they were cut off that trouble you. Let the preacher of another gospel, whether he be man or angel from heaven, be accursed." His Philippian converts have sent him a liberal contribution from the depths of their own poverty to relieve his wants: he has all, and abounds; he is rich. But their messenger who brought the contribution has fallen sick; the friends who sent him have heard of the sickness of their messenger, and are deeply distressed on his account, for he is near death. The sick man recovers: God has mercy, not on Epaphroditus only, but on Paul also, lest he should have sorrow upon sorrow. Loving friends of the Apostle, aware of coming dangers, try to dissuade him from encountering them. The man of firm resolve stands erect, but deeply moved. "What mean ye to weep and to break my heart? for I am ready, not to be bound only, but also to die at Jerusalem for the sake of the Lord Jesus." The Apostle, in his travels, has been the instrument of rescuing from the downward course which leads to destruction a runaway slave who had robbed his Christian master. To that master he sends him back with a letter, "Brother," says he, "who owe to me yourself, receive back and forgive your repentant slave. Refresh my spirit: he has wronged you; though old and a prisoner, I promise you I will repay the debt. I write this promise under my own hand. Do more; receive him as myself. I forbear to command; I entreat for the sake of love. Refresh my spirit in the Lord." Some members of the Corinthian church are doubtful, after all, whether the man who laboured with his own hands for a maintenance, and who pretended to take no pecuniary remuneration from them, that he might preach the gospel freely, instead of being the disinterested person he professed to be, may, after all, have been no better than a cunning impostor. He had probably followed the example of Gehazi, who had relieved Naaman of some of his money, though Elisha would not. Though he had not taken money himself, he had done so by his subordinates. The Apostle's heart swells within him at the unworthy supposition. " Did Titus make a gain of you? Did I make a gain of you by any of those that I sent? I have supported myself by the labour of my own hands : what they did not supply, I received from the brethren in Macedonia. Why did I take nothing from you? Because I love you not? God knoweth." The person who can read these exquisite touches of the Apostle's character, and fail to discern in them overwhelming evidence of his individuality, must, by enslaving himself to a theory, have become either devoid of head or devoid of heart.

But the presence of an element of individuality is not only found in the writings of St. Paul; it is no less distinctly marked in St. John, St. Peter, and St. James.

Notwithstanding the shortness of St. John's Epistles, they furnish us with distinct traits of the peculiarities of the Apostle's mind. Direct logical sequence between the different sentences of the Epistle there is none. The principle which connects the ideas must be sought for deep beneath in the thought, but nowhere appears on the surface. One clear, self-conscious calmness pervades the Epistle. The vehement emotion, so apparent in St. Paul, has in St. John nearly faded away; the mild shining of divine love alone irradiates the page. No bursts of vehement feeling upheave themselves from the depths of the writer's soul; he lives in a state of calm, habitual certainty. No less characteristic are his modes of conception. With St. John, faith is knowledge; its one manifestation, love. Of divine love other graces are the simple manifestations. Love and holiness are identical. Love is the essence of the nature of God. In that soul where it exists, Christianity has wrought her perfect work. Let slavish fear be obliterated from the list of motives by which Christians must be animated. The Apostle lives in the habitual enjoyment of an inward divine light; out of the fulness of that light flow his assertions of Christian truth. All who are taught of God recognize that truth; they need no other teacher. Antichristian tendencies arise, not from Judaizing views or from subverting the doctrine of justification by faith, but from denying the Father and the Son. The Apostle has, with his eyes, beheld the manifestation of incarnate Deity. The eye of his mind enjoys a clear intuition of its spiritual glories. He asserts, therefore, but does not prove.

In St. Peter's writings we see depicted before us the deeply tried and tempted man—the veritable Peter of the Gospels. He has been sifted as wheat; his faith has failed him. He has learned that the trial of his faith, though tried in the fire, has been more precious than that of perishable gold: it will be found unto praise, and honour, and glory at the appearing of Jesus Christ. Like all men of strong impulse, he has been an unstable and therefore a much-suffering man. Fiery trials are, however, no longer strange things happening unto him, but subjects for rejoicing. He had once dissuaded the Saviour from His cross: he is now a partaker of His sufferings, and a joyful expectant of His glory. He, who was once foremost to rush into temptation, has learned that sobriety and vigilance are Christian virtues. Having had bitter experience that he had exposed himself to the attacks of the unseen spiritual enemy by his rashness in advancing beyond the post where he had been stationed by his Master, he now warns believers that their adversary, the devil, like a roaring lion, walketh about seeking whom he may devour. He must be resisted, stedfast in the faith. On his restoration to his office as an apostle, he had been thrice questioned by his Lord as to the reality of his love, and thrice commanded to feed His flock. Now, not as an apostle, but as a fellowelder, he exhorts the elders to feed the flock of God; not by constraint, but willingly; not for filthy lucre, but of a ready mind. He once eagerly sought the honours of an earthly kingdom; now, through the resurrection from the dead begotten to a lively hope, he is aspiring after an inheritance which is incorruptible, undefiled, and that fadeth not away. He who once thrust himself forward as the first in all things, after many falls, has learned that humility is the chief of Christian graces. With St. Paul humility is one single article out of many in the Christian's attire *; with St. Peter it is his entire dress: " Be ye clothed with humility." Once he had, without authority, drawn the temporal sword in his Master's cause: he now emphatically teaches the duty of obedience to the civil governor, for the Lord's sake. He who once would have been in danger of being seized on a charge of an attempt at murder, but for the prompt interference of his Lord, now gives to Christians the singular precept, " Let none of you suffer as a murderer †, but as a Christian." Formerly he could not endure the idea of separation from his Master; now he can assure believers who had never beheld the wonders of our Lord's earthly ministry, or seen the features of His human countenance, that although they had never seen Him, they yet could love Him, and, believing, they could rejoice with joy unspeakable and full of glory. His own denial, and his Master's patient endurance, had left an impression on his mind which never could be effaced. Christians were called to endure with patience, after the example of Him who, when He was reviled, reviled not again; when He suffered, He threatened not, but who committed Himself to Him who judgeth righteously. Such evidences of the presence of the man Peter cannot be mistaken—the same Peter whom we have read of in the Gospels, whose weaknesses have been effaced by the growth of the opposite Christian virtues.

---

* "Put on therefore, as the elect of God, holy and beloved, bowels of mercies, kindness, humbleness of mind, meekness, longsuffering; forbearing one another, and forgiving one another . . . . . And above all these things put on charity, which is the bond of perfectness." (Col. iii. 12-14.)

† This is certainly the last precept which we should have expected an apostle to give to a body of Christians. It singularly gives a remarkable confirmation to the truth of the history. Many of the references here noticed would never have entered into the head of a forger, least of all the one in question. In the precept not to be a busybody, St. Peter seems also to have had an eye to his own infirmities.

St. James's individuality is most distinctly marked: it is only second to St. Paul's. He is all sententious, vehement, practical. "Count it all joy," says he, "when ye fall into divers temptations. Let patience have her perfect work. Let no wavering man think that he shall receive anything from God. The rich man perishes like the grass under the heat of the burning sun. The man who, while professing to have faith, and, not having works, declares that he believes in God, does well! the devils believe, and tremble. O vain man, faith without works is dead. The wide-spread evil of an unrestrained tongue resembles the wide-spread destruction occasioned by a raging fire. Birds, beasts, and fishes have been tamed by man. The tongue none can tame: it is an unruly evil, full of deadly poison. Let lustful Christians know that the friendship of the world is enmity with God. Let them be afflicted, and mourn, and weep. Go to, ye that lay out your plans for tomorrow, and calculate with certainty on the distant day! What is your life? it is a vapour. You rich oppressors, weep and howl for the miseries which are coming on you. Your wicked acts will be a witness against you, and will consume you like fire. You are feeding yourselves fat against the day for your slaughter."

No less remarkable are the doctrinal statements of St. James as evidences of a distinct personality. With him sin is a breach of positive law. God is not the cause of man's sin: man's wicked lusts are that cause alone. From the Father of lights, who neither changes nor varies, comes down every good. A man must be a doer of God's word, and not a hearer only. A man who makes professions of religion, while he does not restrain his tongue, is a self-deceiving hypocrite. Whoever keeps the entire law, but yet breaks it in one point, is guilty of all. Faith without works is dead. If we draw nigh to God, God will draw nigh to us. If any man err from the truth, and one convert him, let him know that he who converteth the sinner from the error of his way shall save a soul from death, and shall cover a multitude of sins. St. James, with all his vehemence, never personally appears in the Epistle but once, in the opening address.

Such, then, are the marks of individuality presented by the four great writers of the New Testament. We ask, can we be deceived or mistaken respecting the fact? Have they not left the distinct evidences of four distinct personalities? Could their human faces have been more distinguishable from each other than their great mental outlines? We have exhibited before us the minds of the respective writers, their habits and modes of thinking, their intellectual, moral, and spiritual peculiarities. This is so undeniable, that it is observed by the most ordinary reader. Every person, who has read the New Testament with attention, says at once, This is St. Paul; this is St. James; this is St. Peter; this is St. John.

Now what is thus felt by all must be a reality, and no deception. It can be neither fiction nor fancy. It must be either an actual presence of the individuality of the writer or, what we almost shrink from saying, a successful imitation of that individuality.

If it be the veritable presence of the individuality of the writers of the Epistles, it must be a human element in them, in connexion with that which is divine. The individuality, and the distinct mental characteristics, which we have been observing, are those of four distinct men. If what we have been tracing is the very impress of their own minds, the presence of it is destructive to the theory of verbal inspiration. The Spirit of God may have directed this human element to be placed in the apostolic writings for the purpose of exhibiting or containing the heavenly treasure; but it must never be forgotten that the element is human, not divine.

But some supporters of this theory have maintained that the apparent presence of the individuality of an apostle does not negative the idea that the Epistle in which it is found may be the work of verbal inspiration: the Spirit may have actually depicted the four separate individualities themselves, and dictated the whole forms of thought and expression by which they are portrayed.

But the supporters of the theory are unable to deny that the most distinct traces of personal individuality, in the most remarkable forms, do, in point of fact, actually exist in the Epistles. It would be as well to deny the existence of anything which we positively behold with our eyes, or perceive by our other senses.

If all the peculiarities by which the presence of such individuality is proved are not the human personalities of the Apostles, but are the dictation of the Spirit of God, it follows that the Spirit of God has imitated the respective individualities of the four Apostles. Then the forms of thought are not those of the Apostles themselves, but imitations of them in letters bearing their names: they are exact copies of the mode in which the writers would have expressed themselves, if they had employed their own mental faculties. Their readers, unless told to the contrary, could only understand that they were the veritable personalities of the Apostles. It would have been impossible to imitate four handwritings more completely than these imitations of the individuality of the four Apostles. Such an imitation is possible; but it places on the Spirit of God what we shrink from expressing in words.

Now it is a confusion of thought, amounting to a contradiction, to affirm that the individual personality of the sacred writers, as it is expressed in the pages of the New Testament, is inspired in the same sense as their statements of Christian truth are inspired. That which is the result of distinct human personality cannot be a dictation of the Spirit of God. A thing cannot be the result of inspiration, and at the same time the simple portraiture of the working of the human mind. God is not man; man is not God.

To assert that the personality is the pure result of inspiration, without the intermixture of a human element, is a very different thing from admitting that it has been incorporated in the sacred page by the direction of the divine Spirit. It may have been His express intention that the individual personality of each of the sacred writers should be closely interwoven with the structure of the records of a divine revelation: it may have been necessary for the edification of the Church. It has been the Divine purpose, not only to exhibit Christian truth in the form of doctrine or precept, and in the perfect human manifestation of Christ, but also to exhibit it as Christian truth lived and energized in four minds of different characters, orders, and modes of thinking. The inspired doctrines and precepts would thus not only be exhibited in the abstract, but in the life—in the energies, in the being, and in the affections of holy men possessing different forms of mental endowment. Christian truth is thus made intelligible and accommodated to every order of human thought.

But, as far as it is an apostle's individual self, it must be a human element in the sacred page. An apostle's being directed to record what he thought and felt will not make the element divine. "The Spirit," says St. Paul to Timothy, "speaketh expressly, that in the last days troublous times shall come." Here, if the Apostle speaks truth, he received an express illumination as to the distant future from the Spirit: the information did not grow out of the use of any of his natural powers. But can we change the words and say, The Spirit speaks expressly, "The salutation of me, Paul, with my own hand;" or, "For love's sake, I rather entreat thee, being such a one as Paul the aged, and now also a prisoner of Jesus Christ;" or, "I have written it with my own hand; I will repay thee;" or, "I am troubled on every side, yet not distressed; perplexed, but not in despair; persecuted, but not forsaken; cast down, but not destroyed; always bearing about in my body the dying of the Lord Jesus." These are plainly the human manifestations of the holy Paul, not the express declarations of the Spirit of God.

It is impossible that we can have stronger evidence for the existence of any fact, than we have for the presence in the Epistles of the individual personality of their writers. To refuse to admit its existence would be to deny the possibility of truth.

The student of the Epistles, therefore, will observe that they consist of five distinct elements:—1st, statements of Christian doctrine; 2nd, Christian precepts; 3rd, statements of the writer's individuality and experience; 4th, statements of facts; 5th, the union of these two last with statements of Christian doctrine or precept. We must select a few examples of these from the Apostle's writings.

In 2 Cor. i. 5-24, the Apostle writes:—"For as the sufferings of Christ abound in us, so our consolation also aboundeth by Christ. And whether we be afflicted, it is for your consolation and salvation, which is effectual in the enduring of the same sufferings which we also suffer: or whether we be comforted, it is for your consolation and salvation. And our hope of you is stedfast, knowing, that as ye are partakers of the sufferings, so shall ye be also of the consolation. For we would not, brethren, have you ignorant of our trouble which came to us in Asia, that we were pressed out of measure, above strength, insomuch that we despaired even of life: but we had the sentence of death in ourselves, that we should not trust in ourselves, but in God which raiseth the dead: who delivered us from so great a death, and doth deliver: in whom we trust that He will yet deliver us; ye also helping together by prayer for us, that for the gift bestowed upon us by the means of many persons thanks may be given by many on our behalf. For our rejoicing is this, the testimony of our conscience, that in simplicity and godly sincerity, not with fleshly wisdom, but by the grace of God, we have had our conversation in the world, and more abundantly to you-ward. For we write none other things unto you, than what ye read or acknowledge; and I trust ye shall acknowledge even to the end; as also ye have acknowledged us in part, that we are your rejoicing, even as ye also are ours in the day of the Lord Jesus. And in this confidence I was minded to come unto you before, that ye might have a second benefit; and to pass by you into Macedonia, and to come again out of Macedonia unto you, and of you to be brought on my way toward Judæa. When I therefore was thus minded, did I use lightness? or the things that I purpose, do I purpose according to the flesh, that with me there should be yea yea, and nay nay? But as God is true, our word toward you was not yea and nay. For the Son of God, Jesus Christ, who was preached among you by us, even by me and Silvanus and

Timotheus, was not yea and nay, but in Him was yea. For all the promises of God in Him are yea, and in Him Amen, unto the glory of God by us. Now He which stablisheth us with you in Christ, and hath anointed us, is God; who hath also sealed us, and given the earnest of the Spirit in our hearts. Moreover I call God for a record upon my soul, that to spare you I came not as yet unto Corinth. Not for that we have dominion over your faith, but are helpers of your joy: for by faith ye stand."

This passage forms a very remarkable illustration of the Apostle's manner; for, with the exception that he gives no precept, we find all these distinct elements united in it. We will therefore endeavour to analyze the various elements of thought contained in the passage.

1. We find in it assertions of Christian doctrine: "all the promises of God in Him are yea, and in Him Amen, unto the glory of God by us." Here the Apostle makes a distinct statement respecting the faithfulness of God. This leads him to make a further statement respecting God's relationship to the Church. He has established the Church in Christ, and anointed it. He has sealed Christians, and given them the earnest of His Spirit in their hearts.

2. We find in this passage, also, very distinct statements respecting the Apostle's own experience. "As Christ's sufferings abounded in him, so his consolation abounded in Christ." "And our hope in you is stedfast, knowing, that as ye are partakers of the sufferings, so shall ye be also of the consolation." These are assertions of certain feelings which the Apostle declares that he experienced. Of a similar nature is the Apostle's declaration, "For our rejoicing is this, the testimony of our conscience, that in simplicity and godly sincerity, not with fleshly wisdom, but by the grace of God, we have had our conversation in the world, and more abundantly to you-ward."

3. The Apostle also details several facts which came within his own direct knowledge. He reminds the Corinthians of the trouble which came upon him in Asia,—how he was pressed out of measure, above strength, insomuch that he

despaired even of life: "but we had the sentence of death in ourselves, that we should not trust in ourselves, but in God which raiseth the dead." In the latter portion of this passage, the Apostle unites together a statement of fact with a description of his own experience respecting it. In the following clause, he unites this statement of fact with the enunciation of a Christian doctrine: "who delivered us from so great a death, and doth deliver: in whom we trust that He will yet deliver us." A little further on in the passage, the Apostle describes the various purposes of visiting Corinth which had passed through his own mind, and vindicates himself from the charge of fickleness in not having carried them into execution: "in this confidence I was minded to come unto you before, that ye might have a second benefit; and to pass by you into Macedonia, and to come again out of Macedonia unto you, and of you to be brought on my way toward Judæa. When I therefore was thus minded, did I use lightness? or the things that I purpose, do I purpose according to the flesh, that with me there should be yea yea, and nay nay?" He then takes a solemn oath, by God, that his change of purpose was not the result of worldly calculations, but that he was influenced solely by a desire of sparing them.

4. The Apostle combines statements of facts and of his own experience with declarations of divine truth. "Not," says he, "that we have dominion over your faith, but are helpers of your joy: for by faith ye stand." Here we have both interwoven together in the same sentence. At the commencement of the passage we have quoted, a divine truth is inferentially mixed up with a statement of his own experience: "And whether we be afflicted, it is for your consolation and salvation, which is effectual to the enduring of the same sufferings, which ye also suffer: or whether we be comforted, it is for your consolation and salvation." The divine truth interwoven with this statement of his own experience is elsewhere stated in express words: "all things work together for good to them that love God."

This passage, then, contains a very remarkable union of

these various elements, and gives us a striking illustration of the manner in which the divine Spirit worked in conjunction with the human personality of the Apostle.

But sometimes the divine truth and the Apostle's personality are kept almost entirely distinct. The Epistle to the Romans, from the 18th verse of the 1st chapter to the 7th verse of the 15th chapter, is almost entirely occupied by statements of doctrine or practice, with very few intermixtures either of fact or experience. In the remainder of the Epistle the other elements are intermixed, as we have already seen. The 2nd Epistle to the Corinthians contains the most remarkable instance of the intermixture of divine truth with the Apostle's human personality.

The following passage is almost exclusively occupied with statements of experience, personality, and fact: doctrinal and practical truth is only interwoven with it inferentially.

Philippians, i. 3-18:—" I thank my God upon every remembrance of you, always in every prayer of mine for you all making request with joy, for your fellowship in the gospel from the first day until now; being confident of this very thing, that He which hath begun a good work in you will perform it until the day of Jesus Christ: even as it is meet for me to think this of you all, because I have you in my heart; inasmuch as both in my bonds, and in the defence and confirmation of the gospel, ye all are partakers of my grace. For God is my record, how greatly I long after you all in the bowels of Jesus Christ. And this I pray, that your love may abound yet more and more in knowledge and in all judgment; that ye may approve things that are excellent; that ye may be sincere and without offence till the day of Christ; being filled with the fruits of righteousness, which are by Jesus Christ, unto the glory and praise of God. But I would ye should understand, brethren, that the things which happened unto me have fallen out rather unto the furtherance of the gospel; so that my bonds in Christ are manifest in all the palace, and in all other places; and many of the brethren in the Lord, waxing confident by my bonds, are much more bold to speak the word without fear. Some indeed preach Christ even of envy and strife; and some also of good will: the one preach Christ of contention, not sincerely, supposing to add affliction to my bonds : but the other of love, knowing that I am set for the defence of the gospel. What then? notwithstanding, every way, whether in pretence, or in truth, Christ is preached; and I therein do rejoice, yea, and will rejoice."

This passage contains an exhibition of Christian truth, not in doctrine or precept, but as it lived and energized in a holy human personality. It was the purpose of God that truth, not in ideal form, but as it existed in the experience of holy but imperfect men, should form a portion of the record of the Christian revelation. We have here an exhibition of the human Paul, a man of habitual prayer, earnestly desirous of the steady progress of his converts towards increasing degrees of Christian perfection—having them engraven on his heart. Discouragements do not daunt him : his very imprisonment has been conducive to the spread of the gospel. Others have been encouraged by his success to increasing boldness in preaching Christ. Some have preached Him from bad motives; but, whether owing to bad motives or to good ones, Christ has been preached, and this rejoices the Apostle's soul.

The whole passage is one simple statement of the Apostle's experience, of events which have occurred to him, and of his own individuality. It contains no direct enunciation of doctrine or precept. Christian truths can only be deduced inferentially from St. Paul's experience. His prayers were uttered in the light of that divine knowledge which permanently dwelt in his soul, which we have already described as afforded to him by direct illumination from above. But, throughout the whole passage, the divine and the human are woven together in the Apostle's personality; and in that personality we behold, not a divine picture of ideal truth, but of truth as it existed in a holy human breast.

Philippians, ii. 17-30 : " Yea, and if I be offered upon the sacrifice and service of your faith, I joy, and rejoice with you all. For the same cause also do ye joy, and rejoice with me. But I trust in the Lord Jesus to send Timotheus shortly unto

2 B

you, that I also may be of good comfort, when I know your state. For I have no man likeminded, who will naturally care for your state. For all seek their own, not the things which are Jesus Christ's. But ye know the proof of him, that, as a son with the father, he hath served with me in the gospel. Him therefore I hope to send presently, so soon as I shall see how it will go with me. But I trust in the Lord that I also myself shall come shortly. Yet I supposed it necessary to send to you Epaphroditus, my brother, and companion in labour, and fellowsoldier, but your messenger, and he that ministered to my wants. For he longed after you all, and was full of heaviness, because that ye had heard that he had been sick. For indeed he was sick nigh unto death: but God had mercy on him; and not on him only, but on me also, lest I should have sorrow upon sorrow. I sent him therefore the more carefully, that, when ye see him again, ye may rejoice, and that I may be the less sorrowful. Receive him therefore in the Lord with all gladness; and hold such in reputation: because for the work of Christ he was nigh unto death, not regarding his life, to supply your lack of service toward me."

This passage is a more remarkable display of human personality in the Apostle's writings than even the preceding one. The passage immediately preceding it contains an enumeration of the most important Christian doctrines and practical precepts. This quotation is a simple statement of facts, feelings, purposes, and hopes, without being interwoven with either doctrine or precept. But it is particularly worthy of attention in connexion with our present subject, as containing the statement of several contigencies respecting which the mind of the Apostle was in a state of uncertainty. He intended to send Timothy, as soon as he should know how it would go with him. He hoped also to be able to come himself. Respecting neither point had he any supernatural light. We have, therefore, in this assertion the most complete evidence of the human personality of the Apostle.

Colossians, iv. 7-9: "All my state shall Tychicus declare unto you, who is a beloved brother, and a faithful minister and fellowservant in the Lord: whom I have sent unto you for the same purpese, that he might know your estate, and comfort your hearts; with Onesimus, a faithful and beloved brother, who is one of you. They shall make known unto you all things which are done here."

In the former part of the Epistle the Apostle had been treating on the deepest subjects of Christian truth, requiring the aid of the highest form of apostolical inspiration. The passage which we have just cited is a statement of ordinary facts, such as one friend might write to another: "My messengers can tell you everything of a religious interest which is taking place at Rome, as I wish them to learn and report to me everything about you and your affairs."

We cite one more passage in illustration of this subject, 1 Thessalonians, iii. 1-8: "Wherefore when we could no longer forbear, we thought it good to be left at Athens alone; and sent Timotheus, our brother, and minister of God, and our fellowlabourer in the gospel of Christ, to establish you, and to comfort you concerning your faith: that no man should be moved by these afflictions; for yourselves know that we are appointed thereunto. For verily, when we were with you, we told you before that we should suffer tribulation; even as it came to pass, and ye know. For this cause, when I could no longer forbear, I sent to know your faith, lest by some means the tempter had tempted you, and our labour be in vain. But now when Timotheus came from you unto us, and brought us good tidings of your faith and charity, and that ye have good remembrance of us always, desiring greatly to see us, as we also to see you: therefore, brethren, we were comforted over you in all our affliction and distress by your faith: for now we live, if ye stand fast in the Lord."

The Apostle here gives us a simple account of the alternations through which his feelings passed while he was at Athens, and of the measures which he took for the security of the faith of the Thessalonian church, and the joy which he experienced on receiving good news respecting them. The passage contains a distinct presence of the Apostle in his human personality.

It is evident therefore that, in addition to doctrines and

precepts, the Epistles of St. Paul frequently give portraitures of his religious experience, descriptions of his own internal consciousness, accounts of facts known to himself or others, and displays of his own individuality, either separately or interwoven with the proper subjects of Christian teaching. These various subjects differ not only widely in degree, but in character; they range from the disclosure of the highest form of Christian truth to sending a salutation to a friend, or a direction about a matter of ordinary business.

The Apostle has told us in express words by what rule we are to estimate his own experience and example. It is the experience and example of an eminently holy man, whose mind was deeply penetrated with Christian truth. But the Apostle does not claim for his experience or his example absolute infallibility: " Be ye followers of me," says he, " as I am of Christ."

The example of Christ is the only example in the New Testament which can vindicate a claim to absolute infallibility. High as was the Apostle's holiness, it was not perfect. He himself asserts that he was constantly aiming after a higher standard. The Apostle's experience of Christian truth is therefore to be viewed as a very high form of Christian experience—as that of a man preeminently holy, whose mind was illuminated from on high as to the nature of those truths which are revealed by the gospel. But we must beware of assigning to it an absolute authority, which the Apostle himself declares only to belong to the perfect example of the Son of God. The Apostle's experience and example, however elevated, are human, not divine. Why shall we claim for them what he himself disclaims?

As we are imperfect beings, it was highly desirable, not only that we should have an exhibition of Christian principles coexisting with perfection in the person of Christ, but with imperfection as they are portrayed in the persons of St. Paul, St. John, St. Peter, and St. James. In them we see those principles living and energizing in men of like passions with ourselves. A manifestation of Christian truth struggling in imperfect but holy minds is as necessary for our edification as its exhibition in its perfection in the person of the Son of God. In this form, therefore, we find it incorporated in the apostolic Epistles as a most important element of Christian truth.

But this experience is the experience of men : it is an experience which the Apostles actually felt, not an ideal experience which the Spirit of God dictated. It has been recorded, by His direction, for the edification of the Church; but the experience is a human experience, the consciousness is a human consciousness, the individuality is a human individuality. The facts were events which actually occurred. Apostles described what they really felt, not what they merely ought to have felt. St. Paul was at times cast down : it does not follow that the power of gospel promises ought not to have preserved him from such depression.

The point, therefore, for which we contend is, that the displays of personality and individuality contained in the Epistles are not a simple dictation of the Holy Spirit, but originate in the experience of men animated by His sanctifying influences. The personality of the writers, although quickened, animated, and sanctified by Him, was not destroyed, but left entire. They form a grand portrait of the sanctifying influences of the Spirit exerted on human nature.

We will illustrate our meaning by a passage of the Old Testament. Of all the Old Testament writers, the individuality of none appears with such richness as that of the prophet Jeremiah. In one of the portraits of his own individuality occurs the following passage :—

Jeremiah, xx. 14-18 : " Cursed be the day wherein I was born : let not the day wherein my mother bare me be blessed. Cursed be the man who brought tidings to my father, saying, A man child is born unto thee, making him very glad. And let that man be as the cities which the Lord overthrew, and repented not : and let him hear the cry in the morning, and the shouting at noontide ; because he slew me not from the womb ; or that my mother might have been my grave, and her womb to be always great with me. Wherefore came I forth out of the womb to see labour and sorrow, that my days should be consumed with shame?"

These were feelings which the prophet experienced in his struggles; but who will contend that they were feelings which ought to have animated him, or that they were breathed into his mind by the Holy Spirit of God? The prophet may have been directed by the Spirit to record the impatient feelings which animated his breast, yet not as an example to be imitated, but as a solemn warning of what ought to be avoided. It is the representation of a mind stirred to its profoundest depths: it contains the expression of the height of passion under the pressure of a terrific burden.

Now we ask, can one conceive that the different expressions of this passage are such that they could have passed from the lips of man without sin, even when under the severest pressure? Are the wishes holy wishes? Can we conceive them as uttered by our Saviour? Are they not the words of terrific impatience? How unlike to St. Stephen praying for his murderers! It may be said, Christians have learned a higher lesson in the school of Christ. True; but the present question is not what lesson Christians have learned, but were these words and expressions dictated to the prophet by the Holy Spirit? or are they a human element permitted by Him to be incorporated with the prophecy?

Let us briefly examine the expressions in detail. The first wish was that the day on which the prophet was born might be cursed: could such a wish have been suggested to his mind from on high? He desires that that day might never be blessed: was such a desire after the mind of Him who said, " Father, forgive them, for they know not what they do"? The prophet next curses the man who brought his father tidings of his birth: this man surely did him no wrong. He then expresses the fierce desire that that man might be like the cities which the Lord overthrew in His anger, and repented not: such a ruthless wish against one who had done him no injury could not have been dictated by the Spirit of God. He then rises to a height of still more terrific vehemence, and expresses a desire that the man had slain him from the womb, *i. e.* had committed a murder; or that his mother's womb had been always great with him: this wish exhibits the paroxysm of his feelings carried to the extremest height. The prophet could scarcely have realized the idea to which he gave utterance. He concludes by murmuring against Providence, with an angry demand, to know why he had thus been born to shame and sorrow.

It may be urged in the prophet's defence, that these expressions were uttered by him in the utmost vehemence of passion, occasioned by the pressure of the deepest suffering. Such was probably the case. But this proves the point we are seeking to establish. Vehemence of passion is human, not divine: it is man's utterance, not God's dictation. The influences of the Spirit of God are love, joy, peace, longsuffering, gentleness, goodness, meekness.

Although the passage which describes these upheavings and vehement perturbations of the prophet's soul may have been recorded for our admonition, yet the passage itself is human, and not divine: it contains a succession of unholy wishes. Such emotions, such feelings, cannot be prefaced by the expression, "Thus saith the Lord."

Between St. Paul and Jeremiah there is one striking resemblance—the degree in which their respective personalities appear, the one in the Epistle, the other in the prophecy. The prophet, in all the various perturbations of his mind in the alternations of his depressions and his hopes, is continually rising on the scene. But here the resemblance ends. In the Apostle's personality we have the purest exhibition of practical Christianity. In the profoundest depths of trial, he has fought the good fight, he has finished his course, he has kept the faith. He is looking forward to his discharge from warfare, and to the possession of the victor's crown. But, as far as St. Paul's personality appears, the element must be human. The Apostle emphatically warns us against confounding the imperfection of the disciple with the perfection of the Master.

We conclude, therefore, generally, that although the experience of the writers of the New Testament transcends that of the writers of the Old, in being a much nearer approximation to the character of Christ, yet, as being the experience of man, it is the human language of the Apostle and does not consist of ideas introduced into his mind by the direct influence of inspiration.

As we possess the personality of St. Paul in his writings, so they are composed in his human style—a style perhaps intensified by the influence of inspiration, but not superseded by it. The divine truths, as they are presented to us in the sacred page, have passed through his human intellect and received the forms of it. This difference of style in the writers of the New Testament is universally perceived: no reader of the New Testament has failed to recognize it.

Now to what do such phenomena point? of what are they the certain evidence? If we had had no theory to maintain, should we ever have inferred that many styles had one and the same author? or should we not certainly have referred the phenomena to the action of differently constituted human minds? The facts are indubitable; how are we to account for those facts? All experience asserts that such difference is evidence of the presence of distinct and differently constituted minds.

We will endeavour to make this argument plain by an illustration. A large building is before us: on examining it, we discover the presence of different styles of architecture: a considerable portion of it consists of different styles of Gothic; the pillars are Corinthian; some of the ornamental portions are Oriental: we infer from this variety of design that the building is not the work of one architect, but of many; we draw the conclusion that these architects lived at different eras. We enter a picture-gallery: we observe that the pictures divide themselves into distinct classes; some are Italian, some Spanish, some Flemish, some French: we draw the conclusion that these pictures were the work of different orders of mind, and that they could not have been painted by the same person. We enter a court of law, and see a large number of various handwritings produced; skilful judges swear to the identity of some, and to the diversity of others: a jury give their verdict in conformity with this testimony.

Now why should these tests be worthy of all confidence

when applied to the practical affairs of life, and only fail us when they are applied to the elucidation of the New Testament? The style of St. Paul does not less differ from that of St. John than the Gothic style of architecture does from the Grecian, or than the Italian style of painting does from the Flemish, or than the style of Bishop Hall does from that of Addison.

Now distinctive difference of style in composition proves difference of authorship, no less than different styles of building or painting do the existence of different schools of architects or painters. The style, therefore, by which difference of authorship is proved is a human element in a book. If the names of Jeremy Taylor and Dr. Johnson had perished, would it be possible to persuade any one who read their writings that they had been composed by one and the same person?

Now it is perfectly possible to express the same truth in two entirely different styles. Different authors will express the same truth in different ways: one may express it nakedly, the other clothe it in metaphor; one may amplify the truth, the other may express it with sententious brevity. The variations in the mode of the expression of the same truth are endless. Every writer in the New Testament may be recognized by his peculiarities of style and modes of expression.

But what is the necessary consequence of this? The truths brought forward by each writer are the same truths communicated by the Spirit of God to their respective minds. The modes of viewing those truths, and of stating them, are the peculiarities of the authors; the metaphors are their metaphors. The conciseness or the copiousness of diction is that of the respective writers. The presence or the absence of argumentative power is a reflection of the character of their respective minds. The lively question, the abrupt transition, the indignant denunciation, have the same origin. The climax, the vehement burst of feeling, the calmness, the clearness, are transcripts of the individual temperament. The truths are the truths of God; the peculiarities proceed from the human personality.

1 John, iii. 5–10, and Romans, vi. 1–5 and 10–23, form a remarkable illustration of the different modes of stating the same truth adopted by St. John and St. Paul. The truth which both are occupied in enforcing is the impossibility that vital Christianity can coexist with a life of sin.

St. John brings forward our Lord's divine person, and the purpose of His manifestation, as the medium of proof: Christ was manifested to take away sin; He is Himself perfectly sinless. The abiding in Christ, which is the true condition of a Christian man, is incompatible with living in a state of sin. One living in sin has neither seen Christ, nor known Him. He that practises righteousness is righteous, as God is righteous: he that commits sin is of the devil; for it is the devil's nature to sin. Christ appeared to destroy the devil's works. He that is born of God cannot sin. Sin and holiness make manifest who are the children of God, and who are the children of the devil.

In marked contrast is the mode of stating this truth adopted by St. Paul. The logical and argumentative form of putting it is at once adopted by him. In St. John all is calmness; the idea that sin and holiness can be confounded, and that gospel truth can be converted into an encouragement to evil, call forth all the vehemence of St. Paul. His holy indignation is aroused. Shall we continue in sin, that grace may abound? May God avert the thought! Redeemed Christians are dead to sin; how shall they live in it any longer? Was not death to sin the very first truth brought before the convert's mind in baptism? Did not the ascent from the water image the Lord's resurrection? Did not faith in it bind the Christian to a corresponding change from sin to holiness? Christ died to sin: He lives to God. So let the Christian die to sin, and live to God in Christ. Let him no longer submit his members to be made the instruments of its ruling power. Shall a Christian sin because he is no longer under a yoke of legal obedience, but under a dispensation of gracious mercy? May God avert the thought! As for servants, they are servants to their respective masters, whether a man is the servant of sin to death or of obedience to holiness. Ye were once the slaves of sin; now from henceforth be its slaves no longer. From the heart you have obeyed the doctrine of Christ: it has enlisted you in the service of righteousness. What then? I would draw a stronger conclusion if human language and human weakness permitted me. As then you have yielded yourselves and your members instruments unto sin, now yield yourselves and your members servants to God. I appeal to yourselves to say, what fruit had ye in that service of which ye are now ashamed? Its end was death. Now you have obtained freedom from the servitude of sin, and have entered the service of righteousness. You have your fruit to holiness: the end is everlasting life.

Thus strikingly contrasted are the different modes of stating the same truth adopted by the two Apostles. With all this difference of conception and expression, both state the same truth, that true Christian faith is incompatible with an unholy life. In revealing this truth, the Spirit of God has used the instrumentality of men, with their individual peculiarities, as the medium of communicating the heavenly treasure: He has thus met the wants of every form of the human understanding. St. John's mode of stating truth is adapted to one condition of the human mind; St. Paul's to another; St. Peter's to a third; St. James's to a fourth. In this manner, by making the great truths of revelation pass through differently constituted minds, with different intellects, feelings, and affections, instead of one single form of understanding or one single mode of feeling, is made known through the Church the manifold wisdom of God. By speaking with the tongues, the understandings, and the affections, not of angels, not of one man only, but of many men differently constituted, gospel truth has been suited and adapted to every form of the human intellect, is capable of translation into the feelings of every human heart, and is capable of being proclaimed to and embraced by every nation under heaven.

As the mode in which the Old Testament is quoted in the New illustrates the nature of the inspiration possessed by the Apostles, we must not pass it over in entire silence.

The facts of the case, as they bear on this question, admit of no debate. They are as follows :—Sometimes the citations of the Old Testament in the New are exact quotations of the received Hebrew text. At other times the Septuagint version is quoted *verbatim*, even where it gives a different sense from the Hebrew. Not unfrequently the citations are representations of what the writers of the New Testament considered the general sense of the Hebrew or the Septuagint, without quoting the exact words. Occasionally the quotations give a sense differing from anything which can be found either in the Hebrew or the Greek texts as they at present exist. Sometimes the citation of a passage seems to be made as an accommodation.

Such are the facts : the inference which follows from these facts is adverse to the theory of verbal inspiration.

If it be necessary to assume that the writers of the New Testament must have been possessed of a power of discriminating what was the true reading of any particular passage in the Old Testament, and that they always gave the true reading, then it is evident that neither the Hebrew, nor the Greek, nor any existing version with which we are acquainted gives us the text of the Old Testament as it actually issued from the hands of its authors.

Now, if the theory of verbal inspiration be correct, it is evident that, whenever the Old Testament is cited in the New, the quotations must have been made, not by men, but by the Spirit of God; the citations, therefore, must be the exact words used by the writers of the Old Testament. But differences exist, both in words and sense, in these quotations in the New Testament from what we at present read in any copy of the Old; it follows, therefore, if the citations in the New Testament are the very words used by the writers of the Old Testament, that our present copies of the Old Testament are incorrect.

But the passages quoted in the New Testament from the Old bear a small proportion to the whole of the Old Testament Scriptures; we may conclude, therefore, if this supposition is correct, that the errors in question do not exist only in the cited passages, but extend in the same proportion throughout the whole. If this principle be correct, it follows that the true Old Testament must have differed considerably from the one with which we are acquainted. Such a consequence follows inevitably from the theory of verbal inspiration.

But if the quotations of the Old Testament in the New are not strictly accurate citations of the genuine text, it follows that the writers of the New Testament were not endowed with a supernatural power to enable them to distinguish which was the genuine text. They must have quoted from such copies of the Old Testament as they were in the habit of using, or from memory. The citations, therefore, must have been liable to the defects to which such quotations are incident.

Now it is expressly asserted in the New Testament that our Lord did open the minds of the apostles as to the meaning of the Old Testament Scriptures in their reference to Himself. But there is no supernatural aid promised them to help them to ascertain what was the true reading of a passage when their copies disagreed, in the same manner as there is a promise made them of supernatural assistance to enable them to recall the discourses to their memories. The Septuagint version is a standing witness that considerable variations in the copies of the Old Testament must have existed earlier than the times of our Lord.

The mode in which the Old Testament is quoted in the New leads to the following conclusion:—The writers of the New Testament were not aided with supernatural powers to enable them to determine what was the true text of the Old Testament; nor were they endowed with supernatural powers of memory to enable them to quote it, nor were they possessed of such a power for the purpose of enabling them to quote the sense only, without reference to the words. The phenomena presented by the Old and New Testaments negative either supposition. The quotations, as we find them in the New Testament, imply that they were not unfrequently made from memory, and from such copies as they were in the habit of reading. Not unfrequently they appear to have cited the mere general sense of a passage; and at times their quotations seem to have been of the nature of accommodations.

The Book of Revelation occupies a different position from the other books of the New Testament. From the nature of the case, this book, if a divine book, must have been composed under the influence of a very high degree of inspiration. It professes to be a revelation of the future: events buried in the distant future can only be known to Omniscience.

The author of the book informs us that it is the Revelation of Jesus Christ, which God gave to Him to show to His servants things which must shortly come to pass. These communications are made in a succession of emblematical visions: the emblems, therefore, must have formed a substantial portion of the Divine communication; for by them the future is revealed.

This book, therefore, must differ from the other books of the New Testament. As far as the imagery is an emblematical disclosure of the future, it must be an essential portion of the Divine communication; such imagery must therefore have been depicted by the inspiring Spirit before the prophet's mind.

It follows as a consequence from this consideration, that whatever human element exists in the structure of the book, it must lie beyond this boundary and be confined to points unconnected with the future; it must therefore be limited to the personal action of the Apostle, to the human language in which the divine visions are expressed, and to the peculiarities of the Apostle's diction. Even that language is affected by the Divine communications.

We should infer, therefore, that the language used by St. John in the Revelation would differ materially from that employed by him in the Gospel and in the Epistles. Such difference does actually exist. The difference of style and expression between this Book and that of the Gospel and Epistles is so great, that it is the stronghold of those who maintain that the Book of Revelation was not written by the Apostle John. The existence of this difference of style, then, is a remarkable fact, and is precisely that which we ought to have found if our theory of the Apostle's inspiration be correct. This theory, therefore, stands the test of fact.

CHAPTER XX.

THE RESULTS OF THE PRECEDING INQUIRIES ON EXISTING THEORIES OF INSPIRATION.

We must now enter on the inquiry how existing views are affected by this investigation of the New Testament respecting the nature of its own inspiration.

It cannot be denied that a spirit of inquiry has arisen of the highest possible importance on this subject. The results of these investigations are deeply affecting the different views entertained as to the nature of divine truth, and shaking existing forms of belief and modes of interpretation. Many of the established methods of accounting for the differences presented by the Gospels, and for reconciling the discrepancies which are known to exist in them, are felt to be such as would never have been applied to the reconciliation of the difficulties presented by any other body of historical writings. Many feel that the phenomena which the Gospels present cannot be accounted for on the old established theories. Their faith is therefore placed in jeopardy. Careful examination also presents phenomena in the Epistles, though in a degree less striking, which the old theories are impotent to account for.

Such questions are no longer discussed in a corner: the existence of such phenomena is becoming more and more known to the general reader. Formerly these difficulties had been kept out of sight; they were esteemed only proper subjects for the discussion of the learned. Professed students knew them, and meditated on them in silence. Now the progress of knowledge has brought them before the great mass of readers. Every species of ingenuity has been exhausted in endeavouring to account for them in accordance with established theories. Their supporters were probably not well satisfied with the solutions which they had propounded. But ordinary readers had been taught to read the Scriptures in the light of a particular theory. Unpleasant difficulties were therefore kept out of sight: when this was impossible, they were passed over in silence. It was assumed that the usual principles of human judgment must not be applied to a revelation from God. Its divine origin was supposed to place it in such a position that the ordinary principles of interpretation were not applicable to it. It was placed on a pinnacle by itself, and careful inquiry into the phenomena presented by it was represented as profane. Human books might be inquired into, examined, and questioned; but reverence forbade such inquiries with respect to the sacred writings.

It seems never to have occurred to persons entertaining these views that religion is a matter of common sense, and that arguments of this description were only a quiet way of assuming the infallibility of those propounding them. Whence did they learn the correctness of their data? Such a mode of stifling inquiry was the old method of maintaining every established system of error: it was a quiet assumption of their own supernatural enlightenment, and that those who disagreed with them were wandering in darkness. It seems never to have occurred to such persons that the more inestimable the treasure is which is contained in the Scriptures, the more solemn is the duty of a careful and reverent inquiry into its nature, within what limits it is contained, whether it lies on the surface, or requires us to dig deep in order to discover it. Men do not quietly assume the existence of an earthly treasure; if they hear a report of its existence, they think that the truth of the report is worth careful investigation and inquiry. Why should we pursue a different course with a divine and heavenly one? It was generally believed that one simple theory would account for all the facts; why then take the trouble of testing that theory by the facts?

Learned men had their doubts. But what use was learning, or careful study, or deep thought, exerted on the Scriptures? Such things might be requisite enough in the study of human books; but, with respect to the Scriptures, careful inquiry and investigation was only a specious form of unbelief. All that was necessary, according to such teaching, was to take Scripture as it stands, *i. e.* to adopt *our* views respecting it. Inquiry, investigation, reading the Scriptures to see whether these things were so, was pronounced to be profane human wisdom or rationalizing contempt of the Word of God.

But the day when such solutions will satisfy the wants of men has passed away. The difficulties which the New Testament presents must be grappled with and honestly met. The answers must not be evasions, but must go to the root of the matter. Theories of inspiration must not be taken for granted, but tested by the facts. The difficulties must be either solved or acknowledged to exist: if they cannot be explained, they must be candidly admitted. What harm will come from candidly admitting their existence? Is not God's book of nature full of them? It will no longer do to assign as a reason why three names are left out of the genealogy of our Lord, that the persons whose names have been omitted sprang from a wicked marriage with the family of Ahab, as is done with some degree of approbation by Scott.

To many persons it never seems to have occurred that a spirit of inquiry is consistent with a teachable spirit, or that a spirit of investigation may be consistent with humility, or that an ardent wish to have evidence that God has spoken is consistent with a spirit of faith. Still less do some persons appear to have thought that deep investigation into what is truth is a Christian duty, or that a readiness to believe without evidence is not faith, or that the wisdom denounced by St. Paul is not wisdom generally, but a spirit of disputatious wrangling prevalent in the schools of Greek philosophy. Nothing is easier than to denounce everything to which we are opposed as flowing from the spirit of unbelief and human pride. It may be very unpleasant to have old prejudices disturbed: so thought the Jews at Thessalonica. Persons who prefer to slumber in their preconceived notions are ever ready to forget that the Beræans are commended for not rejecting the new because it was new, and for using their reason in comparing the new doctrines which St. Paul taught with the Scriptures of the Old Testament.

But can inquiry be averted? Is it even desirable that it should be? Is not the foundation of Christianity laid on truth and individual conviction, and is not this her highest glory? Her demands on our belief are not founded on the claims of ancestral religion, or expediency, or statecraft, but because our Lord declares that He is able to afford proof that He is a messenger from God. Once there was a time when she had to struggle with all these, and to summon her soldiers to enlist under her standard in the name of the God of truth. All systems of imposture may well shrink from rigid inquiry into their claims; but Christianity challenges all men not to believe on trust, but to sift fully into her credentials.

What, then, has revelation to gain by attempting to conceal the difficulties presented by the sacred volume, or by trying to prevent the fullest investigation into their nature? She gains nothing but the suspicion that her claims will not bear inquiry. She descends from the elevation on which God has placed her, and takes her station among the religions of the world. Readiness to embrace whatever is proposed to our assent is not faith, but credulity. When forgeries are common, a conscientious steward will be careful to ascertain the genuineness of his master's signature before he cashes his draft. Such is the teaching of St. John. "Try the spirits," says he, "whether they be of God: because many false prophets are gone out into the world." Credulity is not the livery of humility or love, but the mark of that steward who is ever ready to waste his master's goods.

The discouragers of investigation have had many impressive warnings. One of these has been supplied by the Church of Rome. She discourages the reading of the Scriptures, except under the safeguard of her own interpretations. What is the inference which common sense has drawn from this her conduct? That her governors are conscious in themselves that her doctrines cannot be found in the Scriptures. She endeavours to stop inquiry into her own miraculous pretensions by asserting that the denial of her miracles must be attended with the denial of the miracles which prove Christianity itself. Unhappily, multitudes who have believed her in little else have taken her at her word here, and have denied both.

It is frequently asserted by those who maintain the theory of verbal inspiration that we must accept this theory, or deny the inspiration of the New Testament. Nothing can be more dangerous than such assertions. Those who make them imitate the Church of Rome in the manner we have stated, and, instead of supporting the evidence of divine revelation, are putting a stumbling-block in the way of multitudes to reject it. Before such assertions are made, it is worth while to ascertain that they at least possess some evidence of truth.

But when it is considered that the assertion is made without any claim of authority from the New Testament itself, on mere grounds of antecedent probability, it is not only dangerous, but presumptuous and essentially rationalistic. We have already shown that it is devoid of all Scriptural evidence.

The assumption of the theory of verbal inspiration exposes Christianity to attacks from which it would be free, but for the assumption of this theory. It causes the quarrel between Christianity and science to be propagated from age to age. The supporters of it are never weary of raising the cry that Christianity is in danger on every fresh discovery of science. Such was the case when the Copernican system of astronomy was first promulgated. The supposed opposition between Christianity and astronomy has now ceased: the theologians have been forced to own that the astronomers were right. But the quarrel has been succeeded by a similar contest between divine revelation and geology. If a work is published in which the received system of chronology is impugned,—if a set of bones are discovered in a cavern,—if some new theory is propounded which is the result of the comparative study of languages,—if weapons are found buried anywhere but in the last-stratified formations,—if the facts and phenomena of the Gospels are carefully sifted and inquired into,—if even it is asserted, what every scholar knows to be a truth, that the existing version of the Scriptures is far from infallible,—it is declared to be a dangerous unsettling of men's faith; nay, it is sometimes represented as imperilling Christianity itself. On what is such faith grounded? Instead of such persons having their faith founded on a rock, it resembles a house built on the sand. The constant cry of such persons is, "Christianity is in danger."

Now it is a question worthy of the deepest consideration, whether the supposed danger which Christianity is so often represented as incurring may not be occasioned by an incorrect view as to the nature of the inspiration under the influence of which the Scriptures have been written. A theory which represents that every sentence in the Scriptures is the result of a divine inspiration, however remotely the particular statement may be connected with the proper subject-matter of the Christian revelation, and which denies the possibility of any human element being present in such revelation, is one of the chief causes of the supposed antagonism between science and revealed truth. The theory of verbal inspiration enormously enlarges the line of defence, without increasing the means or the number of the defenders: it exposes Christianity to attacks at every point. It is one thing to prove that Christianity has been revealed by God for the purpose of throwing light on the spiritual path of man, and making the humble and the teachable wise unto salvation; it is quite another thing to endeavour to prove that every reference made by the sacred writers to philosophy, history, or chronology was dictated to them by the omniscient Spirit, or that every event in the gospel history has been recorded with minute accuracy by each of the Evangelists, or that their separate accounts can be woven into a consistent narrative—that each Evangelist is correct in the order of the events narrated—or that not only the substance of the Gospels, but every expression has been dictated, whole and entire, by the Spirit of God—or that when we observe in the Epistles of the New Testament what in ordinary books would be certain marks of a human personality, the evidence totally fails us, and, notwithstanding all proofs to the contrary, we must infer that they have been dictated, whole and entire, by the Spirit of God.

When men are taught that unless this theory of the composition of the New Testament be correct, its inspiration cannot be maintained, and that, if it be not inspired, it can have no claim to be considered as a divine revelation, and when facts are observed to be at issue with this theory, they are much more likely to question the divine origin of the New Testament than carefully to examine whether the theory has been erected on a solid foundation. The theory of verbal inspiration has proved the fruitful source of scepticism, just as the miracles of the Church of Rome have hurried multitudes into infidelity. Large numbers of the objections of unbelievers against the New Testament are founded on the belief that the theory truly represents the influence under which the Scriptures, if inspired, must have been written; and the objections fall to the ground the moment that theory is abandoned.

It is an undeniable fact that unbelief in a greater or less degree in the inspiration of the Scriptures is extensively diffused among a large number of scientific men. No less certain is it that the progress of human science and many of its fresh discoveries, at least in the first instance, have been strongly opposed by those who have considered themselves as the defenders of revealed truth. It is worthy of deep inquiry whether the fault lies in science or scientific men, or in the theory held as to the nature of the inspiration with which the Scriptures have been composed. In most instances scientific truth has carried the victory, and has established its claims to be received as truth; and a different mode of interpreting Scripture has had to be adopted. It is highly desirable that this unseemly warfare should be brought to an end by determining clearly the limits by which inspiration is bounded.

But it may be justly asked, If the theory of verbal inspiration must be abandoned, is there any view respecting the nature of inspiration, fraught with less danger, which can be substituted for it? We answer emphatically, the view which is presented by the sacred writers respecting their own inspiration. The writers of the New Testament hold no vague language on the subject. The facts of the New Testament are entirely in unison with the language and with the analogies suggested by God's conduct in creation and providence.

In the earlier portion of this work we have endeavoured to show that the great argument of Bishop Butler, in which he has proved that the contents of the Christian revelation, as well as the difficulties presented by it, are in strict conformity with what we know of the Divine character and modes of working in the constitution and course of nature, is no less applicable to the mode in which a revelation would be communicated, and to the degree of inspiration which would be vouchsafed for its discovery. We have seen that our *à priori* knowledge on this subject is extremely limited. We have proved that as God acts in creation and providence, we have every reason to expect that He would act as the Revealer of His will; that if there are things in creation and providence which we should not naturally have expected, we have every reason to expect similar contradictions of what we may esteem as probable in the mode of communicating a revelation; that if God nicely proportions the means which He employs to the purposes which He effectuates in the one case, we shall discover the same careful adaptation in the other; that if it is the Divine purpose in nature that man should be a fellow-worker with Himself, we shall see that purpose exhibited in His mode of communicating a revelation ; and that, to whatever limitations the Creator has subjected the human intellect in the exercise of His sovereign will, these limitations would be observed by Him in His mode of communicating a revelation. With these analogies, derived from the Divine conduct in creation and providence, we have proved that the facts presented by revelation and the assertions of the sacred writers entirely agree. The writers of the New Testament declare that the invisible and incomprehensible God has made His last great manifestation to the finite mind, not by creative acts, not by employing the tongues of human messengers, but in the person of the incarnate Son. Christ, in

His life, in His teaching, in His death, and in His resurrection, forms the great objective manifestation of the Godhead. In Him was exhibited inspiration in its highest form, through the indwelling of Deity in His human nature, and the fullest communication of the gifts of the inspiring Spirit. He is the revealer of the Godhead, and the prophet of the Church. But how have the results of this great revelation been communicated to man? The writers of the New Testament inform us that our Lord appointed His Apostles to be the witnesses of His actions and the authorized teachers of the meaning of His revelation. For this purpose He endowed them with the requisite supernatural endowments. As His Father as Creator proportioned the instrumentality which He employs to the results which He effects, so the Son proportioned His promise of supernatural assistance to the work to which He called the Apostles, and to the necessities of that work. The Apostles were to be Christ's witnesses, both as to what He had done and taught. Their natural powers would have been insufficient accurately to report what our Lord taught: He promised them that their powers of recollection should be supernaturally assisted. They had misunderstood many things which He had done and said: He promised that they should be supernaturally guided into the meaning of the truths of His revelation. Their human testimony might be disbelieved: He promised that their human testimony should be corroborated by the testimony of His Spirit, exhibited in the possession of miraculous power. We have examined the Gospels, and have found that their phenomena are in strict accordance with what these promises presuppose. The narratives of fact present all the phenomena which are the peculiar mark of ocular human testimony. In strict accordance with our Lord's promise, their accounts of the discourses present a greater degree of apparent accuracy than their narratives of the facts, though in every history merely human the reverse is the case. In conformity with our Lord's promise of supernatural guidance into the meaning of the Christian revelation, we have seen that there are certain subjects on which the Gospels preserve an unbroken silence, where, had they been ordinary human writings, their communications would have been full. We have proved that God corroborated the human testimony of the Apostles by signs, and wonders, and gifts of the Holy Spirit, according to His own will. But the Apostles were also to be the teachers of the meaning of the Christian revelation. We have shown that our Lord promised them supernatural guidance into its entire truth; the facts agree with the promise. Our Lord communicated to the Apostles special endowments in the form of spiritual gifts, superadded to their ordinary faculties, but not superseding or overwhelming their individuality, which permanently abode in them as an internal light, leading them into the whole truth of the Christian revelation. That light communicated to them a special and objective knowledge of the great truths of the gospel dispensation. Under the illumination of that light they taught and wrote. Inferior degrees of inspiration were afforded to others; but the Apostles were endowed with one special gift, that of wisdom, which unfolded to their minds an objective knowledge of the deep mysteries of the kingdom of heaven. But as His Father worked in creation and providence, so our Lord worked as the Revealer of His will. He used an adequate instrumentality, but He made no useless expenditure of means. He promised the Apostles supernatural enlightenment respecting the truths which were His, not respecting the truths which were man's. He promised to them guidance. Guidance is a gradual process. In conformity with the promise, the history tells us that the Apostles were gradually guided into the knowledge of the truth, with the exception of St. Paul, who, being appointed for a special work, was at once supernaturally enlightened. The promise was not to make them infallible, or to guide them into universal truth, but into the special truths which Christ came to reveal. Accordingly St. Paul informs us that the spiritual gifts were strictly limited to a special function and a definite subject-matter; and the history distinctly informs us that they gave no illumination on points beyond their range. An apostle was not even inspired on points of conduct which had a direct bearing on questions of Christian truth;

who then shall venture to assert that he possessed a supernatural guidance on questions of physical truth, or philosophy, or history, or poetry, or chronology? In his conduct and in his experience he enjoyed the full benefit of inward illumination, which flowed from the spiritual gifts with which he was invested. But St. Paul only claims on such points the authority of one who had received mercy of the Lord to be faithful, and that believers were to be followers of him, as he was of Christ. The Divine illumination formed a portion of the personality, without destroying or even superseding the individual man. The Divine worker, who has all power and instrumentality at His command, operated, in the communication of objective truth by revelation, so as in the smallest degree to interfere with the exercise of those natural powers which He himself had created. Such is the inspiration asserted in the Scriptures—sufficient for the infallible communication of the gospel of Christ, but leaving unfettered the other agencies of man, and rendering it possible that the student of God's revelation made in the person of His Son, and of God's revelation manifested through creation and providence, might work together, in harmonious unison, in discovering those truths which are "as high as heaven: what canst thou do? deeper than hell: what canst thou know?"

CHAPTER XXI.

THE CHRIST OF THE GOSPELS NO CREATION OF THE UNASSISTED POWERS OF THE HUMAN MIND.

We must now consider how our subject bears on the views of those who assert that Christianity is a human development, evolved in conformity with the laws of human thought. Under this head we include all those who consider that Christianity was not communicated to the minds of the Apostles by an influence acting externally, or that they attained to a knowledge of its truths by the mere use of their unassisted natural powers. Those who maintain that Christianity is a mere human development, without any special interference of God, or that it has been evolved out of previously existing elements of thought by the mere powers of the human mind, must be considered as really denying the claims of Christianity to be viewed as a revelation from God.

Many persons have claimed for various systems of human thought a divine origin, as forming a portion of the great plan of Divine Providence for the education of the world. This is a very favourite mode of viewing the subject at the present day. Such persons maintain that the civilization of Greece (her philosophy, her poetry, her exquisite taste for art), the Roman genius for government, the forms of Oriental philosophy, the Hebrew perception of a personal God, the forms of beauty involved in Polytheism, the freedom of German thought, and the civilization of modern Europe are all divine. Persons who maintain such catholic principles as to what is divine, of course, liberally concede to Christianity a place in their extensive Pantheon, and occasionally use expressions which imply that these, one and all, have been derived from a species of Divine inspiration.

But it is impossible to concede that such persons believe that Christianity is a Divine revelation in any ordinary sense of that term. Such things may form portions of the plan of Divine Providence for the education of the world; but, although they may have been brought about by that providence of God which encircles and directs everything in the universe which He has made, and by which even the free will of man is controlled, yet the notion intended differs widely from what is meant by a revelation from God or an inspiration of His Spirit. It may be perfectly true that men of exalted powers are introduced at special times into the world expressly to effectuate the purposes of Divine Providence. Certain great developments of man may have had an important place in the Divine plans. They may have been specially intended by God to have an important influence as subservient to the introduction of His great revelation into the world. Greek, Oriental, and Roman civilization may have prepared the way for Christianity. But there is a wide distinction between such views and those which maintain that Christianity has been communicated by inspiration from God. Such an expression can only mean an influence exerted by God on the mind, different from the influences exerted by God on the human understanding in the ordinary course of nature.

All attempts, therefore, to place Christianity on a level with other developments of the human mind, and to assert a Divine character for them all, by whatever specious names such a proceeding may be dignified, are virtually to rank it among the unassisted products of the mind of man, and to deprive it of all claim to be viewed as communicated by inspiration from God.

But the existence of the Christian Scriptures, whatever origin we may assign to them, is a fact. Persons who deny their supernatural origin are bound to account for their existence: they cannot have been the result of chance. The inspiration of genius, the power possessed by man of developing himself, the possession of deep spiritual insight, inability to perceive the difference between objective realities and subjective perceptions, the aid of a well-constructed system of myths, all assisted by sudden flashes of light bursting on particular minds, form the usual machinery by the aid of which attempts are made to account for the existence of these curious phenomena, the Gospels and Epistles, on human principles.

Of the origin of any ordinary book and its contents we can give some account. If we cannot give a complete account, we can at least give a probable one. Unless it is the first book in existence of any literature, we can refer the forms of thought to something previously existing. We can make discoveries how the ideas contained in it grew in the mind of the author, and from what sources he derived them. This we can do, in most instances, on evidence which leaves little room for doubt.

But the New Testament Scriptures exist; whence came

they? They contain the character of Christ, which many unbelievers have pronounced to be a very near approach to ideal goodness. Out of what elements did the writers of the New Testament create this character? They contain very extraordinary statements of doctrinal truth: whence were they derived? They exhibit the teaching and practical wisdom of the Apostles. Out of what elements was this practical wisdom developed? The person who denies the account which the New Testament gives, that the whole was derived from preternatural inspiration, is bound to give a distinct account of the sources whence it sprang. It is impossible to say that the means of doing so are deficient: the gospel originated in an age in which the materials of history abound.

Let us examine the Gospels and the Divine character of our Lord, and try to ascertain out of what previously existing elements they could possibly have been developed. If they are not of Divine origin in the sense of having been communicated by a special revelation from God, they must have been developed out of some previously existing human element. Whether we affirm that they were created by the inspiration of genius, or of some deep power of spiritual insight, or that they have originated in myths, as we suppose earlier Greek and Roman history to have originated, or whether they had any other kindred origin, we mean that their origin is owing to some form of mere human development. Genius itself, although it may propel the age which has given it birth a great stage in advance, is yet part and parcel of the age from which it has sprung: it is created out of conditions of thought previously existing. It would effect no great results, if the times had not prepared the way for its appearance. A Napoleon was relative to the age out of which he sprang. Mahommed was an embodiment of Eastern modes of thought. We can distinctly point out the previously existing elements out of which their character was formed. Julius Cæsar, although he exerted a mighty influence in propelling his age, was yet a creation of his age. Alexander the Great was a similar phenomenon. The great poets have been creations of the times in which they lived, and have exerted a mighty influence on those times. Who fails to recognize the forms of previously existing thought out of which Shakspeare and Milton sprang? The way for the Reformation itself was prepared in previous centuries: the corruptions of the Church of Rome had long been growing a more and more intolerable burden to the nations. The Baconian philosophy was no fresh creation unconnected with the present or the past. Sir Isaac Newton, with his mighty powers, was yet clearly connected with the age which brought him forth. The greatest event of modern times, the French Revolution, grew out of elements previously existing. All the mightiest of men have sprung out of the present and the past, and have propelled the world with an increased velocity on the course on which it had already entered. If the gospel has originated in an historic age, out of elements essentially human, the nature of these elements can be pointed out: it must have grown out of the past.

But this argument will tell with additional force, if we assign a mythic origin as a satisfactory account of the source whence the gospel has originated. Nothing is more certain than that all myths arise out of previously existing elements, by a slow and gradual growth. The slowness of their progress differs from the efforts of genius. The growth of myths requires long years of progress. The same remarks will be applicable to any other theory which we may invoke to assist in the solution. If the Gospels have not their origin in a special revelation, they must owe their existence to some definite form of human development.

It is generally held, by those persons who assign this human origin to Christianity, that man, commencing from a low and degraded condition, is by slow and gradual stages undergoing a development towards a condition of an indefinitely remote optimism. Such persons have assigned various theories for the origin of man. The one at present in vogue seems to be to deduce him as a development direct from the brutes. He has probably been developed out of the highest form of monkey. At any rate, his original starting-point has been one sufficiently low and mean*. From this state he has been gradually struggling onwards. Just as the material world has been developing itself to greater and greater stages of perfection, man is actually undergoing a similar development. The present state of his religion and civilization is the crowning result of his past struggles. Future ages will witness his progression to higher forms of being.

It does not fall within our scope to inquire into the truth of such theories, or whether they may be partial manifestations of some ill-apprehended truth. It will be sufficient to observe that the object of the theory is to evolve all existing things one from another by the operation of law, which is supposed to be a necessarily existing property in material things, without any special interference of a Creator. It is conceded that God has first created all things, and by the depths of His wisdom and power has originally impressed on them their eternal laws; but these laws have been sufficient to evolve all things without any special subsequent interference. The Creator has only appeared in His character as Creator once: it would be a reflection on His wisdom or His power to suppose that He had thus exhibited Himself again; it would suppose that the laws which He had once impressed on the universe were unable to effect their purposes, or that they required amendment. In conformity with these views, it is maintained that man is passing through a succession of developments, from the lower to the higher forms. His present growth is a stage of those developments: ages remotely future may find Him developed into a being of a higher class. It will be easily perceived that, if views of this kind

---

* According to Herodotus, Hecatæus scandalized the Egyptian priests by claiming a god for his ancestor at the distance of sixteen generations. The priests thought that the gods had lived on earth at a period much more remote. The general feeling of mankind has imitated Hecatæus in claiming ancestry from some eminent notoriety. Among a certain order of minds, a rage has recently burst forth in a contrary direction, and they seem to esteem it as the highest order of nobility to be able to trace their ancestry to an ape.

are entertained, it forms only a part of the same line of thought that Christianity must have an origin essentially human.

In the history of man, undoubted examples of development may be traced. One form of thought and civilization has been closely connected with the preceding. But while such examples are undoubtedly to be found in history, its pages no less distinctly testify to the existence of retrogressions. Still, with the advocates of this view, all these are asserted to be portions of one great system, which, despite of all retrograde movements, is yet continually advancing. Many great facts connected with the history of man are therefore, by the supporters of this theory, with great discretion, kept in the background.

It will be readily conceded that human society is constructed on the principle of progress. Oriental civilization is a development; so is Chinese civilization; so is Grecian, so is Roman, so is modern civilization. But some of these are still existing, not as advancing systems of human growth, but as systems effete, worn-out, and gradually perishing. Some of them are still exerting powerful influences on the modern world. But the facts of history do not prove that man is advancing by a gradual growth towards perfection. Developments which have been well-ascertained facts have always been effected by very slow and gradual stages of advancement. They do not resemble the rapid springing-up of a fungus, but the slow growth of the stateliest trees; like them, they require long intervals of time. Every stage is attained by fixing its roots deeply into the past: progression is grafted on progression. Similar are the stages of decay. Whenever man has undergone a course of real development, the time which has been occupied in its progress may be either computed or approximated.

Those persons who believe in the gradual development of the universe or of man into their present actual condition from previously existing states of imperfection generally concur in representing that it has required periods of almost indefinite extension for its accomplishment. Those who assert that species have been developed out of species, by laws purely natural, require an immense period of time during which these changes must have been effected. The necessity for periods of time of indefinite extent naturally flows from the fact that no remains of species have ever yet been discovered in actual progress of transmutation. The truths which have been established by geology require periods of time for their accomplishment astounding to human thought, though perhaps not greater than the profundities of space which the science of astronomy positively requires in the other direction. The necessity for the existence of these profound depths, both of time and space, is positively established. But if every species has been developed from previously existing species, there arises a demand for profundities of time still more astonishing. Though geology has not yet succeeded in discovering any species in actual process of transmutation, there is no occasion that any theorizer should be daunted. He has only to double, or treble, to multiply indefinitely the longest geological period, and the necessary time will be obtained for any single transmutation; he has only to multiply again and again, and he will get time enough for any succession of transmutations; he has only to continue multiplying, and sufficient length of duration will be found for the development of the noblest of the sons of men from the most ignoble moss which ever grew on the side of rock. With the bank of eternity to draw on, we can never be in want of any amount of finite duration. If our drafts exceed in number the ultimate particles which compose the system of the solar universe, the bank of infinity cannot break. As far, therefore, as time is concerned, we need not fear our ability to develope a Napoleon, a Newton, or a Shakspeare from a piece of sponge or moss. With eternity behind us, and no fact to obstruct us, as far as time is concerned, all developments are possible.

The bold and determined theorizer who is heartily desirous of assigning the smallest possible amount of action to the Creator in the universe which he dares not deny that he originally created, as long as he has not facts to oppose him, need not be daunted. If he is determined to evolve sponge into a god, time cannot hinder him. But the case is different with respect to the historical developments of man. Man has a history, within which they must have taken place; they, therefore, must be accommodated to the actual facts presented by that history. Great and mighty developments in man, no less than in nature, require intervals of considerable duration for the purpose of effecting them. Of many of the well-known historical developments we know the actual or the approximate length. The stages of the development of the Greek mind are known. The developments through which the mind of the Roman and the modern world have passed can be actually measured by years. Oriental nations may have tried to hide their origin in the hoary past; but increased research is gradually dispelling the thick clouds. In human developments, the actual history of man prevents us from drawing on the indefinite past: we cannot open an account with the bank of eternity; we are compelled to accommodate our views to definite periods of historic time.

As we are prevented, in all questions connected with the developments of man, from drawing on the indefinite past, so we are precluded from assuming that they can take place in periods indefinitely short. Those who endeavour to evolve man, as he is first represented by authentic history, from some previous condition little elevated above the brute, are well aware that such an attempt requires not an inconsiderable period of duration for its accomplishment: they have accordingly demanded for it from twenty thousand to one hundred thousand, or it may be a million of years. Others, who have wished to deduce certain developments of man from certain previous conditions, are obliged to ask for intervals of time for their accomplishment to which historical records return a decided negative. If, therefore, we wish to form an idea of the possibility of developing Christianity out of previously existing human elements, we must keep in mind the time which has elapsed while the known great historical developments of man have been effected. We shall not be able to make demands at pleasure on eternity, but must confine

2 D

ourselves within the strict bounds of a well-known historical period.

Now those who assert that Christianity is not a supernatural revelation, but a human development of some sort, are bound to tell us, in no ambiguous terms, out of what previously existing conditions of human thought and sentiment Christianity has been evolved, and to show us that the time within which Christianity must have been developed is sufficiently long for that purpose. This demand may be made with entire propriety, because the period when Christianity originated was an historical period. If we except certain portions of modern history, we have an equally accurate account of no other period of the history of the world. It was a period of abounding literature. The ideas involved in all the great systems of philosophy are well known. The various religious systems which existed in all the countries connected with Judæa are no dark enigmas. At no period of time have we more accurate information of the real state of the Jewish people. Of the general state of thought and feeling throughout the Greek and Roman world we have ample evidence. History was no child when Christianity arose. Her birthplace was a province of the Roman empire: a Roman governor administered that province. Christianity is totally unlike the religions of Egypt or India, which shroud their origin in a hoar antiquity. It in no respect resembles the theologies of Greece and Rome, which were ushered into existence centuries before authentic history was born. Our knowledge of the systems of theology and philosophy, of the morals, of the literature, of the regions within which Christianity originated is extensive. If, then, it is a mere human development, generated out of previously existing conditions of thought, we have a right to demand a statement out of what conditions of thought then existing, and within what definite period of time, the Christianity of the New Testament was developed.

In asking for such a statement, we only demand what is reasonable: it is a test which, to a great extent, has been applied to many of the great historical developments of man, and in cases where the materials for tracing them are far less rich. The relations existing between all the great systems of philosophy have been ascertained. A sufficient mass of historic evidence exists to determine the relations of all their great principles to each other. We have a general idea of the first systems of Greek philosophy. We know how the system of the Sophists developed itself from that philosophy. The relationship which the Socratic philosophy bears to the Sophists and to the systems of previous philosophers is no dark enigma. The connexion of the systems which followed the Socratic with the Socratic philosophy is well known. The relation, for instance, in which the system of Plato stands to that of his master, and that of Aristotle to Plato, has been pointed out. All the subsequent schools of philosophy are well known to be developments of the systems of previous teachers, acted upon by the tendencies of the age, as they were carried out in different directions by different minds. The nature of the different systems of Oriental philosophy is getting more and more understood. The systems of thought which gave birth to Alexandrine philosophy have been examined and pointed out by learned men. But if Christianity be a development out of previous systems, the materials which exist for pointing out the state of thought and feeling out of which it sprang, and for tracing its progress through its various stages until it culminated in the conception of the Christ of the Gospels, are far more rich than those which exist for pointing out the connexion of any one of these systems with those which preceded it. As St. Paul says, the origin of Christianity did not take place " in a corner;" it happened in an historic age.

Now it must be conceded by those who are acquainted with the conditions of thought in the midst of which Christianity arose, if it was developed out of those conditions, that it was the greatest of developments. If it be supposed to have been developed out of existing elements, the human mind must have made a prodigious leap when the full form of Christianity appeared. The gulf which separates the full idea of Christianity from every element previously existing is one of profound depth. It is not a development which can be compared with that of any one school of philosophy from that which preceded it: it involves new creations of thought and feeling, and these entering on new and successive stages of progress. It differs more widely from any previously existing condition of thought than the philosophy of Epicurus does from the views of human life presented in the "Iliad." Let us compare the Christian Scriptures with any system of thought which existed when Christianity arose. How vast the progression! How prodigiously do the four Gospels differ from any remnant of antiquity! How unlike is the Gospel of St. John to the teaching of Aristotle! How contrasted is St. Matthew's with the speculations of Neo-Platonism! Place the Gospels beside any writing of Academician, or Stoic, or Epicurean, and how profound is the interval which separates them! How different are the speculations of Oriental philosophy from the Gospel picture of the living Christ! How wide is the separation between the Gospels and the systems of the great sects of the Jewish Church—hard Pharisaism, sensual Sadducism, unpractical Essenism! The Gospels present us with the divine picture of Christ—Christ the perfect man, Christ the incarnate God. Out of what element of Jewish thought, or Oriental speculation, or of philosophic scepticism of that age of unbelief has that glorious creation sprung? How did the original inventors of Christianity conceive a Christ? With what plastic hand—out of hard Judaism, or speculative or fanatic Orientalism, or polished scepticism—out of what hardened feelings and dead affections of the age which gave birth to Christianity did its inventors fuse these elements together, and thereout generate the Jesus of the Gospels?

All human developments, whether they be intellectual or moral, require a length of time to effect them in exact proportion to the greatness of the interval which separates the original materials out of which they have originated from the full conception of the developments themselves. To develope an acorn-eating savage into a modern English gentleman, if unassisted in its progress by external influences, would require a long succession of ages. That period might be reduced if external influences and a state of more advanced civilization could be brought to bear. Still the success of the undertaking would be very uncertain, unless we had large periods of time at our command. Although the development of species from species confessedly requires the command of vast intervals of time, yet here the supporter of the theory works at the greatest possible advantage. He has the benefit of an unlimited supply of inconvertible paper money in a past eternity from which he can obtain all the necessary time which he requires. History is unable to prove that his speculations are wrong; for historic fact does not exist. Hence it is no difficult operation to develope a man out of a gorilla, or, if it be preferred, even from a piece of sponge; but it is a very different matter to carry forward an extensive development within periods of authenticated history.

Now the interval which separates Christianity from all previously existing systems of human thought is an interval of greater extent than that which is filled by any historical development with which we are acquainted. If we suppose European civilization to be a regular development from a state in which the human mind had no greater degree of knowledge than that possessed by the most degraded savage, the interval between the perfect Christ of the Gospels and the previously existing forms of human thought with which we are acquainted is no less vast. It is a far larger interval than that which separates the Baconian philosophy from the first dawnings of human speculation, or which separates the whole range of modern science from the systems of the Sophists. Yet these developments have only been effected in successive stages, each forming an advance on that which preceded it, and have not been accomplished at a single bound. Numerous external influences have also lent their assistance. The interval which separates the Church of the middle ages from that depicted in the Apostolic Epistles is a very wide interval. If the one be viewed as a development from the other, the strongest supporter of the theory will grant that it has been assisted in its onward course by many external influences, and is not a direct development out of ideas contained in the New Testament, in which it is difficult to detect the smallest germinations of the full-grown tree. Yet it had to pass through a long succession of stages, and required centuries for its completion. The full idea of a theocratic Church can hardly be conceived of as fully developed before the tenth century; and if we include in our view the dogmatic creeds of the Church of Rome, its complete development must be deferred till after the Council of Trent. Now Christianity, as represented in the New Testament, is a far greater development from any element of human thought previously existing than the full idea of the Church of Rome is from the Church of the Apostolic Epistles; but, instead of one hundred and fifty years, this required fifteen hundred to complete. Even from the state of feeling involved in the religion of the Old Testament the Church of the New Testament stands separated by a vast interval. What a profound depth separates our Lord on the cross, saying, "Father, forgive them, for they know not what they do," from Zechariah the priest invoking vengeance on his murderers—"The Lord look on it, and requite it"! Still more vast is the separation between the Judaism of the time in which the Gospels originated and the Christianity of the Gospels themselves. Let it be granted that the Judaism of the time of the Gospels is a development from the Judaism of the Old Testament. The developers are welcome to all the benefit which they can derive from it; for it is unquestionably a retrograde one; it is a development from a higher to a lower form of spirituality, thought, and feeling.

Now, whether the Gospels are supposed to have grown out of myths or from some other origin, they must have had some starting-place from which the development began. They must have commenced with some one laying the foundation of the myths, and must have been gradually widened, enlarged, and perfected as they spread their influence among ever-increasing numbers. One must have added one piece to the story, and another another. Occasionally a genius must have appeared who contributed some new idea. This idea went on enlarging and receiving successive additions. The result has been that the development, starting from some definite commencement of spiritual and moral feeling, has culminated in the creation of the Christ of the Gospels—the perfect man, or, according to our mode of surveying the Divine reality, the elaboration of the complete conception of the character of God manifest in the flesh.

Now, when we consider the elements out of which this development must have originated, and the ideal of perfection in which it has terminated, the belief in its existence is one which requires prodigious faith in human progress, even if we are supplied with an indefinite period of time for its accomplishment. It is one which could not advance in a single line; it could not have evolved itself from a single idea; it required a succession of fresh creations. It is as great a development, in the moral and spiritual world, as that of a gorilla into a man would be in the natural. The speculator finds little difficulty to conceive the possibility of the one, because he has the immensities of a past eternity during which he may conduct his operations. What cannot be effected in a million years may be brought to pass in that number indefinitely extended. If a retrograde development takes place, abundance of time exists for it to turn in a contrary direction. But, in the case of Christianity, the conditions of the historical problem are distinct. The development of the conception of a Christ out of previously existing elements must be fully accomplished within the definite space of one hundred and fifty years.

Let us endeavour to give a brief view of the difficulties which those persons who effected this great development must have succeeded in surmounting. They must have had a definite starting-point. This must have consisted in the existing habits of Jewish, or Oriental, or Grecian thought immediately preceding the apostolic age, or these forms fused together and united. The Jewish Church of the apostolic age was a retrograde development from the Jewish Church of Isaiah and Ezekiel. Its spiritual elements had declined fearfully; its carnal elements had made a no less portentous growth. It would have been as great a revolution, had a Luther sprung up in the first century before Christ, and carried the Jewish Church back to the state of spirituality of which the writings of Isaiah are the prototype, as that which the actual Martin Luther accomplished when he, and others who aided him in that great work, rescued Christianity from the corruptions with which it was encrusted, and carried it back to the idea of the Christianity of the third century. But what would have been such an attempt compared with the deed of those who evolved the Christ of the Gospels out of previously existing elements, by a development merely human, during the interval of time which the conditions imposed by history require ? Yet the character of the Christ of the Gospels is a fact; the idea has been conceived. All accomplished deeds seem easy after their accomplishment. So did the discovery of America, after it was discovered. We ask, not unreasonably, where did the authors of the Gospels, whoever they were, derive the conception of their Christ? It is difficult for the mind to form a lively picture of the divine character of the God-man, as His glories shine forth in the pages of the Gospels. Till we can do so, we cannot fully estimate the greatness of the creation which the Gospels have accomplished.

Let us survey the last day of our Lord's life, and contemplate the great portrait which these accomplished artists have set before us in their pages. His time is come to suffer and to die. Every event which is to befall Him is clearly seen by Him—the agony, the deriding, the insults, the scourging, the cross. With the calmest composure, He proceeds to eat the passover with His disciples. A disciple, who has been highly honoured by Him, is seated near Him with the secret purpose of the foulest treachery : he recognizes it, and is troubled. But the great purpose for which He came into the world never once loses its hold on His mind. He takes the last opportunity of teaching the disciples humility and love. While He is fully sensible that the Father has given all things into His hands, He performs the office of a servant, and washes His disciples' feet. His soul is possessed with the firmest purpose of self-surrendering love. He steadily perseveres in His determination to die for His people a death of horror, torture, ignominy, contempt, and pain.

While the view of what is coming is before His mental eye, He says to His disciples, " Love one another, as I have loved you." He institutes, in everlasting remembrance of His love, the great ordinance of the Christian Church. He points the traitor out, who instantly departs to execute his dark purpose. While twelve hours at most remain before the hour of suffering arrives, He warns His disciples against contending for the preeminence, and occupies the short time remaining in calmly discoursing with them on the great truths of His heavenly kingdom. He then, the God-man speaking to God, consecrates Himself by the calmest of solemn supplications for the great work of offering the atoning sacrifice to the Father. He deliberately enters the garden where He is to meet His betrayers and murderers. His great work of suffering commences. The darkest cloud of the blackest night of mental agony has enwrapt the Redeemer's soul. The Evangelists do not attempt to depict its inner realities: they can only describe it by its outward manifestations. He sweats as it were great drops of blood. He is sorrowful and deeply oppressed. He is prostrate before His Father:—" O my Father, let this cup pass from me: nevertheless, not what I will, but what Thou wilt." He is strengthened by an angel. He rises from prayer; but it is to return to prayer again, with the profoundest feelings of resignation:—" O my Father, if this cup may not pass from me, except I drink it, Thy will be done." Knowing that a band is at hand to seize Him, He rises from prayer and advances to meet them. They fall to the ground before Him; but He surrenders himself into their hands that they may do their pleasure. He stands with unfaltering calmness before the Jewish council. One question alone He answers:—" Art thou the Christ, the Son of God?" " I am." And this answer is death. He yields himself, without resistance, to the derision of the mob, while He has only to utter one word of prayer to His Father and He will be rescued by twelve legions of angels. He stands before Pilate: He confesses that He is a king, though His kingdom is not of this world. To all other charges He answers not a word. Pilate is bent on releasing Him; neither by word or deed will He contribute to His own escape: He had come to die.

The judge, after the hardest struggles against his own judgment, delivers Him to be crucified. No remonstrance is offered to the judge at his delivering up One whom he pronounced innocent, to a death of torture, to gratify a selfish priesthood and a bloodthirsty mob. He is scourged; but no groan is heard. He is treated with bitter mocking; but no reproach passes His lips. The cross is placed on His shoulders: He faints beneath the burden. Weeping women surround Him, and lament Him: "Daughters of Jerusalem," says He, "weep not for me, but weep for yourselves and for your children." The place of execution is reached. He is offered the malefactor's draught: He will die with the fullest consciousness, even in the profoundest torture. He is nailed to the cross: no malediction is uttered. Words pass from Him which, under such circumstances, never passed before from the lips of man—" Father, forgive them; for they not what they do." The people, the priests, the soldiers, all stand aggravating the torture by insulting taunts. The calmness of resignation, darkened by intensity of suffering, settles on His brow. No word of complaint is heard. But one friend is standing near the cross with her who was His human mother; let her be cared for even in the darkness of that terrible hour: "Woman, behold thy son;" to the disciple He says, " Behold thy mother." But not only do the priests, the soldiers, and the mob revile; a fellowsufferer throws in his bitterest taunt. He endures in silence. That silence, which can be broken by neither taunts nor tortures, is broken by a suppliant's cry. Another sufferer's voice is heard rebuking his fellow, and uttering words of penitence and faith—" Lord, remember me when Thou comest into Thy kingdom." From the cross, from the act of surrendering His life for the sins of the world, with the calmness of conscious royalty, He assures him that the gates of paradise shall open to receive him. Again a dark cloud of the intensity of mental anguish settles on the Redeemer's soul—a darkness like the agony in the garden: nature herself is robed in night. For three hours this anguish, the nature of which the Evangelist describes by a silence followed by a single utterance, enshrouds His soul: " My God, my God, why hast Thou forsaken me?"—deserted, but yet His

God. While dying, with unclouded intellect He is able to survey the secret counsels of the Almighty : He is determined that not one of them shall remain unfulfilled. He surveys the Scriptures. All but one purpose of God is now accomplished; but the smallest of His Father's purposes shall be fulfilled in Him. He says, "I thirst." Vinegar is offered : He receives it. With a loud, triumphant cry, He exclaims, " It is finished. Father, into Thy hands I commend my spirit." He bows His head, and surrenders His spirit unto the Father. But the loud cry of the dying sufferer has shaken the solid ground. Heaven and earth have heard it. It opens the graves. The Temple veil is rent; its dark inner chamber is laid open to the light of day, announcing that, by the accomplishment of the great work of redemption, the veil which shrouds the face of the Eternal is withdrawn, and that the redeemed worshipper may freely approach the presence of the Most High.

Now the ideal of a character resembling this, the Gospels have actually depicted. Out of what elements of thought or feeling then existing, either in the Jewish or heathen worlds, did the conception grow? Was it from Jewish elements or Alexandrine, or Oriental, or Greek, or Roman, or all fused together? Through what mental processes, through what succession of myths, through what successive elaborations, did the humble fishermen of Galilee develope the grand pictorial creation of their imagination—the suffering, the scourged, the crucified, the dying Jesus? An unbeliever has said, "If Socrates died like a philosopher, Jesus died like a God;" and the remark is less than the truth: He died like one whose manhood was united with the Godhead.

But the Evangelists have not only delineated a suffering and dying Jesus; their creation, if a human development, is the conception of a man perfect in every relation of life; nay, they have correctly delineated what " God manifest in the flesh" ought to be, if such manifestation were a possibility.

The vast majority of those persons who have made the Gospels a subject of study, with a few most inconsiderable exceptions, admit that the character of our Lord, as represented in them, is absolutely perfect. In addition to many virtues which were recognized as virtues by the ancient world, it contains an array of perfections which that world did not recognize as perfections, but which, since they have been exhibited in the character of Christ, have been recognized as essential portions of the character of a perfect man. These portions of our Lord's character consist chiefly in the representation of His relationship to the Father, and the consequences flowing from that relationship, and in the display of the milder virtues, with the full riches of which His human character was endowed. These portions of our Lord's character cannot fail to strike every reader of the Gospels.

Now, we ask, from what source did the persons who portrayed the character of Christ, or who elaborated that character from a succession of myths, learn that these were virtues at all, in contradiction to the whole current of opinion and practice of the ancient world? How did they acquire their knowledge—to mix and combine in due proportions these perfections themselves with the other portions of His divine character, so as to form out of the complicated Whole a perfect Christ? The difference between any model which they could have studied and the perfection to which they have attained in their great portrait exceeds that which exists between the daub executed by a savage and the most perfect picture of a Raphael. The perfection of painting is no sudden creation: it passes through regular stages of progress. Artists slowly improve upon their models. One generation carries on to greater perfection the acquisitions of the preceding. Are we then to believe that the elaboration of the perfection of a Christ can be created by a single flash of the human intellect?

Holy and good men have, in lower degrees, embodied in themselves certain portions of our Lord's character. One good man exhibits one portion of His heavenly virtues, and another another portion of them. But where one element of goodness is exhibited in a high degree, we frequently see another element strikingly deficient. Different orders of virtues are exhibited in different holy men. One has the sterner virtues, another has the milder. In ordinary men, certain opposite forms of human perfection seem incapable of being combined in the same person. The sterner virtues and large displays of the mild and loving ones rarely unite. Self-conscious dignity and humility seem almost contradictory. But the persons who conceived the Gospels have succeeded in uniting, in the person of Christ, every form of human excellence in due proportion: the greatest opposites meet in unison in the same person. The Gospels have solved the problem how the highest conceivable justice can coexist with the highest conceivable mercy; how the most exalted holiness can be united with the highest conceivable compassion for the unholy; how One who never once faltered in the path of duty can feel the deepest sympathy with those who are faltering at every step; how severity can coexist with love.

Now what have the Evangelists accomplished? What is the problem which they have solved? If the character of Christ be a mere human development, they have invented virtues which were previously unknown to be such, and persuaded men that their discovery is correct. They have combined those virtues together in the most correct proportions and in the greatest possible perfection. They have combined these virtues with others previously admitted, also in correct proportion and absolute perfection. They have exhibited, in one person, the most opposite forms of perfection. These opposite forms are correctly blended together. Out of them they have created, not merely an ideal, but a living Christ, acting in every relation of life. Varied as are the situations in which they have placed Him, the action of the character is perfect: He never once deviates from consistency or propriety.

Let us endeavour, omitting minor details, to depict the broad outlines of the work which the Evangelists have succeeded in accomplishing. They have drawn the portrait of a man mighty to suffer. They have represented Him as free from the smallest contamination of evil; not guiltless merely, but having every perfection of which man's nature is capable. He is armed with power, to which all nature yields obedience. They have portrayed His soul as sinking beneath the profoundest anguish, but yet possessed of confidence in God absolutely unshaken. They have represented Him, at the very moment that He was conscious of possessing super-human power to crush, as surrendering Himself without an effort into the hands of His bitterest foes. He submits Himself to the grossest insults and the cruellest tortures of mind and body, with the most absolute and unfaltering submission. "When He suffered, He threatened not." He prays for His murderers. In the profoundest depth of suffering, He can attend to the penitent prayer of one dying a like death of ignominy with Himself. In the lowest degradation, He is conscious that He is a king. Torture prevents Him not from distinctly perceiving all things, past, present, and to come. In His lowest depression, He retains the firmest grasp on the glorious issue of His work. With His dying breath, with unhesitating confidence, He commends His soul into His Father's hands.

But they have depicted a character no less perfect in every relation of life. Conscious of the highest destiny, He continues in willing subjection to His mean though reputed parents. Throughout life He is animated with a zeal, which never flagged, for the work of His heavenly Father. He unites the full consciousness of having universal power in His hands, with a readiness to discharge the lowest acts which can teach humility and love. Possessed of the greatest possible knowledge, He bears with the greatest possible dulness (nearly approaching to the moral guilt of inattention), with the mild rebuke of "How is it that ye do not understand?" His hatred of sin is unquenchable; yet He has the deepest feeling of sympathy for the misery of those who, through self-induced sin, are sinking into final ruin. Filled with zeal for His Father's law, He yet invites the weary sinner to find rest in Him. His miraculous power is in constant energy for the relief of others; yet He wrought but a single miracle which has even the appearance of relieving Himself. He weeps for the sorrows and sufferings which sinners are bringing upon themselves. The hardened and obstinate reprobate He curses with a curse reaching even unto hell. Not one act of selfishness or of sinful indulgence disfigures the Saviour's character. The highest benevolence for all is united with the feeling of human friendship for a few. His courage never wavers. Humility, meekness, and mildness are united with the ever-abiding consciousness of the most exalted dignity. His meat was to do His Father's work. He weeps for the weight of human sorrows. Inquiring multitudes resorting to Him are the spiritual harvest He has come to reap.

But we have not only a perfect human Christ brought before us in the pages of the Evangelists; we have a perfect divine Christ represented there. The unbeliever will, of course, not admit that the Christ of the Gospels is divine; but we can ask him to assume, for the sake of the argument, that He is so. Now we wish him to consider, if the Christ of the Gospels be God incarnate, whether, as He is there portrayed, He does not act exactly as it would become an incarnate God? A beggar suddenly raised to royalty makes but a bungling display of dignity: the royal robes sit awkwardly on his shoulders. But the Christ of the Evangelists, the humblest of men, sits with grace on the throne of God. In every position in which the Evangelists have placed Him, He acts as if He had long been seated there. "Whosoever shall be ashamed of me," a Galilean carpenter, "and of my words"—what do we expect the humblest of men will add? I will retire abashed at my own meanness?—"of him will I be ashamed when I come in my own glory and in my Father's with His angels." Whosoever shall deny the Carpenter before men, the Carpenter will deny him when He comes in His Father's glory and His own. As a teacher, the Jewish peasant sits himself down as one who had been habituated to fill a throne higher than Moses' seat. "It was said to them of old time, Thou shalt not commit adultery. I say unto you, Whosoever looketh on a woman to lust after her hath committed adultery with her already in his heart. I say unto you, Whosoever loveth father or mother more than me is not worthy of me. If thou wilt be perfect, sell all that thou hast and give to the poor; take up the cross, and follow me."

The Galilean carpenter, who, in His agony, bowed Himself to the earth before His Father's throne, has never once said, in all His teaching, "Thus saith the Lord," but "I say unto you." He, who was devoured with zeal to vindicate His Father's honour when He witnessed the desecration of His Temple, when He performs a miracle says not, "I perform this miracle in my Father's name," but " I will; be thou clean. Go thy way, thy son liveth. But that ye may know that the Son of man hath power on earth to forgive sins, I say unto thee, Arise, take up thy bed, and go to thine house." To the dead body on the bier he says, " Young man, I say unto thee, Arise." To the body in the sepulchre he cries, " Lazarus, come forth," and His voice is heard in the depths of the unseen world. There is nothing like the expression of borrowed dignity which proceeds from the Saviour when He performs His cures. He does actions which are only the acts of God, and He does them in His own name. He teaches the road to heaven. He announces great principles of morals, the motive of which centres only in Himself; but never does a word escape Him unbecoming one who knew the inmost mind of God. There is no hint of the consciousness of fallibility. He claims allegiance as due to His person; and His claim is so exalted that God Himself can claim no more. The Galilean carpenter is familiar with the things passing in the heavenly world : He knows what is taking place amidst the angels of God. His eye has surveyed the unseen worlds. He has royal dignities at His disposal and at His command; and when He bestows, He bestows them like a king. All judgment in heaven and in earth has been committed into the hands of the Galilean carpenter. He has come forth and taken His seat on the throne of God. All the nations are gathered before Him; all the angels of His might attend Him. His messengers have gone forth and gathered His elect together. The King is come in His glory : He has taken His seat on His glorious throne. Who shall say that He is sitting there in a manner unworthy of " God manifest in the flesh " *?

* Renan and others are never weary of asserting that the discourses in St. John's Gospel were never uttered by our Lord, on account of the

What is the work, then, if the Christ of the Gospels be a mere human development, which the Evangelists have actually accomplished? They have created the idea of the man Christ Jesus, and they have succeeded in investing Him, in every conceivable perfection, with the highest outline of moral and spiritual beauty of which human nature is capable. Everything which is great, holy, and excellent, even where the qualities are so opposite that they appear incapable of coexisting, is yet harmoniously united in His person. To have succeeded in portraying such a character, even with every assistance which poetry or literature could supply, is a work the greatness of which it is not easy to estimate. Few characters of fiction are without a flaw, even when surveyed from the point of view in which their inventor conceived them. The character of Achilles, in the "Iliad," is a great creation; but is it absolutely faultless, even according to Homeric conceptions? The conception was the conception of greatness according to the estimate of the times when the poet wrote. But the Evangelists have not portrayed a Christ fashioned merely in reference to the ideal of the times in which they lived, or formed on any mere partial view of human excellence, but one which faultlessly combines every conceivable variety of human perfection into one harmonious whole. Their creation will be recognized as perfect by the wise and good of every race, of every clime, and of every age.

But they have accomplished a far greater work: not only have they created the idea of human perfection, but they have

declarations made in them respecting our Lord's person, and that they exhibit an entirely different view of it from that which is taken by the synoptic Gospels. They therefore assume that they were inventions of St. John in his old age, or they have been added by other hands. Now it surely matters little whether our Lord is represented as acting God or saying that He is God. We recommend to their consideration the picture of our Lord as drawn in Matthew, xxv., and ask them to state whether anything in St. John's Gospel represents Him as more divine; nay, whether the representation of the great white throne in the Revelation more completely invests Him with the attributes of Deity. Perhaps we shall be told that Matthew xxv. is a mythic addition!

2 E

seated the humblest of men on the throne of God. Yet whether on the throne of God, or as the dutiful son of Mary, or as the friend of the family of Bethany, there is no incongruity in the representation. As a friend, He is loving; as a Son, he is dutiful, while conscious of His higher dignity; as a man, He is humble; as perfectly holy, absolutely beloved of the Father, yet as the sinner's substitute He is bereaved of the light of His Father's countenance; as a worshipper, he is clothed with humility; as possessing Godhead, without the consciousness of robbery He personates equality with God. In every part of the Saviour's character the consistency is perfect.

Such is the problem which the Evangelists have solved. How has this great work been accomplished? The unbeliever shall give his own account of the matter. It has been brought about as other great developments of man have been accomplished. Creative genius has contributed its portion to the sublime representation. It has grown out of a succession of myths. Bright coruscations of light have sprung up in the depth of the human soul; but they have not descended from above! Successive generations have improved the original picture: it has at length culminated into a glorious Christ. Not one writer, but four, have each portrayed the same perfect character without a flaw. Truly Homer, and Æschylus, and Sophocles, and Virgil, and Dante, and Shakspeare, and Milton might unite their intellects into one, and envy the success of the fishermen of Galilee!

But can the theory of development, as applied to account for the origin of the Gospels, stand the test to which every such theory must necessarily be subject? The developments of man take place in definite periods of historic time. No great development has taken place within the lifetime of an individual. All the great developments of thought and feeling have extended over lengthened periods, the duration of which has been actually known. Many have required a long course of centuries for their completion. The greater the interval lying between the first starting-point and the full idea of the development itself, the longer must be the interval of time employed in effecting it. We think it can hardly be disputed that the Christ of the Gospels, if a development, must be the greatest which has ever taken place, which can be recognized as an historical fact, and the extreme limits of which can be accurately ascertained. It must therefore have required a longer interval of time for its accomplishment than any of the great historical developments of man. If it did not require a longer interval of time, satisfactory reasons must be assigned why it has advanced at an accelerated ratio. Historical truth compels us to assign a hundred or a hundred and fifty years at the utmost as the period within which it must have been effected.

Now, if the unbeliever is right in asserting that Christianity has originated by the action of the ordinary powers of the human mind, we make no unreasonable demand in requiring him to point out the distinct elements out of which the conception of the Christ of the Gospels has originated. The truth of history will compel him to reply that it must have developed itself out of Judaism as it existed in the first century before Christ, aided and assisted, it may be, by various elements derived from other quarters. It will not be possible to assert that the chief element out of which Christianity has developed itself must not have been a Jewish element existing in living Jewish men in the latter half of the first century B.C. We cannot concede that it originated out of the Judaism of Isaiah; for that would require a Luther to have arisen in the Jewish Church, to have recalled retrograde Judaism to the Judaism of 800 B.C. Compared with that of Isaiah, Judaism as it existed at the Christian era is the hardest ritualism. But if the developer thinks that he can better his position, we are ready to concede to him not only the Judaism of the Pharisee, the Sadducee, and the Essene, not only the Judaism of Philo and the Alexandrines, not only Oriental philosophy and the entire round of Greek philosophy and poetry, not only the Dualism of the Persians, the scepticism of the apostolic age, and the practical wisdom of the Romans, yet even with the aid of all the myths which the most poetic imagination can invent, within the period of time which history must assign for his operations, the attempt to develope the perfection of the man Christ Jesus, and, as the Evangelists have done, to enthrone Him on the throne of God, will be utterly hopeless.

Let us take a brief survey of some of the great developments of man, and examine the progress which they have made and the time which they have occupied in their accomplishment. The formation of the Egyptian religious system, civilization, and mental phenomena must be admitted to be one of those great developments; but its tendency never took the direction of developing a Christ. The origin both of Egyptian religion and Egyptian civilization is shrouded in a darkness which historical research has yet failed to dissipate. Its great outlines, up to a certain point, are visible; but whether it originated in a higher state of civilization and religious knowledge or a lower cannot yet be solved by historical evidence. Theories are propounded respecting it, according as their propounders believe that the course of human developments has been from a higher to a lower or from a lower to a higher state. All the conjectures which have been advanced on the subject have been founded on the supposition that the development in question has extended over a wide interval of time. Most writers on the subject have made the demand, not of centuries, but of thousands of years for its completion. But supposing the theory true, and the utmost demands which it makes for time conceded, what course has the actual historical development run? The answer is, it has created a complicated caste-system, which has enthralled the myriads who have been the subjects of it in hopeless bondage; it has produced a civilization which advanced to a certain point, and then became stationary, and finally perished for ever; it has originated a mystical and metaphysical theology for the priest, and an innumerable army of monster gods for the people; it has created a reigning priesthood, a subject people, gigantic monuments, a peculiar and characteristic school of art, and a multitude of the conveniences and luxuries of life. Age after age has passed onward in its rolling course. In religion, this nation has developed

an ox, a crocodile, a cat, or a hideous monster into a god.
Souls have run their courses of transmigration. Her civilization has gradually dissolved. Her pyramids testify to the present day to the profound depths of her delusions. But no Christ, nor tendency towards a Christ, developed itself in the mind of priest or people. The mighty power of Rome in the latest period of her history could not deter a fanatic mob from slaughtering a soldier who killed a cat. Such materials would present no elements for developing a Christ, had the national existence been prolonged for an indefinite succession of ages.

We will briefly glance at the great development of the Indian mind. Here a long course through an immense succession of ages has been run. All theorizers demand a long interval of time for working out the system of Indian theology and civilization. What were the forms of thought or feeling prior to the era of the Vedas has been lost in the distance of the past. But within the long historic period no tendency has existed towards the creation of a Christ: Indian developments have long since become retrograde ones. Here again we meet with a complicated system of metaphysical theology for the higher order of minds, and a form of Polytheism exceeding all known forms of worship in the depths of its degradation for the people. Prolific as India has been in the growth of men, she has been far more prolific in the generation of gods—grotesque monsters of frightful depravity and frightful ugliness. The number of her deities is said to be more numerous than the teeming millions of her population; but has one of them the attributes of a Christ? Surely India has had peculiar facilities for developing such an ideal. To her the principle of the incarnation of Deity is not unknown. We will give the developer of Christianity the benefit of the ten incarnations of Vishnu, and tell him that out of such creations of the Indian mind, compounded of the wildest romance, of superhuman wickedness, and bestial lust, he may go on in endless successions of millions of years, but he will not generate a Christ. If he is desirous, he may take to himself the benefit of every incarnation of Buddha, but still the development of the Christ of the New Testament will be an event indefinitely remote: all his efforts will only end in the creation of myriads of demons.

The long development of Chinese civilization has a similar tale to tell. Like India and Egypt, its origin is lost in the hoary past. What it has attained in the historic period is distinct, definite, and known. To reach its present state of stagnant death has required a long lapse of ages. China, indeed, has been less rich in her creations of monster gods; but she has developed a moral and political system by which the energies of man are frozen. She has created a Confucius, or a Confucius has created her; but between Confucius and the God-man, as He is exhibited in the Gospels, is fixed a gulf deep, impassable, and profound.

But perhaps the Persian system, with its eternal warfare between the principles of good and evil, will aid the developer to solve his problem. After long struggles, it has developed a Zoroaster; it has created its heavens and its hells; it has graphically depicted the happiness of the one and the horrors of the other; it has even produced an army of angels; it professes to have a revelation brought down from heaven. Still an awful distance separates between it and the Galilean carpenter seated on His glorious throne—the despised Nazarene hanging on the cross. Its later developments have taken place within a period when they might have been able to derive light from Christianity itself. Still the new cloth agreeth not with the old garment. Before the Persian religion could develope a Christ out of its genuine elements, men must have perished through countless ages without a Saviour, and the cry of the human race would in vain have ascended before God, "O Lord, how long?"

Of all the developments of man, that of the Greek mind is most definitely known, both in its origin, its stages, its progress, and its termination. It claims for itself a large portion of actual historic fact. Greece developed herself with wonderful activity and surprising vigour. Her national life, her poetry, her philosophy, her arts, form one of the richest portions of the growth of the human mind. Of the beauty of the human form she attained a most exquisite perception; but towards the creation of the divine, spiritual, and moral beauty of the God-man she made no perceptible advance. Of riches of mind in almost every other direction she has displayed an endless variety. Her historians are numerous; her poetry most extensive; her philosophy voluminous. In most departments of art she has had few rivals. She has passed through endless diversities of political life. The ideal creations of her poets embody her conceptions of human excellence exhibited on a larger scale than that of ordinary mortals. Her heroes are her men amplified. Her gods are constructed on similar principles, but with enlarged dimensions. But we should greatly prefer as companions her men to her gods or her heroes: they would probably have presented to our view nearly as much of what was good, and far less of what was frightful and deformed.

In dealing with the developments of Greece, we hold communion with actual historic men; we have the means in our possession for estimating their greatness, their littleness, and their degradation. Her own sons have furnished us with the picture. In Socrates, philosophers themselves have drawn the portrait of the noblest development of Grecian men who actually existed. We do not possess, as in the Gospels, four portraits drawn by humble men possessed of little or no education or knowledge of the world, but we have two pictures of him by men possessing the largest acquaintance with poetry and literature, the highest forms of philosophic thought and actual experience of mankind. Perhaps the difference in the line of thought between Plato and Xenophon is quite as wide as that which separates the Gospel of St. John from the other three. Here surely we have an opportunity of seeing what genius could accomplish, by means of the long course of past development of the most fruitful of human races, in the creation of the perfect man. We have the character and the personality of the best of Grecian men, drawn by two profound but widely different minds of her philosophic sons, of one of whom at least the genius was sublime. The character is a noble one; but where is the man Christ Jesus? Where is the carpenter seated on His throne of glory? Where is the mighty sufferer dying on the torturing cross? Nothing but careful study and reflexion on the Socrates of Xenophon and Plato, and the Jesus of the Evangelists, can enable us even approximately to estimate the profundity of the depth which separates the one from the other. We will notice a single point; and the whole of the histories of each are filled with similar divergencies. In the midst of His unspeakable tortures, the Redeemer said to the repentant robber, "Verily I say unto thee, To day shalt thou be with me in paradise." The Socrates of Plato, after discussing the immortality of the soul, and adducing a number of most uncertain arguments in favour of that hope, a little before he drank the hemlock, leaves the question fluctuating between the expectation of immortality and the alternative of annihilation. The last words of Jesus were, "It is finished: Father, into Thy hands I commit my spirit." The last words of Socrates were, "We are indebted a cock to Esculapius. Pay it, and do not neglect it." The one is earthly, of the earth; the other is the language of One who, while expiring in ignominy, was conscious that He could at will dispose of the glories of the unseen world.

The creations of the Greek mind have been prolific; yet, various as those creations have been, they invariably refuse to develope themselves in the direction of a Christ. In historical personages we have constellations of great names. In the production of living men she attained her fullest growth, and then retrograded into slavishness. She produced the founders of the various schools of her philosophy, which, too, she exhibited in the most opposite extremes: it developed into the system of Zeno on the one hand, and that of Epicurus on the other. She produced a Diogenes, with his cynical misanthropy. But the most ardent supporter of the theory of development must admit that, so far from a tendency to develope the Christ of the Evangelists, the conceptions of Zeno, Epicurus, and Diogenes would have had no tendency to produce even the humblest of the Apostles. The Greek morality and the gospel morality run in diverging lines.

But, although Greek men who had an historical existence form materials out of which it is impossible to develope a Christ, her ideal characters will perhaps aid us better, and more nearly approximate to the Jesus of the Evangelists. Here also we have materials by which to test the direction of Grecian thought. Her poets have painted the human character in the utmost variety of aspect; but they show not even a tendency to the conception of a Christ. But what say her philosophers? There is the magnanimous man of Aristotle, embodying all that great philosopher could conceive of as grand and glorious: between this character and that of the blessed Jesus it is hard to conceive of anything, not stained with palpable vice, more hopelessly opposed. There is the wise man of the Stoics: alas! where is the humility? There is that beau ideal of the excellencies of human nature, an Epicurean god. Compound these as you will, give them in their conception an ever wider and wider extension; and the creation which will arise out of them, instead of a tendency to generate a Christ, will only develope itself in a direction more and more remote from that glorious form.

But there is the Alexandrian Neo-Platonic philosophy, that mixture of various systems and tones of thought; will it not help us in our extremity, and create the idea of God manifest in the flesh? Its philosophy is metaphysical, its theology is pantheistic. Out of such elements may spring an abstraction of the Highest, remote from the material universe, absorbed in his pleroma—an impersonal God, without morality or perfections, with long chains of æons forming various successions of links uniting the unknown and unknowable essence of Deity with material things,—but no Christ in the perfection of human nature, living and dying, exalted to the throne of God. Either Galilean fishermen have performed the solitary feat of realizing this conception, thereby distancing alike all poets and philosophers, or it has come down from heaven. Neo-Platonism actually has developed an Apollonius; but who dreams in the present day of comparing the prophet (or rather the impostor) of Tyana with the Jesus of the Gospels?

But the Neo-Platonic philosophy actually encountered historical Christianity : it knocked at the door, and tried to obtain admission into the Church. Philosophers of this school tried hard to weld this system with the Christianity of the Gospels. Their attempts at fusion afford the most conclusive proof of the hopeless irreconcilability of the two systems. So far from the Neo-Platonist being able to develope a Christ, the Jesus of the Gospels was his scandal. The union of a spirit with a material body, says he, is the essential principle of evil. The divine Logos never actually assumed human flesh : it was an appearance, a phantasm, only imposing on the bodily senses of man. Jesus and the Christ must be split into two persons, the one of the earth, the other a divine æon. The Christ has formed a temporary union with the man Jesus. Of the scandal of the cross and the passion who can endure to hear? The exhibition on the cross, therefore, was only a phantom on which the Jews vainly spent their rage; or, if a reality, the divine Christ deserted his former partner in his utmost need, and left him to expire in ignominy and shame. The man Jesus of the Gospels and the mystic æons would not fuse : this attempt to unite them has only exhibited their divergency in a stronger light.

But what shall we say to the practical Roman? He can be seen on the page of history. To spiritual conceptions he was a stranger. He founded empires, but never created thoughts or religious systems. As the historian of the 'Decline and Fall' observes, the gods of the nations met in the Capitol and destroyed one another. The state was his ideal ; this world his portion. He will utterly refuse to aid in the uncongenial work of assisting at the development of a Christ.

If, then, the religious systems of Egypt, of India, and of China afford no aid to the developer,—if the Persian Dualism refuses its assistance,—if, when Greece is interrogated, notwithstanding all the wealth of her poetry and her philosophy, and in the rich developments of her individual manhood, she return for answer an emphatic No,—if the Neo-Platonist insists on metamorphosing the human Jesus into a phantom,— if the Roman decline such uncongenial work, to what nation, race, or line of thought is he to have recourse? If he could start afresh any of these lines of thought which have run their destined course, the development would take a course more and more remote from the Jesus of the Gospels; the divergent lines will increase in their divergency. How shall the water rise above the source from which it flows? How shall an idea, thought, or feeling rise higher than its original level, or burst from its original conception and generate one precisely opposite in its nature? But the Hebrew race yet remains. When the Egyptian, and the Hindoo, and the Chinese, and the Persian, and the Greek, and the Roman, when the philosopher, and the poet, and the vulgar mass, decline the proffered honour, cannot the Jew develope the conception of a Christ? Let, then, the developer of Christianity by the aid of myth and genius, and any influence but the assistance of an actual revelation, attempt the work. We must point out to him the necessary conditions of his undertaking.

If, then, the attempt be made to develope the Christ of the Gospels out of Judaism, the voice of history forbids us to use the brightest periods of the Jewish Church as the point from which the development must begin: the developer must commence his operations with the state of thought and feeling involved in the Judaism of the latter half of the first century before our era. He is always ready to evoke the aid of myth; but myths unfold themselves not in individuals, but in multitudes. The state of thought and feeling then existing in Judæa must be assumed as the point of commencement out of which the conception of the Christ of the New Testament originated; for developments grow not out of the state of things involved in books, but from living realities in the human mind. If a fresh development were to arise in India, the movement would commence not with the religious and moral conceptions contained in the Vedas, but with the actual existing state of Indian thought and feeling. An Indian Luther must arise, to recall the Indian mind to that mental condition which existed when the Vedas were composed, before a state of higher progress can commence. His work could not be effected in a day. In an age like the present, the existence of such a person would not be hidden in darkness, but would be an historical fact.

In a similar manner, had any great reformer arisen, in the latter half of the first century before Christ, in the bosom of the Jewish Church, who reproduced as part of the national feelings the Judaism of Isaiah, history would not have refused all notice of his existence. Retrogression had long been the law of the Jewish nation. Its religious and moral tone is no unknown land, but lies within the confines of authentic history. The voice of psalmists and prophets had long since ceased. Their spirituality of sentiment had gradually congealed into the hardest ritualism and the most exclusive nationality. Morality had become casuistry. The outward habitation in which realities once dwelt had become the only reality recognized by the Jew. Intermixed with feelings of this description, among a small portion of the nation had sprung up a spirit of sceptical unbelief, or mysticism. From elements such as these the development must take its starting-point.

But the life of Judaism, although fallen and degraded, was not extinct. It had for some centuries entered on a development of retrogression. The life of the Jewish race has been less capable of destruction than that of any nation under heaven. Whatever the Jew has embraced, he has embraced with tenacity. The Pharisaism, the Sadducism, the Essenism had a development yet in store; but was that development in the direction of the Jesus of the Gospels? History can inform us not only as to the direction to which Judaism was tending, but what was the harbour to which its voyage carried it, and where it has been anchored ever since: it was Rabbinism. The ritualism of the Jew perished under the powerful hand of Providence. To the Jew, exiled from his country, the performance of the rites of his religion was no longer possible. His Temple was destroyed; after that event no sacrifice could ascend acceptable to Heaven from his hand. His sacred feasts existed only in memorials. Driven from the practice of his ritual worship, did he turn the direction of his thoughts towards the religion of Isaiah and the prophets?

Did he begin to learn that the Almighty preferred mercy to sacrifice? Driven from his ritualism, he developed the hardest system of formal morality which was ever laid on men's shoulders—an endless system of trifling casuistry. His little finger became thicker than his father's loins. He elaborated, not a morality, but its most unsubstantial shadow, ending in the habitual preference of the lesser to the greater duty. He went on binding a burden on his back heavier and heavier, without acquiring an atom of additional strength to support the load. The course of development on which the Jew entered in the period in which Christianity originated, and to which he ultimately arrived, was the exact opposite of the teaching of Him whose yoke is easy, and whose burden is light, and whose service is perfect freedom.

Now, we ask, where shall we find a place in the character of the Jewish nation, at the time when Christianity appeared, out of which, by the aid of myth, or fable, or genius, or inward spiritual insight, there will be even a tendency to generate the Christ of the Gospels? The character of the Jew in our Lord's day is no unknown land affording play for the imagination to people it at pleasure: historians, sacred and profane, alike testify to its nature. If the testimony of the writers of the Gospels must be set aside as that of partial witnesses, we can appeal to the testimony both of heathens and of Jews. St. Paul has written, "They please not God, and are contrary unto all men." A heathen writer declares that towards the human race they were animated by a hostile hatred. The character of the Jew, as represented in the Gospels, can be substantiated by testimony derived from every quarter. Now a character of which Rabbinism was the natural fruit could never, by any ordinary process, develope the idea of a Christ. Into what it might ultimately unfold is not our business to inquire. One thing is certain, that, with eternity at its command, it would never create the Jesus of the Gospels.

But the problem is reduced within very narrow limits. We have not an indefinite period of time at our command: history restricts the interval to one hundred and fifty years.

Within this period of time the image of the glorious Christ of the Gospels must have been completed in all its perfectness. But history testifies that the progress of all well-ascertained developments has been slow. Few even of the more gradual stages of their course have been unfolded in a similar interval. Let the developer point out any great development of man which has taken place within a period of one hundred and fifty years. But the greatest of human developments is small compared with the distance which separates the Judaism of the last half of the first century before Christ from the Christ of the New Testament. The time which such a development must have occupied must have been longer than the longest development of man. It would require an interval compared with which the period required for the growth of Egyptian, or Indian, or Chinese, or Grecian civilization would be relatively short. To develope Judaism into the Jesus of the Gospels in the brief period in which the facts of history prove that the change must have been effected is one which the laws of human progress forbid us to conceive of as possible.

The Greek race has been the subject of a more rapid development than any other race of man. Let us take this race as a standard by which to estimate the demands we must make on time, if we endeavour to develope the conception of a Christ out of Jewish ritualism. The religious ideas and the civilization of the age of Homer differ far less widely from those of the age of Pericles than the ritualism and national exclusiveness of the Jew from the conception of the Jesus of the Evangelists. To produce such a conception out of such a moral and spiritual condition requires not simply a development, but a new creation of the elements of thought and feeling; it involves a long course of changes, rising one above the other in successive stages. If such have existed, they should be pointed out. Those who assert that species have been evolved from species, when they are challenged to produce direct evidence of their assertions, by pointing out geological remains in which species are actually undergoing the specified transformations, are ready enough to reply that a most inconsiderable portion of the earth's crust has yet been examined; and that, while it must be admitted that the small portion which has yet been examined does not supply the required evidence, the absence of these remains is no proof that the theory is not true, for the evidence may be yet supplied in the enormous extent of hitherto unexamined strata indefinitely more extensive than those which have been the subject of examination. But while the advocate of transmutation may take refuge in such an assertion, a similar reason cannot be pleaded by the asserter that the Gospels have been developed out of Jewish ritualism. We have no unknown regions of history to explore. We are in possession of the facts. If we cannot name the stages of transmutation, it will be useless for us to assert that the Jewish mind may have passed through several transmutations with which we are unacquainted. The time which such changes would require sternly refuses to allow the plea. We know what was the actual state of the Jewish mind in the latter half of the first century before Christ. Before the termination of the first century of the Christian era, the conception of the Christ of the Gospels was certainly complete. If then this conception was a human development, the shortness of the time during which it was effected shows that it must have been effected, not through a succession of stages, but by one continuous and steady progression. No new creations of either thought or feeling could have arisen and become inwrought into the national feeling and sentiments. But of such materials, therefore, it is impossible to generate a Christ.

But may not the conception of a Christ have originated in the fusion of various forms of thought, as in physics a new compound arises from the union of various chemical ingredients? We answer, that the supposed physical analogy will not hold. The new chemical compound consists of nothing but the same original materials. In a similar manner, in whatever degree forms of thought may be fused together, no new element, which was not originally there, will be created out of the union. Four or five unholy feelings will not fuse into a holy one: as many material conceptions will not generate a spiritual one. No degree of exclusiveness, mixed with any other human feeling, will generate the character of Him whose life no man took from Him, but who laid it down of Himself. It is impossible, by any fusion of thought or feeling, to produce a new element which arises above the original conception.

The national feeling of England will form an apt illustration. It has been formed by means of a great fusion of races: the Briton and the Roman, the German, the Norman, the Dane, and the Scot have alike contributed their share. The result is, that the English nation differs from any one of the separate elements of which it has been composed; it has assimilated different elements from each nationality; the Dane, the Saxon, the Norman exist no longer, but have been swallowed up in the common character of Englishman. The English race contains several of the finer qualities of the races whose fusion has created the English nation : but those qualities existed in the original separate elements; they are not new creations of what did not previously exist, in thought, feeling, or character. The differences of character possessed by distinct races have been combined and modified merely; and out of this modification has sprung the English nation.

But the formation of the English character has been the result of a long interval of time. The separate elements of which it has been composed long continued to exist in insulation. Amalgamation was effected slowly and with difficulty. The elements had to be brought together and then fused into one great national character. Without the aid of favourable external circumstances, such fusion would have been impossible. In other nationalities similarly composed, the different elements, instead of fusing, have gone on fermenting and warring an interminable warfare. The brief period of one hundred and fifty years would have been utterly insufficient for accomplishing such a fusion.

But even if the idea of a Christ could be obtained out of the fusion of any existing elements, the period of time which history assigns as the only one during which this fusion must have been accomplished is too limited for effecting the work. The English nation has taken centuries to create; but the work in question is a far mightier work than the production of the English nation out of the complicated elements which compose it.

We will therefore concede to the developer the free use of such elements as he can find in the religious systems which were in existence during the latter half of the first century before Christ, and allow him to fuse them together in any manner in which he pleases. Let him make a selection from any form of civilization which had an historical existence—let him be aided by the assistance of genius, or deep spiritual insight, or myth—let him assimilate together Judaism, Orientalism, Greek and Roman thought, and out of these let him form a church. Let this church set itself to the work of fusion. Whatever growth may arise in this church in a period of one hundred and fifty years, we venture to assert that the state of its spirituality, its morals, its feelings, and its sentiments will, at the termination of that period, be indefinitely remote from even a tendency towards the development of the Christ of the Gospels.

The work of constructing such a church out of elements so diverse and antagonistic would be one of no inconsiderable difficulty. Churches are not created in a day. It required years of hard and zealous labour to gather together the elements which composed the Apostolic church. The attempt to construct a new system of philosophy among the speculators of Alexandria by the fusion of all systems previously existing had a short life, and perished. The difficulty of such undertakings is, to breathe life into the elements when united together. It is more likely that the elements composing such a church, instead of combining into an harmonious action, or immediately engaging in the work of generating a Christ, will arise against one another in mutual tumult, and enter on a fierce and destructive war. But perhaps the more fiercely the elements strive together, the more certainly will that great and glorious unity be evolved at last. After the most terrible tempests come the profoundest calms. The more the separate materials are shaken together, the more closely will they cohere. But, however these elements may finally be combined, the result will only be equal to the united action of the whole. Two hatreds will not produce a love. Two adverse forms of pride neither by coalescing nor contending can generate a humility. Scepticism and fanaticism, united in any conceivable admixture, will not produce a holy zeal in the service of God. Never by deifying man in his appetites and passions, such as man actually appears on the page of history, shall we develope the Jesus of the Gospels.

Any church which the developer could collect, consisting of Jews and Orientals, of Greeks and Romans, absorbing into its bosom the most repulsive elements of thought, must enter on its course of development either by contention, by actual separation, or by fusion. Man cannot divest himself of his ideas, his feelings, and his passions, and array himself in new ones, with the same facility with which he changes his attire. The various classes out of which any church could have been composed must have brought their former ideas and conceptions, their feelings, their religion, and their morals, with them into their new communion. But one hundred and fifty years is the whole period which can be conceded for collecting the church together, for fusing its elements, for fresh creations of thought and feeling, for each fresh stage of development, and out of the combined operation creating the conception of a Christ. The person who is prepared to say that out of these elements such a conception has been developed must pardon us for requiring some evidence of the fact. The fusion of such principles into an harmonious whole would have required a longer space than the whole interval which history will allow him for the completion of the development itself. Let us suppose that the new-formed church has coalesced together, and has commenced developing; let myth and fable be freely conceded to her use; let genius lend its utmost assistance, let her absorb the philosopher, the fanatic, the politician, and the degraded mob; yea, and let her gather into her bosom the best elements of society which can be found, provided they are historical existences, and not creations of the fancy. She has before her a long and weary journey, a march which can only be accomplished by various deviations from the direct line of route, by bridging over destructive depths, without having any means of finding a secure foundation on which to support the incumbent weight. But steady marching through a continuous plain will never conduct the church to her journey's end. She has many a dizzy height to scale. She must continue raising herself from elevation to elevation, destitute of ladder or scaffolding with which to aid herself in the ascent. She may develope and develope, but, without the creation of fresh thought and feeling, age after age will roll on in its destined course and no Christ will issue from her bosom; she may cry and travail, but there will be no birth. History defines the problem presented for solution, and our hard-labouring church finds that those who urge her to the attempt are Egyptian taskmasters. That problem is, Produce a Christ out of previously existing elements, such as you find depicted in the four Gospels, within a period of one hundred and fifty years.

But even if we were to concede to the developer the free use of the Old Testament Scriptures, even if we were to allow him to select the brighest stars of the Jewish Church, a company of prophets, with which to enter on his course of development, the shortness of the period which history assigns him for the accomplishment of his work would render his attempt an impossibility. The Old Testament Scriptures profess to shine with a brighter light than the unassisted illumination of the human understanding. If their testimony is of any worth, they declare, "Whatever assistance we can render you in your distress, we do not owe to a development of man." But let the whole company of the prophets be summoned to assist the work. The 53rd of Isaiah is the brightest anticipation of the New Testament Messiah which they can furnish; but how faint is the conception of the yet future suffering and glorious King! how shadowy is the outline, when compared with the substantial form, the Galilean carpenter calmly seated on the throne of God, and acting with suitable grace the part of the universal King, who, while divinely zealous for His Father's honour, never performed a miracle in His Father's name — the outcast, the crucified, and the dying disposing places in paradise in absolute accordance with His will.

Let the developer select any number of Jewish saints he pleases, and incorporate with them all the pagan excellence which history, not fancy, will supply him with, and unite these into a church, and propose to them to develope the Jesus of the Gospels within one hundred and fifty years; if the development is to exclude everything divine, and to follow any ascertained human course, the philosophers and prophets will, with unanimous voice, cry out, " The developer is a Pharaoh who commands us to make brick, and, lo! no straw is given to us."

But a fresh obstacle encounters our developer at every stage of his career. He has to commence his development with the actual Jewish Church. Within a certain period he encounters the actual historic Christian Church. That church, when it emerges into history, seems very unlike a society which had just succeeded in developing a Christ. If it had accomplished this feat, after so great a victory, it must have immediately commenced a movement of a most retrograde description. Memorials of that church exist. The earlier writings are indeed few, but sufficient to give us an idea of its character. They soon become more numerous, and supply us with abundant materials for judging whether the character of those composing its body was such that they could have been recently engaged in creating the conception of a Christ. Nothing more strikes the reader of the writings remaining from the early Church than the enormous interval which separates them from the writings of the Apostles. The sound sense, the practical judgment, of the apostolic writings is wholly wanting. We at once are sensible that we have descended into a lower element of thought and feeling, of judgment and conception. If the sublime conception of a Christ had not previously existed, the fathers of the early Church never would have created it. The character of the primitive Church, as soon as it has become the subject of history, wholly negatives the idea that a Christ could have issued from her bosom.

If then there is no human element out of which, by the ordinary laws of human development, the conception of a Christ could have been created, as a Christ is actually portrayed, in the pages of the Evangelists, invested with everything which is gloriously human, and uniting the human with the Godhead, it follows that the phenomenon, as it actually exists, can only be accounted for by assuming that the assertion of the sacred writer is true, " God, who at sundry times and in divers manners spake in times past unto the fathers by the prophets, hath in these last days spoken unto us in His Son."

THE END.

www.ingramcontent.com/pod-product-compliance
Lightning Source LLC
Chambersburg PA
CBHW022139300426
44115CB00006B/262